Crime Victimization

Crime Victimization

A Comprehensive Overview

SECOND EDITION

Elizabeth Quinn Wright

Sara Brightman

CAROLINA ACADEMIC PRESS

Durham, North Carolina

ISBN 978-1-61163-900-1
e-ISBN 978-1-53100-727-0

Library of Congress Cataloging-in-Publication Data

Names: Quinn, Elizabeth (Criminologist) author.
Title: Crime victimization : a comprehensive overview / Elizabeth Quinn
  Wright and Sara Brightman.
Description: Second Edition. | Durham : Carolina Academic Press, [2018] |
  Revised edition of Crime victimization, [2015] | Includes bibliographical
  references and index.
Identifiers: LCCN 2017044416 | ISBN 9781611639001 (alk. paper)
Subjects: LCSH: Victims of crimes.
Classification: LCC HV6250.25 .Q56 2018 | DDC 362.88--dc23
LC record available at https://lccn.loc.gov/2017044416

Carolina Academic Press, LLC
700 Kent Street
Durham, North Carolina 27701
Telephone (919) 489-7486
Fax (919) 493-5668
www.cap-press.com

Printed in the United States of America

Dedication

To my loved ones—thank you for your unending support and encouragement.
EQW

To my family, my husband, and friends who have always supported me.
SWB

To the victims and survivors who inspire us—we wrote this for you.
EQW & SWB

Contents

SECTION I
History and Measurement of Victimization

SECTION II
Victimization: Consequences, Forms and Underrepresented Populations

Preface

Welcome to *Crime Victimization: A Comprehensive Overview, 2nd edition*! This book was created to provide students with a general background of victimology, an understanding of the amount and major types of criminal victimizations and who they affect, a solid introduction to the Victims' Rights Movement and victims' rights legislation, and what victims need to recover from crime. This book also pays particular attention to the strengths and weaknesses that exist in the interactions between criminal justice and non-criminal justice personnel who provide assistance to crime victims in numerous capacities. Throughout this text, students will find profiles of victimologists, victim activists, and victim advocates. The authors are particularly proud of these Professional Profiles, as we believe they provide the reader with an idea about different opportunities for working with crime victims across a wide spectrum of vocations. Within each chapter we have placed profiles of individuals who have contributed to our understanding of crime victims in a way that is consistent with the chapter. Additionally, in almost every chapter we have included news snippets to illustrate important concepts and real-world issues related to the topic of the chapter. These news segments, titled "In the News," provide students with a clear illustration of particular concepts in the real world and help to identify challenges and progress evident in the treatment of crime victims.

This book is divided into four different sections with a total of 12 chapters overall. Section I, "History and Measurement of Victimization," introduces readers to the definitions of victim and victimization, covers the history of victimology, provides the history of addressing crime victimization and the inclusion and exclusion of crime victims overall, and finishes up with a discussion on the continuum of victims' contribution to the crime event and a discussion of victim blaming. Chapter 2 focuses on how we measure victimization, both in the United States and abroad. It is important to view victimization from a global perspective to both identify prevention strategies that eliminate/decrease opportunities for crime but also to understand common patterns of victimization and cultural nuances surrounding what acts are deemed "crimes" and how important they are to different societies.

Section II, "Victimization — Consequences, Forms, and Underrepresented Populations," is the largest section in this book and delves deep into understanding the effects of crime victimization while also providing a comparison for the student on the similarities and differences in victims' responses to specific types of crimes. Chapter 3 focuses on identifying the spectrum of individuals who are affected by a crime and identifies the major categories of harm from which victims try to recover. The chapter discusses long- and short-term effects and opens up a dialogue about what it is that victims need to start healing and moving on from the crime. Chapter 4 focuses attention on UCR Part I offenses specifically and identifies characteristics of "common" victims and "common" offenders, as well as addressing "victimless" crimes and repeat victimization. Chapter 5 shines a spotlight on vulnerable populations and interpersonal violence, as these are the areas in which we see the majority of victim services being implemented. This chapter helps us to see the impact of crime that is perpetrated by those within our closest circles—our families and partnerships. Chapter 6 provides a focus on two types of crime that have been receiving greater attention in the last decade—white-collar crime and workplace violence—and Chapter 7 provides readers with two additional areas receiving more attention as of late—hate crimes and cybercrimes. Students typically read about victimization as a result of street-level crime, but less often do we see a discussion of cybercrime and white-collar crime victims. Because students of criminal justice, sociology, psychology, social work, and other fields will likely engage with crime victims at some point in their careers, it is important to identify all different types of crime victims so we can begin to examine nuances to appropriately aid these individuals.

Section III, "Victims' Rights," provides an in-depth review of the history of the Victims' Rights Movement starting with a discussion in Chapter 8 of important legislation that has come from the efforts of victim activists, victimologists, and victim advocates. Chapter 9 provides students with a description of some of the most important pieces of victims' rights legislation that have been implemented in the United States and traces victimology history through the decades, identifying important events and organizational creations across time.

Section IV, "Working with Victims and Next Steps," introduces the reader to how victims are treated by the various professions that provide services to them after the crime has occurred. In Chapter 10, the focus is on the interaction between criminal justice personnel and victims—identifying the strengths and challenges within these relationships. In Chapter 11 the text focuses on individuals who work with crime victims in a victim advocacy-type capacity and in other areas that victims commonly seek assistance, including medical services, psychological/counseling services, and faith-based assistance. This chapter also addresses common challenges to assisting crime victims faced by victim advocates and discusses both the positive and negative aspects the media brings to crime incidents and their treatment of crime victims. The final chapter, Chapter 12, highlights burgeoning issues for victim advocates and victimologists identified by the Office for Victims of Crime and the National Center for Victims of Crime. Challenges experienced by special groups of victims, such as victims with disabilities, rural victims, human trafficking victims and immigrant victims (legal and illegal), and victims of mass casualty incidents are discussed, as is the focus on cultural competency for victim advocates. New developments in victim services are highlighted to keep the student abreast of progress in the field, including restorative justice initiatives and the importance of collaborative efforts in victim response, such as Sexual Assault Response Teams and Family Justice Centers. The chapter ends with an introduction of hot topics, such as victimization during disasters and the use of social media to prevent crime and reach out to the public, and a discussion of future considerations such as remaining gaps in service to victims and glimpses into areas upon which victim advocacy and victimology fields are focusing.

The authors are particularly proud of presenting you the second edition of *Crime Victimization*. In this new version, students will find updated crime victimization statistics throughout this textbook (to reflect the most recent year available to us— 2015) and added information on areas not previously addressed, such as sibling on sibling violence, the It's On Us movement, crime against transgender individuals, and victimization by the criminal justice system. Additionally, we've highlighted the topic of mass casualties of violent crime and the efforts of the National Center for Victims of Crime to provide financial assistance to the victims of those crimes and their families.

The overall goal of this book is to provide a history of victimology, victimization, and victims' rights, while also highlighting the needs of victims and illustrating what those who work with crime victims in any capacity can do to positively impact the lives of those victims with whom they come into contact.

Acknowledgments

The authors would like to thank Carolina Academic Press, specifically Beth Hall, who believed in this project from the start and supported our vision for a textbook on crime victimization wholeheartedly. We are forever indebted to photographer Kaitlyn Barlow for creating such an extraordinary image for both editions of Crime Vicitmization; she truly helped us make our vision real. Additionally, we would like to acknowledge Grace Pledger for creating such an amazing book cover and for the incredible patience and guidance shown to us in the process of putting the book together.

We would like to thank our family and friends for providing us with the support needed to continue our efforts to add to the conversation on victimology.

We remain in awe of the victimologists, criminal justice practitioners, and victim advocates who are out in the world trying to make life better for crime victims. A special thank you must go out to Anne Seymour, a woman whose impact on the field of victim advocacy is immeasurable. Her support and guidance on the first edition of this text meant the world to us and we are so grateful she was willing to provide us with her profile so students across the nation can learn of her great works.

We would also like to recognize the trials and tribulations faced by victims of crime in general, and pay our respects to the people working on the front lines to help victims find justice and heal from the acts perpetrated against them. We hope this text will guide future victimologists, criminal justice agents, victim advocates, and all others who work with victims in any capacity to constantly strive to serve crime victims to the best of their abilities and to know that their efforts are noticed and appreciated.

About the Authors

Professor Elizabeth Quinn Wright received bachelor's degrees in psychology and social welfare from the University of Wisconsin-Madison. She earned a master of arts and PhD from Sam Houston State University in August 2004 and began her academic career at Fayetteville State University (FSU), which allowed her to pursue her interest in victimology through research, service, and teaching in immeasurable ways. After eleven years in FSU's Department of Criminal Justice she shifted gears and became a faculty member in the Department of Criminal Justice Administration at Middle Tennessee State University (MTSU). At FSU, she created victimology courses at both the undergraduate and graduate level and has recently proposed an undergraduate victimology course at MTSU. Her interests include victimology and victim's studies, police-community relations and the problem-oriented police officer, spatial analysis of fear of crime and police satisfaction, stress management, and the criminal justice response to disasters. Professor Wright has worked as a corrections liaison with incarcerated boys and girls. Additionally, she worked for a number of years as a rape crisis hotline counselor and support group facilitator and continued her victim advocacy work through the Rape Crisis Volunteers of Cumberland County organization from 2007–2011. In addition to responding to crisis line calls and as an emergency room companion, she served as a member of the board of directors for four years, including appointments as board treasurer and board secretary for three of those years, was a primary grant writer for the organization, and assisted with training and fundraising efforts. In her new state of Tennessee, she has been honored to work with two excellent victim service agencies in the middle Tennessee region.

Professor Wright has worked on projects exploring fear of crime and citizen satisfaction with police for the Fayetteville Police Department, exploring availability and utilization of victim services for domestic violence victims in four counties within North Carolina, evaluating a self-defense program for victims of sexual assault, and assessing teaching at the undergraduate level in criminal justice. She has been published in *Women & Criminal Justice*, *Applied Psychology in Criminal Justice*, *Contemporary Justice Review*, *ACJS Assessment Forum*, and *Crime Prevention and Community Safety* and has written five book chapters exploring different victimological and victims' rights issues, including a problem-oriented policing approach to repeat victimization, and a technical report on the victimization experience presented to the Texas State Legislature.

Professor Sara Brightman earned an undergraduate degree in sociology and women's studies from Central Michigan University. She earned her master's and PhD in sociology from Western Michigan University and has been working in the Department of Criminal Justice at Fayetteville State University since August 2009. Professor Brightman's areas of interest include state and corporate crime as well as the victims of state and corporate crimes. She teaches Victimology (at the undergraduate and graduate levels), Comparative Criminal Justice, and Race, Class and Gender in Criminal Justice. She has also taught Senior Seminar in Criminal Justice and a number of undergraduate core courses. Other areas of interest include international law, human rights, women's rights, social movements, and criminological theory.

Professor Brightman has conducted research on state crimes by police and military in Nigeria as well as state crimes by police and the judicial system in Pakistan. Her recent research focused on eugenics and state crime restorative justice in North Carolina, and her most recent publications can be found in the *British Journal of Criminology* and *Contemporary Justice Review*. Professor Brightman's dissertation addressed the systematic nature of sexual violence against women committed by United States actors, focusing on the military, police, corrections officers, and border control agents.

SECTION I

History and Measurement of Victimization

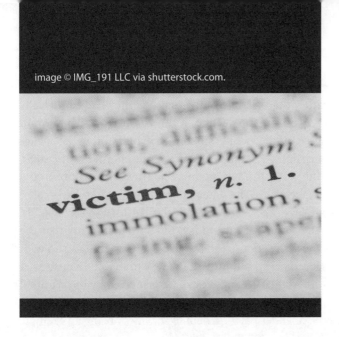

Chapter 1: Background

History of Crime Victimization

Crimes, and therefore victims of crime, have existed throughout human history. Societies have always had the need to control behavior that is deemed harmful to the group and the individual, as well as those behaviors which violate the values and norms of the time. This form of informal social control dominated the regulation of early societies. As societies grew and became more organized, more formal methods of social control became necessary. Originating as early as 4,000 BC in Egypt, the first written codes of law focused mainly on contracts, property crimes, and regulating family life. Actions and behaviors contrary to these laws were seen as the most harmful to individuals as they threatened a person's very survival. They were also very personal, an offense by one against another which threatened to disrupt essential personal and family relationships vital to the community. The personal nature of the process allowed for victims to raise their cases to local leaders individually. Due to the nature of survival at the time, resolution of these types of violations focused on returning all parties involved to the state prior to the violation. Communities would be threatened if those involved were no longer contributing to the greater good. This often meant that the victim was returned their property, plus some for the inconvenience they suffered, and the offender would be required to demonstrate they could continue to participate and contribute to the community. The victim, the offender, and the community were intimately involved with the response to such violations.

A dramatic shift in the treatment of crime and victims occurred with the formation of nation-states in the sixteenth and seventeenth centuries AD. During this period, crime and violations of social norms came to be seen as a threat to the government and to the collective interests of the social order, so crimes came to be redefined as an offence against the state, rather than against individuals, as they had historically been. This shift began to lead to a dramatic decline in the victims' participation in the formal criminal justice process. While victims still brought attention to the crimes committed against them, prosecution was taken over by a representative of the state. It should be noted, however, that even though one may be the *actual* victim in the case, the state now takes on that label as it is the state that prosecutes the crime because the defendant has violated state law. There is a great deal of history that has led to the current case processing system that we have today, but suffice it to say that the reason for naming the state as the victim doesn't necessarily have anything to do with a disrespect for the actual aggrieved party, but instead is a way to maintain our social contract: we give up some of our "rights" so that we can be protected by the criminal justice system. Furthermore, punishment also became less about restoring the victim, and became more focused on the offender paying a debt to society or being an example to others through deterrence.

Victim Participation in the Criminal Justice "Process"

Almost all of us have come into contact with the police through traffic violations or calling to report something we may have heard or seen at a particular place, but having a case processed by the criminal justice system is a very different and oftentimes very lengthy process. Not only is the criminal justice process something that may be new to a victim, the role of the victim within that process and the treatment of the victim by criminal justice personnel are additional things a victim may not be able to anticipate. The purpose of this section is to provide an introduction to how a criminal case proceeds, to discuss what can be expected of criminal justice personnel, and to identify some common interactional issues between victims and criminal justice personnel.

In general, the process of a case includes the following: report of a case to the police, a police investigation, arrest of the suspect, filing of the charge(s), pretrial procedures, plea bargaining or a criminal trial, trial verdict, sentencing, appeal (if sought by the defense), and carrying out of sentence (Boland, 2001). Each step will be discussed briefly along with a discussion about victim-service-provider interactions. One additional thing that should be noted is that all states have something called their victims' bill of rights, which outlines all of the rights crime victims have in relation to the criminal justice system (see http://www.ojp.gov/ovc/rights/legislation.html). In general, these bills state that victims have the right to be treated with respect by criminal justice personnel, that they should be heard by the prosecutor (which doesn't mean their wishes will substitute for what the district attorney is seeking—but it is to ensure that they are part of the process), that they should be informed of all court proceedings, and that they should be informed of the sentence and notified when someone is getting out of prison. These rights are important to know as many crime victims are unaware that they even exist and feel like they are helpless in the process.

The overall job of the police is to take a report of the crime, investigate the claim, collect evidence, and apprehend suspects. The victim and other witnesses will be asked questions that will assist the police in their investigation. The police will ask the victim to tell them about the crime and may ask questions trying to pinpoint certain details. Police are aware that a victim may be in a state of shock and that they may not remember everything. If they seem like they are asking the same question over and over again, or are asking a victim to fill in some blanks for them, it may seem like they don't believe the victim. This is probably *not* the case. It is *more* likely that they are trying to get as much information as they can because the more they have in the beginning of an investigation, the better likelihood that it will be a successful case. There may be things that one does not really think are important, such as what the person smelled like or what was the tone of his voice, but those could be important elements of a case to an investigator. If a victim cannot remember details of the crime it is important that they be honest with the police about that and not try to fill in the blanks on their own.

One of the first things law enforcement will do if they are responding to a victim at the crime scene is to close off the area in which the crime took place. This way anyone coming around the scene won't be able to contaminate it and destroy evidence accidentally. There could be valuable information within the crime scene, such as fibers, hairs, fingerprints, or footprints; signs of a struggle; or bodily fluids and other stains. Evidence is collected and sent to the crime laboratory and will be analyzed there.

For the most serious crimes, such as homicides, rapes and sexual assaults, physical assaults, robbery, and some burglaries, a follow-up investigation will often be conducted by a detective. This is usually a person who has some years on the job and is familiar with the questions to ask and procedures to follow to solve a crime. Since most departments across the United States have 10 or fewer officers employed within them, the follow-up investigator may or may not be called a "detective."

Once a person has been identified as a suspect the police will likely request that the victim identify if that person is the one who she/he believes is responsible for the assault/abuse. This may be done through a lineup down at the police station or through a photo lineup, in which case the victim is shown pictures of a number of individuals, one of whom may be the suspect. If the victim has stated that the perpetrator has a significant identifying feature—say a body piercing, tattoo, or scar—the victim may be shown pictures of individuals with that same, or similar, identifying characteristics. In either case, *the suspect will never have the opportunity to see who is doing the identifying.* Police are very conscientious about keeping the victim and suspect away from each other for the safety and anonymity of the victim.

Once a suspect has been identified and there is enough additional (or corroborating) evidence to substantiate a charge, he or she will be arrested. At that point, the person is booked into custody, may be held in jail and/or may post bond to be released, and then he or she begins the court process. The case then shifts from the police to the legal system as the police supply the district attorney's office with their report. If a suspect is never identified or unable to be located the case may stay open. One common complaint of crime victims is that they feel the police do not give them enough updates as to the status of the case. This can make one feel as if nothing is going on with the case or that the case is unimportant. It is likely that this is *not* the actuality. Instead, the police are following up leads but little information may come from them, they are overburdened by all their cases, and/or they are just as frustrated that a case may be going nowhere. It may be difficult to call a victim to let them know that there is nothing new to report because that could feel like a failure. It is likely that it will partially depend on the police officer — some officers maintain pretty consistent contact with their victims whereas others do not. There are a lot of reasons why one may not hear much from law enforcement, but suffice it to say it may not be because the police are not working or do not care about a victim's case.

Prosecutors have a lot of discretion when it comes to filing charges. They can proceed with the original charge, pursue a lesser charge, or choose not to prosecute at all. Some common reasons for choosing not to prosecute and for pursuing lesser charges include: inadequate evidence or reasonable doubt that the suspect committed the crime, failure of a key witness to testify, characteristics of the case that make it unlikely that a jury will convict the defendant, or the defendant being able to give up information on others involved in the offense.

On television, there are many shows that focus on the courtroom and trials of cases. In reality, only about 5–10% of cases actually go to trial, so the vast majority of cases that are pursued are plea bargained, a process in which the prosecutor and defense agree upon a verdict and propose a sentence to a judge. That means that trial procedures only occur for a small percentage of all cases so it is highly likely that a victim's case will never see the courtroom. When there is a trial, there are a number of hearings that take place prior to the "actual" trial. First is the cause hearing in which a judge or grand jury decides if there is sufficient evidence to charge a suspect. Soon after arrest, the suspect goes before the judge for an arraignment hearing in which he or she officially hears the charges and states their plea (guilty, no contest, or not guilty). If the suspect pleads guilty then a sentence may be handed down right there. The same goes for no contest, except that the defendant is not really admitting their guilt and the plea cannot be used against him or her in a civil trial. If the suspect pleads not guilty the court process continues. There is a bail hearing which will determine if the person is eligible or, because of a number of factors, most notably the seriousness of the charge, not eligible to be released by posting a monetary bond, which is a "deposit" on their reappearance to later court proceedings. Next is a preliminary hearing in which a judge will determine if there is enough evidence to proceed with the case. If so, the case continues towards trial. The defense can then choose to file a number of pretrial motions, including: a motion to dismiss the charge based on a lack of evidence, a motion to suppress evidence that they believe was gathered unethically or in violation of the Constitution *or* is not pertinent to the case, a motion for continuance where there can be a review of evidence or a delay in a witness' availability, a motion for changes of venue which is a request to have the case heard outside of the immediate jurisdiction, and a motion for discovery where the defense requests the prosecution to present them all the evidence they have against the defendant.

At this point there may be additional discussions between the prosecutor and the defense attorney about plea bargaining. The two main types of plea bargains are (1) where a defendant agrees to plead guilty to a lesser offense and (2) where the prosecution and defense agree on a specific sentence in exchange for a guilty plea. Oftentimes, victims are not included in the discussions about plea bargains and/or are not instructed that there will be a meeting to discuss plea bargains. However, it is becoming more and more common for legislatures to include in criminal procedural statutes that prosecutors *must* confer with victims prior to entering into a plea agreement.

One additional way a victim can have an impact on the case is to submit a victim impact statement. In a victim impact statement, the victim is asked to describe what types of psychological, physical, and financial harm they have suffered as a result of the crime. Oftentimes, the victim impact statement is included in the presentence investigation history put together by the probation officer and submitted to the judge. Victim impact statements are used in the sentencing phase of a trial and may be written or spoken (or both). In some states, Texas for instance, the victim impact statement is actually read *after* the sentence has been imposed. There has been a good deal of debate about whether victim impact statements are used appropriately or inappropriately and/or if they might sway a jury or judge based on emotions rather than the law. For the most part, victim impact statements are a symbol that the victim has been included in the process and it gives the victim a chance to be heard, especially if there is no chance for them to testify in court. The district attorney's office is where a victim should find out information about the victim impact statement. Most district attorney's offices have victim-witness liaisons so this is the person who can assist a victim in filling out the form. Additionally, the district attorney's office should make the victim aware of the availability of victim compensation and how to go about filing to receive it. Each state may process victim compensation differently, but it is definitely something each victim should be made aware is available. Additionally, many victim advocacy agencies can assist victims with completing victim compensation forms.

If a case goes to trial, there is a certain progression of events that is pretty consistent across jurisdictions and states. The prosecutor and defense will present opening statements, summing up their cases and presenting their "take" on the charge under review. The prosecutor will present her case, providing a detailed description of the crime and including evidence and witness testimony, at which time the defense can cross-examine (or question) any of the prosecutor's witnesses. Next, the defense will present its case, at which time the prosecutor can cross-examine the defense witnesses. Both parties will present closing arguments and the prosecutor will request that the jury or judge convict while the defense will plead for the jury or judge to acquit (find the defendant not guilty). If the verdict comes back guilty then the court moves on to the sentencing phase. If the verdict comes back not guilty, then the defendant is free to go and cannot be tried for the same crime by the same prosecutor's office ever again.

The federal government and state governments have prescribed penalty tables where a person can serve only a certain amount of time on a sentence as listed by the legislature. You've probably heard about someone being eligible to receive "15–20" years for a crime. That's what we're referring to here. A sentencing hearing will take place in which witnesses can be called to support the position of the prosecutor or defense. Depending on the prescribed penalty, a convicted offender may be required to pay fines, restitution (money) to a victim, conduct community service, submit to the conditions of probation for a period of time, spend time in jail, spend time in prison, or be executed.

If the offender is sentenced to prison, a victim can request to be notified when the offender is going to get released. It is the victim's responsibility to maintain current contact information with corrections officials or state offices of public safety or else notifications may get sent back for lack of an accurate address. A number of states have adopted websites that will allow victims to check on the status of an incarcerated offender. The victim must know the offender's name or criminal identification number and actually register for notifications and the automated system can present information about any upcoming court hearings and release dates for the offender. In some states, the victim can submit their own phone number to the automated system and receive automatic notifications of changes in the status of the offender.

While specific victims' rights legislation and policies will be discussed in further depth and detail in later chapters, it can be seen from this overview of the victim's participation in the criminal justice process that a victim has the potential to come into contact with many professionals in the criminal justice system. However, many other professionals outside of the traditional criminal justice system may also be involved with a victim and their case. For example, medical professionals may become involved in cases of physical or sexual abuse, social workers may be involved in cases where children are victims, a psychologist might be involved in follow-up care, and persons from a community or nonprofit organization may provide victims with additional services.

History of Victimology

Historically, the study of crime, or **criminology**, reflected the focus of the formal criminal justice system on the legal definition of crime and trying to understand the causes of crime by focusing on the offender. Over time, however, the lack of attention to the victims of crime and the importance of understanding both sides of the crime dyad would lead to a more complete picture becoming apparent. Victimology emerged in the field of criminology due to the realization of the lack of attention given to victims of crime. The first criminologist to discuss victims at all was Edwin Sutherland (1924) in his textbook *Principles of Criminology*. Sutherland has been credited with briefly addressing victims in this work, and it by no means focused specifically on

Professional Profile 1.1

Stephanie Frogge
University of Texas at Austin
Institute for Restorative Justice &
Restorative Dialogue

Q: How did you get involved with working with crime victims? In what capacity do you currently work with victims? Have you ever participated in a joint research/practice project? Please describe.

A: I had somewhat of an epiphany in my high school criminal justice course. It occurred to me that we talked about the criminal but never the criminal's victim. Sometime back in the dark ages I also read a *Readers' Digest* article about a police-based on-scene response team and thought, "That's what I want to do!" When picking a major in college I went criminal justice with the (vague) idea of serving victims as a police officer. However, while in college my local community developed its first rape crisis center and I become a volunteer. That opened my eyes to other possibilities and after graduation I was offered a slot in the police training academy and a position with a combined rape crisis/domestic violence program one county over. I went with the latter and have never looked back.

Q: What advice do you have for students interested in working with victims?

A: Volunteer somewhere! This is still a field where there are meaningful opportunities for unpaid staff willing to undergo training. You'll get the experience, the contacts, and be first to know when paid openings occur. You'll also learn about yourself within the context of the work—what you like, what you don't like, where your gifts lie.

Q: What are some challenges for working with victims, especially as it relates to dealing with the criminal justice system and/or lawmakers?

A: I see two overarching issues that represent significant challenges. The first is we've created a system of rights and services based on the needs of high-profile victims, usually homicide survivors. That's been an inductive process where the needs of a few victims became policy and practice. But in a day-to-day context those rights and services are not ones that the majority of victim survivors find meet their needs. A burglary victim, for example, and that's a very common crime type, may be more interested in getting their broken door replaced than in being present at a criminal justice hearing. They may be more interested in an opportunity to ask the burglar what pawn shop they took their heirloom to than in getting to speak at sentencing. And since those rights and services are almost entirely criminal justice-based, they're largely irrelevant to the more than half of all crime victims who don't even report the crime to the police and therefore never enter the criminal justice system. The second over-arching issue is a deductive one. The system itself, including policy makers, typically sees victim survivors only through a punitive, adversarial lens. That lens is a hugely presumptive one in terms of what we think victim survivors want and what is in their best interest. It typically does not allow room for non-criminal justice responses, which we are beginning to understand, may be more advantageous in terms of healing and recovery.

Q: What obstacles have you encountered while striving to assist victims? Have the obstacles changed over the years?

A: The biggest obstacles usually come down to lack of resources, whether political, legislative, training, staff, or financial. For example, it's hard for legislation to keep up with the ways people harm others via technology. What someone does today may not actually be illegal in a particular jurisdiction. In the community where I used to reside, the hospital continues to resist the use of a SANE program in spite of considerable effort to create one. That's a political obstacle. I recently spoke with a victim service provider who told me that it's the policy of her program not to tell survivors of sexual assault about crime victim compensation if they had been drinking at the time of their rape, because their crime victim compensation application will likely be denied. That's simply not true, so it reflects both a policy obstacle as well as lack of training. Here in Texas some of the largest counties in terms of population have only one prosecutor-based victim service provider. One person cannot begin to provide meaningful, let alone mandated, services in literally thousands of felony cases but ostensibly there isn't money to increase staff. That's a financial as well as policy obstacle.

Q: What do you feel is the mark you will have left on the field of victim services? What do you want people to see as your mark? At the end of the day, what do you want your "legacy" to be in the field of victimology/victim services?

A: I can't take credit for any of these advances but I think I was influential during a period of time when we took seriously the notion that impaired driving is a crime and its victim survivors deserved the same rights and services as other survivors. I had some small influence on the creation of early academic initiatives that support this field and I hope to have some influence on broadening our discussion in terms of evidence-based support services, whether or not tied to the criminal justice process, including restorative justice, which believes that response to harm should involve at its core, those parties most impacted by the harm: the victim survivor, the offender, and their communities.

Q: What are some burgeoning issues that you see in the fields of victimology/ victim services?

A: Technology, clearly, and all the ways technology can be used to cause harm, especially among young people who have all the access without the necessary maturity to make good decisions surrounding its use. Another positive issue is a new willingness by leaders in the field to consider offenders within the context of victims. Historically there's been such a chasm between the two but it was an artificial one—today's victim may be tomorrow's offender (or vice versa); a victim and an offender in a particular crime may have a preexisting relationship that has to be taken into consideration; serving offenders does directly impact victims, and so on. The "good victim/bad offender" dichotomy is no longer of service to the field. A third issue that is in no way new, but is so fundamental that the field has to continue its reflection on it, is the question of men's violence against women. Our focus is very much on protecting the individual woman from harm or, if she is harmed, serving her, but less so on the broader question: why do some men harm women in the first place?

Q: Are there groups of victims you think need to be served but are not? Why do you think that way?

A: If I'm interpreting the data correctly, if you're the victim of a crime there's a pretty good chance that you'll be the victim of burglary. That's not a "benign" crime, especially as the homeowner is present in some 50% of burglaries. However, in most jurisdictions that's a crime type that doesn't even rise to the level of meeting the definition of "victim" in terms of rights and services. So if I could wave my magic wand, I'd like to see a cadre of services designed specifically for victim survivors of burglary—both within and without the criminal justice system.

victims, like victimologists later would. One of the earliest works credited to devoting more of its time to the victim was *The Criminal and His Victim* by Von Hentig, published in 1948, where he had one chapter specifically focused on victims, which was a follow up to a 1941 article, "Remarks on the Interaction of Perpetrator and Victim," which focused on the both the offender and the victim (Fattah, 2000; van Dijk, 1999). The first use of the term *victimology* has been credited to Benjamin Mendelsohn in a 1947 speech (van Dijk, 1999). These earliest victimologists' approaches to understanding the dynamic between victims and offenders resulted in a variety of typologies of the victims' role in the criminal event. Mainly, these early typologies focused on victim precipitation of the crime, meaning the victim in some way contributed to their victimization or were somehow in a position to be able to resist the victimization. While some may argue that these typologies were intended to be straightforward explanations of the criminal and victim dyad, they faced many criticisms. From the 1960s through 1980s, these typologies came under fire from several angles, most notably from the Women's and Feminist Movements. They argued that these typologies failed to take into consideration the patriarchal or male dominated nature of society, as well as the idea that crime and victimization represent an asymmetrical relationship, meaning that there is a difference in the balance of power between the offender and victim. While the victim precipitation typologies still hold a place in understanding victimization, as we'll see below, the criticisms of these early victimology pioneers have led to the development of a broader understanding of the experience of victimization.

Specifically, the definition of **victimology** is the scientific study of victims of crime; including identifying and defining forms of victimization; studying the physical, emotional, and financial harms that victims suffer; researching and explaining the causes of victimization, as well as the short-term and long-term consequences of victimization, the characteristics of victims, victim and offender relationships, the risks of victimization, the informal and formal responses to victimization, and victim representation in the media.

An important clarification of terms is needed at this point. Due to the evolving nature of the academic field of victimology, combined with the historical interconnectedness of the discipline with social movements, activism, and service provision, the terminology used is ever changing. The term **victim** will be used throughout this textbook to refer to those individuals who have suffered harm, however the term **survivor** is widely used by practitioners, such as activists and service providers, to describe the same individuals. For some, the term survivor is empowering, symbolizing the stages beyond their victimization, the regaining of control of their lives or other achievements. This can be viewed similarly to the way someone fighting and surviving cancer may use this term. It is critically important to recognize that the term survivor can be subjective. Not everyone will adopt or embrace the term following victimization. Everyone processes their experiences in their own time, if ever, so the term survivor should be used on an individual basis to describe one's self, if appropriate. Language describing forms of victimization have been evolving as well and can be confusing to students in the field. For example, **domestic violence** (DV) was the term traditionally used to describe partner abuse in the home, but more recently the term **intimate partner violence** (IPV) has been substituted to describe the recognition of diversity of types of relationships where violence occurs. For example, early domestic violence laws mainly applied to straight, married couples, thus leaving no protections for dating violence, violence in cohabitating couples, or violence in gay and lesbian couples.

Identifying and Defining Victims of Crime

Alongside the emergence of victimology, new victims and new forms of victimizations were being identified throughout society. Recall that victims and forms of victimization have existed throughout history, however, not all were historically recognized and many changes had to happen so the many types of victims and forms of victimization could be recognized today. For example, victims of various cybercrimes could not have been identified prior to the Internet, so changes in technology and globalization can have an impact on the definitions of crime, along with identification of victims of those crimes.

Social changes and social movements brought more attention to different forms of victimization, and thus led to expanded definitions and changes in the ways different aspects of society were viewed. For example, historically, women and children were seen as property of the head male of the household, and as property he could do anything to them and treat them anyway he wanted to. The notion that the home was the man's domain, and everything within it property, masked the very real experiences of violence some women and children experienced in the home and didn't classify those actions as crimes. While some states began to change their laws in the late 1800s, the movement to characterize violence in the home as domestic violence (and later as intimate partner violence or IPV) didn't emerge until the Women's and Feminist Movements of the 1960s, and by the 1970s more and more states were recognizing this form of violence as a crime.

Another form of violence against women that gained more attention during this time period was that of **sexual violence** against women. While rape and sexual violence has existed throughout history, women's sexuality was such a taboo subject that the problem of sexual violence was rarely, if ever, discussed. As sexual violence began to be talked about and researched following the Women's and Feminist Movements, understanding of this victimization expanded rapidly. As women shared their experiences of these crimes, it was uncovered that not all sexual violence and rapes happen in the same stereotypical way. Fear of the stranger in the dark alley, waiting for a vulnerable woman to violently and forcefully sexually assault began to be seen as making up only one of many ways women's bodies could be violated sexually. Sexual violence in the family and partner relationships began to be explored, as well as the development of the understanding that rapes and sexual assaults could happen through coercion and threat of force. These changes in the understanding of how women experience victimization meant that there might not be any physical evidence of violence, such as bruising or broken bones. This had dramatic implications for the processing of these crimes in the criminal justice system. The violently forced sexual assault in the dark alley provided certain assumptions for law enforcement and the courts, namely that a woman would fight off such an attack or that the attack was so violent that there would be evidence of such violence, such as bruises or a witness who would hear the woman screaming. The absence of this "evidence" would often be grounds for dismissal of a case. However, research on the wide range of how sexual violence is committed has changed the understanding and presumption of what constitutes a victim of sexual violence. Terms such as *date rape* and *marital rape* have entered our lexicon to identify forms of sexual victimization which occur by people known to the victims, and which may occur through coercion or threats. Due to this expansion of understanding of how women experience sexual violence, it is now understood that the stereotypical rape is only one of many ways women experience sexual violence and has changed the standards for law enforcement and the courts in their expectations of what constitutes sexual violence. Further research into sexual violence has exposed the way men and boys experience rape and sexual violence in a variety of contexts, such as within the family, as well as institutional settings, such as schools, churches, and prisons. The identification of these populations of victims have led to revisions in the FBI definitions of rape and sexual assault to expand beyond the traditional idea of rape and sexual violence only occurring to women and girls.

In addition to social change and social movements discovering new forms of victimization, and thus new victims, different professionals were at the forefront of the identification process. For example, it took a radiologist to "discover" **child abuse** (Pfohl, 1977). Family practitioners and other professionals were seen as having an obligation to the parents as their "customers" in the doctor's office, and were willing to believe any story a parent told about their child's injury. But a radiologist, who was detached from the family and only was looking at the film, identified repeat injuries and fractures on children that could only be inflicted by an individual rather than through a fall or an accident, as some parents would contend. This constituted a real shift in the idea about the relationship between parents and their children. Up to this point, it was believed that parents were always the protectors of their children and would never harm them. When a child was a victim of a crime, law enforcement and the state would look outside of the home for the perpetrator. Today, it is much more likely that the family will be investigated first in cases of abuse, neglect, or even kidnappings and homicides involving children.

Recently additional groups within the population have begun to receive attention from victimologists. For example, as people have been living longer and spent more years in assisted living homes, such as retirement and nursing homes, a variety of crimes against the elderly have been identified. Physical abuse by family members and care providers against the elderly or the disabled has been detected with more frequency. From more traditional forms of physical violence, such as slapping or hitting, to various degrees of neglect where an elderly or disabled person who relies on others for food, bathing, and other basic care are not receiving those services, abuse and neglect result in a variety of physical and emotional harms. The elderly or disabled may also be victimized through a variety of financial crimes. In some cases this may be at the hands of children who take control of parent's finances and may mismanage or outright steal from those funds. Care providers may also have access to those funds and severely overcharge patients for care or not provide the care they are being paid for. The elderly may also be more vulnerable to electronic scams, as they come from a generation where technology such as the Internet, email, and Facebook didn't exist. They may not be as aware of or familiar with the types of crimes and scams committed via the Internet, which make them very tempting targets for criminals. For example, scams where an elderly person is asked to help someone they know (although they don't realize the person is an imposter) and send money to help with their situation, play at their sympathies and get them to send large amounts of money to a complete stranger. Depending on the scam, the money may not be traceable.

Professional Profile 1.2

Anne Seymour
National Crime Victim Advocate
Justice Solutions

Q: How did you get involved with working with crime victims? In what capacity do you currently work with victims? Have you ever participated in a joint research/practice project? Please describe.

A: I began in 1984 working for the new National MADD where, five weeks after joining MADD, we were in the White House Rose Garden where President Reagan was signing the "21 Drinking Age" bill. Two years later, I co-founded the Sunny von Bulow National Victim Advocacy Center (now National Center for Victims of Crime). In both organizations, I specialized in media relations, communications, and public policy development—which are still three of the foundational hallmarks of our field's progress and success.

I have participated in many research/evaluation projects, most notably *Rape in America*, published in 1992, which, for the first time ever, accurately defined the scope and impact of rape. I also worked with the MUSC National Crime Victims Research and Treatment Center on a project to encourage partnerships between researchers and practitioners, which are extremely important to our field.

Q: What advice do you have for students interested in working with victims?

A: Crime victim assistance is one of the most noble, rewarding, and challenging pursuits one can have. The needs of victims who are traumatized and affected by crime are immense, and today we have a strong, vibrant profession that works together to identify and address victims' most salient needs. I always advise students about the importance of listening to victims, as the "power of the personal story" has been the driving force in our field since its inception. I have yet to meet a survivor who did not teach me something that strengthened me personally and professionally.

I also advise students to take care of themselves. Working with victims leaves one prone to vicarious trauma and, without skills to cope, young advocates can become quickly overwhelmed and burnt out.

Q: What are some challenges for working with victims, especially as it relates to dealing with the criminal justice system and/or lawmakers?

A: The majority of victims do not report crimes, so there are countless survivors who do not benefit directly from our efforts. I always keep this in mind in my work, so that our policy and outreach initiatives can positively affect their lives. The criminal justice system remains a maze for many victims, and much of our work seeks to ease the process of their understanding of and participation in the system. We have spent 30 years trying to break down the "silos" of the justice system so that we can provide "seamless" victim service delivery to achieve this goal (while we are not entirely successful, we are heading down the right path!).

Q: What obstacles have you encountered while striving to assist victims? Have the obstacles changed things for the better over the years?

A: The biggest early obstacle was the people simply didn't want to talk about or hear about victimization and its impact. This has profoundly changed, due in large part to victims speaking out ("the power of the personal story"), and to the fact that (I believe) today everyone *is* or *knows* a victim of crime. We have indeed reached a "tipping point" where victims and their advocates are no longer simply an "afterthought" in justice policy and practices, but are considered to be key stakeholders in their outcomes.

Obstacles today (again) include the large number of victims who do not report crimes and sometimes do not access supportive services; and underserved victim populations, which differ across jurisdictions but include victims of juvenile offenders, elderly and child victims, and victims of color. Our field works very hard to form partnerships with allied professionals and "gatekeepers" who serve these populations, so that we can proactively reach them with services and support.

The obstacles have indeed changed over the years. I always quote Bob Dylan relevant to the pioneer days of our field: "When you got nothing, you got nothing to lose." Over 30 years ago, there was next to nothing available to assist victims, which made our pioneers quite fearless, creative, and assertive. While we still have these core tenets, we have over the years professionalized our field, gained respect from allied professions, and worked in partnerships that strengthen victim assistance programs and services.

Q: What do you feel is the mark you will have left on the field of victim services? What do you want people to see as your mark? At the end of the day, what do you want your "legacy" to be in the field of victimology/victim services?

A: My personal legacy is simply being a mentor to thousands of survivors and advocates across my thirty-plus-year career. I was truly blessed to end up in this amazing field, and feel an obligation and receive great strength from "paying it forward." Since I have worked nationally and internationally my entire career, I have the capacity to be a "connector" for advocates and survivors who are seeking information and referrals across our nation and world.

I think my other legacy is helping to develop the field of post-sentencing victim advocacy. When I began, only one Department of Corrections had a victim assistance program and, today, they are sponsored in 49 states (with the final state developing one right now!). Victim assistance in the post-sentencing phases of cases is critical to survivors' ability to be and feel safe, and to be highly involved in case outcomes.

Q: What are some burgeoning issues that you see in the fields of victimology/ victim services?

A: The most important issue I see is our capacity to identify and promulgate evidence-based practices. I think our field was a bit slow in the research area, and we are making up for lost time! To be effective in advocacy, policy, and education, we need to be able to prove the efficacy of our work with survivors.

Another issue is to ensure that we continue to push victimology as a profession, and within higher education. We are seeing success in this effort, with victimology majors available at some universities, and victimology courses infiltrating criminal justice, corrections, social work, psychology, and other curricula. State Victim Assistance Academies provide quality basic education to newer advocates to strengthen their capacity and encourage their long-term commitment to our amazing field.

Other vulnerable populations in society have also been targeted for victimization, but due to various factors or circumstances are woefully undercounted when it comes to victimization experiences. The homeless, for example, are not likely to be counted in victimization surveys because they tend to focus on "households" and use addresses to conduct their research. Additionally, given their potentially high levels of interaction with the police due to the criminalization of homelessness and mental illness in the country, they may be reluctant to report crimes committed against them. In particular, the homeless have been targeted by teens and young adults causing violence for thrills or to capture the abuse on cameras as the novelty of technology has expanded. In addition, the homeless have been the target for bias or hate crimes.

Another population that is underrepresented is immigrants and other individuals for whom English might be a second language. For example, women crossing the border from Mexico into the US have reported experiencing sexual victimization when captured by border patrol agents (Human Rights Watch, 1992) and female immigrant workers in California have reported experiencing sexual harassment in their work environments (Waugh, 2010). Due to language barriers, the stigma, and potential illegality of immigration, as well as the intimidation from the aggressors, these victims are reluctant to report to the authorities and are isolated in ways that prevent them from participating in victimization surveys. Victims of human trafficking, either for sex work or labor, are also vulnerable to victimization, difficult to detect, and are underreported due to language barriers.

Some populations of victims may not, on the surface, appear to fall under the scope of victimologists. In 2005, Hurricane Katrina hit several states along the Gulf of Mexico, causing loss of life and massive property damage. The country was captivated by the failure of the response from local, state, and federal organizations. In New Orleans, the devastation was widespread and thousands of people found themselves trapped by the floodwaters, while thousands of others took refuge in the crumbling Superdome. In the aftermath, hundreds of thousands of people across the Gulf Coast were left victims of the massive storm, requiring services similar to those of victims of crime. They had to deal with the loss of life, of their homes, businesses, and property, much like victims of crimes. At the same time crime itself continues to occur, so they may be forced to deal with multiple traumatic situations. The emotional, physical, and financial costs of natural disasters are something that victimologists and victim service providers are equipped to deal with in ways other emergency responders may not be. In fact, emergency responders themselves may also be in need of the types of services victimologists and victims' service providers can offer due to experiencing the trauma of working in such emotional conditions. Working with organizations who have contact with victims of natural disasters, such as emergency management and first responders, can help victims by providing best practices assistance and connecting with established victims' services, similar to those which crime victims utilize.

In 2007, reports of a dog fighting ring organized by NFL quarterback Michael Vick gripped the nation's attention and ignited a national discussion about animal abuse and neglect. Although the American Society for the Protection of Animals (ASPCA) was established in 1866, the treatment of animals and where brutality against animals fits into criminal laws remains unclear, and there have been repeated attempts to protect animals from victimization. States have passed laws about the treatment of pets, from laws prohibiting chaining animals outside to criminalizing horrific acts of violence, such as burning or disfiguring animals. In addition to the harm caused to animals, the study of animal abuse and its relationship to other forms of violence have been increasingly discussed. For example, the abuse of animals has been linked to forms of human violence, such as child and partner abuse (American Humane Society, n.d.).

Another way new victims were discovered is because not all crimes were historically studied by criminologists. Often, the field of study was constrained by what was characterized as crime by the criminal justice system or as defined by criminal law. This study of victims of crime based on legal definitions has been termed by some to be *penal victimology* (van Dijk, 1999). Edwin Sutherland has been credited with breaking out of this mold and began a movement to study the crimes of the powerful with his 1939 speech to the American Sociological Association. Due to the positions these individuals held, their actions were not always technically defined as crimes; it was up to criminologists and victimologists to study their actions and consequences for individuals and society. Sutherland argued that these individuals held high-status positions or positions of such respected authority that many in the public would never think these individuals would commit a crime. However, the fact was that the crimes these individuals were committing may not even have been defined as crimes in the traditional sense of the criminal justice system. Sutherland also argued that, by virtue of their positions, they were able to commit crimes that the lower class didn't have the access to commit, such as financial crimes like embezzlement or insider trading. These types of crimes, committed by individuals by virtue of their positions in business or government, are today termed **white-collar crimes**. From these beginnings, identification of crimes by the powerful has expanded and terms for **state crimes**, **corporate crimes**, and **state-corporate crimes** have emerged, and with them, the study of the individuals and groups who are harmed by them. These new categories expanded upon Sutherland's original definitions of individual crimes committed within organizations, to the study of organizations as criminogenic, termed **organizational crimes**. Through these new definitions, understanding crime moved from an individual phenomenon to one that also includes an organization and multiple levels of accountability. Today, this expansion has led to the study of a much larger population of victims in society than what was traditionally studied by criminologists and early victimologists, which has been mainly termed *street crime*. Victims of wars and genocide are now being studied as victims of state crimes, and victims of financial crimes, such as the ENRON scandal, consumer fraud, and medical malpractice are studied as victims of corporate crimes, as well as victims of environmental crimes.

Another example of the ways and reasons victimologists are still recognizing new victims and new forms of victimization is because of changes in technology. For example, all Internet forms of victimizations, such as identity theft, cyber bullying, and stalking, were not even possible prior to the invention of the Internet. As these crimes began to be committed, and people began to be victimized, the process or recognition and study of these victims began. As was the case with white-collar and organizational crimes, the definitional process through the law is on the one hand a limitation of victimologists' ability to study these crimes, as well as a limitation to victims having any legal recourse for their victimization. As technology continues to progress, this discovery process will continue to expand our understanding of online victims and victimizations.

Changes in technology and the process of globalization have facilitated the discovery of other categories of crime and thus, new categories of victims. **Transnational crimes**, defined as crimes that cross international borders, may have victims from multiple countries or in multiple locations that can also be categorized into several emerging groups. For example, **organized crime**, once characterized by American "mobs" or "mafias" during and after prohibition, has expanded into a global phenomenon that is not contained by the borders of nation-states. Today, these crimes have the potential to cross multiple national and international borders, and can also occur in the virtual world. **Transnational organized crime** groups tend to operate in three criminal theaters: trafficking in guns, drugs, and people. In addition, transnational crimes have also been linked to the identification of new global terrorist networks after the events of September 11, 2001, in New York City, Washington, DC, and Pennsylvania.

As evidenced by the events of that day, these types of crimes can result in large numbers of victims, but also has a ripple effect throughout the society and the rest of the world. The ramifications of that event are still being felt in the world today, and multiple victims and forms of victimization have been expanded upon as a result.

In addition to transnational crimes, **international crimes** have gained attention by victimologists in recent decades. Defined as crimes against the peace and security of mankind, international crimes include many of the previously discussed crimes of the state, such as wars and genocide, as well as slavery and torture. The foundations for identifying international crimes are based on agreements, treaties, and conventions negotiated by nations through the international body of the United Nations (UN). Beginning in the late 1800s, the international community started laying the foundations for the creation of an international organization aimed at creating global peace and security. The first International Peace Conference was held in 1899 and began to codify rules of warfare to attempt to prevent or end wars peacefully. Following World War I, the League of Nations was established by the Treaty of Versailles in 1919, however, the organization was dissolved once it was deemed ineffective due to the start of World War II. Due to the need to end the war and find a path to future peace and security, 50 countries met in 1945 and drafted the United Nations Charter, which was signed on the 26th of June, 1945. In 1948 the Universal Declaration of Human Rights was adopted by the General Assembly of the UN, which outlined the basic protections for all people. In 1985 the UN General Assembly adopted the Declaration of Basic Principles of Justice for Victims of Crime and Abuse of Power, and then in 2005 the General Assembly adopted the Basic Principles and Guidelines on the Right to a Remedy and Reparation for Victims of Gross Violations of International Human Rights Law and Serious Violations of International Humanitarian Law.

Explaining Victimization

Many approaches have been taken to understand and explain victimization, as well as to reconcile the limitations of early victimology typologies that were criticized for blaming the victim. This section will discuss victims' contribution to the crime perspectives, such as victim-blaming and precipitation, Routine Activities Theory, Lifestyle and Deviant Place Theories, Critical Theories, as well as State, Corporate, and State-Corporate Crime Victimization Theories.

Continuum of Victims' Contribution to Crime

As the study of victims came into focus as part of the crime equation, the role of the victim began to be scrutinized and perspectives that blamed the victim began to emerge. Today, these perspectives can be viewed as a continuum of the victims' contribution to crime. This continuum encompasses many different types of victims; from the completely innocent victim, absolved of any responsibility for the crime committed against them, to those who are viewed as contributing significantly to their own victimization. On the one hand, those seen as the most vulnerable in our society, children, the elderly, and the disabled, tend to be viewed as the most innocent victims, contributing nothing to the victimization against them. On the other hand, individuals who are viewed as criminals or those who have initiated the actions which resulted in their victimization are viewed as being partially or even wholly responsible for their situation. Examples of this are the drug dealer who is beaten and robbed of his money or drugs, or the drunk at the bar who is picking fights all night and is sent to the hospital once he has gone too far with another patron. Other victims may land anywhere between these on this continuum.

Perspectives that focus on the victim's role in the crime dyad tend to be characterized as **victim-blaming** or **victim precipitation** approaches. They often focus on what the victim could have or should have done to avoid the victimization they experienced. On the one hand, **passive precipitation** places the least amount of perceived blame on the victim for their victimization. These can range from carelessness, such as leaving keys in a running car during a quick stop to the store, to neglect, such as leaving a window in the home open. **Active precipitation**, on the other hand, can be characterized by those victims who are viewed as being the most responsible for bringing about their own victimization, such as the drug dealer or the bar patron discussed earlier. In some way they are seen as an active participant in the crime against them.

Another way of looking at the victims' contribution to the crime problem is through the level of perceived "responsibility" the victim contributed to the event (see Figure 1.1). Mendelsohn (as cited in Miethe, 1985) suggested a typology of victims based on their relative contribution (or lack thereof) to the criminal incident that unfolded. The range of contribution goes from complete innocence to fabricated victimization and includes three additional levels in between, victim facilitation, victim precipitation, and victim provocation. **Complete innocence** suggests that there was nothing that the victim did to contribute to the criminal event. Victims of 9/11 may have boarded a plane to arrive at an alternate destination, but their actions did not result in a victimization through negligence or purposeful behavior. **Victim facilitators** and **precipitators** are akin to those defined within passive precipitation, wherein an individual may have neglected to do something that could have prevented a victimization, such as locking one's car door. Victim precipitators are sometimes perceived as a bit more culpable than facilitators because they may have played a more active role in the event that ended up resulting in harm. However, they are seen as reacting to situations and not creating them, similar to facilitators. For instance, someone may lend a somewhat untrustworthy friend his laptop computer to finish an assignment, but the friend ultimately pawns it for ready cash. The victim willingly gave up the computer, and may have been leery about the exchange, but could not have expected the computer to be stolen by said friend. Victim blamers may suggest that this individual "should have known better" and thus attribute more blame to him than someone who accidentally left a car door unlocked. **Victim provocateurs**, on the other hand, create behavior that could lead to a criminal event and fits within the active precipitation category previously mentioned. Probably the best example of a victim provocateur is the

Figure 1.1: Continuum of Victims' Contribution to Crime

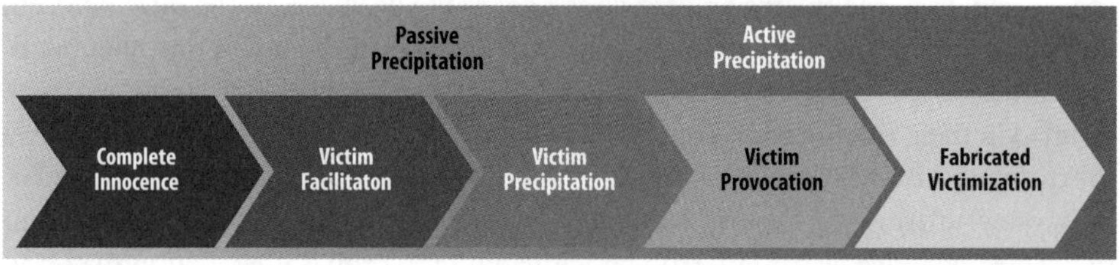

individual who starts a fight with someone in a bar and ends up getting stabbed. The person may be seen as both an offender and a victim at the same time, as he may have initiated the event, but also experienced harm as a result of it (and perhaps greater harm than the other victim). Finally, there are those individuals who **completely fabricate** a crime, and their so-called victim status, for many different reasons—to cover up a crime, to garner sympathy from others, or for some type of financial gain. For example, a person may report that her vehicle was stolen so she could receive an insurance payment, but she may have arranged to have someone take it and dispose of it or there may be no true vehicle (beyond a fabricated paper trail) in the first place.

At any given point on the victim-blaming and precipitation continuum, observers may argue that these individuals are responsible for their own victimization. This approach is one of the ways many in society justify their own lack of victimization, thinking they are too smart to do such a thing. This can also be viewed as the "**just world outlook**" or "**just world philosophy**," which reinforces in the mind of the observer that the victim must have done something to bring the crime on themselves, that they got what they deserved based on their own actions, behaviors, or neglect and can reassure the observer that they themselves are safe from harm. The just world outlook has somewhat of a Karmic approach to victimization, in that in some ways people get what they have coming to them.

Victim representations in the media tend to focus on the extreme ends of this continuum, often defending those characterized as the most vulnerable victims and discrediting those victims seen as contributing to their victimization. However, these characterizations have often been inaccurate, based on unfounded stereotypes, and in fact have been harmful to victims who seek justice. One example of this that has had some official remedies for the victim, at least in the court process, are victims of rape and sexual assault. Female rape victims have been characterized in some situations as "asking for it" because of their actions and behaviors. Some have argued that the way a woman dresses, or going out drinking at the bar, or coming home late, or even walking alone, is asking for sex. The criminal justice system has responded by enacting rape shield laws, protecting these victims at trial from having these factors brought up. Through research, victimologists have demonstrated that rapes and sexual assaults are not about sex, how a woman dresses, or what she has to drink, but they are about the offender and power.

On the other side is the **offender-blaming approach**. This approach reflects some of the more traditional criminological perspectives which seek to explain all crime

"In the News" Box 1.1

On May 10, 2014, Salisbury, MD, *Daily Times* journalist Vanessa Junkin published an article entitled "Victimized Twice: Accuser Blamed in Rape Case." The article discusses the case of a 15-year-old girl raped in the hallway of her high school during school. The local news station posted their own story on their Facebook page and the comments focused not on the offender, but on the victim's "poor" or "lack of appropriate" behavior. According to the article, comments that were posted focused on why she didn't yell, if was she lying, why wasn't she in class … and so on, all illustrating that the focus of the public was on blaming the victim. One source in the article, Lisae C. Jordan, both the executive director of and legal counsel for the Maryland Coalition Against Sexual Assault, suggested that people blame the victim because it "distances themselves from the reality of what occurred." Furthermore, Jordan states that when these types of victim-blaming events happen "(s)urvivors are often discouraged from reporting sex crimes because of a lack of perceived support or a fear of ridicule." It was noted that unlike other crimes, such as burglary, the character of victims of sex crimes was often questioned, leading to victim blaming. It wasn't all bad news, however, as some of the posts on the news station's Facebook page offered support and comfort for the victim, things she likely needed very much.

To view the full article go to: http:// archive.hattiesburgamerican.com/usatoday/ article/8955585.

thorough the offender's actions, placing no responsibility on the victim. This perspective is most commonly used for those victims society or the media may deem most undeserving or most innocent. When the victim is a child, elderly, or otherwise vulnerable in the eyes of society or the media, the attention quickly turns to blaming the offender. For example, early Classical theories and later Rational Choice theories explain that crime is based off of a cost-benefit decision by would be offenders. According to these theories, if the gain of the crime outweighs the potential costs of punishment, there is the potential for a crime to occur. The particular victim or target may have little to do with that decision, according to these theories. General Strain Theory also explains crime through the offenders' perspective. Strain theories argue that individuals in society are trying to reach a variety of goals within society, which could be money or social status, and when the socially legitimate pathway to achieving those goals are blocked, such as education or stable employment, one result could be crime. Once again, this theory doesn't take into consideration the victim or their role in the crime. Overall then, the offender-blaming approach can be characterized as some of the criminological explanations of crime, which focus on why people offend, rather than contributing to the understanding of victims, victimization, or how victims are targeted.

Routine Activities Theory (RAT) (Cohen and Felson, 1979) attempts to explain the crime and victimization as the coming together of several factors. The first is the presence of a **motivated offender**. An offender may be motivated by a variety of factors, such as being poor or desperate, a feeling that they won't be caught or punished, excitement, or boredom. The second factor is the presence of a **suitable target**. A target may appear suitable to an offender because they may be considered among the weak in society (women, children, the elderly, or disabled), they are vulnerable, alone, appear trusting, they may be wealthy or appear to be new to the area (e.g., out of their element, a tourist), or they may have a highly desirable object, such as a car or electronic device. The third factor is **insufficient guardianship** or the lack of capable guardianship. The notion of guardianship often brings to mind a person, such as a parent, police officer, or security guard, and these are certainly some aspects of the concept. However, target hardening, such as locks, security cameras, or dogs, can provide guardianship of persons or property.

There are several limitations to RAT and explaining/understanding victimization. For one, some see RAT as a victim-blaming approach. No matter how motivated the offender, some would argue, it is the victim's responsibility not to make themselves a target and they should just increase their guardianship to avoid being the victim of a crime. However, there are certain societal value and status differences that are not recognized which undermine these assumptions. For instance, differences in social class or employment may have an impact on what women, for example, make a suitable target. A woman from a lower social class may have no other option but to work late into the night at a waitressing job, and because of the low pay must make the trip to and from work alone and in the dark, whereas an upper-class woman may have the ability to get home from work before dark and drive safely in her nice car to her gated community, where everyone who enters and exits is monitored. In these cases, differences in social class and status can provide differential opportunity of increasing guardianship for similar targets.

Lifestyle theories explain crime and victimization as consequences of the different ways people live their lives. Individuals who are seen as living quieter lives, such as those who are married, have children, are home by sundown and not out late on the weekends, are believed to be less likely to be victims of crime. People who are seen as being irresponsible or making bad choices, such as going out to bars or clubs during all times of the night and associating with people who might themselves be involved in criminal behavior, are believed to be more likely to be victims of crime. **Deviant Place Theory** is linked to lifestyle theories in that it connects the place where victimization may occur to the lifestyle one leads. Some examples of deviant places may be the bars or the clubs previously discussed, or known drug and party houses. These theories suffer from several limitations similar to RAT because they tend to assume that the same choices in life are desirable or available to everyone.

Conflict and Critical theories (Marxist, Critical Race, and Feminist theories) encompass a number of theories or perspectives, but what they all have in common is a focus on social inequality and its consequences. These perspectives don't view either the victim or the offender as fully to blame, and focus more on the impact of the larger social system for explaining criminal behavior and victimization. Also known as **system-blaming** approaches, these view both the victim and offender as products of their social and cultural environments. Most conflict/critical theories have their roots in Marxism, which critiques the capitalist system and argues economic structures are the root of inequality in society. According to Marxism, the elimination of private property and a return to a more equitable human society would eliminate crime. Extensions of this theory have argued that the powerful class (Marx's *bourgeoisie*) creates laws to protect their own (financial) interests and therefore create a class of criminals. The larger social structure ensures that these divisions are maintained through lack of education, lack of social mobility, unequal access to property ownership, and the negative and longer term effects of criminal labeling and incarceration in order to sustain a perpetual "criminal class."

Since the time of Marx, Conflict theories more generally refer to a struggle for power in society between different groups or classes of people. This struggle could be conceptualized in the traditional sense of a struggle between the social classes, but also encompasses the struggle for power between the dominant and minority races/ethnicities (Critical Race theories) as well as between the sexes/genders (Feminist theories).

Shifting traditional perspectives of crime and victimization in the ways that Conflict and Critical theories do have significant consequences for the discussion of crime and victimization so far. Let's return to the example of the drug dealer who was robbed. Traditional perspectives might blame this victim for engaging in criminal behavior, but a Critical theory perspective might question the racial and classist creation and enforcement of drug laws to begin with. Rather than focus on the individual drug dealer, a critically oriented victimologist might argue that these laws create more crime and victimization than they prevent, and, furthermore, concentrate the victims among a particular population in society. In addition, this approach creates a class of victims not previously considered: victims of the "system"—the criminal justice, economic, racial, patriarchal, or heterosexual system or some other system. For example, the destruction of thousands of lives due to the War on Drugs and mass-incarceration has created a class of victims of the criminal justice system.

Summary and Conclusion

Victims of crime have been around throughout history and their treatment has been evolving. The emergence of the field of victimology, apart from criminology, has grown into an expansive area of study, identifying the scope and scale of victimization, as well as offering explanations for victimization. Social movements and advocacy groups have called attention to forms of victimization and offered remedies in a variety of forms.

Going forward, the need for victimology and victimologists continues to grow. New populations of victims continue to emerge, the media will continue to shape the public's understanding of crime and victims, and additional legislation needed for victims and victims' service organizations will continue to expand.

Key Terms

Criminology	Victim-blaming
Victimology	Victim precipitation
Victim	Passive precipitation
Survivor	Active precipitation
Domestic violence (DV)	Complete innocence
Intimate partner violence (IPV)	Victim facilitators and precipitators
Sexual violence	Victim provocateurs
Child abuse	Just world outlook/Just world philosophy
White-collar crimes	Offender-blaming approach
State crimes	Routine Activities Theory
Corporate crimes	Motivated offender
State-corporate crimes	Suitable target
Organizational crimes	Insufficient guardianship
Transnational crimes	Lifestyle theories
Organized crime	Deviant Place Theory
Transnational organized crime	Conflict and Critical Theories
International crimes	System-blaming

Discussion Questions

1. Describe the treatment of victims prior to the development of nation-states and formal criminal justice systems.
2. Identify the role of victim participation during the different stages of the American criminal justice system.
3. Describe the similarities and differences between criminology and victimology.
4. Identify and discuss why the discovery of new populations of victims is an ongoing process.
5. Describe the continuum of victims' contribution to crime.
6. Identify and discuss alternative explanations and theories for victimization.

Websites for Further Information

Academy of Criminal Justice Sciences, Victimology Section: http://www.acjs.org/pubs/167_2134_14479.cfm.

American Society of Criminology, Division of Victimology: http://www.ascdov.com/.

World Society of Victimology: http://www.worldsocietyofvictimology.org/index.html.

References

American Humane Society. (n.d.) Facts about the link between violence to people and violence to animals. Retrieved from https://www.animalhumanesociety.org/webfm/574.

Cohen, L. E., & Felson, M. (1979). Social change and crime rate trends: A routine activity approach. *American Sociological Review, 44*(4), 588–608.

Fattah, E. A. (2000). Victimology: Past, present and future. *Criminologie, 33,* 17–46.

Human Rights Watch. (1992, May). *Brutality unchecked: Human rights abuses along the U.S. border with Mexico.* Retrieved from www.hrw.org/sites/default/files/reports/US925.PDF.

Miethe, T. D. (1985). The myth or reality of victim involvement in crime: A review and comment on victim-precipitation research. *Sociological Focus, 18*(3), 209–220.

Pfohl, S. (1977). The "discovery" of child abuse. *Social Problems, 24*(3), 310–323.

Sutherland, E. H. (1924). *Principles of criminology.* Chicago: University of Chicago Press.

van Dijk, J. J. M. (1999). Introducing victimology. The Ninth International Symposium of the World Society of Victimology.

Waugh, I. M. (2010). Examining the sexual harassment experiences of Mexican immigrant farmworking women. *Violence Against Women, 16*(3), 237–261.

Chapter 2: Measurement of Victimization

The study of victims of crime is similar to other academic areas of study, in that it has its origins in the positivist scientific tradition. However, because of the highly sensitive nature of victimization, combined with the myths and stereotypes of victims and victimizations, victimologists sometimes experience a heightened level of scrutiny in their work, along with accusations that they may be overly sympathetic to victims and too harsh on offenders. As with any research, victimologists strive for the highest level of objectivity in their work, but claims of bias abound. A particular challenge for victimologists can come from their personal experiences with victimization, which may drive some into this area of study, and can lead to claims that they lack objectivity. However, many scientists and researchers may have personal experience with their area of study but are not attacked as being biased. For example, the cancer researcher who is so passionate to find a cure because of the loss of a loved one to the disease is not very likely to be accused of bias when they have a research breakthrough. The same ought to be true for victimologists because of the nature of all scientific research. The same standards hold true for both the cancer and sexual violence researchers—they are both held to standards of review from their peers and replication of their research. Neither one would benefit from falsifying their research to fit their personal beliefs and perspectives.

Victimologists' research includes a wide array of areas of study. The extent of victimization includes how many victims of specific crimes occur annually, the rates of victimization in different areas, what patterns of victimization occur and how patterns might be changing over time. The types of harm experienced by victims, such as physical, emotional, psychological, and financial harms, are also studied by victimologists. Understanding how victims are harmed and that victims may experience multiple types of harm is essential to providing proper services to victims. Victimologists must study the impact of victimization on secondary victims, such as family members and the community, as well as the impact on first responders and those in victims' services. Researchers also study the treatment of victims from a variety of angles, such as treatment by first responders, the criminal justice system, victim service and treatment programs, family and community responses, as well as media responses and the portrayal of victims in the media. Through their research, victimologists have also been at the forefront of identifying new forms of victimization and played an active role in the process of defining those harms and advocating for their inclusion in the definitions of crime. For example, rape historically was defined in a very gender-specific way and only included penile-vaginal penetration in the definition. However, the research done by victimologists identified more ways victims were penetrated and also identified that men could also be victims of rape. This type of research helped lead to the FBI's revision of the definition of rape in March of 2012 (implemented in January of 2013 and to be reflected in the 2013 Crime in the United States report) to include these variations from the original definition. Starting from the point of harms inflicted on victims has also led to the identification of actions and behaviors that didn't fall under the purview of traditional criminology or traditional definitions of crime, such as the victims of human rights abuses, war crimes, state crimes, corporate and white-collar crimes, and victims of organized crime and terrorism, as well as identifying new areas to extend the notion of victim to, including animals and the environment.

Sources of Data on Victims

The **Uniform Crime Report (UCR)** is prepared every year by the Federal Bureau of Investigations (FBI) and has been a source of data for many researchers. It is compiled of voluntary data on arrests submitted by police departments around the country. It contains data on Part I index crimes, which include homicide, forcible rape, robbery, aggravated assault, burglary, larceny-theft, motor vehicle theft, and arson. The UCR has a variety of limitations when it comes to studying crime because it only includes crimes reported to the police and leaves out the "**dark figure**" of crime, or those crimes that are not reported to the police. Another limitation is that the UCR utilizes the **hierarchy rule**, meaning that only the most serious crime in a series of crimes will be counted in the UCR. For example, if an individual steals a car, commits a burglary and then commits a homicide, only the homicide will be counted by the UCR. This is not to say that the person cannot be charged with the other crimes, only that the most serious will be counted for the purposes of UCR reporting. For victimologists the limitations are far more severe, since the UCR doesn't collect data on any victims other than homicide victims.

Victimologists have had to rely on data in addition to the UCR to study victimization. Developed in the 1970s, one of the main sources of this data is the **National Crime Victimization Survey (NCVS)**. The NCVS is a survey that directly asks respondents about their victimization experiences. Households are randomly selected to participate in the study for a period of three years, and they are interviewed twice a year during that period. The selection process, by phone numbers or addresses, can be a limitation of the NCVS due to the exclusion of individuals who don't have a permanent address or phone number. Furthermore, a self-selection bias may be present, in that the victimization experiences by those individuals who choose to participate may be significantly different from those individuals who decline participation. Members of the household who are interviewed are restricted to those individuals over the age of 12, which can be a limitation to understanding children's victimization in and out of the home. Additionally, some family members may be hesitant to report victimizations to the researchers due to the presence of the victimizer during the interview.

"In the News" Box 2.1

Attorney General Eric Holder Announces Revisions to the Uniform Crime Report's Definition of Rape

Data Reported on Rape Will Better Reflect State Criminal Codes, Victim Experiences

US Department of Justice January 06, 2012
Office of Public Affairs (202) 514-2007/TDD (202)514-1888

WASHINGTON—Attorney General Eric Holder today announced revisions to the Uniform Crime Report's (UCR) definition of rape, which will lead to a more comprehensive statistical reporting of rape nationwide. The new definition is more inclusive, better reflects state criminal codes, and focuses on the various forms of sexual penetration understood to be rape. The new definition of rape is: "The penetration, no matter how slight, of the vagina or anus with any body part or object, or oral penetration by a sex organ of another person, without the consent of the victim." The definition is used by the FBI to collect information from local law enforcement agencies about reported rapes.

"Rape is a devastating crime and we can't solve it unless we know the full extent of it," said Vice President Biden, a leader in the effort to end violence against women for over 20 years and author of the landmark Violence Against Women Act. "This long-awaited change to the definition of rape is a victory for women and men across the country whose suffering has gone unaccounted for over 80 years."

"These long overdue updates to the definition of rape will help ensure justice for those whose lives have been devastated by sexual violence and reflect the Department of Justice's commitment to standing with rape victims," Attorney General Holder said. "This new, more inclusive definition will provide us with a more accurate understanding of the scope and volume of these crimes."

"The FBI's Criminal Justice Information Services (CJIS) Advisory Policy Board recently recommended the adoption of a revised definition of rape within the Summary Reporting System of the Uniform Crime Reporting Program," said David Cuthbertson, FBI Assistant Director, CJIS Division. "This definitional change was recently approved by FBI Director Robert S. Mueller. This change will give law enforcement the ability to report more complete rape offense data, as the new definition reflects the vast majority of state rape statutes. As we implement this change, the FBI is confident that the number of victims of this heinous crime will be more accurately reflected in national crime statistics."

The revised definition includes any gender of victim or perpetrator, and includes instances in which the victim is incapable of giving consent because of temporary or permanent mental or physical incapacity, including due to the influence of drugs or alcohol or because of age. The ability of the victim to give consent must be determined in accordance with state statute. Physical resistance from the victim is not required to demonstrate lack of consent. The new definition does not change federal or state criminal codes or impact charging and prosecution on the local level.

"The revised definition of rape sends an important message to the broad range of rape victims that they are supported and to perpetrators that they will be held accountable," said Justice Department Director of the Office on Violence Against Women Susan B. Carbon. "We are grateful for the dedicated work of all those involved in making and implementing the changes that reflect more accurately the devastating crime of rape."

The longstanding, narrow definition of forcible rape, first established in 1927, is "the carnal knowledge of a female, forcibly and against her will." It thus included only forcible male penile penetration of a female vagina and excluded oral and anal penetration; rape of males; penetration of the vagina and anus with an object or body part other than the penis; rape of females by females; and non-forcible rape.

Police departments submit data on reported crimes and arrests to the UCR. The UCR data are reported nationally and used to measure and understand crime trends. In addition, the UCR program will also collect data based on the historical definition of rape, enabling law enforcement to track consistent trend data until the statistical differences between the old and new definitions are more fully understood.

The revised definition of rape is within FBI's UCR Summary Reporting System Program. The new definition is supported by leading law enforcement agencies and advocates and reflects the work of the FBI's CJIS Advisory Policy Board.

http://www.fbi.gov/news/pressrel/press-releases/attorney-general-eric-holder-announces-revisions-to-the-uniform-crime-reports-definition-of-rape

Reprint permission granted by the FBI.

The study of crime and victims globally has been growing, and the area of comparative criminology has contributed to this growth and provided the tools needed for global analysis. Comparing crime, crime victims, and criminal justice systems provides a variety of benefits for countries around the world. We can learn from each other the best practices for reducing crime and serving victims. We can also learn from the problems and failures of others, as well as learning to see our own practices from a different perspective. Studying victimology and victimization globally presents its own set of challenges. Definitions of crime vary globally, which impacts the definition of victims for formal data collection. For example, cultural and religious differences can mask crimes such as rape in countries that have no definition for such a crime; where, in fact, Western researchers would consider the victims (mostly women) as victims, they are instead defined as the offenders under adultery laws. Furthermore, individual countries have a variety of capabilities and motivations for collecting and reporting data on different forms of victimization. The International Crime Victimization Survey (ICVS), UN Interregional Crime and Justice Research Institute (UNICRI), the World Health Organization (WHO), and the United Nations Office on Drugs and Crime (UNODC) are a few of the most complete and reliable sources for international crime data.

Overview of Victimization in the United States and Globally

Homicide

You wouldn't believe it based on watching the news or television crime shows, but becoming the victim of a homicide is the least likely crime for a person to experience. According to the UCR expanded homicide data from 2015, the FBI estimates that nearly 15,696 people were murdered in the United States that year (FBI, 2015, Crime in the United States Table 1). The FBI provides estimates to fill in for missing data from various police departments who may not yet have reported for the year or may only have reported on a few months out of the whole year. Police departments reported 15,696 murders to the FBI for 2015. The number of murders for which full supplemental data was received from police departments was 13,455 (FBI, 2015, Expanded Homicide Data: Table 1). The FBI definition for murder includes "nonnegligent manslaughter as the willful (nonnegligent) killing of one human being by another" (FBI, 2015h). Other types of deaths, such as negligence, suicide, accidents, or justifiable homicides, are not included in the homicide reports. Significantly, the Supplementary Homicide Data does provide information about the victims of homicide, their relationship to the offender, the situations the homicide occurred under, and with the types of weapon used, unlike all other crimes.

The largest percentage of homicides in 2015 occurred in the South (45.9%), followed by the Midwest (21.5%) and the West (20.2%) with the lowest percentage of homicides

Professional Profile 2.1

John Dussich
California State University, Fresno
Tokiwa International Victimology
Institute, Mito, Japan

Q: What got you into the field of victimology and/or working with crime victims?

A: I was a graduate student at Florida State University where I met Professor Stephen Schafer in 1961. He taught a criminology theory course and in it mentioned a new field of victimology. We became friends and some years after obtaining my master's degree, I returned to FSU for a PhD and simultaneously was working full time in the governor's office as a corrections planner. On a trip from the Miami jail, it occurred to me that so much was being done for offenders and nothing for victims. During the flight back, I jotted down a concept for providing victim services within a police agency and sent it to him. He convinced me to present my idea at the First International Symposium on Victimology 1973 in Israel. Eventually I was able to get this idea funded as the first victim advocate project (Ft. Lauderdale, FL) in 1974. That led to creating the National Organization for Victim Assistance (NOVA) in 1976. The rest is history.

Q: What advice do you have for students interested in working with victims and/or becoming victimologists?

A: Become well versed in sociology, psychology, and criminal justice. Then get a master's degree in social work, marriage and family counseling, or in criminology. Be sure to participate in a dynamic internship in your undergraduate program. Try to participate in a NOVA conference (if you are interested in working directly with victims). If you are interested in research, then go on to get a PhD with victimology at the core of your studies. Attend at least one International Symposium on Victimology hosted by the World Society of Victimology, and try to attend one of the regional two-week courses on victimology and victim assistance also hosted by the WSV. Select an area you would like to specialize in and find a mentor with that specialty; then, try to study with him/her. I also advise students to look beyond their own state or country. These days it is amazing what is being done in other counties to help victims.

Q: What are some challenges to studying crime victims that you have encountered or seen?

A: Perhaps the biggest challenge is trying to implement a victim assistance project that your research has indicated is needed, but the funding is not available and/or some of the community leaders are not willing to change the system. The resistance to change is oftentimes difficult to overcome. This has been especially hard in working at the international level with developing countries.

Q: What obstacles have you encountered while striving to study crime victims?

A: One serious obstacle has been trying to gather data from victims who have been seriously impacted without re-victimizing them with the data collection process. Most universities have Institutional Review Boards which require students and faculty conducting research not to injure in any way the subjects of their research. The challenge for the researcher is to find a way to collect data that answers important questions within these limits. Another obstacle is finding adequate time and funding to collect data from large samples with good research methods that produce significant and meaningful findings that can be used to make effective programs, policies, and laws.

Q: What do you feel is the mark you will have left on the field of victimology? What do you want people to see as your mark? At the end of the day, what do you want your "legacy" to be in the field of victimology/victim services?

A: I would like to be remembered as: an innovator of the American Victim Advocate Concept; as the creator of the National Organization for Victim Assistance; one of the founding officers of the World Society of Victimology, which was instrumental in nurturing to fruition the United Nations Declaration of Basic Principles of Justice for Victims of Crime and Abuses of Power; having created the Psycho-Social Coping Theory to explain all forms of victimizations and which can be used to facilitate their recovery regardless of the type of force that caused the victimization (crime, disasters, wars, human rights violations, traffic accidents, and other stark misfortunes); the creator of the first victim assistance certificate for practitioners offered by a university in the US at the California State University, Fresno; as a co-founder of the American Society of Victimology; as the director of the first fully operating International Victimology Research Institute; and, as someone who has been a disaster responder, having logged many hours in the USA and abroad: Bosnia (war); Japan (Kobe earthquake); New York (terrorist attacks on 9/11); China (Chendu earthquake); El Salvador (San Salvador earthquake); Japan (triple disasters—earthquake, tsunami, and nuclear accident on 3/11); and in Juarez, Mexico, and Guatemala City, Guatemala (femicide).

Q: What are some burgeoning issues that you see in the field of victimology?

A: Today a burning issue concerning victims' rights has yet to be resolved. The most important and most compelling challenge is to give crime victims real legal standing in our courts. Roughly 30 years ago there were no victims' rights; today our country has a wide range of crime victims' rights. However, these rights are only of value if they are upheld in the courts; unfortunately, they are not all being supported as they were intended to be. Another ubiquitous issue facing victimology is the need to expand the concept of victimology to include all forms of significant injuries and killings regardless of the source of the harmful force. This would place the victim at the center of victimology and formally recognize the commonalities of all forms of victimizations. The last compelling issue I would like to mention revolves around the theme of repeat victimizations. The research findings have given us new (and surprising) insights. It has also provided us with the wherewithal to understand the unique vulnerability of specific categories of people. Not only can we change the future repeat victimizations of those already victimized, but we have a responsibility to create effective strategies to change how this small number of vulnerable persons who are disproportionately being victimized behave so as to avoid their first victimization. Too long has crime prevention centered on the behaviors of pre-offenders and avoided the behaviors of pre-victims.

Q: What areas within victimology do you think are neglected?

A: With the exception of sexual assault, men are disproportionately victimized in the US; yet, research, special victim services, and specific rights for women disproportionately outnumber those for men. In my judgment, victimology should study those victims that represent the most serious problems. When we consider the untreated victimization of males (especially as children) and the long-term negative consequences of males' victimization with special regard for the conversion of victim trauma to victim offending, male victimization is the most serious form and it is under studied, under treated, and under legislated. Another area of victimology that needs to be addressed is the lack of grand theories. Most of the theories used to explain victim behavior either come from outdated one-dimensional postulates from the early pioneers, or they are variants of simplistic criminological theories which were created to explain criminal behavior. Victimology as a discipline needs a comprehensive grand theory to fully explain the common behaviors of all forms of victims.

occurring in the Northeast (12.4%) (FBI, 2015, Crime in the United States Table 3). Of the 13,455 homicides in 2015, more men (10,608) were victims of homicide than women (2,818) (FBI, 2015, Expanded Homicide Data Table 2). Of those men, the majority of them were between the ages of 20 to 24 years old (2,102) (FBI, 2015, Expanded Homicide Data Table 2). For women, most homicides occurred between the ages of 25 to 29 (338), but was followed by women between the ages of 20 to 24 (329) (FBI, 2015, Expanded Homicide Data Table 2). Black males made up a larger number of victims (6,115) than White males (4,117), but there were more White female victims (1,734) than Black female victims (923) of homicide (FBI, 2015, Expanded Homicide Data Table 1). Most homicides are intraracial, meaning they occur within the same race, rather than the victim and offender being of different races or interracial. In 2015, 2,574 White males were killed by other White males, and 2,380 Black males were killed by other Black men (FBI, 2015, Expanded Homicide Data Table 6). When it comes to gender, men kill other men (3,845), but men are also killing more women (1,554) than are other women (151) (FBI, 2015, Expanded Homicide Data Table 6). Children under the age of 18 accounted for 1,093 of the homicides for the year (FBI, 2015, Expanded Homicide Data Table 2). In most cases, the victim-offender situations occurred with a single victim and a single offender (6,137 or 45.6%) followed by single victims, but unknown offender or offenders (4,239 or 31.5%) (FBI, 2015, Expanded Homicide Data Table 4). In 1,551 cases there was a single victim and multiple offenders and 835 instances where there were multiple victims and a single offender (FBI, 2015, Expanded Homicide Data Table 4). A very consistent trend in homicides is that the majority of homicides are committed with a firearm. In 2015, of the 13,455 homicides for which law enforcement have data, 9,616 or 71.5% were committed with firearms, of which 6,447 were committed with handguns (FBI, 2015, Expanded Homicide Data Table 7 & 8). The rest of the homicides committed with firearms were mostly split between rifles (252) and shotguns (269), or other guns (171) and firearms not stated (2,447) (FBI, 2015, Expanded Homicide Data Table 8).

Trends in Homicide Rate across Time

The rate of homicide has been steadily decreasing since the mid-to-late 1990s. (See Table 2.A and Figure 2.1). Despite an increase of approximately 56 million people from 1996–2015, the homicide rate declined, at first rather sharply and then more moderately, with some small increases in the mid-2000s.

Blumstein and Rosenfeld (2008) suggest that there are a number of contributing factors to why the homicide rate declined in three major periods of time from 1980 through the early 2000s. They proposed that there was a major incline in crime rates prior to and into the 1980s due to the boom in population brought about by the baby boomer generation (particularly from the 1960 birth cohort). There were both more people who could participate in crime and more competition for jobs, which contributed to more crime on the whole. They suggest that in and around 1980, the 1960 birth cohort was starting to "age out" of criminal behavior, which resulted in a

Table 2A: Change in Homicide Rate 1996–2015

Year	US Population	Raw Number of Homicides	Rate of Homicides
1996	265,228,572	19,645	7.4
1997	267,783,607	18,208	6.8
1998	270,248,003	16,974	6.3
1999	272,690,813	15,522	5.7
2000	281,421,906	15,586	5.5
2001	285,317,559	16,037	5.6
2002	287,973,924	16,229	5.6
2003	290,788,976	16,528	5.7
2004	293,656,842	16,148	5.5
2005	296,507,061	16,740	5.6
2006	299,398,484	17,309	5.8
2007	301,621,157	17,128	5.7
2008	304,059,724	16,465	5.4
2009	307,006,550	15,399	5.0
2010	309,330,219	14,722	4.8
2011	311,587,816	14,661	4.7
2012	313,914,040	14,846	4.7
2013	316,497,531	14,319	4.5
2014	318,907,401	14,164	4.4
2015	321,418,820	15,696	4.9

Source: FBI, UCR—Crime in the United States, 1996–2015.

decline in crime between 1980 and 1985. The increase in the homicide rate from 1985 to the mid-1990s is attributed primarily to the increase of young people recruited to deal crack in the inner cities. The authors suggest that the older drug dealers were being sent to prison so there was a need for the positions to be filled with younger people in the neighborhoods. There was an increase in the use of firearms as protection for both the drug dealers and others in the community who wanted to protect themselves against the drug dealers. Some researchers also suggest that youth were recruited because they would face lesser penalties in the juvenile justice system and were used to protect the older drug dealers who would have been processed in the adult court system and likely given stiff, longer term penalties (National Gang Intelligence Center, 2011). Blumstein and Rosenfeld (2008) suggest that employment

Figure 2.1: Homicide Rate and Raw Number Change over 20 Years

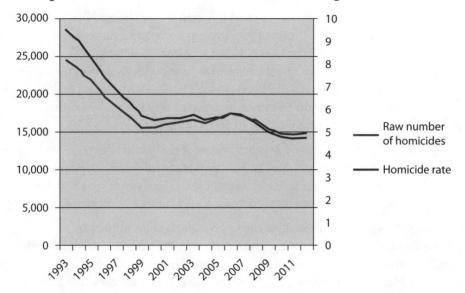

opportunities opened up rather drastically for both African American and Hispanic young men in the mid-1990s and that many of the older drug dealers were being incarcerated, along with a decline in the demand for crack cocaine. It is suggested that all of these factors contributed to a decrease in the need to pursue financial gain in illegal markets.

The same trends in the increases and declines in homicide have been found elsewhere, as Thompson and Gartner (2014) illustrate in their analysis of homicides in Canada and the United States. Whereas the dynamics of motive appear to be different across the countries (i.e., guns are not legal in Canada and the crack cocaine market does not exist as it does in the US), we see the same pattern of increases and decreases of homicide across the last half a century.

Harris, Thomas, Fisher, and Hirsch (2002) suggest that the homicide rate has declined as a result of advances in medical technology, specifically improvements in emergency room technology. Therefore, those acts that could have led to the death of an individual because the physical harm perpetrated was so traumatic ended up as aggravated assaults (or attempted homicides) because emergency room medical personnel were able to treat the harm and eliminate a homicide result.

Finally, Dugan, Nagin, and Rosenfeld (1999) suggest that a portion of the homicide rate may also be declining due to the decrease in the number of homicides as a result of intimate partner violence. Specifically, Dugan et al. (1999) state that three factors have led to a decrease in homicides of intimate partners by their significant others (most drastically noted in a decrease of female perpetration of homicides): a decrease in domesticity (relationships resulting in cohabitation and/ or marriage), increases in employability of women, and the availability of domestic violence victim services.

Homicide in a Global Context

Globally, homicide data is collected and reported by the United Nations Office on Drugs and Crime (UNODC) and the most recent complete data report is the 2013 Global Study on Homicide. The UNODC report is compiled from data collected by criminal justice agencies from member countries along with data from public health organizations representing a total of 219 countries. The UNODC definition of homicide generally is the "unlawful death purposefully inflicted on a person by another person" (p. 9). More specifically, the definition includes three elements:

- The killing of a person by another person (objective element).
- The intent of the perpetrator to kill the victim (subjective element).
- The intentional killing needs to be against the law, which means that the law considers the perpetrator liable for intentional homicide (legal element) (p. 102).

The UNODC report intentionally aims to provide data on homicides which could be described as interpersonal violence, meaning, they exclude the forms of intentional killing which may be a result of wars and conflict, terrorism, and other types of mass intentional killings such as genocide. This is not unusual, as the deaths resulting from the 9/11 terrorist attacks were not included in the FBI UCR homicide data for 2001 (FBI, 2001). Similar to the FBI UCR, the UNODC Homicide Report also excludes other forms of death resulting from suicides, accidents, and negligence.

For 2012, the UNODC reports a total of 437,000 homicides worldwide. When breaking this number down by region we can see that homicides are not equally distributed throughout the world. The Americas accounted for the largest portion of homicides at 36% or 157,000, while Africa contributed the second largest portion at 31% or 135,000. Asia followed in third with 28% or 122,000, and Europe was substantially below the rest of the world accounting for only 5% or 22,000 of the world's homicides. To account for variation in population size, rates per 100,000 are needed for accurate comparisons. The average homicide rate for the world is 6.2 per 100,000 and gives a baseline for regional comparisons. The Americas had the highest homicide rate at 16.3, followed by the Africa at 12.5, both which are above the global average.

Globally, homicides are a male phenomenon, with men making up large portions of both victims and offenders. According to the UNODC 2013 Global Homicide Report, men make up 79% of all the victims of homicide globally. The risk for homicide victimization for men decreases as they age. Men are at the greatest risk for victimization between the ages of 15 and 29, with a homicide rate of 16.7 per 100,000 compared to men between the ages of 60 to 69, whose rate is 5.6 per 100,000. Much of the driving force behind such male victimization due to homicides are factors relating to access to and contact with firearms, as well as involvement in organized crime or gang-related activity. While men tend to be victims of homicide committed by acquaintances or person's unknown to the victim, women are more likely to be victims of homicides committed by a family member, an intimate partner, or a formerly intimate partner. The UNODC 2013 Global Homicide Report "estimated that of all the women killed in 2012 (93,000 women), 43,6000 (47 per cent) were killed by their family members or intimate partners, whereas 20,000 of all male homicide victims (6 per cent) were killed by such perpetrators" (p. 53). The 2013 World Health Organization (WHO) report "Global and Regional Estimates of Violence against Women: Prevalence and Health Effects of Intimate Partner Violence and Non-partner Sexual Violence" found that overall, 13% of homicides involved an intimate partner, with 38% of women who were murdered were killed by a partner compared to 13% of male victims.

According to the UNODC 2013 Global Homicide Report, the type of weapon used in homicides varies depending on the region of the world. Overall, the percentage of homicides committed with a firearm globally is 41, with the remaining committed by means that fall into a large category of "other means." These include methods such as bodily harm or injury, such as fights or strangulation, and sharp or blunt instruments, such as knives or baseball bats. In the Americas, the percentage of homicides committed with a firearm is high compared to the global figure (66%) with Europe being below at 13%.

Sexual Violence

As seen earlier this chapter, in 2012, the FBI revised the definition of rape, and data collection under the new definition began in 2013. According to the FBI, the legacy (i.e., prior to the 2012 change) definition for forcible rape "is the carnal knowledge of a female forcibly and against her will" (FBI, 2015, Forcible Rape). Under the new, and current, definition "forcible" was removed, so the definition of rape is "penetration, no matter how slight, of the vagina or anus with any body part or object, or oral penetration by a sex organ of another person, without the consent of the victim" (FBI, 2015, Forcible Rape). Any other sexual crimes, such as statutory rape without the use of force, are included as Part II offenses. In 2015, the FBI UCR estimates 90,185 forcible rapes (under the legacy definition), or 28.1 per 100,000 in the population, which is up 6.3 percent up from 2014, and 7.1 percent above 2011, although overall 4.5 percent below 2006. The FBI has also been reporting data on rape under the new definition since 2013 and we see a different picture emerge. In 2013, the data estimates 113,695 rapes (35.9 per 100,000) compared to 82,109 under the legacy definition of forcible rape (25.9 per 100,000). In 2014, under the new definition of rape, the FBI reports 118,027 (37.0 per 100,000) compared to 84,864 forcible rapes under the old definition (26.6 per 100,000). The pattern continues for the 2015 data, reporting 124,047 rapes under the new definition (38.6 per 100,000). It should not be surprising that a change to expand the definition of a crime would result in higher numbers, but the challenge of acquiring accurate numbers for this crime remain. According to Kreisel (2009), rape/sexual assault is the most underreported crime to police; thus, it is necessary to rely on measures of both reports to police and self-reports in victimization surveys to best understand this particular type of crime. Among personal victimizations, sexual assault has the lowest reporting rate, per the NCVS, overall (see Figure 2.2.).

Figure 2.2: Percent of Violent Crimes Reported, 1993–2012, NCVS

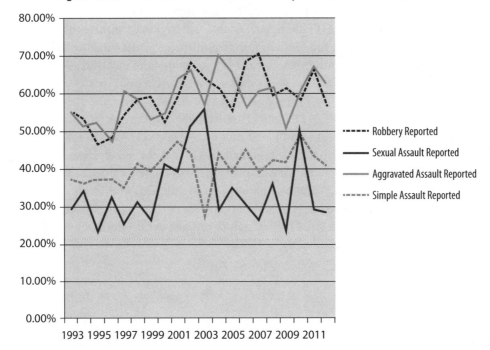

The NCVS (Truman & Morgan, 2016) paints a very different picture than the UCR for 2015. It is important to acknowledge that the NCVS uses an expanded definition, which combines rape and sexual assaults, compared to the UCR. The NCVS defines rape as:

> The unlawful penetration of a person against the will of the victim, with use or threatened use of force, or attempting such as act. Rape includes psychological coercion and physical force, and forced sexual intercourse means vaginal, anal, or oral penetration by the offender. Rape also includes incident where penetration is from a foreign object (e.g., a bottle), victimization against male and female victims, and both heterosexual and homosexual rape. Attempted rape includes verbal threats of rape (Truman & Morgan, 2016, p. 15).

And the NCVS defines sexual assault:

> Across a wide range of victimizations, separate from rape or attempted rape. These crimes include attacks or attempted attacks generally involving unwanted sexual contact between a victim and offender. Sexual assault may or may not involve force and includes grabbing or fondling (Truman & Morgan, 2016, p. 15).

According to the NCVS 2016 report (for 2015), there were 431,840 rapes and sexual assaults, a rate of 1.6 per 1,000 (which translates into 160 per 100,000 in comparison to the UCR reporting method). Comparing the total number of rapes reported by these two organizations, as well as the rates, we can see the very real problems of how rape is defined by the different organizations, as well as the large amount of under-reporting for this particular crime.

In March of 2013, the US Department of Justice (Planty, Langton, Krebs, Berzofsky, & Smiley-McDonald, 2013) released a Special Report on Female Victims of Sexual Violence for the years 1994–2010. The report looked at changes in sexual violence against women over time, as well as specific characteristics of the victims, such as age and income. The report was limited to females due to the low numbers of male sexual violence, which only accounted for 9% of the NCVS victims or a rate of 0.1 per 1,000 in 2010, whereas females had a rate of 2.1 per 1,000. Defined in the report as "sexual violence against females includes completed, attempted, or threatened rape or sexual assault," sexual violence against women declined from 1995 to 2005 by 64%, but then remained stable until 2010. Across all the time periods, the highest rates of sexual violence were found among younger women and girls ages 12–17, and declined with age. From 2005–2010, the rates for 12–17-year-olds was 4.1 per 1,000, for 18–34-year-olds the rate was 3.7 per 1,000, for 35–64-year-olds the rate was 1.5 per 1,000, and for 65 or older, the rate was 0.2 per 1,000. The rates by race declined in all categories from 1994–2010, but women who identified as American Indian or Alaska Native, as well as women who identified as two or more races, consistently had the highest rates of sexual violence victimizations. During the period of 2005–2010, American Indian or Alaska Native women experienced rates of sexual violence at 4.5 per 1,000, compared to White women at a rate of 2.2 per 1,000, Black women at a rate of 2.8 per 1,000, Hispanic or Latina women at a rate of 1.4 per 1,000. and Asian or Pacific Islander women at a rate of 0.7 per 1,000. Marital status was also shown to have variation over the time period from 1994–2010. In 2005–2010, married or widowed women experienced lower rates of sexual violence, 0.6 per 1,000 for married and 0.8 per 1,000 for widowed, than women who were divorced/separated, 4.4 per 1,000, or never married, 4.1 per 1,000. Women in the lowest household income bracket, or below $25,000 per year, experienced the highest rates of sexual violence from 1994–2010. Even though the rates dropped for all income categories over time, women in the lowest bracket still experienced the highest rates of victimization from 2005–2010, at 3.5 per 1,000, compared to women who's household incomes were $25,000–$49,000, with a rate of 1.9 per 1,000, and women with a household income of $50,000 or more, with a rate of 1.8 per 1,000. One very important piece of the data, which showed very little variation over the time period, was the number of offenders and the relationship of the offender to the victim. From 1994–2010, 90% of the violent sexual victimizations involved a single offender and in 75% of cases or higher the victim and the offender had a non-stranger relationship, meaning the offender was an intimate partner, a relative, or an acquaintance (Planty, Langton, Krebs, Berzofsky, & Smiley-McDonald, 2013).

According to NCVS figures overall, about 35% of sexual assault victims report their crimes to police. Reporting is more likely when there is injury involved, but the majority of rape/sexual assault victims do not report to police. Also according to the NCVS, in 1995 about 5 in every 1,000 females were raped or sexually assaulted, had a rape/sexual assault attempt occur, or were threatened with rape or sexual assault.

By 2010, this number had decreased to about 2.1 per 1,000 (Planty, Langton, Krebs, Berzofsky, & Smiley-McDonald, 2013). Therefore, it appears that rape and sexual assault are on a bit of a decline, consistent with the general crime rate in the United States. A *Washington Post* article by Fahrenthold (2006) quotes criminologists and sexual assault victim advocates as stating that the decline could be for the same reasons that crime is general is declining—namely that the youth population is declining, that more criminals are in prison, and that the crack epidemic is subsiding. Others in the article suggest that there has been a vast increase in school programs teaching kids about safe relationships and clearly defining consent. Finally, still others argue that with the highly publicized treatment of rape and sexual assault victims in the media, many victims are both failing to report these crimes to police and to admit to them at all for fear of public scrutiny and stigmatization.

Intimate Partner Violence

Often referred to as domestic violence, **intimate partner violence (IPV)** refers to the violence experienced in current or former relationships by a partner or a spouse and applies to same-sex or opposite-sex partners. The forms violence can take are not only physical violence, such as hitting, slapping, punching, choking, and sexual violence, but also include emotional, psychological, and financial violence; threats of violence; and stalking (NIJ, 2017). While anyone can be a victim of IPV, historically women have been the primary victims of such violence, but men can also be victims. Throughout history the nature of the marital relationship was such that a woman was considered a man's property, similar to a slave, and so he could treat his property in any way he wished, whether it be violently or sexually. The Women's Rights and Gay Rights Movements questioned this history, as well as the singular focus on heterosexual relationships, to expand the definitions to what we know today. Sexual violence in intimate relationships can take the form of rape (termed *marital rape*) and sexual assault as traditionally defined, but also may include threats or manipulation, as well as sex while intoxicated. The Women's Rights Movement brought to the forefront the issues of rape in marriage, arguing that the marital contract was not a contract for indefinite sex. They empowered women to take control of their sexuality and sex lives and require consent for each sexual encounter in marriage. Psychological, emotional, and financial violence in relationships are much harder to detect than much (but not all) of the physical violence. Psychological and emotional violence includes many of the strategies and techniques that trap many women into IPV relationships. Women can be broken down psychologically to be made to feel they are unworthy of love, that they are unattractive and be made to cut off emotional connections and relationships with others outside of the relationship. The isolation victims experience can prevent them from leaving the relationship because they feel friends and family don't care about them or they simply no longer have access to them. Other psychological and emotional strategies may be to threaten violence against a victim's loved ones, including children, family, and even pets, to maintain control over the victim. The abuser also may take control of all the money in a relationship, so the victim has no resources to leave the situation, which can be compounded by having children to take with them and provide for.

The NCVS (Truman & Morgan, 2016) measures domestic violence overall, which includes numbers of IPV, as well as violence against other family members, and found virtually no change from 2014 to 2015. According to the NCVS (Truman & Morgan, 2016), IPV-capturing violence inflicted by both current and former spouses as well as boyfriends and girlfriends, did increase from 634,610 in 2014 to 860,050 in 2015. This means that in 2015, the IPV rate was 3.0 per 1,000 (Truman & Morgan, 2016).

Overall, serious IPV has been declining since the 1990s according to a US Department of Justice Special Report (Planty, Langton, Krebs, Berzofsky, & Smiley-McDonald, 2013). The report found a 72% decline in serious victimizations against women from 1994 to 2011, a decline from 5.9 per 1,000 to 1.6 per 1,000. Simple assaults against women also declined during the time from 1994–2011 by 70% over the same period, from 10.3 per 1,000 to 3.1 per 1,000. Men also experienced a 64% decline in serious IPV from 1994–2011, starting at 1.1 per 1,000 and going down to 0.4 per 1,000. Simple assaults against men also declined by 44% from 1994 to 2005, and then stabilized through 2010 when it increased from 0.7 per 1,000 to 1.1 per 1,000 (Planty, Langton, Krebs, Berzofsky, & Smiley-McDonald, 2013).

Gender-Based Violence in a Global Context

In 1979, the United Nations adopted The Convention on the Elimination of All Forms of Discrimination against Women (CEDAW). According to the text, discrimination against women is defined as "… any distinction, exclusion or restriction made on the basis of sex which has the effect or purpose of impairing or nullifying the recognition, enjoyment or exercise by women, irrespective of their marital status, on a basis of equality of men and women, of human rights and fundamental freedoms in the political, economic, social, cultural, civil or any other field." In 1993 the UN adopted the Declaration of the Elimination of Violence against Women (DEVAW) which defines "any act of gender-based violence that results in, or is likely to result in, physical, sexual or psychological harm or suffering to women, including threats of such acts, coercion or arbitrary deprivation of liberty, whether occurring in public or private life." Article 2 of the DEVAW specifically identifies, but does not limit gender-based violence to:

(a) Physical, sexual and psychological violence occurring in the family, including battering, sexual abuse of female children in the household, dowry-related violence, marital rape, female genital mutilation and other traditional practices harmful to women, non-spousal violence and violence related to exploitation;

(b) Physical, sexual and psychological violence occurring within the general community, including rape, sexual abuse, sexual harassment and intimidation at work, in educational institutions and elsewhere, trafficking in women and forced prostitution;

(c) Physical, sexual and psychological violence perpetrated or condoned by
   the state, wherever it occurs.

These documents are significant because they recognize and condemn gender-based
violence in a variety of contexts, including the home and family, which historically had
been hidden from the public or ignored by authorities as "private matters." The document
also recognizes gender-based violence by the state and state actors, which is significant,
as women are victimized by the state in their home countries, for example as prisoners,
or in armed conflict as is the case with genocidal rape. While many forms of gender-
based violence continue to be hidden and under reported, the UN and World Health
Organization (WHO) publish several reports on gender-based violence globally.

The WHO 2013 report on Violence against Women found that, when looking at
the data combining physical and sexual violence by intimate partners and sexual
violence committed by non-partners, 35.6% (that's more than one in three) of women
globally have experienced one or both forms of victimization. Africa was the region
with the highest percent of women experiencing one or both (45.6%), followed by
Southeast Asian (40.2%), and European women experiencing the least (27.2%), even
when compared to high income regions (32.7%).

According to the 2013 WHO report "Global and regional estimates of violence
against women: Prevalence and health effects of intimate partner violence and non-
partner sexual violence," when looking at women who were ever in a partner relationship
globally, 30% experienced some form of physical or sexual violence by an intimate
partner. This was higher (37%) in the regions of Africa and the eastern part of the
Mediterranean as well as Southeast Asia. The Americas region was consistent with
the global average of 30%, but lower in the higher income countries (23%), along
with the European region (25%), and Western Pacific (25%).

Globally, data on sexual violence and rape come from a variety of sources. One
source is from the United Nations Office on Drugs and Crime 2004–2005 report,
Criminal Victimization in International Perspective. The 2004–2005 report covers
30 different countries (about 2,000 respondents each) and 33 cities (about 800
respondents in each). Once again, addressing the definition used by the report is the
first thing to take into consideration. For this victim survey, interviewees were asked
"first, a rather personal question. People sometimes grab, touch or assault others for
sexual reasons in a really offensive way. This can happen either at home, or elsewhere,
for instance in a pub, the street, at school, on public transport, in cinemas, on the
beach, or at one's workplace. Over the past five years, has anyone done this to you?
Please take your time to think about this" (p. 76). The question was asked to both
male and female respondents, and globally found an average of 0.5% of male and
1.7% of female respondents reported experiencing sexual victimization. The United
States and New York City topped the country and city lists of sexual assaults against
women with 1.4% and 1.5% respectively. Iceland (1.4%), Sweden (1.3%), and Northern
Ireland (1.2%) followed the US on the countries list, and Copenhagen (Denmark)
followed in the city category with 1.4% of women experiencing sexual assaults, then
Helsinki (Finland), also with 1.4%, and Reykjavik (Iceland) with 1.3%. The Criminal
Victimization in International Perspective report provides a valuable snapshot of the

international data on sexual violence, but has several limitations including the small number of developing countries included, as well as the small sample size within countries and cities.

Another source of international sexual victimization data comes from the World Health Organization (WHO) World Report on Violence and Health, 2002. Compared to all the sources of data previously discussed, the WHO report includes categories and situations of sexual violence not previously discussed. For example, sexual violence experienced by sex workers and those trafficked into sex work are included, sexual violence experienced during wars and armed conflict, sexual violence against children, such as forced marriage, female genital cutting, or virginity tests, as well as ignoring women's rights to contraception or forced abortions. In 2013 the WHO released the report "Global and regional estimates of violence against women: Prevalence and health effects of intimate partner violence and non-partner sexual violence" and found that 7.2% of women globally have experienced sexual violence not committed by an intimate partner. The WHO 2013 report found great variation based on different regions, with high-income regions reporting the highest sexual violence at 12.6%, along with the African region (11.9%), and the lowest levels in the Southeast Asia region (4.9%). As previously pointed out, reporting of sexual violence is among the lowest of all crimes, and can have great variability based on the culture, with many parts of the world lacking comparable reporting mechanisms or there being such severe consequences for women who report, that it just isn't likely to occur.

"In the News" Box 2.2

On April 24, 2014, Lusakatimes, an Internet news source in Zambia, a country located in the southern part of Africa, published an article entitled "U.S. and U.K. Announce Additional $10 million for Helping Survivors of Gender-Based Violence." The article discusses funding for eight additional one-stop centers in Zambia that would assist in the treatment related to and the eradication of gender-based violence. The article suggests that the funding would bring the country's total one-stop centers to 16, double its number at the time. The centers housed both medical and criminal justice personnel to better serve victims of gender-based violence. According to the article, at each center, multiple services were provided, including: "medical help from professionals; collection of criminal evidence by police; legal advice and crime reporting guidance; and psychological care through counseling and access to survivor support groups."

The one-stop center idea is being used across the globe and will be discussed more in-depth in Chapter 12.

To read the article in its entirety, visit http://www.lusakatimes.com/2014/04/24/ u-s-u-k-announce-additional-10-million-helping-survivors-gender-based- violence/.

Women are also disproportionately impacted by sexual violence experienced due to **human trafficking**. Human trafficking is defined by the UN Protocol to Prevent, Suppress and Punish Trafficking in Persons in Article 3, paragraph (a), "as the recruitment, transportation, transfer, harbouring or receipt of persons, by means of the threat or use of force or other forms of coercion, of abduction, of fraud, of deception, of the abuse of power or of a position of vulnerability or of the giving or receiving of payments or benefits to achieve the consent of a person having control over another person, for the purpose of exploitation," which includes "at a minimum, the exploitation of the prostitution of others or other forms of sexual exploitation, forced labor or services, slavery or practices similar to slavery, servitude or the removal of organs." A commonly held myth about trafficking is that people are moved or transferred out of the country they live in to a different country, and while this is certainly the case in many instances, a person can be trafficked in their own state and community; in fact, a person can be trafficked from one side of the street to the other. According to the UNODC 2016 Global Report on Trafficking in Persons, women and girls make up roughly 70% of victims of trafficking worldwide. Children make up 25 to 30% of the victims of trafficking. The majority (54%) of trafficking is for sexual exploitation, with 36% of trafficking in different forms of forced labor. Women and girls make up the largest percent of victims of trafficking and, since sexual exploitation, including prostitution, is the largest area of trafficking, one might assume that all women and girls end up in sex trafficking. However, women and girls are also considered valuable domestic laborers, in cleaning industries or garment industries. These workers are trafficked from their home countries, stripped of identification, made to fear law enforcement, remain unfamiliar with the local language, and may spend years working in the homes of others or caring for their children. According to the UNODC 2016 Global Report on Trafficking in Persons, the majority of traffickers, 60%, are men. According to the report, females make up an average one third of traffickers, but in some countries the number was higher. Traffickers tend to be so successful at recruiting women and children because they target the most vulnerable and marginalized with the promise of a better life and opportunities that they can't get by staying where they are. This promise of a better future is how and why parents may willingly hand over their children to traffickers because of the fraud, lies, and deception traffickers use to lure people in.

Robbery

Robbery and burglary are two crimes that are often confused by people who are not familiar with the criminal justice system. A person who has an item taken from them may declare "I've been robbed! Call the police!" However, if that item was taken from an apartment and they never saw who took it, that person was in fact burgled. The FBI "defines robbery as the taking or attempting to take anything of value from the care, custody, or control of a person or persons by force or threat of force or violence and/or by putting the victim in fear." Therefore, the key distinction between robbery and burglary is the confrontation between the offender and the victim with an element of force, actual or threatened. Understandably, the police reaction will be very different if they believe they are responding to a robbery or a burglary; therefore, 911 operators will try very hard to clarify with a caller what specifically happened before they dispatch officers.

According to the FBI there were 327,374 robberies in 2015, which is up 1.4% from 2014 and but down 7.7% from 2011. Robberies can happen in variety of locations, but the most common in 2015 (39.8%) occurred on a street on highway, followed by miscellaneous (19.1%) and residences (16.5%), then commercial houses (14.4%), convenience stores (5.7%), gas or service stations (2.7%), and, lastly, banks (1.7%) (FBI, 2015, Table 23). The average value a robber made off with in 2015 was $1,190, with the highest amount being that taken from banks, which is surprisingly low at $3,884 (FBI, 2015, Table 23). Similar to homicides, robberies are committed using a variety of weapons: 40.8% are committed with firearms, followed by other weapons (9.1%), and then knives or cutting instruments (7.9%) (FBI, 2015, Robbery Table 3). Interestingly, in 2015 the majority of robberies (42.2%) were committed by strong-arm, rather than any weapon (FBI, 2015, Robbery Table 3). The type of weapon or strategy used varies by region of the country. In the South (51.4%) and the Midwest (46.5%), you are most likely to be confronted by a robber with a gun, whereas in both the Northeast (51.7%) and the West (49.9%) you are more likely to be confronted by a strong-arm robber (FBI, 2015, Robbery Table 3). This data may be a function of the different gun laws in these regions, but in either case, a confrontation with a threatening robber is terrifying for a victim.

According to the NCVS (Truman & Morgan, 2016), there was a decline in robberies from 2014 to 2015. In 2014, there were 664,210 robberies at a rate of 2.5 per 1,000 and in 2015 there were 578,580 robberies with a rate of 2.1 per 1,000 (Truman & Morgan, 2016). However, there was a slight increase in the percentage of robberies reported to the police from 2014 to 2015, with 60.9% of victims reporting to the police in 2014 and 61.9% in 2015 (Truman & Morgan, 2016).

Trends of Robbery across Time

Between 1993 and 2012, the rate of robbery has declined by 44% from 256 per 100,000 people to 112.9 per 100,000 people (see Figure 2.3: Crime rates across time, 1993–2012). Despite a momentary increase from 2005–2008 it appears to have declined rather steadily over a twenty-year period. Robbery has a relatively good reporting rate to police with approximately 58.5% of victims reporting between 1993 and 2012 (see Figure 2.2 in the discussion on Sexual Assault).

Robbery in a Global Context

The United Nations Office on Drugs and Crime 10th Survey of Crime Trends and Operations of Criminal Justice Systems (UN-CTS) covers data collected over 10 years, from 1996 to 2006. The survey defined robbery as "theft of property from a person, overcoming resistance by force or threat of force" (p. 27). The definition used here

Figure 2.3: Type I Crime Rates, 1993–2012

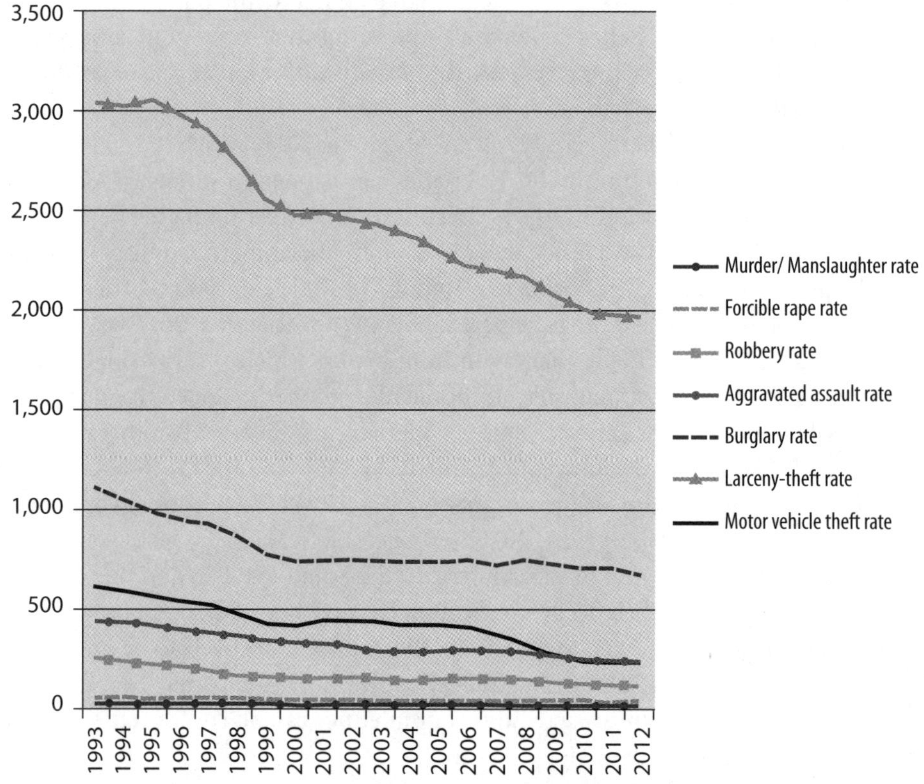

is not far off from that used by the FBI for the UCR; however, in addition to the basic definition, some countries, such as Poland, assign a monetary amount to the definition, below which is not counted among robbery data. Among the 35 countries surveyed, the trend is that robberies have increased over the ten-year study period, with Southern African states leading globally followed by the Americas (first Latin America and the Caribbean followed by North America). Central and South Asia have the lowest rates.

Another resource from the United Nations Office on Drugs and Crime is the Criminal Victimization in International Perspective 2004–2005 report. Respondents were asked, "Over the past five years has anyone stolen something from you by using force or threatening you, or did anybody try to steal something from you by using force or threatening force" (p. 73)? The research found a global average for robbery at the country level of 1%, but the average for cities was higher at 2.4%, which is consistent with what is expected when comparing rural and urban areas. Countries considered developed had generally low risks for robberies, at about 0.5% or below, with the lowest risks identified in Japan, Italy, Finland, Germany, Austria, and the Netherlands. Generally, robbery has trended downwards, particularly in Spain, the US, and Poland, while they have remained mostly stable or experienced only slight increases in countries such as England, Wales, Northern Ireland, and Sweden. The United States was below the global average at 0.6%, and New York was slightly below the city average at 2.3%. Mexico was the highest at 3%, followed by Ireland at 2.2%. Warsaw, Poland, topped the list of cities at 2.8%, along with Tallinn, Estonia, but cities in developing countries were much higher, with Buenos Aires topping the list at 10%. Globally on the country level, weapons were used in robberies 28% of the time, with knives used in 14% of the total robberies and guns in 5.5% of total robberies. Variation in use of a weapon to commit robbery was significant across countries, from Japan, the lowest at 0%, to Mexico (with the highest percentage of robberies), where a weapon was used in 63% of robberies. For cities, 19% of robberies were committed using a knife compared to 12% with a gun. In cities such as Rio, Sao Paulo, Phnom Penh, Lima, Rome, Madrid, Istanbul, New York, and Johannesburg, half of all the robberies involved some type of weapon, and in cities such as Phnom Penh, 66% involved a gun, compared to New York where 27% of robberies involved a gun.

Aggravated Assault

The FBI defines aggravated assault as "an unlawful attack by one person upon another for the purpose of inflicting severe or aggravated bodily injury" and "is usually accompanied by the use of a weapon or by other means likely to produce death or great bodily harm." The FBI also includes attempted aggravated assault in this category, but an aggravated assault combined with larceny-theft will be classified as robbery. In 2015 the FBI estimates 764,449 aggravated assaults in the US, a rate of 237.8 per 100,000, the highest rate of violent crimes covered so far (FBI, 2015, Table 1). While this is a 4.6% increase from 2014, it is a 12.5% drop from 2006. The majority of aggravated assaults were committed using weapons classified as other (31.4%), such as blunt objects or clubs, while the next highest amount were committed with personal weapons (26.3%), such as fists or feet (FBI, 2015, Aggravated Assault Table). Firearms were used in 24.2% of aggravated assaults and, finally, knives or cutting instruments 18.1% of the time (FBI, 2015, Aggravated Assault Table). For 2015, the NCVS (Truman & Morgan, 2016) reported 816,760 aggravated assaults, a rate of 2.1 per 1,000, which is lower than the UCR rate when converted (210 per 100,000 for the NCVS and 237.9 for the UCR). Aggravated assaults are one of the crimes most likely to be reported to the police, particularly in the violent crime category. In 2015, 61.9% of aggravated assaults were reported to the police, which as equal to the reporting of robbery for the year, with only the property crime of motor vehicle thefts (69%) ahead of them in reporting (Truman & Morgan, 2016).

Trends of Aggravated Assault across Time

UCR data shows that the aggravated assault rate has declined significantly from 1993 to 2015. In fact aggravated assaults in 2015 account for only 75% of the number in 1997. In the last ten years of the timeframe (2007–2016) there was a 13.5% decline, which indicates that the 11-year period between 1997 and 2006 saw sharper decreases in aggravated assault. One should note, however, that from 2012–2016 and 2015–2016 the aggravated assault rate has increased by over 5%. NCVS data illustrate that from 1993–2002 strangers accounted for approximately 50% of aggravated assaults, but from 2003–2015 that trend started to decline, with only about 32–45% of aggravated assaults committed by strangers most of the time with the exception of the years 2012 and 2015. Acquaintances account for between 25–35% of assaults across the 23-year period and intimates and other relatives account for an additional 10–25%, depending on the year. Pittman and Handy (1964) stated that there were gender differences in aggravated assault, however. They found that assaults against men took place more often out in the open, in a public arena, whereas assaults against women took place indoors, and more often by a familiar than a stranger. Lauritsen and Heimer (2008) note that even though the aggravated assault rate has declined, there continue to be major gender differences that need serious attention as we progress in the twenty-first century. Lauritsen and Heimer (2008) conducted a 30-year assessment of aggravated assault and found that while men's rates of victimization declined significantly, women's rates of victimization declined less drastically, indicating that while violence against men has declined, violence against women is still a serious problem. Domestic violence assaults are often included in aggravated assault figures, which Lauritsen and Heimer (2008) suggest may be contributing to the closing gender gap for this particular crime. Lauritsen and Heimer (2008) further suggest that explanations for these gender differences should include both structural explanations (decline in crack cocaine market, increased incarceration, more police) and exposure explanations (women have more opportunities for employment and self-sufficiency and have greater access to domestic violence programs and hence they are less reliant on male partners and have more resources when separating from an abusive partner).

Aggravated Assault in a Global Context

The International Statistics on Crime and Criminal Justice 2010 report defined assault for respondents as a "physical attack against the body of another person, *including* battery but *excluding* indecent assault"; however, comparison globally is quite limited as some countries make distinctions between more simple assaults (involving slapping or verbal threats) and aggravated (wounding or maiming) while others group the whole range into assaults. While Oceania (the region in the Pacific Ocean including Australia and New Zealand, as well as many of the islands to the east) appears to have the highest numbers of assaults, the majority of those are classified as simple assaults (International Statistics on Crime and Criminal Justice 2010, Figure 1). However, when looking at major assaults, Oceania drops to third, with North America second, and West, Central, and Southern Africa as a single region in first (International Statistics on Crime and Criminal Justice 2010, Figure 2). The incidence of total assaults rose from 1996 to 2006, but major assaults in the 10 countries with the highest rates only rose from 1996 to 2001, when they leveled off (International Statistics on Crime and Criminal Justice 2010, Figure 3).

According to the United Nations Office on Drugs and Crime Criminal Victimization in International Perspective 2004–2005 report, respondents were asked: "have you over the past five years been personally attacked or threatened by someone in a way that really frightened you, either at home or elsewhere, such as a pub, in the street, at school, on public transport, on the beach, or at your workplace?" (p. 79). Globally, 3.1% of those interviewed responded that they had experienced an assault by force or threat. Countries with responses of 4% or higher included the United States, the Netherlands, New Zealand, Ireland, England and Wales, Iceland, and Northern Ireland, with the highest at 6.8%. Belfast in Northern Ireland was also the highest city at 9.2%, followed by London, England, and Reykjavik, Iceland. Developing countries were higher at 6.1%, with Johannesburg, South Africa, being the city with the highest at 11.2%. Respondents indicated that a weapon was used in 17% of incidents at the country level, most commonly a knife in 6.4% where as in 2.4% of incidents a gun was used. The country where guns were used the most was Mexico with 16% of incidents, followed by the United States and Northern Ireland tied with 6%. In cities, respondents indicated a weapon was used in 22.6% of incidents, knives in 9.4%, and 5% for guns. Rio de Janeiro and Sao Paulo, both in Brazil, had the highest incidents involving a gun at 39% and 35%, respectively. At the country level, respondents indicated they knew the victim 50% of the time, with women being more likely to know the offender than men.

Burglary

A burglary, for the purpose of the FBI UCR reporting, is defined as "the unlawful entry of a structure to commit a felony or theft" and defines "structure" as including an "apartment, barn, house trailer or houseboat when used as a permanent dwelling, office, railroad car (but not automobile), stable, and vessel (i.e., ship)." In 2015, the FBI estimates 1,579,527 burglaries occurred in the US, which is a rate of 491.4 per 100,000 (FBI, 2015, Table 1). This indicates a continued decrease since 2006 estimates, a decline of 28% since that year (FBI, 2015). While this number might seem alarming at first, we'll begin to see that overall, people in the US are most likely to be victimized by a property crime, rather than a violent crime. What might not come as a surprise is that the majority or burglaries (999,446) were committed in a residence/dwelling (FBI, 2015, Table 23). The NCVS numbers for household burglary are far higher than for the UCR. In 2015 the NCVS reported 2,904,570 household burglaries, or a rate of 22 per 1,000 (2,200 per 100,000). Of those, the NCVS found that 50.8% of burglaries were reported to the police (Truman & Morgan, 2016).

Trends across Time for Burglary

Burglaries rates have experienced a 56% decrease from 1994 to 2011 (Walters, Moore, Berzofsky, & Langton, 2013). The pattern illustrating the type of burglary has persisted across that same time period, however, with completed unlawful entries accounting for the majority of burglaries, followed by completed forcible entry, and attempted forcible entry. Essentially that means that most burglars are gaining access to structures through unlocked portals (which could be good news for crime prevention experts as the fix may be "simple"—lock up). Similar to its cousin robbery, victims reporting completed burglaries to police have remained in the 50–58% area, with greater reporting happening at the tail end of the 18-year period. Over 80% of victims who suffered a loss of $1,000 or more reported the crime to police. Victims who lost between $500 to $999 appeared to report the crime around 60% of the time, while victims who suffered no loss appeared to report the crime approximately 45% of the time. Interestingly, victims who lost between $1 and $499 had the lowest reporting rates, with a reporting rates in the 35–40% area. One interesting finding was that in about 4% of all burglaries, a firearm is one of the items taken (Langton, 2012). According to the NCVS, approximately 4 out of 5 of those firearms are never recovered; this equates to about 186,000 missing firearms *each year*.

Burglary in a Global Context

The definition of burglary, according to the International Statistics on Crime and Criminal Justice 2010 report, is "to gain access to a closed part of a building or other premises by use of force with the intent to steal goods" (p. 27). The definition intended to focus mainly on structures, and excludes such things as automobiles or vending machines. The region with the highest rate of burglaries was Oceania, specifically Australia and New Zealand, followed by North America, where the United States and Canada had highest rates, with South Africa being the region with the third highest rates. South Asia had the lowest rates of burglary, followed by the Near and Middle East/Southwest Asia, with the exception of Israel. Significantly, the report found most burglaries occurred in commercial and business properties, rather than in homes.

For the 2004–2005 Criminal Victimization in International Perspective report from the United Nations Office on Drugs and Crime, the focus was on attempted or completed entry into a household. Overall at the country level, 1.8% of households reported a completed burglary and 1.7% of households reported failed burglary attempts. Reports were higher in main cities compared to country-level data, with 2.3% in cities in developed countries and 6.4% in cities in developing countries. Some of the countries above the average for burglaries include the United States (2.5%), Australia (2.5%), Mexico (3.9%), and England and Wales (3.5%). Several countries fell below the average for burglaries, including Japan (0.9%), Finland, and Spain (both 0.8%), and Sweden at the lowest (0.7%). Cities in developed countries with the highest percentages were Istanbul, Turkey (4.6%) and London, England (4.5%) and the lowest were Lisbon, Portugal (0.7%) and Hong Kong, China (0.6%).

Larceny-Theft

According to the FBI, larceny-theft is the "unlawful taking, carrying, leading, or riding away of property from the possession or constructive possession of another," such as bicycles, shoplifting, and pick-pocketing. The main distinction from previous forms is the absence of the use or threat of force. Larceny-theft also excludes thefts by fraud and forgery. In 2015, the FBI recorded 5,706,346 larceny-thefts at a rate of 1,775.4

per 100,000 (FBI, 2015, Table 1). The majority of larceny-thefts recorded came from the catchall "all others" category (1,521,226) and next were of thefts from a motor vehicle (1,203,497) with the average value of the items taken at $782 (FBI, 2015, Table 23) and the highest percentage occurred in the West (29.7%) (FBI, 2015, Larceny-theft table). Third most common larceny-theft was shoplifting (1,118,390) and the average value of items taken was $262 (FBI, 2015, Table 23) with fairly small range across regions of the country (21.5–23.5%%) (FBI, 2015f, Larceny-theft Table). Thefts from buildings were the next most common (582,055) with the second highest average cost at $1,394 (FBI, 2015, Table 23) and were regionally highest in the Northeast (18%) (FBI, 2015f, Larceny-theft Table). In 2015 the NCVS found much higher numbers for this property crime than those reported for the UCR. There were 11,142,310 thefts reported for the NCVS, or a rate of 84.4 per 1,000 (8,440 per 100,000). Of those thefts, the NCVS found that only 28.6% were reported to the police (Truman & Morgan, 2016).

Trends across Time for Larceny-Theft

Larceny-theft has seen a consistent and significant decline since 1995, from a rate of 3,043.2/100,000 to 1,959.3/100,000 in 2012. In the ten-year period of 2003–2012 alone, the rate dropped by 18.9% according to the UCR. The NCVS also showed a decline in larceny-theft from 1993–2012, with a bit of an increase in 2012 (about 3,000,000 more reports than in 2011). Even with the increase, however, the amount reported in 2012 is significantly less than what NCVS victims reported for 1993. As with other crimes, the decline in crime is attributable to more law enforcement on the streets, decline in the demand for crack cocaine, and higher incarceration rates (Kearney & Harris, 2014). Larceny-theft crimes have a relatively low reporting rate, with averages in the mid-late 1990s being around 27% with some increase in the 2000s in the 29–32% range.

Larceny-Theft in a Global Context

Globally, thefts are looked at slightly differently than in the United States, where the personal property was taken from automobiles, stores, or buildings. According to the United Nations Office on Drugs and Crime Criminal Victimization in International Perspective report for 2004–2005, in one third of thefts around the world the victim was carrying what was stolen, resulting in many of the cases of theft being recorded as pick-pocketing. For overall thefts, including pick-pocketing, at the country level an average of 3.8% of respondents reported being victimized compared to 1.7% for pick-pocketing alone. Ireland (7.2%) and Iceland (6.9%) experienced the highest percentage of overall thefts and the United States (4.8%) was above the average. The countries with the lowest percentage of overall thefts were Japan (0.3%), Portugal (1.6%), and Spain (2.1%). For cities in developed countries, London, England (10.2%) topped the list of overall thefts, followed by Tallinn, Estonia (9.6%), Reykjavik, Iceland (8.2%), and New York City in fourth (7.7%). The cities with the lowest overall thefts in developed countries were Lisbon, Portugal (2.4%), and Helsinki, Finland (3.0%). When looking at cities in developing countries, Phnom Penh, Cambodia (12.8%), was highest in overall thefts, followed by Lima, Peru (12.3%), and Maputo,

Mozambique (9.9%). When looking only at pick-pocketing, Greece (4.3%), Estonia (3.3%) and Ireland (3.0%) were in the top three, with the United States falling below the average with 1.2%. Japan was once again the lowest (0.4%), followed by Mexico (0.6%) and New Zealand (0.7%), for pick-pocketing alone. For only pick-pocketing in developed cities, number one and number two for overall thefts switched places; Tallinn, Estonia (6.5%), and London, England (5.2%), were still at the top, followed by Brussels, Belgium (3.8%), with New York City (3.3%) falling lower on the list. Similarly, in developing countries number one and number two also switched places, with Lima, Peru (11.4%), being the highest for pick-pocketing, followed by Phnom Penh, Cambodia (11.3%) and Maputo, Mozambique (8.2%), staying at number three.

Motor Vehicle Theft

For the purposes of the UCR, the FBI limits the definition of motor vehicle theft to those vehicles operated on land and excludes vehicles on rails. This includes cars, trucks, SUVs, ATVs, buses, snowmobiles, and motorcycles. Large vehicles, such as construction equipment or airplanes are excluded, as well as watercraft, such as boats or jet skis. In 2015, the FBI estimates 707,758 motor vehicle thefts, which is a rate of 220.2 per 100,000, the lowest of the property crimes (FBI, 2015, Table 1). Motor vehicles were the most likely property to be recovered locally with 58.2% of vehicles recovered, which is above the average of overall property recovered (26.1%) (FBI, 2015, Table 24). Automobiles were the most likely motor vehicle stolen, overall accounting for 74.7% of thefts compared to trucks and buses at 14.8% and other vehicles totaling 10.5% (FBI, 2015, Motor Vehicle Theft Table). Regionally, automobiles were most likely to be stolen in the Northeast (83.9%), while theft of trucks and buses was highest in the South (18.8%) (FBI, 2015, Motor vehicle theft table). The NCVS found 564,160 motor vehicle thefts in 2015, which is the lowest rate found by the NCVS among property crimes at 4.3 per 1,000 (430 per 100,000) and also the highest percentage reported to the police (69%) (Truman & Morgan, 2016).

Trends across Time for Motor Vehicle Theft

Motor vehicle theft has demonstrated a significant decline in rate from 1993–2012 (606.3/100,000 to 229.7/100,000) with a slight resurgence between 2001 and 2003. For property crimes, motor vehicle theft has the highest associated dollar loss, which in 2012 was $6,019 per vehicle, with a total 2012 loss of $4.3 billion. Consistent with other crimes, some explanations for the decline in motor vehicle theft include the decreasing population of youth, the decline in the crack epidemic, and the increased incarceration rate. Some additional reasons have been suggested that are also compelling. The auto industry has gone to great lengths to manufacture cars that are incredibly difficult, if not impossible, to hot-wire (Klein & White, 2011). Private companies sell security packages that allow for a stolen car to be tracked via GPS technology and in some cases even have the power to automatically shut down a car so the thief cannot effectively drive it away. Police have also acquired new technology that allows them to scan license plates to detect stolen cars (as one of the goals of the technology). In a study by the Police Executive Research Forum (2012), it was found that when law enforcement used the license plate scanners they were able to scan eight times as many cars compared to a manual check, perform four times as many hits on stolen automobiles, and make two times as many arrests and vehicle recoveries compared to manual checks where an officer manually types in each license plate into the cruiser's mobile data unit (Cover & Koper, 2012). Police have also utilized the "bait car" tactic, in which a police-owned vehicle was rigged with surveillance and the keys were left in it in a high-crime area. This enabled the police to track down car theft rings (Klein & White, 2011). Special units have been created to address motor vehicle theft and state law enforcement agencies have created specialized law enforcement units within their Departments of Motor Vehicles focusing specifically on license and theft issues. So, the interaction between car companies using increasing sophisticated technology in the cars themselves and law enforcement utilizing specialized technology and focused units to address motor vehicle thefts have significantly contributed to the decline in motor vehicle thefts. This has, however, created the unfortunate effect of car thieves turning to additional types of crime to secure keys for cars since the newer cars are difficult or impossible to hot-wire (Copes & Cherbonneau, 2006). Copes and Cherbonneau (2006) suggest that car thieves are now engaging in burglaries, robberies, and/or fraud to acquire keys, which illustrates the highly adaptive nature of this particular group of criminals.

Motor Vehicle Theft in a Global Context

Motor vehicle thefts globally take on a different character than in the United States. The United Nations Office on Drugs and Crime report, *Criminal Victimization in International Perspective* (2004–2005) devotes an entire chapter to "Victimization by Vehicle Related Crime" and includes sections on theft of cars, thefts from or out of cars, and motorcycle and bicycle thefts. Thefts of cars globally have been decreasing since the 1990s even as car ownership has increased. Much of the decline can be attributed to increases in vehicle security, such as car alarms, steering wheel locks such as the "Club," and new electronic and computerized ignition systems. At the country level, 0.8% of respondents experienced a motor vehicle theft, whereas in cities 1.3% of citizens reported a car theft. Countries experiencing the highest vehicle thefts were England and Wales (1.8%) and New Zealand (1.8%), followed by Portugal (1.5%), with the United States above the average with (1.1%). The lowest countries for car thefts were Austria and Japan, both only reporting 0.1%. For cities in developed countries the average was 1.1% with Rome, Italy, topping the list (3.4%), followed by Dublin, Ireland (3.0%), Buenos Aires, Argentina (2.1%), and New York City in the ninth spot (1.6%). The average for cities in developing countries was 1.8% and Sao Paulo, Brazil (4.2%), was leading the list, followed by Johannesburg, South Africa (2.6%).

In the FBI UCR data, we saw that in the United States the second highest category of larceny-thefts occurred from a motor vehicle, but the UNODC Criminal

Victimization in International Perspective 2004–2005 report collects separate data on thefts from cars, which also includes parts stolen off of cars. The global average for countries reporting thefts from cars was 3.6%, which is more common than the theft of cars (0.8%), with New Zealand (6.6%) at the top of the list, followed by England and Wales (6.0%) tied with Estonia. Ireland and the United States tied with 5.2% of the population experiencing thefts from cars. The countries experiencing the lowest thefts from cars were Japan (1.1%), Greece (1.8%), Germany (2.0%), and Hungary (2.1%). For developed cities the average was 4.4% of the population experiencing thefts from cars, with London, England (8.5%) highest on the list, followed by Tallinn, Estonia (8.4%), Belfast, Northern Ireland (6.7%), and New York City (6.6%). The two developed cities to experiencing the lowest rate of car thefts were Hong Kong, China (0.5%), and Copenhagen, Denmark (1.5%). In the developing cities the average was 4.7% of the population experiencing thefts from cars with Buenos Aires, Argentina (7.2%), and Sao Paulo, Brazil (7.2%), tied at the top of the list and Rio de Janeiro, Brazil (1.2%), lowest on the list.

Compared to the United States, much of the rest of the world relies on two wheel transportation, such as motorcycles or bicycles, rather than personal cars. At the country level, the global average for motorcycle thefts was 0.3%, with Italy, the most common country for ownership with 33% of citizens having motorized two wheel vehicles, topping the list (1.0%), followed by England and Wales (0.8%) and Japan (0.7%). The United States fell at the average with several other countries, such as Denmark and France. The average for cities in developed countries was 0.3%, the same as for countries. Paris, France (1.0%), took the number one spot, followed by Rome, Italy (0.9%), and Zurich, Switzerland (0.8%). Not surprisingly, New York City didn't even register, reporting 0.0% motorcycle thefts. For cities in developing countries the average for motorcycle thefts was 1.3%, but Phnom Penh, Cambodia, far surpassed the average with a whopping 6.6% of respondents reporting motorcycle thefts.

Of the vehicle types discussed, bicycle theft posed the highest risk, with a global country average of 2.9% of citizens experiencing bicycle thefts. This might come as a surprise to American readers, however, in countries such as the Netherlands, Sweden, and Denmark, 80% or more of the population owns bicycles and when used as a primary mode of transportation is more likely to be reported than in the states where a bicycle is more commonly used for recreation. Given this, the Netherlands experienced the highest bicycle thefts, with 6.6% of the population reporting thefts, followed by Denmark (6.0%) and Finland (5.2%). The United States was at the average, with 2.9% of the population reporting bicycle thefts. Looking at the data for developed cities, it is not surprising that Amsterdam, in the Netherlands reported 12.0% of the population experiencing bicycle thefts, compared to the city average of 3.5%. Other cities in countries with the highest ownership also topped the list, such as Copenhagen, Denmark (9.3%), and Stockholm, Sweden (7.0%). New York City landed below the average with 3.0% of the population reporting bicycle thefts. The average bicycle theft for cities in developing countries was 2.7% with residents in Phnom Penh, Cambodia, experiencing 5.3%, followed by Buenos Aires, Argentina (4.2%).

Arson

According to the FBI UCR (2015), the "willful or malicious burning or attempting to burn, with or without intent to defraud" defines arson. Arson can be committed against a variety of property types, including homes, public buildings, automobiles, airplanes, and other personal property of another individual. This particular crime poses some challenges for data collection and FBI reporting. First, local law enforcement and fire officials must determine through investigation that a fire was intentionally set. Any suspicious fires or those ruled unknown in origin are not included in the data. Second, while 13,443 law enforcement agencies reported data on arson, not all agencies reported expanded data with details of the types of structures or value lost in the fire. In total, 41,376 arsons were reported by law enforcement to the FBI for 2015, and of those the FBI received expanded data on 36,757 arsons. The majority of the arsons for which expanded data is available, 16,809 or 45.7%, were committed against some type of structure, while 8,895 or 24.2% were mobile (automobile and "other" mobile combined), and 11,053 or 30.1% were categorized as "other" (FBI, 2015, Arson, Table 2). The average dollar amount lost per arson was $14,182, but for commercial structures the average loss was $51,231, with the highest losses coming from industrial/manufacturing at $270,462.

Summary and Conclusion

Data on crime victims, both in the US and globally, come from a variety of sources. In the US, the UCR and NCVS are two of the main sources of crime data, but data on victims in the UCR is limited. Internationally, the UN provides global crime and victimization data on a variety of areas. Comparing data on victimization in the US and globally can help to recognize trends in victimization, detect areas of weakness, as well as identify new and emerging victim populations.

Key Terms

Uniform Crime Report (UCR)
"Dark figure" of crime
Hierarchy rule
National Crime Victimization Survey
   (NCVS)
Homicide
Sexual violence
Intimate partner violence (IPV)

Gender-based violence
Human trafficking
Robbery
Aggravated assault
Burglary
Larceny-theft
Motor vehicle theft
Arson

Discussion Questions

1. Identify and describe the main sources of crime data in the United States.
2. Discuss strengths and weaknesses of each of the main sources of crime data in the United States.
3. Define the "dark figure" of crime.
4. Discuss why it is important to study crime and victimization internationally.
5. Compare and contrast homicide data in the United States and internationally.

Websites for Further Information

Access the UCR through the FBI website: http://www.fbi.gov/.

Access the NCVS through the Bureau of Justice Statistics website: http://bjs.gov/.

Access the NCVS survey instrument: http://www.bjs.gov/content/pub/pdf/svs1_06.pdf.

Access the ICVS: http://www.unicri.it/services/library_documentation/publications/icvs/publications/.

Access the UNODC: http://www.unodc.org/.

References

Blumstein, A., & Rosenfeld, R. (2008). Factors contributing to U.S. crime trends. In A. S. Goldberger & R. Rosenfeld (Eds.), Understanding crime trends: Workshop report, (pp. 13–43). Washington, DC: The National Academies Press.

Boland, M. L. (2001). *Crime victims' guide to justice* (2nd ed.). Naperville, IL: Sphinx Publishing.

Bureau of Justice Statistics. (2013). *National Crime Victimization Survey*. Retrieved from http://www.bjs.gov/index.cfm?ty=dcdetail&iid=245.

The Convention on the Elimination of All Forms of Discrimination against Women (CEDAW). (1979). Retrieved from http://www.un.org/womenwatch/daw/cedaw/cedaw.htm.

Copes, H., & Cherbonneau, M. (2006). The key to auto theft: Emerging methods of auto theft from the offenders' perspective. *British Journal of Criminology, 46*, 917–934.

Cover, C., & Koper, C. (2012). *Critical issues in policing series: "How are innovations in technology transforming policing?"* Washington, DC: Police Executive Research Forum.

Dugan, Nagin, and Rosenfeld (1999). Explaining the decline in intimate partner homicide: The effects of changing domesticity, women's status, and domestic violence resources. *Homicide Studies*, 3(3), 187–214.

Fahrenthold, D. A. (2006, June 19). Statistics show drop in U.S. rape cases. *The Washington Post*. Retrieved from http://www.washingtonpost.com/wpdyn/content/article/2006/06/18/AR2006061800610.html.

FBI. (2001). Crime in the United States, Section V: Special Report. Retrieved from http://www.fbi.gov/about-us/cjis/ucr/crime-in-the-u.s/2001.

FBI. (2015a). Crime in the United States, Aggravated Assault Table. Retrieved from https://ucr.fbi.gov/crime-in-the-u.s/2015/crime-in-the-u.s.-2015/offenses-known-to-law-enforcement/aggravated-assault.

FBI. (2015b). Crime in the United States, Arson: Table 2. Retrieved from https://ucr.fbi.gov/crime-in-the-u.s/2015/crime-in-the-u.s.-2015/offenses-known-to-law-enforcement/arson.

FBI. (2015c). Crime in the United States, Burglary. Retrieved from https://ucr.fbi.gov/crime-in-the-u.s/2015/crime-in-the-u.s.-2015/offenses-known-to-law-enforcement/burglary.

FBI. (2015d). Crime in the United States, Expanded Homicide Data: Tables 1, 2, 3, 4, 6, 7 & 8. Retrieved from https://ucr.fbi.gov/crime-in-the-u.s/2015/crime-in-the-u.s.-2015/offenses-known-to-law-enforcement/expanded-homicide.

FBI. (2015e). Crime in the United States, Forcible Rape. Retrieved from https://ucr.fbi.gov/crime-in-the-u.s/2015/crime-in-the-u.s.-2015/offenses-known-to-law-enforcement/rape.

FBI. (2015f). Crime in the United States, Larceny-Theft. Retrieved from https://ucr.fbi.gov/crime-in-the-u.s/2015/crime-in-the-u.s.-2015/offenses-known-to-law-enforcement/larceny-theft.

FBI. (2015g). Crime in the United States, Motor Vehicle Theft. Retrieved from https://ucr.fbi.gov/crime-in-the-u.s/2015/crime-in-the-u.s.-2015/offenses-known-to-law-enforcement/motor-vehicle-theft.

FBI. (2015h). Crime in the United States, Offences Known to Law Enforcement: Murder. Retrieved from https://ucr.fbi.gov/crime-in-the-u.s/2015/crime-in-the-u.s.-2015/offenses-known-to-law-enforcement/murder.

FBI. (2015i). Crime in the United States, Offenses Known to Law Enforcement: Tables 1, 23, 24 Retrieved from https://ucr.fbi.gov/crime-in-the-u.s/2015/crime-in-the-u.s.-2015/offenses-known-to-law-enforcement/offenses-known-to-law-enforcement.

FBI. (2015j). Crime in the United States, Robbery: Table 3. Retrieved from https://ucr.fbi.gov/crime-in-the-u.s/2015/crime-in-the-u.s.-2015/offenses-known-to-law-enforcement/robbery.

Harris, A. R., Thomas, S. H., Fisher, G. A., & Hirsch, D. J. (2002). Murder and medicine: The lethality of criminal assault 1960–1999. *Homicide Studies, 6*(2), 128–166.

Kearney, M. S., & Harris, B. H. (2014). Ten economic facts about crime and incarceration in the United States. Retrieved from http://www.hamiltonproject.org/papers/ten_economic_facts_about_crime_and_incarceration_in_the_united_states/.

Klein, A., & White, J. (2011, July 23). Car theft tamed by technology, aggressive police work. *The Washington Post.*

Kreisel, B. W. (2009). Police and victims of sexual assault. In F. P. Reddington & B. W. Kreisel (Eds.), *Sexual assault: The victims, the perpetrators and the criminal justice system* (pp. 337–357). Durham, NC: Carolina Academic Press.

Langton, L. (2012). *Firearms stolen during household burglaries and other property crimes, 2005–2010.* Washington, DC: US Department of Justice, Office of Justice Programs, Bureau of Justice Statistics. NCJ 239436.

Lauritsen, J. L., & Heimer, K. (2008). The gender gap in violent victimization, 1973–2004. *Journal of Quantitative Criminology, 24,* 125–147.

National Institute of Justice. (2017). Intimate partner violence. Retrieved from http://www.nij.gov/topics/crime/intimate-partner-violence/Pages/welcome.aspx.

Planty, M., Langton, L., Krebs, C., Berzofsky, M., & Smiley-McDonald, H. (2013). *Female victims of sexual violence, 1994–2010.* Washington, DC: US Department of Justice, Office of Justice Programs, Bureau of Justice Statistics. NCJ 240655.

Thompson, S. K., & Gartner, R. (2014). The spatial distribution and social context of homicide in Toronto's neighborhoods. *Journal of Research in Crime and Delinquency, 51*(1), 88–118.

Truman, J., & Morgan, R. (2016). *Criminal victimization, 2015.* Washington, DC: US Department of Justice, Office of Justice Programs, Bureau of Justice Statistics. NCJ 250180.

United Nations Office on Drugs and Crime (UNODC). (2007). *Criminal victimization in international perspective: Key findings from the 2004–2005 ICVS and EUICS.* Retrieved from http://unicri.us/services/library_documentation/publications/icvs/publications/ICVS2004_05report.pdf.

United Nations Office on Drug and Crime (UNODC). (2008). *United Nations Office on Drugs and Crime 10th United Nations survey of crime trends and operations of criminal justice systems.* Retrieved from http://www.unodc.org/unodc/en/data-and-analysis/Tenth-United-Nations-Survey-on-Crime-Trends-and-the-Operations-of-Criminal-Justice-Systems.html.

United Nations Office on Drug and Crime (UNODC). (2012). *Global report on trafficking in persons.* Retrieved from https://www.unodc.org/unodc/data-and-analysis/glotip.html.

United Nations Office on Drug and Crime (UNODC). (2014). *Global study on homicide 2013: Trends, contexts, data.* Retrieved from https://www.unodc.org/documents/gsh/pdfs/2014_global_homicide_book_web.pdf.

UN Protocol to Prevent, Suppress and Punish Trafficking in Persons. Retrieved from http://www.uncjin.org/Documents/Conventions/dcatoc/final_documents_2/convention_%20traff_eng.pdf.

Walters, J. H., Moore, A., Berzofsky, M., & Langton, L. (2013). *Household burglary, 1994–2011.*

Washington, DC: US Department of Justice, Office of Justice Programs, Bureau of Justice Statistics. NCJ 241754.

World Health Organization (WHO). (2002). *World report on violence and health, 2002.* Retrieved from http://whqlibdoc.who.int/hq/2002/9241545615.pdf.

World Health Organization (WHO). (2013). *Global and regional estimates of violence against women: Prevalence and health effects of intimate partner violence and non-partner sexual violence.* Retrieved from http://www.who.int/reproductivehealth/publications/violence/9789241564625/en/.

Victimization: Consequences, Forms and Underrepresented Populations

image © Semmick Photo via shutterstock.com.

Chapter 3: Victims and Victimization — Definitions and an Overview

Definition of Victim and Victimization

As discussed in Chapter 1, the term **victim** suggests that harm has been experienced by an entity, whether that be a person, business, or community. People are victims of accidents, harmful behavior perpetrated toward them (criminal or otherwise), disasters (natural or manmade), and other such events. Just like with people, a business could experience harm due to a particular type of event. For instance, a business could be the victim of a crime, such as burglary, robbery, vandalism, fraud, embezzlement or numerous other offenses. A business could also be a victim of a natural disaster. Though there are humans who own the business it is the institution of the business that is harmed. Effects of the harm may be passed along to consumers in the form of increased prices or the inability of that business to serve its consumers as it once did (or perhaps not at all). A **crime victim** is an entity that has been harmed by an act that breaks a criminal statute (sometimes along with other legislative guidelines) for a particular jurisdiction. Perpetrators of crime can be individuals, groups, businesses, organizations, and even entire governments (as will be discussed in Chapter 6). Crime itself can happen anywhere and is not limited to just what we can physically "see." As you'll learn in Chapter 7, one does not have to be within the same physical space as a victim to be able to perpetrate a crime on an entity. This can add additional complexities to solving crime when the perpetrator lives in one jurisdiction and the victim lives in another. So far, this discussion has centered on what we would call the **primary victim**, meaning the intended target of the criminal act, but the harm of a criminal act permeates beyond the primary victim to others.

Primary, Secondary, and Tertiary Victimizations

As stated, the primary victim is the intended target of the criminal act. However, the harm that comes from that act is not limited to the primary victim alone. Oftentimes, there are others who feel the effects of the crime, but they may not be recognized as needing assistance because they did not experience the actual crime itself. There are two additional categories of individuals that may experience harm from the criminal incident; these are called **secondary victims** and **tertiary victims**.

Secondary victims are those who are closely related to or involved with the primary victim. These could include family members, friends, or coworkers/colleagues. When the primary victim is harmed, there can be psychological, physical, and financial implications following the crime. As will be discussed shortly, there are a variety of psychological/emotional effects of crime that could influence a primary victim to act differently and/or to change his or her behavior. Depression and manifestations of post-traumatic stress disorder (PTSD) or obsessive-compulsive disorder (OCD) can be seen in some victims that may alter the way they behave. For instance, a victim of sexual abuse, sexual assault, or rape may feel like she can't get clean and/or wash off the scent or feeling of the perpetrator. This may lead the victim to compulsive cleaning behaviors as a way to eliminate the feeling that the perpetrator is still there (A.A.R.D.V.A.R.C., n.d.). The family member or friend of the primary victim may perceive this as uncharacteristic or even annoying and it may require that the secondary victim adjust his or her own behavior to accommodate the primary victim's behavioral modifications. The secondary victim may experience a lack of caretaking or be subject to a change in behavior or mood that seems foreign to them and that they may not be able to understand, but that they definitely feel. Consider the case of a rape victim who is also the mother of small children. The depression and PTSD symptomology she may exhibit after the rape could alter her ability to care for her children in the same manner as she had previously, which may deprive them of the nurturing environment they were used to. Secondary victims may experience harmful effects from the potential financial harm that could occur because of a crime. If the main breadwinner of the family is not able to work due to recovery from a criminal incident, is fired because he or she can no longer work or needs to replace missing items due to loss from a criminal incident, this could impair the ability of that individual to take care of basic needs of others in the family — thus those individuals become financially affected by the crime and are considered secondary victims in this instance.

Tertiary victims are those that may also experience harm or set back due to the victimization of a primary victim. Most notably, tertiary victims are those that feel the tangential effects of crime — the community, the consumer, and the first responder/victim advocate. The community could be negatively affected by the impact crime

"In the News" Box 3.1

On April 22, 2014, *The Guardian* journalist Lucinda Hardwick published an article entitled "Kindness Can Be Cruel: Experiencing Trauma by Proxy." The article discusses the concept of vicarious trauma—when providing assistance to people in need starts to take both a psychological and a physical toll on the aid giver. The article focuses mainly on humanitarian aid, although, as you will have learned in this chapter, vicarious trauma has the same effects of burnout but may have "a more rapid onset of symptoms." It is noted in the article that humanitarian aid workers are instructed to be neutral, but the practicality of that expectation is unrealistic, just as it is in criminal justice. The article states that possible side effects of providing aid and assistance include the potential for emotional disconnection (as a means to safeguard oneself from the suffering experienced by those they serve), resentment toward one's client base, intrusive thoughts, anxiety, PTSD, and cynicism, among others. The article closes with a list of strategies to prevent and treat vicarious trauma, a relatively recent idea that has received a great deal of attention.

To access the article in its entirety, visit http://www.theguardian.com/global-development-professionals-network/2014/apr/22/vicarious-trauma-humanitarian-workers.

has on it in many ways, including visibly affected properties (perhaps due to vandalism, other destruction of property, break-ins, etc.), decrease of property values, witnessing the visible effects of crime on the primary and secondary victims within one's own neighborhood, watching or reading the news and learning of crime victimizations that occur, the loss of a productive community member who may choose to leave due to the criminal incident, abandoned homes, and the list goes on. The consumer could feel the effects of crime through the increased costs for items at a store that was burglarized. The store owner may need to increase prices to be able to stay in operation. Additionally, the consumer may have to deal with the loss of a business that closed down due to victimization, which could require that the consumer travel further to receive a service or pay more to receive a service. The first responder or victim advocate may be especially affected by one case in particular or as a function of their overall job by working with multiple people who are themselves dealing with crisis situations. The literature calls this **compassion fatigue, burnout**, and **vicarious trauma**. This occurs when an individual sees so much harm and trauma that it affects their ability to respond in a compassionate manner and affects their mental health. Phelps, Lloyd, Creamer, and Forbes (2009) suggest that compassion fatigue, burnout, and vicarious trauma are manifested in many aspects of a person's health and mental health as they may affect the physical, cognitive, and behavioral domains. Specifically, a person could exhibit signs of fatigue, have trouble sleeping, and just feel overall

Figure 3.1: Harm Including Primary, Secondary, and Tertiary Victims

Primary
Victim

Secondary Victims   Tertiary Victims

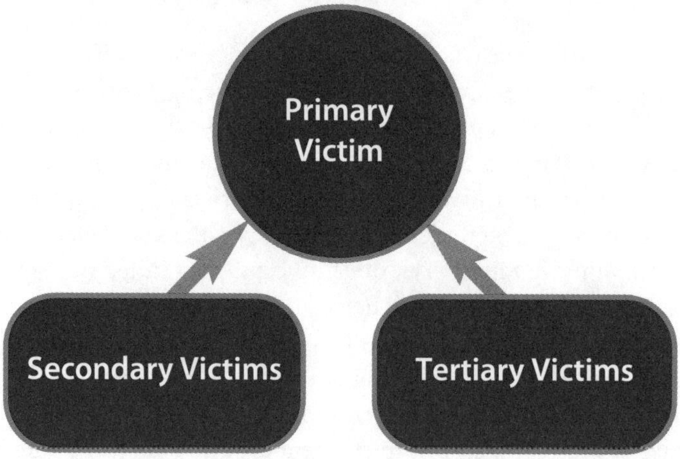

achy on a physical level. He or she could have trouble making decisions, exhibit attention deficits, demonstrate an inability to trust, and become suspicious of everyone on a cognitive level. And the first responder or victim advocate could become detached and withdraw from regular pastimes and activities on a behavioral level. Additionally, they may be giving of themselves so much on the job that they have little to give to the people in their personal lives. Whereas the end results of compassion fatigue, burnout, and vicarious trauma may be very similar and are all work-related stress reactions, there are also some subtle nuances that differentiate these three concepts. **Burnout** may be more of a response to an accumulation of stress from the job, whereas **compassion fatigue** is directly related to the emotional output given to the clients of the job, and **vicarious trauma** appears to more deeply affect one's overall view of the world and self (Phelps et al., 2009). How prevalent is tertiary victimization? In one study, 70.2% of respondents indicated that they experienced some type of secondary traumatic stress when working with individuals experiencing some type of trauma (e.g., victimization, disasters, war, terrorism) (Bride, 2007). Bell (2003) found that whereas 43% of family violence victim advocates could name positive and negative effects of their work, only 10% indicated their work had a negative impact on them.

In sum, crime victimization most often becomes known once the primary victim has reported it and it may appear that the greatest level and amount of harm occurs to the primary victim; however, the ripple effect of harm permeates beyond the primary victim to secondary and tertiary victims as well and should not be discounted.

The Effects of Victimization

When we discuss the effects of victimization it is important to address the three main realms in which harm is manifested: physical harm, psychological or emotional harm, and financial harm (Wallace, 2007). More recently some have taken to investigating a potential fourth realm of harm that occurs to crime victims, the realm of social harm (Lasslett, 2010). **Physical harm** occurs when an individual suffers from minor or major physical injuries as a result of a crime (Wallace, 2007). Examples range from a scratch, bruise, or broken limb, to a change in personality due to traumatic brain trauma, to the destruction of reproductive organs, thereby preventing someone from producing biological offspring, to death—the most grave form of physical harm. **Psychological or emotional harm** occurs when an individual suffers distress as a result of the crime (Wallace, 2007). Examples range from sadness, anxiety, and anger, to slight modifications in behavior patterns in response to crime—such as checking doors and windows more often to ensure they are locked, to more significant changes in behavior—such as avoiding places or activities that once were commonly enjoyed, to diagnoses of mental illness including depression and post-traumatic stress syndrome. Research into the psychological harms experienced by crime victims illustrates that this type of harm can affect one's physical well-being in the long run, as stress, anxiety, and sadness can significantly alter one's chemical makeup, thereby affecting their immune system, cardiovascular health, and neuro-chemistry. **Financial harm** occurs when a victim experiences some type of monetary loss due to a crime victimization (Wallace, 2007). Financial harm runs the gamut from direct monetary and/or property loss, to having to pay for repair or replacement of items stolen, altered, or destroyed, to losing wages in the workplace, to being pursued by collection agencies for debts incurred through accounts created by an identity thief, to the loss of pensions, stock holdings, or retirement plans due to corporate malfeasance. The last realm, social harm, is actually an old idea newly connected with victimization, especially in the contexts of state and corporate crime, and in the effect of crime on communities. **Social harm** occurs when the social structure (social relations, social processes of human beings) is disrupted, or more severely set back, so that the normal day-to-day functioning of an organization or community is significantly altered, which in turn changes the way that organism operates as a result of crime (Lasslett, 2010). Consider the terrorist attack on 9/11/2001. As soon as the first plane hit the North Tower of the World Trade Center, life as we knew it changed. Businesses stopped functioning, people all over the world focused their attention on the attacks, the FFA shut down all flights, significant numbers of police and fire personnel diverted their attention to the World Trade Center, people within the buildings stopped what they were doing and attempted to evacuate or get to what they thought would be a safe place ... and ultimately, a large number of people lost someone who significantly contributed to their emotional and financial well-being. It is safe to say that when that crime happened the normal day-to-day functioning of many organizations and communities were significantly altered. On a smaller scale, though no less significant, when someone loses another to homicide that person's life is likely turned upside down, and the person has to learn to live a new life, sometimes making drastic changes to accommodate the loss.

Impact of Harm

When talking about the harms associated with crime victimization, it is important to note that though we will be talking about the types of harm separately, victims rarely experience only one type of harm. Physical, psychological, financial, and even social harms can intertwine in different ways depending on the victimization that occurred and the resources (emotional, social, and financial) of the victims themselves.

Physical Harm

According to the NCVS for 2015 (Truman & Morgan, 2016), 1,303,290 non-fatal injuries were experienced as the result of violent crime. Just under half of those (658,040) were attributable to rape/sexual assault, robbery, and aggravated assault alone. The ultimate physical harm is death, the complete loss of life. In Chapter 2 you discovered the trends in homicide and are now aware that it is (1) the least likely crime to occur and (2) the numbers continue to decline from year to year. Still, 15,696 people were killed through a violent act in the United States in 2015, which constitutes a rate of 4.9 homicides per 100,000 people (FBI, 215, Crime in the United States Table 1). A report conducted for the World Health Organization provides an even clearer picture of violence-related deaths on a global level. According to Krug, Dahlberg, Mercy, Zwi, and Lozano (2002) there were approximately 1,659,000 violence-related deaths across the globe in 2000, broken down into homicide (520,000), suicide (815,000), and war-related deaths (310,000). Even though self-directed violence accounted for about half of all global fatalities due to violence, interpersonal and community violence accounted for a large number of violent fatalities overall. Over 91% of the deaths took place in low-middle level economic countries.

As cited in a Bureau of Justice Statistics report, Simon, Mercy, and Perkins (2001) reviewed the prevalence and types of injuries experienced by crime victims in the mid-1990s; they suggested that approximately 2.6 million crime victims suffered from injuries each year between 1992–1998. Of those, 480,000 crime victims (about 20% of crime victims injured annually) spent time in a hospital to receive treatment for their physical injuries due to crime (BJS, 2001). It was estimated that about 14% of victims had severe injuries, including gunshot or knife wounds, broken bones and lost teeth, and/or internal bleeding, which means that the vast majority of injuries were less severe. Over 50% of victims with severe injuries indicated that a weapon was used. When a weapon was used it was usually a knife, other sharp object, or a blunt instrument. Less than 15% of the time was a firearm the weapon used to inflict the non-fatal injury. Female victims were more likely to be injured by someone they knew, whereas males were more likely to be injured by a stranger. A startlingly large percent of victims had been previously victimized by the perpetrator who injured them in a later victimization (1 in 3 victims). Even though people experienced injuries due to victimizations, only about 75% of those severely injured and less than half of those with minor injuries actually reported their crimes to the police.

An analysis of NCVS data over the years 1996–2015 shows an interesting picture for victims who experienced physical harm. For all individuals who were injured, it appears they are more likely to utilize victim services than those who are not injured.

Year to year it appears that approximately 23–30% of victims of violent crime experience injuries as a result of the crime. This trend has stayed consistent over the years (see Table 3A).

Examining the crimes of rape/sexual assault, robbery, aggravated assault, and simple assault, it appears that rape/sexual assault has the highest percentage of injuries associated with it, with robbery and aggravated assault victims reporting about the same amount of injury and simple assault victims reporting the least. Victims that were harmed reported that the most likely weapon to be used to impart the injury was "other weapon" (pipe, blunt instrument, etc.), followed by a knife, firearm, and unknown weapon type. When it was a serious victimization (rape/sexual assault, aggravated assault, or robbery) it appeared that firearms were the second most often used weapon in the incident.

It is important to assess whether victims who are injured have a higher likelihood of reporting the crime to police and/or seeking out assistance from victim service agencies and/or personnel. NCVS NVAT Analysis for 1996–2015 shows that victims who are injured, regardless of the type of violent victimization, have higher reporting patterns than those not injured (see Table 3B).

Broken down into serious violent victimization, it appears that injured robbery victims are most likely to report to police, followed very closely by injured aggravated assault victims, whereas injured rape/sexual assault victims are least likely to report to police. For those reporting injury, approximately 16.9% reported utilizing victim services as well, while 83.1% do not utilize victim services (Truman & Morgan, 2016). Is this very different from victims who don't report injuries? The answer is *yes*. When we add in both victims with and without injury, the percentage that utilize victim services decreases to approximately 9%. This means that there is a far greater percentage of non-injured victims who do not utilize victim services. Truman and Morgan (2016) report that from 2014 to 2015, it appears that there was a greater increase in victim service utilization by individuals who were harmed in incidents where a weapon was used. This accounts for the most significant increase in victim service utilization across victim types.

When we break it down to serious violent victimization, rape/sexual assault victims appear to use victim services more so than robbery and assault victims. On average, however, robbery and aggravated assault victims tend to use victim services more so than simple assault victims overall. In all crime types, victims who were injured appeared to use victim services more than those who were not injured (see Table 3C). Perhaps it is the type and severity of injury that exists that determines whether a victim will utilize services or not. For instance, rape/sexual assault victims interact with medical personnel for injury assessments and treatment and evidence collection; medical staff could put them in touch with other victim services as it is not uncommon for a victim advocate to be called to provide support to a victim during the evidence collection process. The advocate may inform the victim about the services that are available in the community (and from their agency), which may lead to greater service utilization overall.

Table 3A: Percent Injured by Violent Crime Type, 1996–2015 (NCVS — NVAT)

Year End	96	97	98	99	00	01	02	03	04	05	06	07	08	09	10	11	12	13	14	15
Violent Victimization	100	100	100	100	100	100	100	100	100	100	100	100	100	100	100	100	100	100	100	100
Not Injured	76.6	73.6	76.6	76.6	76.1	71.6	74.5	73.6	70.5	74.7	69.7	74.2	77.3	73.9	73.9	75	77	73.8	74.3	74
Injured	23.4	26.4	23.4	23.4	23.9	28.4	25.5	26.4	29.5	25.3	30.3	25.8	22.7	26.1	26.1	25	23	26.2	25.7	26
Rape/Sexual Assault	100	100	100	100	100	100	100	100	100	100	100	100	100	100	100	100	100	100	100	100
Not Injured	58.3	47.6	49.5	50	42.8	32.4	61.7	39.4	57.1	35.3	46.2	47.8	39.3	65.1	44.1	48.6	58.5	49.1	54.3	63.4
Injured	41.7	52.4	50.5	50	57.2	67.6	38.3	60.6	42.9	64.7	53.8	52.2	60.7	34.9	55.9	51.4	41.8	50.9	45.7	36.6
Robbery	100	100	100	100	100	100	100	100	100	100	100	100	100	100	100	100	100	100	100	100
Not Injured	73.9	63.2	67.9	61.4	70.3	62.8	66	63.2	67.7	57.3	62.8	66.5	65	62	65.1	75.7	61.8	61	65.6	63.9
Injured	26.1	36.8	32.1	38.6	29.7	36.2	34	36.8	32.3	42.7	37.2	33.5	35	38	34.9	24.3	38.2	39	34.4	36.1
Aggravated Assault	100	100	100	100	100	100	100	100	100	100	100	100	100	100	100	100	100	100	100	100
Not Injured	65.8	67.6	66.1	68	72.4	68.2	68.8	63.6	63.4	71.8	68.7	66.7	67.7	60.8	62.7	59.3	66.5	66.3	69.4	64.3
Injured	34.2	32.4	33.9	31	27.6	30.8	31.2	36.4	36.6	28.2	31.3	33.3	32.3	39.2	37.3	40.7	33.5	33.7	30.6	35.7
Simple Assault	100	100	100	100	100	100	100	100	100	100	100	100	100	100	100	100	100	100	100	100
Not Injured	81.3	78.6	81.9	32.1	80.1	77.2	78	79.6	73.9	80.1	73.3	78.9	84.4	80.3	80.8	80.8	82.9	79.3	79.4	79.7
Injured	18.7	21.4	18.1	16.9	19.9	22.8	22	20.4	26.1	19.9	26.7	21.1	15.6	19.7	19.2	19.2	17.1	20.7	20.6	20.3

Source: Bureau of Justice Statistics, NCVS, NVAT, visited 3/6/2017.

Table 3B.1: Physical Injury and No Injury and Reporting Patterns, 1996–2005 (NCVS — NVAT)

Year End	96	97	98	99	00	01	02	03	04	05
Violent Victimization	100	100	100	100	100	100	100	100	100	100
Not Injured	76.6	73.6	76.6	76.6	76.1	71.6	74.5	73.6	70.5	74.7
Reported to Police	28.7	28.4	31.5	30.4	32.6	33.5	34.9	32.8	32.4	30.7
Injured	23.4	26.4	23.4	23.4	23.9	28.4	25.5	26.4	29.5	25.3
Reported to Police	11.6	13.6	13.9	12.7	13.4	15.5	15.8	14.7	18	15.1
Rape/Sexual Assault	100	100	100	100	100	100	100	100	100	100
Not Injured	58.3	47.6	49.5	50	42.8	32.4	61.7	39.4	57.1	35.3
Reported to Police	15.1	9.7	12.4	7.6	16.7	13.7	33.5	23.4	10.6	14.2
Injured	41.7	52.4	50.5	50	57.2	67.6	38.3	60.6	42.9	64.7
Reported to Police	16.9	15	18.7	18	24.4	25.6	21.8	33.1	18.8	20.9
Robbery	100	100	100	100	100	100	100	100	100	100
Not Injured	73.9	63.2	67.9	61.4	70.3	62.8	66	63.2	67.7	57.3
Reported to Police	32.3	26.5	38.7	37.2	32.5	32.2	396.8	32.9	38.3	28.7
Injured	26.1	36.8	32.1	38.6	29.7	36.2	34	36.8	32.3	42.7
Reported to Police	16.3	27.6	19.2	22.2	19.3	26.9	28	31.3	22.2	26.7
Aggravated Assault	100	100	100	100	100	100	100	100	100	100
Not Injured	65.8	67.6	66.1	68	72.4	68.2	68.8	63.6	63.4	71.8
Reported to Police	29.7	40.6	36.5	31.8	40.3	42.7	43.8	35.4	42.5	42.9
Injured	34.2	32.4	33.9	31	27.6	30.8	31.2	36.4	36.6	28.2
Reported to Police	17.6	19.6	21.2	21.6	14.1	20.3	22	20.4	27.3	22.1
Simple Assault	100	100	100	100	100	100	100	100	100	100
Not Injured	81.3	78.6	81.9	32.1	80.1	77.2	78	79.6	73.9	80.1
Reported to Police	28.5	25.8	30.1	30.9	31.5	33	32.1	32.7	29.5	28.4
Injured	18.7	21.4	18.1	16.9	19.9	22.8	22	20.4	26.1	19.9
Reported to Police	8.8	9.6	10.9	8.4	11.6	11.6	12.3	9.9	14.3	11

Source: Bureau of Justice Statistics, NCVS, NVAT, visited 3/6/2017.

Table 3B.2: Physical Injury and No Injury and Reporting Patterns, 2006–2015 (NCVS — NVAT)

Year End	06	07	08	09	10	11	12	13	14	15
Violent Victimization	100	100	100	100	100	100	100	100	100	100
Not Injured	69.7	74.2	77.3	73.9	73.9	75	77	73.8	74.3	74
Reported to Police	29.8	31.6	33.8	29.7	34	33.8	30.7	31.1	31.9	31.7
Injured	30.3	25.8	22.7	26.1	26.1	25	23	26.2	25.7	26
Reported to Police	16.8	13.3	12.6	14.4	17.1	15.2	13.5	14.5	14.1	14.8
Rape/Sexual Assault	100	100	100	100	100	100	100	100	100	100
Not Injured	46.2	47.8	39.3	65.1	44.1	48.6	58.5	49.1	54.3	63.4
Reported to Police	9.8	17.8	16.4	15.9	27.9	11.9	18.6	10.1	15.1	23.2
Injured	53.8	52.2	60.7	34.9	55.9	51.4	41.8	50.9	45.7	36.6
Reported to Police	20.2	23.8	22.8	6.9	20.7	14.9	9.6	24.7	18.5	9.3
Robbery	100	100	100	100	100	100	100	100	100	100
Not Injured	62.8	66.5	65	62	65.1	75.7	61.8	61	65.6	63.9
Reported to Police	29.3	41.1	35.5	36.7	33.6	48.4	34.8	41.32	34	36.7
Injured	37.2	33.5	35	38	34.9	24.3	38.2	39	34.4	36.1
Reported to Police	16.7	29.3	23.1	24	24	18	21.1	26.8	26.9	25.2
Aggravated Assault	100	100	100	100	100	100	100	100	100	100
Not Injured	68.7	66.7	67.7	60.8	62.7	59.3	66.5	66.3	69.4	64.3
Reported to Police	30.9	35.1	37.8	25	32.9	36.6	38.6	39.9	40.9	37.1
Injured	31.3	33.3	32.3	39.2	37.3	40.7	33.5	33.7	30.6	35.7
Reported to Police	25	14.8	22.7	25.5	27	29.9	23.8	24.4	17.5	24.8
Simple Assault	100	100	100	100	100	100	100	100	100	100
Not Injured	73.3	78.9	84.4	80.3	80.8	80.8	82.9	79.3	79.4	79.7
Reported to Police	31.3	29.9	34	30.9	34.9	32.3	29.3	28.9	30	30.5
Injured	26.7	21.1	15.6	19.7	19.2	19.2	17.1	20.7	20.6	20.3
Reported to Police	13.8	9.6	8	10.3	13	10.9	10.4	9.6	10	11.1

Source: Bureau of Justice Statistics, NCVS, NVAT, visited 3/6/2017.

Table 3C: Victims of Violent Crime and Their Patterns of Victim Service Utilization, 1996–2015 (NCVS — NVAT)

Year End	96	97	98	99	00	01	02	03	04	05	06	07	08	09	10	11	12	13	14	15
Violent Victimization																				
Not Injured/Services Received	5.6	9.6	6.2	8.5	6.6	7	9.5	10	8	7.6	6	8	7.7	6	7.4	7	6.2	7	9	6.3
Injured/Services Received	12.8	17	17.5	19.7	17.1	17	10	18	17	16	13	13	13.6	15	12	14	15	17	15	17
Rape/Sexual Assault																				
Not Injured/Services Received	17	14	8	3	8	23	36	15	5	12	2.4	12	1.3	7	43	30	9	4.6	29	8
Injured/Services Received	33	38	21	41	49	40	21	22	58	25	36	35	32	5	33	16	40	33	38	37
Robbery																				
Not Injured/Services Received	5	12	8	12	6	5	18	13	14	7	14.6	15	4.6	23.3	4.3	8.4	5.8	16	9	12
Injured/Services Received	13	19	20	18	11	10	13	21	9.5	17	6	9	13.7	6.3	8.8	5.3	7	32	15	11
Aggravated Assault																				
Not Injured/Services Received	5.3	7.8	7.5	5.9	3.7	10	5	6	4	11	7	5.9	5.9	1.1	4.4	60.4	3.6	2.2	3.4	5.6
Injured/Services Received	9.6	12	18.2	18	6	13	6	28	22	20	10	4.8	10.5	14.5	7.7	12.2	16.4	14	17	29
Simple Assault																				
Not Injured/Services Received	5.4	10	5.6	9	7	5.8	8.2	10	8.5	6.8	4.3	7.2	8.6	4.3	6.8	5.6	6.5	6.7	9.6	5.4
Injured/Services Received	12	16	16.5	9	17	13	9.5	11	12	12	12	15	9	20	10	16.7	12	11	9.2	8.3

Source: Bureau of Justice Statistics, NCVS, NVAT, visited 3/6/2017.

Financial Harm

Klaus (1994) purported that 71% of personal crime victims and 91% of property crime victims surveyed for the 1992 version of the NCVS indicated they suffered some type of economic loss associated with their victimization. But what is economic loss associated with victimization? Economist David Anderson states that there is a great deal to consider when developing a definition for "economic loss" and an estimate for an overall "cost of crime" (PRWeb, 2012). There are the direct costs of crime to the victim for medical expenses or property loss/damage, direct costs to the victim through loss of workdays, expenditures by the government for the criminal justice system, costs associated with public and private crime prevention strategies to thwart crime, costs related to medical and psychological well-being affected by crime, costs to enforce compliance of laws and regulations (outside of the criminal justice system), and costs associated with the loss of potentially productive members of society displaced when they are sent to prison (PRWeb, 2012). Including the various avenues described above by Anderson in his 2012 report in *Foundations and Trends in Micro-economics*, he proposed that the annual cost of crime in the United States is estimated to be *$3.2 trillion*. McCollister, French, and Fang (2010) proposed that when looking at just economic losses to victims and expenditures by government to operate the criminal justice system, the cost of crime in 2008 was *$194 billion*. Wright and Vicneire (2010) suggest that the combined tangible and intangible costs associated with crime are estimated at approximately *$795 billion*. These three numbers alone demonstrate the difficulty associated with producing a true number addressing the financial harm generated by crime.

Perhaps the best way to look at the costs of crime is to break it down into two general categories: *tangible*, including direct victim costs, criminal justice system costs, crime career costs, and *intangible* costs (McCollister, et al., 2010).

Tangible costs are those costs for which we can ascribe a specific amount in the form of services rendered, cash losses, property costs (damage or loss), lost earnings, and other crime-related costs for which a distinct total could be identified. Lost productivity, the salary that would have been earned by a murder victim had the crime not occurred (calculated from approximate time period of death to typical working life span), and other such costs are also considered tangible. Within tangible costs we can include *direct victims costs*, *criminal justice system costs*, and *crime career costs*. Direct victim costs include money that victims have to expend to recover from the criminal incident and/or money that may have been taken directly from the victim; criminal justice system costs include the money that is allocated for police services, court and other legal services, and corrections; and crime career costs are those costs associated with the loss of productivity due to incarceration. **Intangible costs** include expenses that are attributable to a criminal incident and are incurred by the crime victim, a secondary victim, or society itself. Intangible costs include estimates for things that are not easily quantifiable or may not have a "set price" associated with them. For instance, pain and suffering is included in intangible costs and is often estimated by what a jury has chosen to award a crime victim in a civil court. Miller,

Table 3D: Tangible and Intangible Costs of Crime by Crime Type

Offense Type	Average Tangible Cost by Crime Type per Victim	Average Intangible Cost by Crime Type	Total Cost
Murder	$1.28 million	$8.4 million	$8.9 million
Rape/Sexual assault	$41,252	$199,642	$240,776
Robbery	$21,398	$22,575	$42,310
Aggravated assault	$19,537	$95,023	$107,020
Motor vehicle theft	$10,534	$262	$10,772
Arson	$16,429	$5,133	$21,103
Household burglary	$6,462	$321	$6,462
Larceny/theft	$3,523	$10	$3,532
Stolen property	$7,974	N/A	$7.974
Embezzlement	$5,480	N/A	$5,480
Forgery and Counterfeiting	$5,625	N/A	$5,625
Fraud	$5,032	N/A	$5,032
Vandalism	$4,860	N/A	$4,860

Reproduced from McCollister, French, and Fang (2010), p. 25.

Cohen, and Wiersema (1996) suggest that for victims, the costs associated with crime that occurs to them come from three main areas: (1) out-of-pocket expenses due to medical bills and/or property loss and/or damage, (2) reduction in productivity, and (3) costs associated with the effects of victimization, including pain and suffering and decreased quality of life. Whereas victims incur very real direct and indirect costs associated with crime, society (as a tertiary victim) also incurs costs in the form of maintaining a criminal justice system and as a response to fear of crime (paying for various private security measures, altering behavior, etc.).

McCollister et al. (2010) prepared an estimate of both the tangible and intangible overall costs of crime using 2008 dollars estimates, through their analysis of various official crime data (UCR, NCVS, USFA, NIBRS, and works by other researchers). Using 2008 dollars estimates, personal crimes tended to have the highest overall costs associated with them when compared to property crimes (see Table 3D) with murder, the least likely crime to occur, having the highest costs per victim and larceny/theft, the most likely crime to occur, having the lowest average costs per victim. The reason murder has such a high overall cost is because the remainder of lifetime earnings of the homicide victim is included in the tangible cost estimate.

Looking at loss reported just to police for crimes in 2015 in which a victim (personal or business) reported some type of theft (robbery, burglary, larceny-theft, and motor vehicle theft) it appears that the average loss ranged from $262 for shoplifting to $7,001 for motor vehicle theft (FBI, 2015, Table 23). In 2015, 284,772 robberies took place. The average property loss in dollars for robbery was $1,190, with the range including $623 in losses from convenience store robberies to $3,884 losses from bank robberies. Burglary crimes accounted for 1,395,913 crimes overall and residential burglary victims faced an average loss of $2,296, with daytime burglaries costing slightly more than nighttime burglaries ($2,316 versus $1,904, respectively). Non-residential burglary victims (stores, office, etc.) experienced an average loss of $2,366 with daytime burglaries once again doing slightly more damage than nighttime burglaries ($2,244 versus $2,154 respectively). The most common crime committed in the United States, larceny-theft, accounted for 5,014,269 offenses in 2015 and the average loss to the victim was $929. Larceny-theft encompasses a number of different activities from shoplifting and theft from motor vehicles to pocket-picking and stealing from coin-operated machines. The costs reported here include the tangible costs only.

Crime victims providing information for the NCVS in 2008 (most recent data available for economic loss) reported an average loss of $238 per person for personal crimes, with robbery victims reporting an average loss of $1,167, and property crime victims reporting an average loss of $993. Approximately 50% of both personal crime and property crime victims experienced a loss of under $250 overall (52% of personal crime victims and 48.5% of property crime victims) (Robinson, 2010).

Psychological Harm

The vast majority of victims experience some type of psychological or emotional harm associated with the victimization that has occurred to them, regardless of whether the crime was a personal or property crime (DeValve, 2004). Common reactions for both include fear, anger, violation, guilt, grief, loss of trust, disbelief, and sadness. Short-term and long-term effects of victimization, including a more in-depth discussion of psychological or emotional reactions, will be discussed below.

Short- and Long-Term Effects of Victimization

Kennedy and Sacco (1998) state that crime deprives victims of their emotional well-being, regardless of the type of crime committed. The victimization can create a feeling of disorientation wherein the victim examines why it happened and what, if anything, could have been done to prevent it. In this sense, victims may examine their own behavior to assess their vulnerability and/or contribution to the event through to the offender's motivation and perhaps even a broader view into societal roles and legislation surrounding crime. Kennedy and Sacco (1998) further suggest that victims may engage in a couple different types of self-blame to examine the event. When victims engage in **behavioral self-blame**, they set out to learn what they could have done differently to prevent the crime. In these cases, it appears that victims, in general, are better equipped to ward off longer term effects of victimization. When victims engage in **characterological self-blame** they examine the aspects of their personalities that may have contributed to the event and may lead victims to believing they cannot fend off future victimization attempts. Victims may also engage in cognitive restricting, wherein they examine the crime itself to understand what happened and why, and how they can cope with the victimization itself. When they search for meaning in the event and/or compare themselves with others who have been similarly victimized, they may be able to put the victimization in a context that allows them to stabilize the effects of the victimization and ward off longer term effects. Additionally, the effects of crime on the victim may also be mitigated or aggravated by the type of social support received from significant others. Kennedy and Sacco (1998) suggest that victims who receive advice, emotional support, and tangible assistance (financial, resources, etc.) may be better equipped to deal with the distress caused by the crime. However, some people may be more likely to withdraw from contact with the victim because the topic makes them uncomfortable as it forces them to look at their own vulnerabilities. Distancing themselves from the victims allows them to maintain their "just world" philosophy and retain the relative calm they believe they have constructed in their own lives. The **"just world" philosophy** espouses that good things happen to good people and bad things happen to bad people. Typically, people who have been victimized learn that life flips this philosophy on its head (Gray, 2009). In these instances, victims may not get the social support they need, which might exacerbate the negative aspects of dealing with victimization in the first place.

Common Short-Term Effects of Crime

Kilpatrick (2000) (as cited in Wasserman & Ellis, 2007) suggests that crime victims achieve a considerable level of recovery within three months after the criminal incident; therefore, when considering the short-term effects of crime it is reasonable to define "short-term" as approximately three months post-victimization. In their materials for first-responders, the Office for Victims of Crime (OVC) suggests that immediate responses to victimization may include shock, surprise, fear, a feeling of unreality ("is it really happening?"), physiological effects (such as hypertension, anxiety, helplessness), and physical pain (in those victims experiencing injury) (Woods, 2010). Williams (1999) suggests that victims may also experience feelings of resentment, shame, anger, and humiliation. Common short-term effects include preoccupation with the crime; flashbacks/bad dreams; insomnia; being easily startled and jumpy; having a heightened concern for self and loved ones; fear that they will be blamed, were actually at fault, or won't be believed; fear of law enforcement (particularly if a pre-existing poor relationship exists); lack of ability to trust; and fear of the next attack (Woods, 2010; Williams, 1999). Williams (1999) adds that they may withdraw from their regular lives and activities to avoid reminders of the crime itself, but may also be in denial that they were actually victims of a crime in the first place.

Common Long-Term Effects of Crime

It's not always possible to envisage all the long-term effects of victimization when one is first victimized. It may be impossible to predict the extent and types of harms that are directly attributable to the victimization that one will experience over the course of time. The loss of a bread-winning family member may affect the survivors immensely as this may immediately affect their ability to sustain the lifestyle they were living. The loss or destruction of property may require an immediate financial commitment to replace or repair the items affected, and this may hamper a victim's ability to "catch-up" or stay on track with bills and future financial planning (child's college funds, saving for a home, etc.). An injury incurred in the victimization may lead to prolonged medical treatment, which may or may not have been able to be included in the initial case, which might lead to prolonged payment of medical bills related to the crime. Victim compensation, a topic that will be discussed in Chapter 10, may help to assuage the financial costs of crime, but there are limits on that and the victim will be responsible for anything above and beyond that covered by the program. Additionally, victim compensation is a "payment of last resort," meaning that all other avenues must be explored prior to submitting a claim for consideration. The discussion of long-term effects of victimization must include within it the understanding that we may not always be able to assess the true long-term effects of victimization. Additionally, "feeling" the effects of victimization may persist for quite some time and in areas one may not have originally anticipated; therefore, it is somewhat easy to understand the depth of the effects and how victims may ultimately cope with victimization across time.

The long-term effects of victimization may be influenced by how one copes with victimization, the supports that exist in the victim's life to assist him/her through the recovery process, and how that coping and the victimization itself can affect the psychological and physical well-being of a victim (Kennedy & Sacco, 1998). Wasserman and Ellis (2007) suggest that when the trauma experienced by crime victims is not addressed appropriately, those initial reactions to crime can turn into long-term effects. Some of the more long-term effects of victimization include major depression, suicidal ideation and attempt, substance abuse, relationship problems and sexual dysfunction, anxiety disorders, panic disorders, and increased vulnerability for additional victimizations (Wasserman & Ellis, 2007). Obsessive-compulsive disorder (OCD) and post-traumatic stress disorder (PTSD) are two long-term effects associated with crime victimization (Woods, 2010; Williams, 1999; Kennedy & Sacco, 1998). Obsessive-compulsive disorder occurs when a person feels that he or she must engage in repetitive behavior in order to feel comfortable or "normal" (A.A.R.D.V.A.R.C., n.d.).

Post-traumatic stress disorder (PTSD) is defined as a disorder that is experienced by individuals who have suffered a traumatic event, the byproducts of which persist after the event and in which the individual re-experiences the traumatic event through a variety of ways (Kennedy & Sacco, 1998). The person may have flashbacks or dreams putting her "back" in the traumatic situation; specific cues can also bring the victim back to the event, such as smells, sounds, phrases, etc. Persons affected by PTSD may avoid places they believe may be associated with the event, and may experience difficulty sleeping, fear, nervousness, anxiety, depression, paranoia, as well as another negative affect symptoms (Kennedy & Sacco, 1998). Crime victims that have higher incidences of PTSD are primarily personal crime victims, especially those who are victims of sex crimes. Childhood sexual abuse survivors, rape and sexual assault victims, victims of interpersonal violence, and victims of aggravated assaults have been reported to experience PTSD at higher rates than other crime victims and non-victims in general.

Whereas crime victims across the spectrum tend to experience similar psychological effects, for property crime victims those effects may manifest themselves in some areas a bit more than others.

Property Crime Victims

Though much research is done exploring the effects of crime on personal/violent crime victims, a decent amount has been conducted on property crime victims as well. Kennedy and Sacco (1998) suggest that guilt, a sense of violation, fear, and grief are notable common reactions for property crime victims. The victims may experience guilt as they assess the situation and attempt to determine what they could have done to prevent the crime in the first place. The intrusion of offenders into one's home often leaves property crime victims feeling violated and their homes unsafe. In the OVC video *Listen to My Story*, one burglary victim suggested that even if she were to receive her property back she would wonder what the burglars had done with it while they had it. Did they watch the videos on the camcorder they stole, did they go through her documents on the computer ... did they alter them in some way? Another common reaction is grief. When property crime victims either lose or have damaged an item of particular significance to them they grieve for the loss of that item. The item could have been something that was irreplaceable—a family heirloom, a special gift, a recording of a memory—and in those instances there is not only the loss of the item itself, but the loss of the attachment to the item and the realization that it is gone. Van den Bogaard and Wiegman (1991) suggest that property crime victims experience a loss of control over their own lives as well. The perception of a stranger breaking into one's secure abode has a tendency to make the property crime victim become distrustful of strangers overall and can deteriorate social behavior of the victims themselves. Williams (1999) suggests that property crime victims may spend a good amount of time, effort, and money on securing their property, and that they may feel uncomfortable leaving at all, thus becoming shut off from social interactions. Additionally, when the victim is one with limited resources the effects of the crime itself can be exacerbated as seemingly small losses can have considerable consequences.

Social Harm

Because the concept of social harm as it relates to victimology is relatively new, one must look back at the previous discussion regarding the physical, psychological, and financial harm experienced by victims to see the impact these things could have on the fabric of society and the ability of a society to function as a whole. When a great deal of money is spent by a government on crime-related necessities, it takes away from the ability to spend that in other areas, such as education, healthcare, aid to other countries, etc. Perhaps if we were able to decrease crime, we would be able to reinvest in other more elevating institutions within the social world and see improvement in education, healthcare, quality of life of citizens, and economic well-being overall, which would increase the society's ability to thrive.

What Do Victims Need to Recover?

Recovering from crime victimization is a process that requires both time and understanding (going through one phase only to return to it briefly when there is a need to do so). There are four general phases of recovery for crime victims (Daane, 2009). The *first phase* includes crisis management, which entails the victim coming to a basic understanding about what happened to him/her. During this phase the victim may experience fear, guilt, shame, exhaustion, helplessness, shock, anxiety, confusion, and vulnerability. The *second stage* is composed of a face-level adjustment, wherein the victim may not feel him or herself yet, but is bending to the expectations of society to appear recovered and/or dealing with the crime. The victim may still be experiencing great psychological damage, but may likely be simply going through the motions in order to get by day to day. The *third phase* is a more active phase in which the victim begins to make changes in his/her life in response to the victimization, but this may include changes in his/her behavior towards those with whom she has relationships. Lastly, in the *final phase* the victim is likely experiencing anger, anxiety, and depression and may be searching for something that can help him/her regain control of her life. It is the second through final phases in which victims may start to think about and seek out ways to help cope and recover from the offense.

The Office for Victims of Crime has put together a number of guides helping practitioners understand the needs of crime victims so the victims can be best served and assisted on their road to recovering from the criminal incident they experienced. Three major needs exist, with specific components within that assist victims with recovering from the criminal event that occurred; they include (1) to feel safe, (2) to express emotions, and (3) information (Woods, 2010).

Feeling Safe

Research suggests that all victims experience some type of trauma after a crime, regardless of the type of crime that was perpetrated. Fear is a common reaction to being victimized. This typically leads to a feeling, whether short-term or long-term, that they are no longer safe in the environment in which they felt safe previous to the event. Victimization makes people feel violated, vulnerable, and scared. For example, burglary victims may feel that their homes have been violated and that their space is no longer a safe haven for them, cybercrime victims may feel especially vulnerable after their personal information and resources have been taken without their knowledge, assault victims may fear the next attack and may be hypersensitive to loud sounds and unfamiliar noises, and rape victims may be fearful of being in the same proximity with people. All of these reactions are normal, as discussed previously in this chapter. In order to feel safe once again, it is important for victims, and those working with victims, to work towards the individual *regaining control, building trust,* and *overcoming communication barriers* (OVC, 2005). The reassurance to a victim that he or she is safe, after assessing where and with whom the person is, can be a great help. Making sure to keep one's tone of voice even and calm can provide that safety reassurance even without the word "safe" being used. A practitioner aiding a victim can do little things to help the victim feel like he or she is regaining control of the situation. Simple things like explaining their role and telling the victim why they are there and what they may need can give victims a message that the situation is in their hands and won't add to the confusion a victim may be feeling. Body language can also help to illustrate that the environment is a safe one. Standing or sitting at the same level as the victim can help to eliminate feelings of being talked down to. Nodding one's head and providing affirmative sounds can also help that victim feel as if he or she is being heard and that their story is important. Asking victims what they want—if that means helping them contact someone that can help them, asking them how they would like to be addressed, asking if the victim wants someone to stay with him or her, and conducting interviews in a private area of the victim's choosing can help to communicate that the situation is coming back under their control and that their safety is important to the person helping out.

Express Emotions

It is important to victims that those who work with them *listen to them with compassion* (and without judgment) and *understand the impact that trauma* may have on a person. This could even include having some basic knowledge about the effect that trauma has on memory and how that might affect the ability of a victim to provide important information to a first responder immediately after the crime (Campbell, 2012). While it is important for first responders to gather specific pieces of information (if there is injury and where, details about the offense that occurred, where there may be evidence) it is equally important for the victim to feel heard by the people he or she has contacted for assistance. Victims may simply just need to purge—to get the story out about what happened to them and how it is affecting them. They need to feel that they are believed, or at least not being judged or perceived as a liar. It's important for personnel working with victims to explain *why* they're asking questions so that the victim does not feel like they are being disbelieved, which may lead to them shutting down completely. Victims may experience a range of emotions from fear and anger, to numbness, to laughter, or just no affect at all. What is being shown on the outside does not necessarily reflect all that is going on in the inside and may not seem "normal" to the outsider's view. What is important is that the practitioner understands that each person's reaction to a traumatic event can vary and that any reaction short of self-harm or harm to others, is normal.

It is important when victims are expressing emotions to not interrupt them or cut them off. Active listening skills are important for hearing what the victim has to say and giving them the space in which to say it.

Information

For those victims that report the crime to police, it is especially important that we understand that they likely have no idea how the criminal justice system processes cases. There are a plethora of crime shows on television which make it look like the process moves extraordinarily quickly and that evidence and information is easy to locate, but this is simply not the reality. Therefore, it is important to let victims know "what's next." They need to know what the general process is and what they can expect at each point in the process. As you will read in Chapter 10, one of the biggest areas of dissatisfaction among victims is the lack of communication, and/or consistent communication, that they get from members of the criminal justice system. When victims don't hear anything, they tend to assume that means nothing is being done on their case. This may not be the fact at all — there may be a great deal of activity surrounding a case, but no solutions or new information gathered, so the criminal justice practitioner may not feel as if there is anything worthwhile to inform the victim about. It is important that this be communicated to victims up front — that not hearing anything does not mean the case isn't being pursued. This simple piece of information could put a victim's mind at ease and may help them to understand that not hearing from a criminal justice person for a period of time is normal.

It is also important to help victims understand common reactions to being victimized, such as experiencing an inability to concentrate, memory loss, depression, physical ailments, etc. They need to know about any services that are available to them that they could seek out immediately or down the road. Providing this information in some type of written form can be especially helpful as simply telling them may become a casualty of memory loss. Letting them know what they have to do next (file a restraining order, file the police report with their insurance company, see a doctor about physical injuries, etc.) can also be helpful. Again, they may have no idea what they should be doing so even something that seems obvious to a criminal justice practitioner may not be obvious to someone in the general public. It can also be helpful to ask them if they want contact information for the person(s) who will be working on their case and/or if they want someone to follow up with them to make sure they're OK and to address any additional questions they may have.

Summary and Conclusion

Victims of crime can be directly or indirectly affected by the criminal event. Most victims experience a combination of physical, psychological/emotional, financial, and social harm as a result of the victimization. While most victims will begin to recover from the crime within a short period of time, some victims are affected more dramatically and may suffer from disruptions in their mental health; some may even experience symptoms of post-traumatic stress disorder. Knowing what a victim needs to recover can greatly assist in the healing process for a victim. Most importantly, victims need to feel safe, to be able to express their emotions, and to receive information related to the crime committed against them.

Key Terms

Victim

Crime victim

Primary victim

Secondary victims

Tertiary victims

Compassion fatigue

Burnout

Vicarious trauma

Physical harm

Psychological or emotional harm

Financial harm

Social harm

Behavioral self-blame

Characterological self-blame

Just world philosophy

Tangible costs

Intangible costs

Discussion Questions

1. What is the difference between a primary victim, secondary victim, and tertiary victim? Could the same person be all three at different times in their life?
2. Which type of harm do you think is the most detrimental, or do you think they impact victims equally?
3. What types of intangible costs do you think are most difficult to illustrate for a crime victim?

Websites for Further Information

Office for Victims of Crime: http://www.ovc.gov/welcome.html.

National Center for Victims of Crime: http://www.ncvc.org/.

National Organization for Victim Assistance: http://www.trynova.org/.

References

A.A.R.D.V.A.R.C. (n.d.). Obsessive compulsive behaviors. Retrieved from http://www.aardvarc.org/rape/about/ocd.shtml.

Bell, H. (2003). Strengths and secondary trauma in family violence work. *Social Work, 48*(4), 513–522.

Bride, B. E. (2007). Prevalence of secondary traumatic stress among social workers. *Social Work, 52*(1), 63–70.

Campbell, R. (2012). *The neurobiology of sexual assault: Implications for first responders in law enforcement, prosecution, and victim advocacy.* Washington, DC: US Department of Justice, Office of Justice Programs, National Institute of Justice. Retrieved from http://nij.ncjrs.gov/multimedia/video—campbell.htm.

Daane, D. M. (2009b). Victim response to sexual assault. In F. P. Reddington & B. W. Kriesel (Eds.), *Sexual assault* (2nd ed.). (pp. 79–111). Durham, NC: Carolina Academic Press.

DeValve, E. Q. (2004). *Through the victims' eyes: Towards a grounded theory of the victimization experience.* Sam Houston State University, ProQuest, UMI Dissertations Publishing, 2004. 3143578.

FBI. (2015). Crime in the United States, 2015, Table 1. Retrieved from https://ucr.fbi.gov/crime-in-the-u.s/2015/crime-in-the-u.s.-2015/tables/table-1.

FBI (2015) Crime in the United States, 2015, Table 23. Retrieved from https://ucr.fbi.gov/crime-in-the-u.s.-2015/tables/table-23.

Gray, J. M. (2009). What shapes public opinion of the criminal justice system? In J. Wood & T. Gannon, *Public opinion and criminal justice* (pp. 73–95). Portland, OR: Willan Publishing.

Kennedy, L. W., & Sacco, V. F. (1998). *Crime victims in context.* Los Angeles, CA: Roxbury Publishing.

Klaus, P. A. (1994). *The costs of crime to victims (Crime Data Brief).* US Department of Justice, Bureau of Justice Statistics, NCJ 145865.

Krug, E. G., Dahlberg, L. L., Mercy, J. A., Zwi, A. B., & Lozano, R. (2002). *World report on violence and health.* Geneva: World Health Organization.

Lasslett, K. (2010). Crime or social harm? A dialectical perspective. *Crime, Law and Social Change, 54*(1), 1–19.

McCollister, K. E., French, M. T., & Fang, H. (2010). The cost of crime to society: New crime-specific estimates for policy and program evaluation. *Drug and Alcohol Dependence, 108*(1–2), 98–109: doi: 10.1016/j.drugalcdep.2009.12.002.

Miller, T. R., Cohen, M. A., & Wiersema, B. (1996). *Victim costs and consequences: A new look.* Washington, DC: US Department of Justice, Office of Justice Programs, National Institute of Justice. NCJ 155282.

Office for Victims of Crime. (2005). *Listen to My Story: Communicating with Victims of Crime.*

Phelps, A., Lloyd, D., Creamer, M., & Forbes, D. (2009). Caring for careers in the aftermath of trauma. *Journal of Aggression, Maltreatment & Trauma, 18,* 313–330.

PRWeb. (2012, September 28). New study estimates the annual cost of crime to be $3.2 trillion. Retrieved from http://www.prweb.com/releases/2012/9/prweb9947109.htm.

Robinson, J. E. (2010). *Crime victimization in the United States, 2008, Tables 81 & 83.* Washington, DC: US Department of Justice, Bureau of Justice Statistics. NCJ 231173.

Simon, T. R., Mercy, J. A., & Perkins, C. (2001). *Injuries from violent crime, 1992–1998.* Washington, DC: US Department of Justice, Bureau of Justice Statistics, NCJ 168633.

Truman, J., Langton, L., & Planty, M. (2013). *Criminal victimization, 2012.* Washington, DC: US Department of Justice, Bureau of Justice Statistics, NCJ 243389.

Truman, J. L., & Morgan, R. E. (2016). *Criminal victimization, 2015.* Washington, DC: US Department of Justice, Bureau of Justice Statistics, NCJ 250180.

Van den Bogaard, J., & Wiegman, O. (1991). Property crime victimization: The effectiveness of police services for victims of residential burglary. *Journal of Social Behavior and Personality, 6*(6), 329–362.

Wallace, H. (2007). *Victimology: Legal, psychological, and social perspectives* (2nd ed.). Boston, MA: Allyn and Bacon.

Wasserman, E., & Ellis, C. A. (2007). *Impact of crime on victims* (Chapter 6, Participant's Text, 2007 National Victim Assistance Academy, Track 1, Foundation-Level Training). Retrieved from http://www.ccvs.state.vt.us/sites/default/files/resources/VVAA%20Ch%206%20Impact%20of%20Crime.pdf.

Williams, B. (1999). *Working with victims of crime: Policies, politics and practice.* London, UK: Jessica Kingsley Publishers, Ltd.

Woods, T. O. (2010). *First response to victims of crime, Guidebook.* Washington, DC: US Department of Justice, Office of Justice Programs, Office for Victims of Crime. NCJ 231171.

Wright, E., & Vicneire, M. (2010). Economic costs of victimization. In B. Fisher & S. Lab (Eds.), *Encyclopedia of victimology and crime prevention* (pp. 344–348). Thousand Oaks, CA: SAGE Publications, Inc. doi: 10.4135/9781412979993.n110.

Chapter 4: Understanding Victimization across the Crime Spectrum

Violent Crime Victimizations versus Property Crime Victimizations

As you learned in Chapter 2, the UCR provides us with the general crime rate for the United States and generates that rate from Type I offenses, which include four personal crimes and four property crimes. The personal or violent crimes are murder/manslaughter, forcible rape, aggravated assault, and robbery; and the property crimes are burglary, motor vehicle theft, larceny-theft, and arson. Property crimes account for about 88% of crime rather consistently, leaving violent crime accounting for about 12% of crime overall. This chapter will focus on some key identifiers for the seven most common UCR Type 1 crimes (excluding arson) for an understanding of characteristics and motives of perpetrators, differential risk of victims, and points of information that are unique to each particular crime in order to facilitate an overall better understanding of the crimes themselves, how we understand the crimes, and how those crimes impact crime victims. Additionally, this chapter will address victimization on a continuum from "victimless" crimes, where the perpetrator is also the "victim," to repeat victimization, a concept that has been studied more and more since the mid-1990s and which illustrates the need to explore not only single victimizations but overall victimization rates and the compounding effects of multiple victimizations.

Homicide

As you learned previously, homicide is the least likely crime to occur to an individual, but the resultant act of the crime is the elimination of a human being from existence, an act that is irreversible and around which the primary victim's life cannot be adapted because that life has been extinguished.

Circumstances/Motives for Homicide

According to UCR data, approximately 15% of homicides in 2015 were committed in the course of another felony, with "other" felony, robbery, and narcotic drug felonies accounting for the vast majority of these types of homicides. 44.2% of homicides were committed for reasons other than a felony. 25.4% of all homicides were the result of some type of argument, including "other" arguments, arguments over money or property, romantic triangles, and brawls due to the influence of a substance (alcohol or illegal drug). Gang killings (adult and juvenile gangs) accounted for 5.8% of homicides overall and "other—not specified" accounted for 12.5% of all homicides. 39.8% of homicides occurred where the motive was unknown. This suggests that for all known explanations, arguments are the most common reason that homicides occur. Cooper and Smith (2011) suggest that between 1980 and 2008 the circumstances (or motives) surrounding homicides have changed. Whereas gang activity has consistently accounted for the least amount of homicides there has been a shift in the most common circumstances explaining homicide. Arguments were the most common circumstance within which homicides occurred until the year 2000, at which time "unknown" surpassed that explanation and continues to remain the primary circumstance for homicides. Felonies and "other" have remained as the third and fourth most common explanations for homicide across the 28-year period.

Ouimet (2012) suggests that one of the best predictors of homicide is income inequality within the populace. In an analysis of 165 different countries, Ouimet found that those countries that have vast income inequalities have higher rates of homicide compared to nations in which the income inequalities are less drastic. Ouimet (2012) proposed that income inequality could also be an indicator of other social ills which may lead to violence.

Firearms account for the most commonly used weapon in homicides consistently across time, followed by knife or blunt object, personal weapon (feet, hands), and other non-personal weapon (poisons, narcotics, fire, explosives, etc.) (Smith & Cooper, 2013).

Differential Risk for Homicide

The trend of males accounting for the majority of homicide victims and offenders has persisted for decades. From 1980–2010, males accounted for both the majority of victims (77%) and offenders (90%) of homicide (Cooper & Smith, 2011). In that

Figure 4.1: Number of Homicides, by Circumstance, 1980–2008

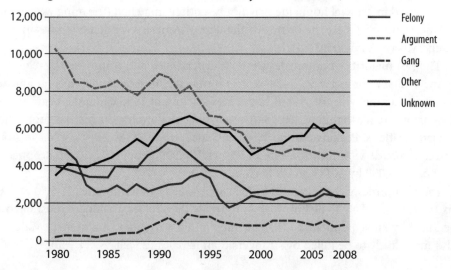

Note: Arguments include brawls due to the influence of narcotics or alcohol, disagreements about money or property, and other arguments. Felony types include homicides committed during a rape, robbery, theft, motor vehicle theft, arson, and violations of prostitution and commercial vice laws, other sex offenses, narcotic drug laws, and gambling laws. Gang homicides include gangland killings and juvenile gang killings.

Source: Cooper, A., & Smith. E. L. (2011). Homicide trends in the United States, 1980–2008. Bureau of Justice Statistics.

same time period, males had a victimization rate of 11.6 per 100,000 compared to females whose rate was 3.4 per 100,000.

In terms of race, Blacks are disproportionately represented as both victims and offenders of homicide. Cooper and Smith (2011) found that 47.4% of homicide victims and 52.5% of offenders from 1980–2008 were Black. This is a vast overrepresentation compared to their representation in the general population (which accounted for 12.6%). Conversely, Whites and those in the category of "Other" (American Indians, Native Alaskans, Pacific Islanders, Native Hawaiians, and Asians) were disproportionately underrepresented, with Whites accounting for 50.3% of victims and 45.3% of offenders, and "Other" accounting for 2.3% of victims and 2.2% of offenders. Homicide is primarily an intraracial crime, meaning that victims are most often killed by someone within their own racial group. In 2016, 81.5% of White victims were killed by another White person and 89.5% of Black victims were killed by another Black person. 15% of White victims were killed by Black offenders, and 8% of Black victims were killed by White offenders (FBI, 2016). While the majority of homicides of those in the "Other" category appear to follow this pattern, it is at a much lower percentage. 56% of homicides of those in the "Other" category were committed by an offender in the "Other" category. 23% of the time a White offender was the perpetrator and 20% of the time a Black offender was the perpetrator of the homicide of someone in the "Other" racial category. It should be noted that because there are five different groups included within the "Other" racial category, the 56% of perceived interracial homicide may not be entirely matched (meaning we can't tell if American Indians are the primary offenders of American Indian victims since the category is not disaggregated).

The vast majority of homicides are both experienced and committed by teens and young adults. Prior to 1985, 25–34-year-olds were the most likely victims of homicide, but co-occurring with the rise of homicides starting in 1985 came the beginning of the current trend, that in which 18–24-year-olds account for the highest proportion of victimizations. Peaking around 1994/1995, people in the 18–24-year-old age group had a homicide victimization rate of 25 per 100,000 people. This rate dropped to 11.9 per 100,000 by 2011 (Smith & Cooper, 2013).

Female murder victims are most likely to be killed by an intimate (41.5%) and are six times more likely to be killed by an intimate than males; males are most likely to be killed by an acquaintance (56.4%), most often a friend/acquaintance. Males are also more likely to be killed by strangers than females (25.5% vs. 11.9%).

Did You Know ... ?

Unlike the patterns seen in homicide in general, victims of serial murder are primarily female, with female prostitutes accounting for a disproportionate percentage of overall victims (Quinet, 2011). In her analysis of 502 solved serial murder cases, Quinet (2011) found that 85% of the time, female victims were targets of serial killers, either exclusively or in addition to male victims (*note*: a serial killer case includes all murders committed by a single serial killer or team of serial killers). Additionally, Quinet (2011) suggests that serial killers who target prostitutes also have a higher overall number of victims and perpetrate for a longer period of time, most likely because crimes against prostitutes are among the "missing missing" — meaning that these individuals are missing but are not reported as such, so choosing them as targets may be strategic on the parts of the killers. Quinet (2011) found that though cases of serial killers have declined since the 1980s, there has been a strong increase in targeting of female prostitutes as time has progressed. For instance, in the 1970s 16% of serial murder victims were female prostitutes, compared to 30% in the 1980s, 46% in the 1990s and 69% in the first decade of the 2000s. Quinet (2011) cautions that currently, a higher proportion of prostitutes who were victims of serial killers in later decades were also listed as homeless, which could be an additional risk factor leading to the perception that they are "easy targets."

Rape, Sexual Assault, and Other Sex Offenses

Rape and other sexual offenses have the unfortunate distinction of being the victimizations most likely to be doubted by criminal justice personnel, hospital personnel, and the general public. In fact, Garland (2009) points out in the 1942 publication of

Henry Wigmore's *Evidence in Trials at Common Law* text prosecutors were instructed to consider *not* bringing a rape case to trial unless the victim's background and mental health had been thoroughly analyzed by a qualified physician. It is clear that this has been a long-standing perception of rape/sexual assault victims within the system and may help to explain why sex crimes have some of the lowest rates of reporting to law enforcement.

Circumstances/Motives for Sex Crimes

Sex crimes occur out of a need for a perpetrator to acquire and demonstrate power, act on feelings of anger, and/or fulfill an urge experienced as a result of a type of paraphilia or other psychological disorder (Garland, 2009; Laufersweiler-Dwyer & Dwyer, 2009). The primary motive is *not* sexual gratification, as is demonstrated by many bits of evidence, not the least of which are that the perpetrator does not always attempt to reach orgasm, may not climax at all, and that many sex offenders are in relationships within which they have access to a consensual sexual partner. Numerous typologies of sex offenders exist, usually focusing on the motivation of the offender, but Laufersweiler-Dwyer and Dwyer (2009) caution against focusing specifically on motivation, as many sex offenders have multiple reasons for the acts, so placing them into a specific category within a typology may limit our true understanding as to why individuals commit sex crimes. Laufersweiler-Dwyer and Dwyer (2009) suggest that the Prentky, Knight, and Rosenberg Motivational Typologies may be the most comprehensive typology of sex offenders as it includes biological, psychological, and cultural factors in its design. This model breaks down offending behavior by three things: (1) aggression level in the offense, (2) sexual component of the offense, and (3) impulsivity of the offender, and suggests nine distinct types of motivations for sex offenses (Laufersweiler-Dwyer & Dwyer, 2009).

Differential Risk for Rape/Sexual Assault

Lifetime estimates of rape suggest that 1 in 5 women and 1 in 71 men will have been raped or sexually assaulted in their lifetimes (The White House Council on Women and Girls, 2014). Unlike other crimes, females are the primary victims of rape/sexual assault. Planty et al. (2013) report that approximately 91% of rape or sexual assault victims are female and 9% are male. From 1994–2010, it was reported that individuals aged 12–17 were at the highest risk of rape or sexual assault (rate: 11.3/1,000 for 1994–1998, 7.6/1,000 for 1999–2004, 4.1/1,000 for 2005–2010), followed by 18–34-year-olds (rate: 7.0/1,000 for 1994–1998, 5.3/1,000 for 1999–2004, 3.7/1,000 for 2005–2010). Individuals 35 years and older have consistently had the lowest rates of rape or sexual assault (rate: 2.3/1,000 for 1994–1998, 1.8/1,000 for 1999–2004, 1.5/1,000 for 2005–2010) (Planty et al., 2013). This crime appears to affect females across racial and ethnic categories equally, a pattern that was found consistently from 1994–2010. Females who had never been married or were divorced or separated had the highest rates of rape or sexual assault, as compared to married and widowed women. Females in the lowest income bracket (earning below $25,000/yr.) appear to be more at risk of rape or sexual assault at a rate of 3.5/1,000, compared to 1.9/1,000 for the middle-income bracket and 1.8/1,000 for households making $50,000 or more. Whereas in the mid- to late-1990s victims were more often located in urban areas, by the end of the 2000s victims in rural communities had a higher rate of sexual violence.

So where do the victimizations take place? The vast majority of rapes and sexual assaults occur at or near the victim's home or the home of a friend/relative/acquaintance (60–67% of the time from 1994–2010). Most victims were sleeping or doing another activity at their home at the time of the offense (41–48%), or were out of the home engaged in some type of work, school, or leisure activity (29–35%).

Planty et al. (2013) report that most offenders are 30 years of age or older (43–51% of the time from 1994–2010), White (57–70% of the time), are acting on their own (90–93% of the time), and do not use a weapon (other than their physical body) in the offense (83–88% of the time). Whereas Whites make up the vast majority of offenders, Black males account for a disproportionately larger percentage of offenders given their overall representation in the general population (18–27% of the time versus 12.6% distribution in the general population). The offender is known to the victims 3 times out of 4, and is usually a well-known/casual acquaintance (38–42% of the time) or a current or former intimate partner (28–34% of the time) and alcohol or drug use by the offender is often reported by the victim (37–40% of the time).

Though rape and sexual assault are primarily "female adult-victim" crimes, it is important to address the similarities and differences that might exist for children and male victims; therefore a section has been included below to address issues for children and male rape and sexual assault victims.

Compounding Factors for Children and Males

Although the responses to the assault/abuse and common psychological reactions to the assault/abuse immediately after the act *are consistent* across victims of sexual violence there are a couple of things to keep in mind when the victim is a child or male.

Oftentimes, adult victims of sexual violence consider not reporting the offense to law enforcement because they don't feel like they will be believed. This is particularly the case when it comes to children. There is a common perception that children do not have the memory tools that adults have because their brains aren't developed completely yet, and this leads some to suggest that children might "make something up" or misinterpret an action. Some children may not be able to articulate what happened to them other than to say that something bad happened. They very well may not have the vocabulary that will assist them and attempts by adults, familial and professional, to help them verbalize the abuse may be seen as "coaching" and thus invalidated or looked at skeptically in the criminal justice process. Despite this obstacle, it is still important to listen to and investigate claims by children of sexual abuse. Children who are sexually abused often experience physical and psychological issues that affect their development and their lives well through adulthood (Dunlap, 2009). For instance, for a child who has been raped, no matter who the perpetrator may be, there may be an aversion to medical exams and in particular, gynecological exams because of their sensitivity to being touched. Additionally, the stress experienced as a result of the abuse may affect their immune systems, just like it can with adults. However, the length of time that children who experience sexual abuse have to deal with the abuse can take a toll on them physically and psychologically. In Chapter 3 you learned about common psychological and physical reactions to crime. These effects can be exacerbated for children as the victimizations are often experienced for years without the ability to seek out healthy assistance on one's own. That is why it is important to address claims of child sexual abuse immediately so that the child has a chance to recover and grow into adulthood stronger and with healthy coping mechanisms.

Much of what is known about male sexual assault comes as a result of data gathered from relatively small samples of men who came in to clinics or sexual health centers (Allen, 2004). As these samples are self-selected and may well be very different from the "typical" male sexual assault victims (e.g., because respondents came to a medical care facility, it is likely they were injured in the assault), results from such research may not represent all male victims, but it does give us an idea as to some of the special issues that must be considered. One of the reasons that males choose not to report to law enforcement is because of the additional stigma that is attached to male sexual assault victims which makes some believe that the victims must be homosexual and/ or weak. Since the majority of rapes of male victims are perpetrated by male offenders this is somewhat understandable, though unfortunate (Allen, 2004). The perception in society of males as strong, sexual individuals who should be able to fight off an attack seems to fall into question when a man is a victim of rape. This challenging of one's masculinity is well known as a reason for deciding not to talk about the victimization to anyone (Daniel, 2004). Additionally, although some studies have found that male sexual assault is marked by greater physical violence, other studies have found physical harm to be the same as that for female acquaintance sexual assaults, or even less (Stermac, Del Bove, & Addison, 2004). All of this is not to say that male sexual assaults are not violent, because indeed many are extraordinarily brutal. But because male sexual assaults range in tone from violent, hate-motivated gang attacks on men who are perceived to be gay, attacks on heterosexual men to demonstrate power and domination, and to intimate partner assaults by female or male perpetrators, arguing for a "typical" male sexual assault has little credibility. Differences that do exist among the many kinds of male sexual assault seem to stem from victims' perceptions of self, the assailant, and the interpretation of the event. Heterosexual males who are raped by men may feel less "masculine" in a traditional sense, and that their manhood has been plucked from them; viewing the measures taken by the assailant (e.g., extreme force, drugs, coercion) as unfair may neutralize heterosexual survivors' sense of loss of their masculine identity. Additionally, research indicates that heterosexual males may also start to question their own sexual orientation after the assault, which exacerbates the psychological impact of the rape as well (Daniel, 2004). Homosexual survivors in one study did not appear to link their victimization with a loss of masculinity, and tended to neutralize the events as miscommunication (Allen, 2004). For male homosexual victims of sexual assault there is the added obstacle that they may not be believed because they could just be blowing that mis-communication out of proportion. In this case it could be a he said/he said obstacle, similar to females who are hesitant to report for fear of not being believed. Additionally, because homosexuality is not widely accepted in the United States, some male homosexual victims of sexual assault may be resistant to coming forward as the crime may "out" them and cause additional stressors and potentially violence in their lives. One final obstacle for male victims of sexual assault is that the rape crisis services that are available are often perceived to cater only to females. Whereas the crisis line, emergency room, legal companionship, and one-on-one counseling *are* available for male victims it is unlikely that support groups for male victims exist on a consistent basis or at all. They may also perceive that the services are not for them and may, therefore, not attempt to reach out.

Did You Know ... ?

In the early discussion of rape/sexual assault, the issue of false accusations was noted. Because this is such a prominent issue when the topic of rape/sexual assault comes up, it is necessary to truly examine the phenomenon of false rape accusations. Interestingly, there is a great deal of suspicion in this area for both rape/sexual assault allegations and childhood sexual abuse allegations (Gross, 2009). There are a number of reasons why there may be the perception that the number of false rape allegations is off the charts; first, the empirical evidence is not conclusive, with estimates ranging from 1–90% of cases being fabricated (Saunders, 2012; Gross, 2009); second, despite evidence to the contrary, there is a perception by some criminal justice practitioners that "most" rape victims are lying or lying "in part" and the term "false" has multiple meanings (Saunders, 2012); and third, there is confusion with the terms *unfounded, defounded,* and *false* (Saunders, 2012). Garland (2009) purports that the belief that the majority of rape accusations are false is the most widely touted rape myth of all. She states that an article in the *Colombia Law Review* from the 1960s portrayed women as "crying rape" for reasons of guilt and vengeance—that women who accused men of rape were either reframing what happened because they felt ashamed of themselves after the fact or that they created an act that never occurred because they had been spurned (see also Saunders, 2012; Gross, 2009). In an effort to determine the true prevalence of false rape/sexual assault claims, the FBI looked to the UCR to evaluate the percentage of cases that were listed as "unfounded." According to the UCR, unfounded means that the case is false or baseless (End Violence Against Women International, 2013, www.evawintl.org). An analysis of 1991 cases resulted in the FBI reporting that 8% of cases were unfounded. However, previous research on unfounded rape cases suggests that all the cases weren't necessarily false, some were labeled unfounded through mistakes—inappropriately collecting evidence, sending victim reports to the wrong department, and a victim not participating as a witness in the case (Garland, 2009).

It appears that most studies on false allegations of rape tend to find that between 2–11% of rape allegations are false (Saunders, 2012). In her interviews of police officers and judges, Saunders (2012) found that criminal justice practitioners classified cases as "false" if they were either: (1) false in and of themselves, meaning no crime occurred and the complainant was making something up (i.e., the false complaint), or (2) the act may have occurred but the complainant included false or misleading information within the recounting of the incident (i.e., the false account). In the false account, the victim could have problems remembering the incident correctly or could be omitting information that could be damning to them for a different reason (for instance, they may have engaged in illegal behavior, i.e. drugs, underage drinking, etc., that could make the complainant believe that she or he would not be believed). This could help to explain why criminal justice researchers and criminal justice practitioners held different understandings of how many "false allegations" actually occurred.

Oftentimes, cases that the FBI lists as "unfounded" are confused to mean "false," which is not the case (Gross, 2009). Generally, "unfounded" means that there is not substantial evidence to secure a belief that the crime occurred (Gross, 2009). This is very different from establishing that a crime did not occur at all. A victim could un-wittingly identify the wrong suspect or may recant her claim for any number of reasons, thus lending the case to be listed as "unfounded" (Gross, 2009). A case can also be "unfounded" if it does not meet the strict definition of the crime, for instance, a weapon was not used, physical force was not applied to compel the act, if the victim did not fight back and does not have physical injuries, or if there was a prior relationship between the accused and the perpetrator (Gross, 2009). Gross (2009) suggests that only those cases that have the element of intentionally stating a falsehood should be considered false allegations, and that they should not be confused with cases that are listed as "unfounded." Specifically, those cases in the following areas should be considered false allegations:

- Victim knowingly alleges that a sex crime occurred when it did not;
- A rape did occur, but the victim alleges that a person who she/he knows did not commit the crime is the perpetrator; and
- Consensual sex occurred but the victim does not want to admit that after the fact and thus files a rape accusation.

Policy emerged in response to these types of accusations about rape victims, which often required that rape cases, in particular, had to rely heavily on corroborated evidence rather than the victim's statement. Additionally, until relatively recently rape victims were required to take a polygraph examination to assess the validity of their claims, *unlike any other crime victim*. As a part of the 2005 reauthorization of the Violence Against Women Act, however, all law enforcement agencies interested in re-ceiving STOP Program or Arrest Program grant money from the act had to create policies strictly forbidding the use of polygraph examinations of rape/sexual assault victims given the lack of admissibility of such reports, the trauma it created for the victims, and the numerous problems inherent with trusting the results of polygraph tests, including:

- Nervousness, anxiety, and emotional state
- Anger
- Self-blame of victim (belief that he or she may have done something to contribute to the offense)
- Physical discomfort
- Too many questions
- Medication use by the victim, and
- Poor question phrasing by the polygraph administrator (Houser & Dworkin, 2009).

Given the recent research by Rebecca Campbell (2012) on the neurobiology of sexual assault, what may have appeared to law enforcement as the victim "lying" can now be understood as the effects of the neurochemicals released during trauma. For a long time, a major critique of rape victims by law enforcement is that their stories seemed to change from interview to interview (Campbell, 2012). From their view, it appeared that the victim was lying, and thus the victim was disbelieved. However, Campbell (2012) found that the neurochemical response in the brain prohibits rape/sexual assault victims from being able to easily piece together the events in a sequential order for a time after the victimization occurs (not permanently). Campbell equates it to writing down a story on a series of post-its. Once the story is written, you should crumble up the post-its and throw them in the air. When they land the story is now jumbled and no longer in sequential order. Some pieces may have even fallen underneath a desk or chair, and not located until a later time. Dr. Campbell suggests that this is what happens to the memories of those in extremely traumatic situations (so this could apply to other personal crime victims as well—attempted homicide, aggravated assault, robbery). When the victim is asked by law enforcement to tell them what happened, he or she is doing his or her best to tell it like they remember ... but the chemical soup in their brains may not be letting them access everything they need, hence it looks like their "story is changing" when they meet up with law enforcement again and talk about the case with more or different information.

Often compounded by the perceived (or actual) doubt a rape/sexual assault victim may feel is coming from criminal justice and medical personnel is the self-blame rape victims oftentimes experience. One may wonder if she or he drank too much, shouldn't have used drugs, shouldn't have worn a particular item of clothing, shouldn't have talked to or danced with or kissed the person who ended up being a perpetrator. If an individual believes that there is something wrong with her or his character—like she or he believes that they are "easy" and have a tendency to get involved in sexual relations with people too quickly—this will exacerbate the self-blame that is attributed. Society tends to encourage self-blame of sexual abuse/assault victims in that the people who respond to aid the victim may ask questions implying that they shouldn't have been doing a certain thing, or asking if they forcefully said no or fought back. As stated earlier, this is one of the most unique aspects of sexual abuse/assault—the victim has to go on the defensive almost immediately to prove that it wasn't something she or he "asked for." Self-blame is also associated with guilt feelings and a devaluation of oneself.

Professional Profile 4.1

Rebecca Campbell
Michigan State University

Q: What got you into the field of victimology and/or working with crime victims?

A: In college, I took a women's studies course and we were encouraged to become involved with a community group/ organization that addressed a "woman's issue." I volunteered at a domestic violence shelter/rape crisis center and was forever changed by what I saw there and I knew that's what I wanted to focus on in my career. And by the way, the field has changed a lot since then and no longer refers to gender-based violence as a "woman's issue"!

Q: What advice do you have for students interested in working with victims and/ or becoming victimologists?

A: Get out into the world and *be* with victims. Volunteer in organizations, do front-line work—this is not something that can be understood, or changed, or ended by sitting at a desk. Listen to survivors, be humbled by what you see, bear witness to what they tell you. And, take good care of yourself in the process, because it is hard to do this.

Q: What are some challenges to studying crime victims that you have encountered or seen?

A: This is emotionally draining work—it can be very fulfilling and meaningful, and it can also make you go fetal sometimes. There are, of course, practical challenges in doing this work (access to key populations, sufficient resources, etc.), but the main challenge I have always faced is the challenge to keep going when I feel tired, overwhelmed, and burned out.

Q: What obstacles have you encountered while striving to study crime victims?

A: Access to key data sources is always challenging—police records, prosecutorial records, social service records, other records, professionals willing to be interviewed, survivors willing to be interviewed.

Q: What do you feel is the mark you will have left on the field of victimology? What do you want people to see as your mark? At the end of the day, what do you want your "legacy" to be in the field of victimology/victim services?

A: The concept of "secondary victimization"—that how we, as a society, treat victims is all too often a "second assault" or a "second rape." Our understanding of trauma is incomplete without this—victims' post-assault disclosure and help-seeking experiences can be traumatic and we need to document this harm and *change* these practices.

Q: What are some burgeoning issues that you see in the field of victimology?

A: Understanding the neurobiology of trauma and how and why victims behave as they do and what they can remember about the assault. This information is critical for front-line practitioners and victimologists need to be providing practitioners with sound science on the biological, physiological, and psychological underpinnings of trauma.

Q: What areas within victimology do you think are neglected?

A: Strong, empirically based models of sexual offending and serial sexual assault, particularly in non-stranger perpetrated crimes.

In regard to guilt, there is guilt that the incident took place, guilt that someone "got in trouble," and guilt that you may not have been as careful as you now think you should have. In terms of devaluation, some people may start to feel as if they are cheap or "dirty" after the fact and start to integrate that into their self-concept.

The most recent, and most predominant finding, behind the "usefulness" of self-blame is that it has a tendency to make the victim fail to see the trauma that has occurred to her or him. Some have argued in the past that self-blame might actually make one feel like they have a stronger ability to prevent a future sexual assault or abusive act, but that doesn't seem to play out across the board (Daane, 2009). It seems that the common belief now is that self-blame tends to lend itself to longer recovery periods in which self-destructive coping skills may be utilized (such as alcohol and drug use) which will further exacerbate the negative self-concept one has adopted.

Oftentimes it is encouraged that the victim focuses her blame on external, or outside, factors. This could be the perpetrator (rightfully so), a non-offending family member or friend (less clear), or society in general. This could lead to healthy responses to recovery (blaming the perpetrator), a rift in a potential support system (if blaming family and friends who are supportive of the victim), or a belief that there is no way to control what happens and that a future assault/abusive act could happen no matter what the individual does to prevent it. This last issue tends to exacerbate depression in victims and can impede the healing process.

Aggravated Assault

Aggravated assault accounts for the greatest amount of violent crime in the UCR Type I Index. Whereas simple assault is more prevalent, aggravated assault tends to carry with it a greater chance of injury and markedly different injuries, since the perpetrator typically utilizes some type of weapon or more aggressive posture toward the victim.

Circumstances/Motives for Assault

Pittman and Handy (1964) conducted one of the earliest assessments of the motives behind aggravated assault and found that verbal arguments (between familiars, acquaintances, or strangers) were the precursors to the vast majority of aggravated assaults and that most assaults have one victim and one offender. Lopez (2000) suggests that when alcohol and narcotics are introduced into the mix, this enhances the chances of an aggravated assault occurring. Sweeney and Payne (2011) found this same link between alcohol and assault in Australia, with the median number of drinks consumed being 14. It appears that whereas there are "motives" for other crimes, with aggravated assault we're looking more at common circumstances within which these acts transpire—namely after arguments and often when alcohol or drugs are involved.

Differential Risk for Assault

Pittman and Handy (1964) found that the majority of aggravated assaults happen on the weekends, at night, and are more frequent in the warmer summer months (as this increases the overall interactions between people, particularly in settings where alcohol and other substances are available and their use is encouraged). Forty years later, Lauritsen and White (2014) noted the same pattern—that aggravated assaults are more likely to occur in the summertime, at night, and on the weekends. Cochran et al. (1999) suggests that proximity to an alcohol outlet significantly increases the likelihood of aggravated assault, with each new establishment increasing the number of aggravated assaults by 8.

Males are the most likely victims of aggravated and simple assault, per the Sourcebook of Criminal Justice Statistics (2008a). White males had a victimization rate of 18.1/1,000, whereas Black males had a rate of 21.3, indicating that Black males are more likely to be victimized in this manner. For females, there is a similar pattern; White females had a victimization rate of 13.7, whereas Black females had a victimization rate of 16.2/1,000. Both males and females were more at risk of simple assault overall, and when assaulted (either aggravated or simple) injury was not likely to occur. Both males and females in the age range of 20 to 24 had the highest rates of aggravated assault (8.2 and 9.3 respectively), whereas 12- to 15-year-olds had the highest rates of simple assault overall (males 32.4/1,000 and females 25.5/1,000) (Sourcebook of Criminal Justice Statistics, 2008b). Both males and females are most likely to be assaulted by someone they know (Males: 49% nonstrangers vs. 37% strangers: Females: 54% nonstrangers vs. 38% strangers) (Sourcebook of Criminal Justice Statistics, 2010). Conversely, in the case of simple assault, males are more likely to be assaulted by a stranger (46% of the time vs. 42% by nonstrangers) than females (68% of perpetrators are nonstrangers vs. 26% nonstrangers) (Sourcebook of Criminal Justice Statistics,

2010). For both aggravated and simple assault, when the perpetrator is a nonstranger, intimate partners are responsible more often for females than males (24% aggravated, 22% simple vs. 7% aggravated, 4% simple for males). Taken together with the information about rates of simple assault for 12- to 15-year-olds, this information suggests that dating violence may be a real problem for teenage females. In both aggravated and simple assault, when a victim fought back this helped the situation about two thirds of the time (Sourcebook of Criminal Justice Statistics, 2008c).

Did You Know ...?

Because aggravated assault includes within its definition assault with a weapon it's important to consider what might fall within the "other" category. Typically, official statistics create specific categories for firearms and knives (NCVS—NVAT), using the catch-all phrase of "other" to include other instruments. Knives may include other sharp objects, such as a broken bottle, an ice pick, or scissors (Perkins, 2003). More commonly used blunt instruments include rocks, blackjacks, metal pipes, bats, bricks, and unbroken bottles (Perkins, 2003). Perkins (2003) reports that the "other" weapons category accounts for slightly more assaults than the blunt object category. In the "other" category the NCVS includes "ropes, chains, poison, martial arts weapons, BB guns, and objects that could not be classified" (Perkins, 2003, p. 3). It appears that items we may not think of are being used to perpetrate aggravated assault more recently. A recent Internet news article (Fox, June 3, 2013) reported that biting someone with false teeth constituted aggravated assault and in another case hot vegetables were used as the offending weapon (see the news article box on "Hot Vegetables" used in an aggravated assault). What this all suggests is that almost anything can be used as a weapon, if the perpetrator has the mindset to do so.

Robbery

Robbery is a unique personal crime in that the "victims" are both humans and businesses. As you learned in Chapter 2, the definition of robbery per the FBI is: "the taking or attempting to take anything of value from the care, custody, or control of a person or persons by force or threat of force or violence and/or by putting the victim in fear" (FBI, 2013). Therefore, though the "victim" may technically be a business, it is a human who is threatened or forced to "give up" the item(s) of value to the perpetrator.

Circumstances/Motives for Robbery

In the majority of cases, the motive for robbery is theft. The robber uses violence or the threat of violence to secure something he or she wants. Some researchers have suggested that there may be other or additional motivations for committing robbery.

"In the News" Box 4.1

Hot Vegetables Thrown during Argument
Result in Aggravated Assault Charge

By Linda A. Moore
Posted April 18, 2014 at 3:44 p.m.

A 43-year-old man was charged on Friday with aggravated assault after he allegedly threw a pot of hot mixed vegetables on his uncle's girlfriend.

Officers responded to a disturbance call at a house on the 600 block of Pope and heard the victim yelling that her face was burning.

She said that Ronnie Beasley had thrown the vegetables on her neck and back during an argument. The victim is the live-in girlfriend of Beasley's uncle and the three live in the house together. The uncle told police that he heard the two arguing, and police found a pot of mixed vegetables in the kitchen sink.

She was taken by ambulance to the Regional Medical Center in noncritical condition with blisters on her neck and back.

Beasley was taken to the Shelby County Criminal Justice Center.

Reprint permission granted by the Memphis Commercial Appeal.

http://www.commercialappeal.com/news/2014/apr/18/hot-vegetables-thrown-during-argument-result-in/.

Bennett and Brookman (2009) interviewed 55 offenders in the United Kingdom (UK) involved in robbery and assault and found that for those who commit robbery approximately 39% suggested they included violence in their act to secure the goods they sought, and that was it. 21% suggested that using violence to commit a robbery also gave them a "buzz" and that in some instances the financial gain gotten from the robbery was secondary to the excitement they felt when they were fighting. 15% suggested that they started committing violent street robberies to gain a reputation for being tough and to increase their status among their peer group. Finally, 25% suggested that they engaged in violent street robberies to both secure the item or financial gain they wanted but also because the person they robbed was someone who had done them or someone close to them wrong—so they sought street justice. Jacobs and Wright (2008) reported a similar pattern in their examination of moralistic street robbers in St. Louis, Missouri. Their offenders were steeped in the drug market and thus robberies were often focused on drug dealers. Moralistic street robberies included elements of both traditional robbery (getting the goods they wanted) and an attempt to get even. Jacobs and Wright (2008) fit their moralistic street robberies into three areas, similar to Bennett and Brookman—market-related violations, wherein the offender was previously robbed by a person (and was thus a victim) and set out to rob their offender as payback and to emphasize that that person messed with the wrong person; status-based violations, in which one party felt that another was devaluing his or her role in either a street-level hierarchy or in their role as a user or dealer; and personalistic violations, wherein the robber used the robbery as a means to get revenge on the "victim" for an egregious offense he or she had perpetrated either on the robber or a loved one of the robber. Similarly, Felson, Baumer, and Messner (2000) found that in acquaintance robberies (robberies in which the victim and offender knew each other) that there were two main motives: (1) the offender had inside information about the "goods" the victim was holding which made the victim a more attractive target, and (2) the "known" victim was targeted specifically so the robber could pay back the victim for a previous falling out. So, it appears that in addition to securing the item(s) the offender wants through threat or force, that status, reputation, and street justice may be additional, perhaps secondary, motivations for committing robbery.

Differential Risk for Robbery

As previously noted, humans and businesses can be "victims" of robbery. According to the UCR for 2015, in both counties and in cities with a population of 10,000 or more the primary type of robbery that occurred was street/highway robbery. This was more prominent as the size of the city grew, for instance in cities with a population of 250,000 or more 54.4% of robberies were street/highway. In contrast, in cities with a population of 10,000–24,999, street/highway robberies accounted for 29.2% of all robberies. Therefore, despite the fact that street/highway robberies ranked first in type of robbery, there was a significant difference in the amount of robberies that fell within that category. When locations are looked at together, miscellaneous location is the second most common location for robberies (19.1%), and residence is the third most likely location (16.5%) (*note*: Miscellaneous refers to any location not listed in the other categories, such as a university, an office, etc.). Commercial house locations accounted for 14.4% of robberies, convenience stores accounted for 5.7% of robberies, gas stations accounted for 2.7% of robberies, and banks accounted for 1.7% of robberies (*note*: A commercial house is an establishment where business takes place in which a monetary transaction will occur, like a hair salon/barber shop, restaurant, etc.). The average value for property (including cash) stolen was $1,190, with banks reporting an average loss of $3,884. Both strong-arm tactics and firearms were used about equally to carry out the robbery (42.2% and 40.8% respectively); knives and other dangerous weapons were each used less than 10% of the time.

In their examination of the 2009 NCVS results, Truman and Rand (2010) reported that street robbery victims are predominantly male (2.7/1,000 rate vs. 1.6/1,000 for females), and disproportionately Black or two or more races (5.6/1,000 and 5.2/1,000 respectively versus 1.6/1,000 for Whites, and 0.5/1,000 for other races). Hispanics also reported higher rates of robbery than non-Hispanics (3.4/1,000 vs. 1.9/1,000). The age group most at risk for robbery was 16–19-year-olds with a rate of 5.2/1,000, followed by 20–24-year-olds (3.5/1,000), 12–15-year-olds, and persons 25 and older. Individuals aged 35 and older appeared to be least at risk for robbery. Felson, Baumer, and Messner (2000) found that approximately one-third of street robbery victims knew their perpetrators and Truman and Rand (2009) reported that one-third of male victims and just under half of female robbery victims knew their perpetrators of robbery. Tompson and Bowers (2012) suggest that darkness is the robber's friend—more robberies were committed in the winter time and after the sun set than in daytime.

For commercial robberies a number of indicators may make a commercial establishment more attractive than others for a robbery. Establishments that are either open 24 hours a day or have late hours, have a single attendant, and have a ready amount of cash that a robber believes is possible to access are at heightened risk for robbery. Though exhibiting many of the components listed, Exum, Kuhns, Koch, and Johnson (2010) found that convenience stores and fast-food establishments had significantly different indicators that made them attractive targets for robbers. In the convenience store setting, Exum et al. (2010) found that the presence of ATMs and the use of and signage indicating there was a drop-safe decreased the risk of robbery (a drop-safe is a safe into which someone can deposit money, typically through a slit in the safe, but only the person with a key can open the safe). It was thought that perhaps locating an ATM inside the establishment would bring in more legitimate clientele who could act in the role of capable guardians and thus deter motivated offenders from robbing the establishment. The presence of a public pay phone and a nearby public transportation depot increased the chances of robbery for convenience stores and fast-food restaurants, possibly because the traffic of motivated offenders was greater. The presence of police, but not security guards or armed security personnel, decreased the risk of robberies of fast-food establishments. The researchers found that methods of deterrence that might work at one type of establishment may do nothing for another type of establishment.

Demographic characteristics of robbery offenders were not as easy to come by. According to the NCVS for 2008, in single-offender robberies (both completed and attempted), perpetrators were most often male (85.8%) and most often fell in the 21–29-year-old age group, with 30 years and older encompassing the second greatest percentage of offenders. However, when the incident was a multiple-offender robbery, perpetrators were predominantly male (79.3%), but the presence of females increased in the form of male-female teams of offenders. Perpetrators were significantly more likely to be between the ages of 12–20 for both completed and attempted robberies. In that same year, for single-offender victimizations, Black perpetrators accounted for 42% of robbery offenders, followed by 36.6% White offenders, 9.7% other race, and 11.8% unknown. For multiple-offender victimizations in 2008, 53% of offenders were Black only, 15.7% were mixed races, 9.9% were White only, 1.8% were other races, and 20.1% were unknown. An interesting finding for that year was that White perpetrators were significantly more likely to injure their victims than Black perpetrators for both attempted and completed robberies in both single-offender and multiple-offender victimizations. So, one could conclude that despite more robbery offenders being Black, one is more likely to be injured in any type of robbery situation if the offender is White.

Did You Know ...?

According to Alitzio and York (2007), convenience store employees are more likely to be injured in robberies where the offender is taking goods only, as opposed to money or a combination of money and goods. Another interesting fact is that bank robberies tend to have one of the highest clearance rates of all crimes, perhaps because they are conducted most often during the day, are reported while in progress, and security images of the offenders are usually readily available (Alitzio & York, 2007).

Burglary

Many people get burglary and robbery confused and will use the terms interchangeably, similar to how the terms *prison* and *jail* are used interchangeably though they mean distinctly different things. How many times have you heard someone say something akin to "I always lock my doors, so my house doesn't get robbed." To set the record straight, one commits a burglary when he or she unlawfully enters a structure for the purpose of committing a felony or theft. The entrance can be made with force, though force is not necessary, or may be an attempted entry with the use of force. Robbery, on the other hand, exists when someone forcefully or with threat takes belongings from a person. Therefore, burglary is focused on a place whereas robbery is focused on a person. According to the UCR for 2015, of all Type I property crimes, burglary is the second most common type of property crime and in 2015 accounted for 19.8% of property crime overall. The average dollar loss for burglary offenses in 2015 was $2,316, which is over double that of the most common property crime, larceny-theft ($929), and almost double that of robbery ($1,190). Similar to robbery, businesses can also be burglarized; whereas 71.6% of burglaries are of residences, 28.4% are committed in nonresidential structures (stores, offices, etc.).

Circumstances/Motives for Burglary

Verhage and Ponsaers (2009) suggest that there are about four main motives surrounding a similar theme explaining why burglars engage in burglary: (1) survival, (2) to live, (3) to live life with more amenities, and (4) as a means to support an addiction. Essentially, all of these motivations suggest that burglary is a crime in which individuals get money from the goods and cash they take so that it will support them in a variety of ways. The authors suggest that additionally, some burglars, especially young ones, have reported getting an adrenaline rush or "kick" from burglaries and that the fantasy goal is to "hit the jackpot."

Differential Risk for Burglary

Similar to robbery, the majority of burglaries (as indicated) occur in what one might call one's "intimate" property, or for lack of a better term, one's "personal space." Just under three out of every four burglaries occurs in one's residence, and most residential burglaries occur during the day (52.3%), whereas slightly more nonresidential burglaries occur at night (41.9% of nonresidential burglaries versus 35.3% during the day). According to Catalano (2010), there appears to be a vulnerability enhancement when the household is headed by a single male or single female (with or without children). If over 52% of burglaries to residences are happening during the day, it would make sense to target households headed by single adults because there is a greater likelihood that they will be out at work and that there will be a sure absence of an adult in the home. This seems to be confirmed by additional information suggesting that only approximately 28% of burglarized households had someone home at the time of the burglary, which means the majority of burglaries are done when people are away. In approximately 7% of household burglaries, a member of the household experienced a violent victimization, most often simple assault (15%) followed by robbery (7%) and sexual assault (3%) (Catalano, 2010). Victims typically knew who the offender was in a household burglary when violence was involved (65% of the time), but tended not to know the offender in nonviolent burglaries. For the most part, burglars did *not* enter a home armed with a weapon (61%) (Catalano, 2010).

Individuals reporting two or more races currently have the highest rate of household burglary, followed by American Indian/Alaskan Natives, Blacks, Hispanics/Latinos, Whites, and Asians/Native Hawaiian/Pacific Islanders. Household burglary disproportionately affects heads of household who are 19 years and under, followed by 20–29-year-olds and continuing to decrease as one gets older (Catalano, 2010).

Urban residents are more likely to be vulnerable to household burglaries, followed by rural households, with suburban households experiencing the lowest rate of burglary. In 2011, rural households actually had a greater amount of household burglary than urban households. Though it may seem counterintuitive, households with an average income of $14,999 or less experience the highest rate of burglaries across time. Rental properties had a significantly higher rate of burglary than owned properties (32.7 vs. 18.3 per 1,000). Perhaps this coupled with the age that is most vulnerable suggest that college students and/or young adults out on their own are particularly vulnerable to household burglary (Catalano, 2010).

Did You Know ...?

We've all read about the use of DNA in identifying and convicting offenders in personal crime cases such as murder and sexual assault, but a recent study funded by the National Institute of Justice has found that DNA is effective at solving burglary cases too (Ritter, 2008). In a five-city experiment it was found that when DNA evidence was collected at the scene of burglaries it increased the identification of suspects by two times that of traditional investigations, the amount of arrests of suspects rose by two times, and the number of cases the prosecution took on increased by two times (Ritter, 2008). Cases in which DNA evidence identified a suspect appeared to identify suspects with more serious criminal histories (5.6 prior felonies for DNA-identified suspects vs. 1.7 prior felonies on traditional investigation-identified suspects). Some interesting findings of the experiment included: DNA collected by patrol officers or detectives was just as useful as evidence collected by crime scene technicians (meaning, almost anyone could be taught how to collect DNA evidence effectively); scenes in which blood and/or saliva were collected yielded a higher likelihood of obtaining DNA versus collecting samples of cells on items that were touched or handled; collection of an entire item versus taking a swab, was more likely to yield a usable DNA sample; and crime scenes where entrance was made through an unlocked portal were not likely to yield usable DNA samples. These results could have serious implications for law enforcement as they could help to determine when a case should attempt to utilize DNA collection for burglary cases. One of the main issues being examined as a result of this study is the financial cost and collateral "burden" on the justice system that use of DNA for burglary cases could lead to. If we're more successful at identifying suspects, and habitual offenders at that, is the criminal justice system going to be able to shoulder the costs that come with it?

Motor Vehicle Theft

Probably one of the most reported crimes, due to the necessity of individuals to make insurance claims and the importance of a vehicle to attend to many of life's necessary activities (work, school, etc.), motor vehicle theft reporting rates are in the mid 70% to low 80% range pretty consistently from 1993–2015, with 2015 listing the lowest rate of 69% and 2004 recording the highest reporting rate of 85.6% (NCVS Victimization Analysis Tool, utilized 03-06-2017).

Circumstances/Motives for Motor Vehicle Theft

Gant and Grabosky (2001) suggest that individuals engage in motor vehicle theft for two main reasons: opportunity-oriented reasons, including joy-riding and transport from one area to another, and instrumental-oriented reasons, basically, for profit. They estimate that 75% of motor vehicle theft is done for opportunistic-oriented reasons and 25% is for instrumental-oriented reasons. When cars are stolen for profit, Gant and Grabosky (2006) suggest that the cars are dealt with in one of two ways— altered to be sold as a legitimate vehicle or chopped up into spare parts.

Differential Risk for Motor Vehicle Theft

When discussing the most likely "victim" in motor vehicle theft, we've got to focus on the most oft-stolen vehicles. Automobile thefts account for 73.9% of motor vehicle thefts overall, trucks and buses account for about 14.2%, and "other" vehicles (including SUVs, motorcycles, scooters, ATVs, and snowmobiles) account for approximately 9.2% of motor vehicle thefts. Within automobile thefts, some automobiles have a higher rate of theft, even though their raw number may not be as great as other vehicles, but instead the rate is based on the number of those cars available in the population. According to the National Highway Traffic Safety Administration (2014), the top ten cars with the highest rate of theft (per 1,000 cars) include, in descending order:

1. Dodge Charger (4.82)
2. Mitsubishi Galant (4.24)
3. GM Cadillac STS (3.88)
4. Lamborghini Gallardo (3.86)
5. Hyundai Accent (3.51)
6. GM Chevrolet Impala (3.43)
7. GM Chevrolet HHR (3.36)
8. GM Chevrolet AVEO (3.35)
9. Nissan Infiniti FX35 (3.13)
10. Nissan GT-R (3.07)

Motor vehicle theft seems to be a predominantly male-perpetrated crime, with males accounting for 83% of arrests. While the median age of arrestees was 23, the peak age for arrestees of motor vehicle theft was 18, with 22% of motor vehicle thefts being committed by juveniles.

Carjacking is another method by which an offender can steal a motor vehicle. Klaus (2004) provided an analysis of carjackings between 1993 and 2002. According to Klaus (2004), there was an average of 38,000 carjacking incidents annually. Again, men were the primary perpetrators of carjacking acts (93%), with Blacks accounting for 56% of carjacking arrestees, Whites accounting for 21% of arrestees, Asian or American Indian accounting for 16% of arrestees, and mixed races/didn't know accounting for about 7% of all arrests. Sixty-three percent of carjackings took place within 5 miles of the victim's home, and 25% of cars were recovered undamaged. 78% of carjackings resulted in partial of complete recovery of property, overall. Only 45% of carjackings were completed. Victims resisted in 67% of attempts and 32% of completed carjacking victims and 17% of attempted carjacking victims were injured. Weapons were used in about 74% of carjackings, with the primary weapon being a firearm.

Victims of carjackings were predominantly Black (rate of 3.3/10,000) and Hispanic (2.6/10,000), and were more likely to be male (2.3/10,000 vs. 1.1/10,000 females). Most victims were also either divorced/separated or never married, 5.7/10,000 overall. Carjackings were most likely to happen at night (68%) and 44% occurred out in the open or near public transportation. 98% of completed carjackings were reported to the police, but only 58% of the attempted carjackings were reported.

Did You Know ... ?

According to McDonold (2014), president of the International Association of Auto Theft Investigators, the advent of technology, along with increased sales markets on the Internet, have opened the door for motor vehicle theft and the sale of stolen vehicles. Popular sites, such as Craigslist and eBay Motors allow for motor vehicle thieves to set up transactions in which they can set up an appointment with a buyer, take the car for a test drive and never return, or pay for the car with a bad check only to disappear after the check has been deposited. Additionally, they can conduct the transaction over the Internet, pay for it, and arrange for transport, but never receive the vehicle. Rental car agencies are also victims of motor vehicle theft, as McDonold reports that rental cars are easy to rent and never return. Some rental car agencies have resorted to placing GPS devices in their cars to track them when they don't return at the arranged turn-in time. In one case, a Maryland car rental agency located some of its stolen vehicles in Ghana, Africa (McDonold, 2014).

Larceny-Theft

Larceny-theft accounts for the largest amount of crime within the overall crime rate. For the year 2015, 5,706,346 larceny-thefts were reported to police (as reported in the UCR) and 11,142,310 larceny-thefts were recorded in the NCVS. As you learned in Chapter 2, larceny-theft includes "the unlawful taking, carrying, leading, or riding away of property from the possession or constructive possession of another" (FBI, 2013). Larceny-theft captures a number of different activities, including bicycle theft, stealing parts off of motor vehicles, shoplifting, pick-pocketing, and the stealing of property or articles without the use of force or violence. In 2015, larceny-theft accounted for 71.4% of all property crime reported in the UCR, and the average amount "lost" for each offense was $929. In 2015, there were just under 8 million property offenses reported to police, which is estimated at about $14.3 billion in overall losses for that year (FBI, 2013b). For the 5,104,269 larceny-thefts upon which information was recorded, at least 34.1% of larceny-thefts occur to businesses in the form of shoplifting (22.3%), theft from buildings (11.6%), and theft from coin-operated machines (0.2%), with the remaining 65.9% experienced by private individuals. Twenty-four percent of lar-ceny-theft occurs in thefts from motor vehicles with an additional 6.9% of lar-ceny-theft including motor vehicle accessories thefts (hub caps/rims, etc.). This has been a consistent pattern since 1973 (Sourcebook of Criminal Justice Statistics Online, Table 3.146, 2010). 30.3% of larceny-thefts are reported as "other," so it is difficult to estimate the true amount that occurs to businesses and private indi-viduals. In the NCVS, theft rose from 138.7/1,000 persons to 155.8/1,000 from 2011 to 2012 and was the main contributor to a slight increase in the property crime rate (Truman, Langton, & Planty, 2013). More recently, larceny-theft appears to have dropped rather dramatically, with the 2015 rates being 84.4/1,000 persons (Truman & Morgan, 2016).

Circumstances/Motives for Larceny-Theft

The motives for the different types of larceny-theft may vary based on the type of crime committed. For instance, Kulbarsh (2013) suggests that only 5% of shoplifting is committed for financial need, while the remaining 95% can be explained by compulsive behaviors, supporting a drug/gambling habit, thrill seeking, absent mind-edness (or cognitive impairment), kleptomania, and professional shoplifting. Keister (2007) suggests that theft from cars is done strictly for the profitability of the items stolen. Katz (1988) suggests that larceny-theft is done for the thrill, particularly for younger people (teens). Jenson (2010) reports that employee theft (shoplifting) occurs because employees may need the items to survive, but also may feel that they are entitled to the items because of low pay. What these articles demonstrate is that there are numerous reasons why larceny-theft occurs, and those reasons often vary based on the type of crime within the category of larceny-theft itself.

Differential Risk for Larceny-Theft

Mustaine and Tewksbury (1998) suggest that the majority of larceny-thefts (when perpetrated on individuals) occur near people's homes (but not in them), in a parking lot or parking garage, or at school. Additionally, they report that higher income homes and African Americans have higher risks of victimization. As noted above, there are many different acts that fall within the definition of larceny-theft; therefore, there may be different characteristics as to when, where, how, and who is at risk for larceny-theft. In terms of when these crimes typically occur, over 50% of purse snatching/pocket picking happens during the day (6am–6pm) and an additional 30% occurs between 6pm and midnight; this makes sense since this is when greater numbers of people are out and about and may be at vulnerable to this type of theft (Matson & Klaus, 2006). Slightly less than 40% of theft (from a motor vehicle, from the work environment, objects taken from the outside of the home, etc.) occurs during the daytime with ap-proximately 44% occurring in the evening hours (between 6pm and 6am). In some instances, people are unaware of when the theft happened as they may not notice an item has been taken until well after the event occurred (Matson & Klaus, 2006). According to NCVS results for 2005, purse snatching/pocket picking is most likely to occur in a restaurant/club or other commercial building (51% of reports), followed by a parking lot or garage (14.2%), on a street not near one's home (10.2%), on public transportation (7.9%), and in other areas outside of the home. Theft, on the other hand, is most likely to occur at (10.1%) or near (38.4%) one's home, with the next most likely place being a parking lot or garage (12.7), at school (8.8%), and in other venues away from one's residence. Victims of purse snatching/pocket picking are typically out for entertainment (45%) or shopping/running errands (25.5%) at the time of the offense, whereas other theft victims are most often sleeping (29.2%) or conducting other activities at home (12.2%), participating in a leisure activity (13.1%) or working (11.7%).

Individuals who self-identify as two or more races are almost twice as likely to be victims of theft (rate of 219.7/1,000 persons) followed by Whites (119.6/1,000), Blacks (96.9/1,000), and other races (89.5/1,000). Youngsters (12–19-year-olds) are almost twice as likely to be victims of theft as well (rate of 238.7/1,000), and one's risk declines as one ages (140.1/1,000 for 20–34-year-olds; 136.8/1,000 for 35–49-year-olds; 98.8/1,000 for 50–64-year-olds; and 51.4/1,000 for 65-year-olds and over). Interestingly, individuals with household incomes of $75,000 or more and $7,500 and under share the highest levels of risk of being victims of theft (134.6/1,000 and 132.4/1,000, respectively). The more people that live in a household, the more likely someone is going to experience a theft (1 person: 66.1; 2–3 people: 106.1; 4–5 people: 171.9; and 6 or more people 246.9). So, the overall profile of the most likely theft victim is young, biracial, and lives in a large household. Alternatively, Black females have a rate double that of Black males and White males and females when it comes to purse snatching/pocket picking (2.2/1,000 for Black females versus 1.1/1,000 for Black males and 0.9/1,000 for White males and females). Similar to theft in general, victims of purse snatching/pocket picking are typically young (16–19 and 20–24 having the highest rates of victimization). Not surprisingly, from 1993–2012 strangers overwhelmingly were the perpetrators of purse snatching/pocket picking (on average 95% of the time) (NCVS Victimization Analysis Tool, calculated 6/12/2014). In 2003, 2007, and 2008 nonstrangers appeared to perpetrate a higher number of purse snatchings/pocket pickings (19% in 2003 and 2007 and 35% in 2008). Unfortunately, the NCVS does not collect information on the victim-offender relationship for theft.

Snyder (2012) states that there has been a growing trend in female arrests for larceny-theft, as their rate of arrest has only dropped 8% between 1990–2010, versus a 34% drop for males in that same period. In 2010, females accounted for 44% of arrests, which was starkly different than their proportion of arrests for other property crimes, including burglary (17%) and motor vehicle theft (15%). Snyder (2012) suggests that patterns for larceny-theft arrests are more similar to those found for fraud (particularly forging checks and using others credit cards) which was 42% for females in 2010. Since 1990, juveniles were the most likely offenders of larceny-theft offenses, though adults have become increasingly arrested for these offenses in the last 10 years. Eighteen-year-olds had the highest rates of arrest for larceny-theft offenses. So, it appears that larceny-theft is a young adult crime.

Did You Know ... ?

According to Hollinger (2002), employee theft accounts for the single largest proportion of larceny theft to businesses. In his 2002 assessment of retail theft he estimated that employee theft accounted for $15 billion of loss for businesses, whereas shoplifting by "customers" accounted for $10 billion only. Hollinger (2002) found that 82.5% of convenience stores surveyed indicated that employees steal from within. The next closest commercial victim was grocery stores at 59%. Langner (2010) suggests that employees steal when they are dissatisfied with their job or work environment. They could feel that they are being treated unfairly by their employer or they may retaliate against the employer for perceived unfairness.

"Victimless" Crimes

It may seem counterintuitive to discuss so-called "victimless" crimes in a book about victimology, however, now that you have an understanding of the different categories of victims who may experience harm (primary, secondary, tertiary) it is important to examine whether "victimless" crimes truly have no victims. Typically **victimless crimes** are those crimes in which the primary "victim" is engaging in some type of law-breaking, so he or she is both the offender and the victim of the crime at the same time. Schur (1965) defines it as engaging in a consensual illegal act that does not have a complainant and is thus only discovered when the offending behavior comes to the attention of law enforcement. Veneziano and Veneziano (1993) further distinguish "victimless" crimes as those acts that may cause some type of harm, but more importantly are activities that are looked down upon by the majority of society. They suggest that there are many activities that are not looked down upon but may cause a great deal of harm and have impacts on society (i.e., fast food restaurants, smoking and alcohol use/abuse), but because they are accepted by the overwhelming majority they are not judged as criminal. Crimes that fall within the "victimless" category include drug use, prostitution, gambling, and adult pornography.

Critics of categorizing "victimless" crimes as truly victimless suggest that each of the crimes listed previously do have victims, namely secondary and tertiary victims (Veneziano & Veneziano, 1993). Family and friends of drug users who become addicted may be subject to erratic and perhaps violent behavior and/or theft by the drug user. Individuals who engage in acts with prostitutes may be putting loved ones in jeopardy of sexually transmitted diseases, including HIV. It has been argued that drug use, prostitution, and gambling can exact a huge financial burden on the loved ones of the persons engaging in these activities, so financial harm, along with psychological harm, is reasonable to propose. On a societal level, critics suggest that taxpayers may end up paying for medical treatment of drug abusers and those that engage the services of prostitutes, and that prostitution and adult pornography contribute to the degradation of women in society so tertiary victimization may be occurring as well. Overall, though "primary" victimization may not be occurring in the traditional sense, secondary and tertiary victimization is somewhat easy to see.

Repeat Victimization

In studies of criminal justice we tend to focus on decreasing crime by focusing efforts on repeat (habitual) offenders since they are a small proportion of all criminals who account for a great deal of crime that occurs (Moffitt, 1997). Another approach that could help us both with decreasing crime and helping victims recover from crime is to address **repeat victimization**. Similar to the proportion of repeat offenders in the overall offender base, repeat victims occupy a relatively small percentage of all victims, but they account for a surprisingly large amount of victimizations that occur. Farrell (1992) suggests that "if repeat of multiple victimization can be prevented, a large proportion of all crime might be prevented" (p. 85).

Defining Repeat Victimization

One of the overarching questions about repeat victimization is how it is defined. Some researchers have suggested that the term *repeat victimization* is best defined as a catch-all phrase, while others have suggested that the term *repeat* intimates that the victimization is the same from time to time and that when one is a victim of many different crimes the term *multiple victimizations* is a better identifier. Ken Pease and Graham Farrell have conducted a great deal of research on the problem of repeat victimization. To them, repeat victimization is best defined as "multiple criminal incidents experienced by either a person or place" (Farrell, 1992, p. 86; Farrell & Pease, 2001). As is plain to see in the Farrell and Pease definition, one does not need to be a victim of one type of crime with the same offender to be considered a repeat victim. Their definition of repeat victimization includes a wide spectrum of repeats—same crime, same offender through multiple crimes, and different offenders. It makes sense to adopt this more broad definition of repeat victimization as the effects of repeat victimization are consistent no matter if the offense and/or offenders are the same or different. Farrell and Pease are also not particular about limiting the terminology to just repeat victimization, but instead suggest that the terms *multiple victimization*, *recidivist victimization*, *multi-victimization*, and *repeat victimization* can all mean the same thing (DeValve, 2004).

Prevalence of Repeat Victimization

Discussion about the definition of repeat victimization is important because it is often difficult to identify repeat victims in both police records and victimization surveys. If we can't identify repeat victims in practice or research it is difficult to assess the true prevalence of repeat victimization and to determine the effects of repeat victimizations as well. What has been able to be discovered, however, is that consistently across the globe, a seemingly small percentage of people tend to account for a disproportionate amount of victimizations (Ellingworth, Farrell, & Pease, 1995). For instance, Ellingworth, Farrell, and Pease (1995) analyzed 10 years' worth of responses for the British Crime Survey (BCS) and found that 24% of property crime victims and 38% of personal crime victims experience five or more offenses against them each year. Additionally, Farrell (1992) found that in the 1982 BCS alone, 14% of victims experienced over 70% of all offenses. In an assessment of the International Crime

Figure 4.2: Repeat Victimization Percentages by Country from ICVS 2000

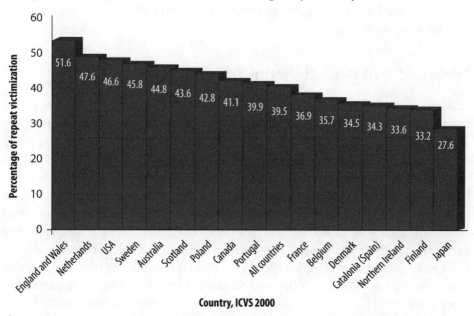

Reproduction of Farrell, G., Tseloni, A., & Pease, K. (2005). Repeat victimization in the ICVS and the NCVS. *Crime Prevention and Community Safety: An International Journal, 7*(3), 7–18. Figure 1. Repeat victimization by country: ICVS 2000 percentage of all crimes that are repeats (p. 9).

Victims Survey (ICVS) Farrell and Bouloukos (2001) found that repeat victimization was a widespread phenomenon across industrialized countries. Additionally, they found that victims of personal crime had higher rates of repeat victimization than victims of property crime. For instance, they found that a small percentage of women experienced between 40–60% of sexual incidents and a similarly small percent of assault victims experienced 30–40% of assaults and threats. They also found that for countries with low crime rates overall (e.g., Japan) those people or places that were victimized accounted for a great deal of the overall victimization. Farrell, Tseloni, and Pease (2005) found that for 17 countries surveyed in the ICVS, 40% of crime overall was the result of repeat victimization. England had the highest amount of repeat victimization and Japan had the lowest (see Figure 4.2). As can be seen in Figure 4.2, most countries report that at least 33% of crime is due to repeat victimization.

Using Vancouver police records Frank, Brantingham, and Farrell (2012) found that 1% of dwellings that experienced burglaries were victimized two or more times, accounting for 20% of burglaries overall. Utilizing the Recorded Repeats Adjustment Calculator (RRAC), a device that predicts the actual amount of overall crime based on percentage reported to police and raw number reported to police, the authors suggested that households that reported 5 or more burglaries accounted for 1% of the overall burgled households, but were estimated to experience over 20% of the actual burglaries overall. Looking at these numbers overall, it is easy to see that if time is spent with individuals who experience two or more offenses in a given time period, we could dramatically change the crime rate and decrease the harm produced through victimization.

Time Order of Repeat Victimization

Another issue to consider when talking about repeat victimization is the time period in which a subsequent victimization should occur in order for someone to be considered a "repeat" victim. When a repeat is going to happen, research has shown that it will happen relatively quickly, usually within one month (see discussion in DeValve, 2004). Most research discusses the time frame of repeat victimizations occurring between one month and a year. For instance, Anderson, Chenery, and Pease (1995) (as cited in Ratcliffe & McCullagh, 1998) found that 40% of repeat burglaries were committed within one month of the first and that for school burglaries there was an even higher percentage, with 79% of repeats occurring within one month (Burquest et al.—as cited in Ratcliffe & McCullagh, 1998). Ratcliffe and McCullagh (1998) suggest that most true repeats (first victimization and subsequent victimizations are linked in some manner) occur within six months and after that, the likelihood that one will be victimized again matches the likelihood of being victimized in the first place.

Why Are Targets Repeatedly Victimized?

Research has shown that we can improve our understanding of repeat victimization if we include an analysis of repeat victims within hot spots as part of the discussion, as well as addressing the topic of "near repeats." **Hot spots** are areas of high crime intensity (Ratcliffe, 2004) and have been noted as areas in which a great deal of repeat victimization is likely to occur (Farrell & Sousa, 2001). Oftentimes, police administration target these hot spots for directed patrols to prevent new crimes from happening and to seek out "super-predators," prolific repeat offenders. Farrell and Sousa (2001) suggest that if they shift some of their focus to include working with repeat victims, an already identified and perhaps captive audience, to prevent additional crimes happening to that population then they can bring down the crime rates within those areas as well. Think of it this way: police may be in these hot spots trying to prevent new crimes and seeking out habitual offenders—two things that may not be easy to do because they are waiting for these things to be noticed in order to take action. However, repeat victims are already identified in the police system, if they have reported the crime, and thus they can watch and work with these people and places to ward off additional crimes from happening, which is a more proactive approach to crime control.

Just as it is important to address the potential for repeat victimization to the primary target of a previous offense, Bowers and Johnson (2004) have identified that it is also necessary to address the issue of **near repeats**. In their study of burglary victims, they identified that those nearest to the initial target have a heightened risk of being targeted shortly after the initial crime because of the proximity to the primary target. For instance, a burglar may ultimately focus on one residence, but in his assessment of that residence he may also look at residences nearby and identify the potential for future burglaries there as well. Johnson and Bowers (2004) suggest that the risk is communicable, meaning that within one month's time the risk for the initial target and those nearby are heightened for additional victimizations. Think of it this way: when a loved one gets sick that makes him or her more susceptible to additional illnesses and you become susceptible to that same illness based on the proximity you have to that person. When that sickness goes away, you are both at the same "risk" level for contracting that illness as you were in the first place. In this sense, near repeats are similar to hot spots in that a specific geographic area is pinpointed as being at high risk for future criminal victimizations due to past victimizations in the same or surrounding areas. Bowers and Johnson (2004) have developed a spatial analysis technique that was able to predict 90% of future burglaries based on the "near repeat" principle, a technique that has been better than general hot spot directed prevention overall.

So, what makes a target enticing for repeated victimizations to a prospective offender? Bowers and Johnson (2004) suggest that there are two hypotheses that account for this phenomenon; they are **boost** and **flag** explanations. The **boost** explanation (also known as **event dependence**) originates out of the field of epidemiology and suggests a contagion-like phenomenon in which people or places that have been victimized are attractive for additional future victimizations. In the case of burglaries, the attractiveness of that place is "boosted" because the goods taken have likely been replaced in a relatively short period of time, typically one month, thereby making the risk of another burglary high (Johnson, 2008). Johnson (2008) provides an example in which he suggests that a burglar walks down the street and identifies a probable suited property (for victimization) and probable unsuited property and burgles the probable suited place. Shortly thereafter he walks down the same street and sees a known suited (the place he originally burgled), a probable suited, and a probable unsuited property. He is likely to focus on the known suitable since he is familiar with that abode, thus the risk for that establishment is *boosted*. In the case of personal crime, the target has made him or herself attractive as a vulnerable entity and is thus repeatedly victimized by the offender because of this vulnerability—particularly if nothing has been done to decrease the level of vulnerability of the victim (Tseloni & Pease, 2003). For instance, if a batterer beats his partner and nothing is done about it, then he doesn't believe that there is heightened risk that his behavior will be stopped and the target is attractive for continued beatings in the future. In the boost explanation, repeat victimizations by the *same offender* are more likely. The **flag** explanation (also known as **risk heterogeneity**) suggests that an entity is perceived as attractive to multiple offenders just based on its characteristics and advertises its attractiveness in potentially unsecured or easy to manipulate ways (as if those characteristics "flag" the target for victimization). That target has heightened risk of becoming a victim because of those attractive features (e.g., valuable goods that are highly visible and relatively unsecured, physical characteristics that suggest weakness) from multiple offenders who aren't relying on their knowledge of that target from a previous victimization. In this sense, flag explanations are more likely to account for repeated criminal activity perpetrated by *different offenders.*

Police Response to Repeat Victimization and Victims' Expectations of and Satisfaction with Police

One of the problems recognized in the United Kingdom by many researchers was that when police responded to victimizations they did so in a reactive, single-event mind frame, thereby eliminating the ability to determine connectedness between events and thus the need for crime prevention strategies for future victimizations (Farrell, Tseloni & Pease, 2005; Bowers & Johnson, 2004). No doubt police are familiar with those establishments and people that have called for service repeatedly, but police policy may have dictated that each offense be dealt with in a singular manner. Furthermore, Bracey (1996) suggests that police responses may be no more than symbolic, because unless there are good leads on the perpetrator of a crime, there is a limited amount of resolution police can bring to the case after the fact. This is especially true for burglaries, for without good evidence linking a person (or persons) to an offense, the only thing the police may be able to do is to document that items once there are now missing.

In those cases where police are familiar with the victim it has been proposed that discussions on crime prevention strategies would be very helpful to decrease future victimizations and repeated harm. In fact, a project in Huddersfield, England, entitled "Biting Back" demonstrated just that. "Biting Back" ran from October 1994–March 1996 in Huddersfield, England, an area with a population of about 220,000. The project required that police work with victims by taking an initial burglary call and providing them with crime prevention advice on one of three levels: after first victimization labeled as "bronze" (letter to victim with security advice, discount vouchers for security equipment, Cocoon Watch—wherein neighbors of the victim were informed of the event and an informal type of individualized neighborhood watch developed); after second victimization labeled as "silver" (wherein the victim was loaned temporary security equipment, a visit from a Crime Prevention Specialist, and twice weekly police watch visits); and after third victimization labeled as "gold" (increased police watches (daily), installation of high-tech security equipment by police, and another visit from the Crime Prevention Specialist). A similar system was introduced for victims of thefts from cars with increased security equipment and interaction with crime prevention specialists. Some of the technology implemented also helped to identify the offenders. Index Solutions provided a dye that would be invisible in normal lighting but would show up under specialized lighting and marked offenders when they attempted to burglarize an establishment. Tracker was a device that was installed on the most oft targeted items of burglaries and would lead police to the item and ultimately to the offender. Both of these techniques were implemented at the Gold stage of the project. The result of this focused effort on crime prevention for repeat victims was a reduction of domestic burglaries by 30% and thefts from cars by 20%. One could surmise that by implementing Cocoon Watch the police were also addressing possible near repeats, as the knowledge that a burglary occurred may have encouraged some to be on alert for their own homes as well (Chenery, Holt, & Pease, 1997). In a satisfaction survey sent out to victims in the Huddersfield area of West Yorkshire, where the experimental aspect of the study took place, and surrounding areas within West Yorkshire where no changes were made, victims reported 20% greater satisfaction with police than in the surrounding areas, where a 2% decrease in satisfaction was found from previous surveys. This suggests that focusing efforts on repeat victims can have both an effect on crime rates and satisfaction of victims overall.

In general, repeat victims tend to contact the police more often and with greater demands of police than singular or first-time victims (van Dijk, 2001). In his analysis of repeat victims in the International Crime Victim Survey, van Dijk (2001) found that repeat victims in developed countries were more likely to contact police than those in transitional or developing nations. In developed countries, victims were more motivated to contact police because of a belief in the duty to report and to comply with insurance procedures (as applicable). For those in transitional or developing countries victims typically reported crimes to police so they could recover their items, so the offender could be brought to justice, and to avoid future victimizations. Repeat victims in the ICVS also noted that they were less satisfied with police overall, though those in developed nations listed higher levels of satisfaction than those in transitional or developing nations. Van Dijk (2001) suggested that repeat victims were less confident that the police could actually help them and reported feeling revictimized by their experiences with police more often than first-time victims. However, he stated that when they did report they wanted more services and protection from police. Perhaps the case of Huddersfield illustrates that when repeat victims do perceive they are receiving more services and protection they feel their cases are taken more seriously and are thus more satisfied overall.

Summary and Conclusion

In Chapter 3 you learned about common reactions to victimizations as experienced by both personal/violent and property crime victims. In this chapter you learned about specific issues for each of the Type I offenses and discovered that there are some crimes that are not addressed as fully by the criminal justice system as they could be (white-collar crimes) and the effects that can have on victims and society overall. Additionally, when we discuss "victimless" crimes it is important to consider all the levels of victims that exist, as discussed in Chapter 3, and note that primary victims are not the only ones that may need assistance recovering from a criminal incident. Finally, understanding repeat victimization helps us to understand those groups of individuals who may be suffering at a disproportionate rate to the rest of the victim population and how repeated victimizations can leave even more lasting harm. Actions by criminal justice personnel do seem to better serve these populations, repeat victims in particular, which should be a focus in the system overall.

Key Terms

Hot spots

Flag or risk heterogeneity

Near repeats

Victimless crimes

Boost or event dependence

Repeat victimization

Discussion Questions

1. What are the primary reasons suggested for the overall drop in crime rates from the mid-1990s to the mid-2010s?
2. Who is most likely to be a victim of crime for each of the seven crimes discussed? How can that inform us in terms of crime prevention and/or marketing of victim services?
3. Given what you learned in Chapter 3 about the different types of victims (primary, secondary, tertiary), how do you think "victimless" crime and repeat victimization affect those different parties?

Websites for Further Information

Federal Bureau of Investigation, Crime Stats: http://www.fbi.gov/stats-services/crimestats.

Bureau of Justice Statistics, National Crime Victimization Survey: http://www.bjs.gov/index.cfm?ty=dcdetail&iid=245.

Center for Problem-Oriented Policing: http://www.popcenter.org/.

References

Alitzio, A., & York, D. (2007). Guide No. 49: The problem of robbery of convenience stores. Center for Problem-Oriented Policing. Retrieved from http://www.pop center.org/problems/robbery_convenience/.

Allen, S. (2004). Male victims of rape: Responses to a perceived threat to masculinity. In C. Hoyle & R. Young (Eds.), *New visions of crime victims* (pp. 23–48). Portland, OR: Hart Publishing.

Baumer, E., Lauritsen, J. L., Rosenfeld, R., & Wright, R. (1998). The influence of crack cocaine on robbery, burglary, and homicide rates: A cross-city, longitudinal analysis. *Journal of Research in Crime and Delinquency, 35*(3), 316–340.

Bennett, T., & Brookman, F. (2009). The role of violence in street crime: A qualitative study of violent offenders. *International Journal of Offender Therapy and Comparative Criminology, 53*(6), 617–633.

Blumstein, A., & Rosenfeld, R. (2008). Factors contributing to U.S. crime trends. In A. S. Goldberger & R. Rosenfeld (Eds.), *Understanding crime trends: Workshop report*, (pp. 13–43). Washington, DC: The National Academies Press.

Bowers, K. J., & Johnson, S. D. (2004). Who commits near repeats? A test of the boost explanation. *Western Criminology Review, 5*(3), 12–24.

Catalano, S. (2010). *Victimization during household burglary. Special Report, National Crime Victimization Survey.* Washington, DC: US Department of Justice, Office of Justice Programs, Bureau of Justice Statistics. NCJ 227379.

Chenery, S., Holt, J., & Pease, K. (1997). *Biting back II: Reducing repeat victimisation in Huddersfield.* Crime Detection and Prevention Series Paper 82, Police Research Group.

Cochran, J. K., Rowan, K., Blount, W. R., Heide, K., & Sellers, C. S. (1999). Beer joints and badasses: An aggregate-level assessment of alcohol availability and violent crime. *Criminal Justice Policy Review, 9*(3 & 4), 465–495.

Cooper, A., & Smith, E. L. (2011). *Homicide trends in the United States, 1980–2008: Annual Rates for 2009 and 2010.* Washington, DC: US Department of Justice, Office of Justice Programs, Bureau of Justice Statistics. NCJ 236018.

Copes, H., & Cherbonneau, M. (2006). The key to auto theft: Emerging methods of auto theft from the offenders' perspective. *British Journal of Criminology, 46,* 917–934.

Cover, C., & Koper, C. (2012). Critical issues in policing series: "How are innovations in technology transforming policing?" Washington, DC: Police Executive Research Forum.

Daane, D. M. (2009b). Victim response to sexual assault. In F. P. Reddington & B. W. Kreisel (Eds.), *Sexual assault* (2nd ed.), (pp. 79–111). Durham, NC: Carolina Academic Press.

Daniel, E. (2009). Sexual abuse of males. In F. P. Reddington & B. W. Kreisel (Eds.), *Sexual assault* (2nd ed.), (pp. 133–140). Durham, NC: Carolina Academic Press.

DeValve, E. Q. (2004). Through the victims' eyes: Towards a grounded theory of the victimization experience. Sam Houston State University, ProQuest, UMI Dissertations Publishing. 3143578.

Dugan, L., Nagin, D. S., & Rosenfeld, R. (1999). Explaining the decline in intimate partner homicide: The effects of changing domesticity, women's status, and domestic violence resources. *Homicide Studies, 3*(3), 187–214.

Dunlap, A. G. (2009). Child sexual abuse. In F. P. Reddington & B. W. Kreisel (Eds.), *Sexual assault* (2nd ed.), (pp 27–53). Durham, NC: Carolina Academic Press.

Ellingworth, D., Farrell, G., & Pease, K. (1995). 'A victim is a victim is a victim?' *British Journal of Criminology, 35*(3), 360–366.

End Violence Against Women International. (2013, August). *Training bulletin: Unfounding: False vs. baseless reports.* Retrieved from www.evawintl.org.

Exum, M. L., Kuhns, J. B., Koch, B., & Johnson, C. (2010). An examination of situational crime prevention strategies across convenience stores and fast-food restaurants. *Criminal Justice Policy Review, 21*(3), 269–295.

Fahrenthold, D. A. (2006, June 19). Statistics show drop in U.S. rape cases. *The Washington Post.* Retrieved from http://www.washingtonpost.com/wp-dyn/content/article/2006/06/18/AR2006061800610.html.

Farrell, G. (1992). Multiple victimization: Its extent and significance. *International Review of Victimology, 2,* 85–102.

Farrell, G., & Pease, K. (2001). Why repeat victimization matters. In G. Farrell. & K. Pease (Eds.), *Repeat victimization,* (pgs. 1–4). Monsey, NY: Criminal Justice Press.

Farrell, G., & Sousa, W. (2001). Repeat victimization and hot spots: The overlap and its implications for crime control and problem-oriented policing. In G. Farrell & K. Pease (Eds.), *Repeat victimization,* (pgs. 221–240). Monsey, NY: Criminal Justice Press.

Farrell, G., Tseloni, A., & Pease, K. (2005). Repeat victimization in the ICVS and the NCVS. *Crime Prevention and Community Safety: An International Journal, 7*(3), 7–18.

FBI. (2013a). *Crime in the United States, 2012, Aggravated Assault Overview.* Retrieved from www.fbi.gov.

FBI. (2013b). *Crime in the United States, 2012, Robbery Overview.* Retrieved from www.fbi.gov.

FBI. (2013c). *Crime in the United States, 2012, Larceny-Theft Overview.* Retrieved from www.fbi.gov.

FBI. (2016). *Crime in the United States, 2016,* Expanded Homicide Data Table 3.

Felson, R. B., Baumer, E. P., & Messner, S. F. (2000). Acquaintance robbery. *Journal of Research in Crime and Delinquency, 37*(3), 284–305.

Fox, D. (2013, June 3). Biting someone with false teeth is 'aggravated assault' in Louisiana. Retrieved from http://965kvki.com.

Frank, R., Brantingham, P., & Farrell, G. (2012). Estimating the true rate of repeat victimization from police recorder crime data: A study of burglary in Metro Vancouver. *Canadian Journal of Criminology and Criminal Justice, 54*(4), 481–493.

Gant, F., & Grabosky, P. (2001). *No. 215, The stolen vehicle parts market.* Australian Institute of Criminology.

Garland, T. (2009). Rape myths. In F. Reddington & B. Kreisel (Eds.), *Sexual assault* (2nd ed.), (pp. 11). Durham, NC: Carolina Academic Press.

Gross, B. (2009, Spring). False rape allegations: An assault on justice. *The Forensic Examiner*, 66–70.

Harris, A. R., Thomas, S. H., Fisher, G. A., & Hirsch, D. J. (2002). Murder and medicine: The lethality of criminal assault 1960–1999. *Homicide Studies, 6*(2), 128–166.

Hollinger, R. C., & Davis, J. L. (2002). *2002 National Retail Security Survey: Final Report*. Gainesville, FL: Security Research Project, University of Florida.

Houser, K., & Dworkin, E. (2009). *The use of truth-telling devices in sexual assault investigations*. National Sexual Violence Resource Center: Critical Issues, National SART Toolkit.

Jacobs, B. A., & Wright, R. (2008). Moralistic street robbery. *Crime & Delinquency, 54*(4), 511–531.

Jensen, C. (2010, May 10). Employee theft: 5 things you ought to know. *The Huffington Post/AOL Small Business*.

Johnson, S. D. (2008). Repeat burglary victimization: A tale of two theories. *Journal of Experimental Criminology, 4*, 215–240. doi: 10.1007/s11292-008-9055-3.

Katz, J. (1988). *Seductions of crime: Moral and sensual attractions in doing evil*. New York, NY: Basic Books, Inc., Publishers.

Kearney, M. S., & Harris, B. H. (2014). *Ten economic facts about crime and incarceration in the United States*. The Hamilton Project, Brookings Institute. Retrieved from http://www.brookings.edu/research/reports/2014/05/10-crime-facts.

Keister, T. (2007). Guide No. 46: Thefts of and from cars on residential streets and driveways. Center for Problem-Oriented Policing. Retrieved from http://www.popc-enter.org/problems/residential_car_theft/.

Klaus, P. (2004). *Carjacking, 1993–2002. Crime Data Brief, National Crime Victimization Survey*. Washington, DC: US Department of Justice, Office of Justice Programs, Bureau of Justice Statistics. NCJ 205123.

Klein, A., & White, J. (2011, July 23). Car theft tamed by technology, aggressive police work. *The Washington Post*.

Kreisel, B. W. (2009). Police and victims of sexual assault. In F. P. Reddington & B. W. Kreisel, *Sexual assault: The victims, the perpetrators and the criminal justice system* (pp. 337–357). Durham, NC: Carolina Academic Press.

Kulbarsh, P. (2013, April 10). *The shoplifters on your beat*. Retrieved from http://www.officer.com/article/10915657/the-shoplifters-on-your-beat?page=2.

Langner, D. (2010). *Employee theft: Determinants of motive and proactive solutions*. University Libraries, University of Nevada, Las Vegas, UNLV Theses/Dissertations/Professional Papers/Capstones, Paper 543.

Langton, L. (2012). *Firearms stolen during household burglaries and other property crimes, 2005–2010*. Washington, DC: US Department of Justice, Office of Justice Programs, Bureau of Justice Statistics. NCJ 239436.

Laufersweiler-Dwyer, D. L., & Dwyer, G. (2009). Sex offenders and child molesters. In F. P. Reddington & B. W. Kreisel (Eds.), *Sexual assault: The victims, the perpetrators, and the criminal justice system* (2nd ed.), (pp. 239–265). Durham, NC: Carolina Academic Press.

Lauritsen, J. L., & Heimer, K. (2008). The gender gap in violent victimization, 1973–2004. *Journal of Quantitative Criminology, 24,* 125–147.

Lauritsen, J. L., & White, N. (2014). *Seasonal patterns in criminal victimization trends. Special Report.* Washington, DC: US Department of Justice, Office of Justice Programs, Bureau of Justice Statistics. NCJ 245959.

Lopez, J. J. (2000). Assault. In L. S. Tumbull & E. H. Hendrix (Eds.), *Atlas of crime: Mapping the criminal landscape* (pp. 30–36). Phoenix, AZ: Oryz Press.

Lord, W. D., Boudreaux, M. C., & Lanning, K. V. (2001, April). Investigating potential child abduction cases: A developmental perspective. *FBI Law Enforcement Bulletin,* 1–10.

Matson, C., & Klaus, P. (2006). *Crime Victimization in the United States, 2005, Statistical Tables. National Crime Victimization Survey.* Washington, DC: US Department of Justice, Office of Justice Programs, Bureau of Justice Statistics. NCJ 215244.

McDonold, C. T. (2014, May). The changing face of vehicle theft. *The Police Chief: The Professional Voice of Law Enforcement.* Retrieved from http://www.policechiefmagazine.org/magazine/index.cfm?fuseaction=display_arch&article_id=2420&issue_id=72011.

McNamara, J. J., McDonald, S., & Lawrence, J. (2012). Characteristics of false allegation adult crimes. *Journal of Forensic Science, 57*(3), 643–646.

Moffitt, T. E. (1997). Adolescence-limited and life-course persistent offending: A complementary pair of developmental theories. In T. Thornberry (Ed.), *Developmental theories of crime and delinquency,* (pgs. 11–54). New Brunswick, CT: Transaction Publishers.

Mustaine, E. E., & Tewksbury, R. A. (1998). Specifying the role of alcohol in predatory victimization. *Deviant Behavior, 19*(2), 173–199.

National Highway Traffic Safety Administration. (2014). Vehicle-related theft. Retrieved from http://www.nhtsa.gov/theft.

Ouimet, M. (2012). A world of homicides: The effect of economic development, income inequality, and excess infant mortality on the homicide rate for 165 countries in 2010. *Homicide Studies, 16*(3), 238–258.

Perkins, C. (2003). *Weapon use and violent crime, Special Report, National Crime Victimization Survey, 1993–2001.* Washington, DC: US Department of Justice, Office of Justice Programs, Bureau of Justice Statistics. NCJ 194820.

Pittman, D. J., & Handy, W. (1964). Patterns in criminal aggravated assault. *Journal of Criminal Law, Criminology & Police Science, 55,* 462–470.

Planty, M., Langton, L., Krebs, C., Berzofsky, M., & Smiley-McDonald, H. (2013). *Female victims of sexual violence, 1994–2010*. Washington, DC: US Department of Justice, Office of Justice Programs, Bureau of Justice Statistics. NCJ 240655.

Quinet, K. (2011). Prostitutes as victims of serial homicide: Trends and case characteristics, 1970–2009. *Homicide Studies, 15*(1), 74–100.

Ratcliffe, J. (2004). The hotspot matrix: A framework for the spatio-temporal targeting of crime reduction. *Police Practice and Research, 5*(1), 5–23.

Ratcliffe, J. H., & McCullagh, M. J. (1998). Identifying repeat victimization with GIS. *British Journal of Criminology, 38*(4), 651–662.

Ritter, N. (2008, October). DNA solves property crimes (But are we ready for that?). *NIJ Journal, 261*. NCJ 224084.

Saunders, C. (2012). The truth, the half-truth, and nothing like the truth. *British Journal of Criminology, 52*(6), 1152–1171.

Schur, E. M. (1965). *Crimes without victims: Deviant behavior and public policy*. Englewood Cliffs, NJ: Prentice Hall.

Smith, E. L., & Cooper, A. (2013). *Homicide in the U.S. known to law enforcement, 2011. Patterns & Trends*. Washington, DC: US Department of Justice, Office of Justice Programs, Bureau of Justice Statistics. NCJ 243035.

Sourcebook of Criminal Justice Statistics. (2008a). Table 3.10.2008: Estimated number and rate of personal victimization; by type of crime, and sex and race of victim, United States.

Sourcebook of Criminal Justice Statistics. (2008b). Table 3.7.2008: Estimated rate of personal victimization; by sex and age of victim, and type of crime, United States.

Sourcebook of Criminal Justice Statistics. (2008c). Table 3.20.2008: Estimated percent distribution of violent victimization in which self-protective measures were employed; by person taking measure, type of crime, and outcome of measure, United States.

Sourcebook of Criminal Justice Statistics. (2010). Table 3.16.2010: Victim-offender relationship in violence victimization; by type of crime and sex of victim, United States.

Snyder, H. N. (2012). *Arrest in the United States, 1990–2010. Patterns & Trends*. Washington, DC: US Department of Justice, Office of Justice Programs, Bureau of Justice Statistics. NCJ 239423.

Stermac, L., Del Bove, G., & Addison, M. (2004). Sexual assault of adult males. *Journal of Interpersonal Violence, 19*(8), 901–915.

Sweeney, J., & Payne, J. (2011). *Alcohol and assault on Friday and Saturday nights: Findings from the DUMA program. Research in Practice*, Duma quarterly report, no. 14. Australian Government: Australian Institute of Criminology.

Thompson, S. K., & Gartner, R. (2014). The spatial distribution and social context of homicide in Toronto's neighborhoods. *Journal of Research in Crime and Delinquency, 51*(1), 88–118.

Tompson, L., & Bowers, K. (2012). A stab in the dark? A research note on temporal patterns of street robbery. *Journal of Research in Crime and Delinquency, 50*(4), 616–631.

Truman, J. L., Langton, L., & Planty, M. (2013). *Criminal victimization, 2012.* Washington, DC: Department of Justice, Bureau of Justice Statistics, NCJ 243389.

Truman, J. L., & Morgan, R. E. (2016). *Criminal victimization, 2015.* Washington, DC: Department of Justice, Bureau of Justice Statistics, NCJ 250180.

Truman, J. L., & Rand, M. R. (2010). *Criminal victimization, 2009. Bulletin, National Crime Victimization Survey.* Washington, DC: US Department of Justice, Office of Justice Programs, Bureau of Justice Statistics. NCJ 231327.

Tseloni, A., & Pease, K. (2003). Repeat personal victimization: 'Boosts' or 'flags'? *British Journal of Criminology, 43*, 196–212.

Walters, J. H., Moore, A., Berzofsky, M., & Langton, L. (2013). *Household burglary, 1994–2011.* Washington, DC: US Department of Justice, Office of Justice Programs, Bureau of Justice Statistics. NCJ 241754.

The White House Council on Women and Girls. (2014). *Rape and sexual assault: A renewed call to action.* Retrieved from http://www.whitehouse.gov/sites/default/files/docs/sexual_assault_report_1-21-14.pdf.

van Dijk, J. J. M. (2001). Attitudes of victims and repeat victims toward the police: Results of the International Crime Victims Survey. In G. Farrell & K. Pease (Eds.), *Repeat victimization,* (pgs. 27–52). Monsey, NY: Criminal Justice Press.

Veneziano, L., & Veneziano, C. (1993). Are victimless crimes actually harmful? *Journal of Contemporary Criminal Justice, 9*(1), 1–14.

Verhage, A., & Ponsaers, P. (2008). Power-seeking crime? The professional thief versus the professional launderer. *Crime, Law & Social Change, 51*, 399–412.

image © ambrozinio via shutterstock.com.

Chapter 5: Vulnerable Populations and Interpersonal Violence — Children, Adolescents, Intimate Partners, the Elderly, and Animals

Impacts of victimizations and reactions to crime are relatively consistent across the different populations of crime victims, as discussed in the previous four chapters. However, there are some populations who are particularly vulnerable to abuse given the amount and type of dependence they have on adult caregivers, the intimate nature of the relationships, and/or the obedience that is expected of them when it comes to their relationships with adults. This chapter will focus on special issues for child and adolescent crime victims, intimate partner violence, elderly victims, and animals as victims. Given that most crime is perpetrated by individuals we know, particularly in a domestic situation, it is important to recognize and understand how dependence can create an environment in which victimization can thrive and recovery is complicated. Until the 1970s, issues such as child abuse and domestic violence (which will be used interchangeably with intimate partner violence) were issues that the criminal justice system tended to leave alone, suggesting that these were matters that were best dealt with in family court or by the family themselves (Gosselin, 2005). Stalking, elder abuse, and cruelty to animals are more recently developed areas of concern as our understanding of the violence that occurs within "households" and amongst those in/or seeking to begin relationships develops. The Office for Victims of Crime, Training and Technical Assistance Center (OVC-TTAC) put together resource papers for participants of the National Victim Assistance Academy trainings to further their understanding of child abuse, intimate partner violence, and elder abuse. These resources will be utilized heavily in the discussion of violence against "familiars" in this chapter.

Children as Victims

Children are particularly vulnerable to crime because of their dependence upon others to care for them. They are typically helpless as well, as they may not know that what they are experiencing is "wrong" and could thus grow up believing that the harm they have experienced is "normal" and that everyone experiences the same thing. Child victimization can severely affect the lives of those harmed, as they are more likely to become involved in the criminal justice system, to experience violence and victimization as adults, to have substance abuse and drug dependency issues, to become pregnant as teens and/or to engage in sexually promiscuous behaviors that expose them to risk for sexually transmitted diseases, and to continue the cycle of violence on to their own children (Childhelp.org, n.d.). Fang et al. (2012, as cited by Childhelp.org, n.d.) reports that in 2008, child maltreatment cost the United States approximately $124 billion for services to address the harm after it occurred. The immediate and snowball effects of child victimization illustrate how important it is for the criminal justice system and related agencies to respond to and prevent these incidents from happening.

Types of Abuse

Gosselin (2005) indicates that there are four main types of abuse that children experience that fall within **primary maltreatment** of children (which includes active maltreatment and passive maltreatment). **Active maltreatment** includes acts that are purposeful and direct and require some type of action or interaction between the perpetrator and the victim. Emotional or psychological abuse, physical abuse, and sexual abuse fall under active maltreatment. **Passive maltreatment** occurs when a caregiver fails (purposefully or recklessly) to provide a child with the necessary elements of survival such as food/water, shelter, clothing, supervision, education, and medical care, as well as emotional care. Clearly, neglect is the form of abuse reported within passive maltreatment. **Secondary maltreatment** occurs when a child is exposed to violence, in the form of domestic violence between adults and/or homicide of a caregiver. Gosselin (2005) further suggests that children who are victimized often experience multiple forms of abuse/neglect, a term referred to as **polyvictimization**. However, when we look at national statistics on child abuse and neglect they are typically reported independently, so it may be difficult to determine, at first glance, how much polyvictimization occurs.

Before we go much further it is important to define the four main categories of abuse (*note:* these same definitions will be used for understanding elder abuse and animal cruelty/abuse). **Emotional or psychological abuse** is behavior toward a child that damages his or her emotional development and/or sense of self-worth (Gaboury, Seymour, McCown, & Modell, 2012). Acts that are categorized as emotional abuse include "constant criticism, threats, or rejection, as well as withholding love, support, or guidance" (Gaboury, Seymour, McCown, & Modell, 2012, p. 4). Oftentimes it is difficult to prove emotional abuse as the telltale signs are not visible to the naked eye or to physical examination.

Physical abuse occurs when injury is experienced by a child in a non-accidental context (Gaboury, Seymour, McCown, & Modell, 2012). Examples of physical abuse include hitting, shaking, slapping, pushing, choking, biting, burning, poisoning, suffocating, and the forceful holding of a child underwater. Signs of physical abuse include bruises, broken bones, burns, cuts, welts, internal injuries, and death. When a child is repeatedly injured there may be physical signs of repeated injuries over time (varying shades of bruises and healing patterns of cuts/scrapes, varying stages of recovery of bones), which is commonly referred to as **battered child syndrome** (Gaboury, Seymour, McCown, & Modell, 2012). Bruising goes through a gradation of color changes: red in the first two days, blue/purple from days 2–5, green from days 5–7, yellow from days 7–10, and brown from days 10–14. Most bruises disappear in two to four weeks (Gosselin, 2005). One thing that is difficult with determining physical injury is whether the injury was accidental or purposefully inflicted. Where the injury occurs on the body may help in this determination, as injuries on the arms and legs are more commonly associated with general play and accidents, whereas injuries in the torso, back, buttocks, earlobes, cheeks, and neck are not commonly associated with accidents (Gosselin, 2005).

Sexual abuse includes incidents of sexual assaults, sexual abuse, and sexual exploitation. Sexual assault of a child includes the touching and fondling of a child for the sexual gratification of the adult or older youth (laws may depend on the state) (Gaboury, Seymour, McCown, & Modell, 2012). Categories within sexual assault include molestation (indecent touching), rape (insertion of an object into any orifice), voyeurism (watching a child in any stage of undress for the sole purpose of sexual gratification of the perpetrator), exhibitionism (exposing one's genitalia so a child might see it), pornography (recording sexual abuse), and forced prostitution (Gosselin, 2005). Sexual abuse includes acts that are not as obvious as those within sexual assault and may include tickling, sexual propositions, unwanted touching/hugs/pinching, and/or making a child watch sex acts (Gaboury, Seymour, McCown, & Modell, 2012). Sexual exploitation includes using a child in a sexual manner for financial or commercial gain. These acts could include pictures or other forms of child pornography (as described above), forcing the child into a child sex ring, and prostitution (also mentioned above) (Gaboury, Seymour, McCown, & Modell, 2012).

Neglect is by far the most common form of child mistreatment, the consequences of which could lead to emotional harm and even death, accounting for approximately 75% of calls to Child Protective Services agencies in 2015 nationwide (U.S. Dept. of Health and Human Services, 2017). Gosselin (2005) suggests that a true definition is difficult to come by because there is not a consensus as to what specific acts or failures to act are considered neglectful. However, most definitions of neglect suggest that it is the failure of a caregiver to provide a child with his/her basic needs, in a socially acceptable manner. One may want to consider, however, if the neglect must be purposeful or if it can simply be circumstantial. Take the case of a single mother who has lost a job and has no support system in her community. She may become homeless, and by extension so do her children. Given the current economic state of the early to mid-2010s, many people who held secure positions were laid off and have run out of unemployment without being able to secure new employment. In that example is the mother truly "neglectful" or has her employment situation led to her failure to provide consistent shelter, food, clean clothing, etc. for her children?

All states require that children attend school until the age of 16, so a caregiver who fails to enroll a child in school, ensure he or she is attending school, and/or fails to provide children with special needs the service and/or attention needed is guilty of neglect. Caregivers must provide children with food, water, shelter, and clothing since children are unable to secure those things for themselves. The failure to provide these things for children could lead to cognitive, social, and behavioral deficits, particularly in the case of food and water. When a child is ill, a caregiver must provide the child with medical care to treat the illness, though this may vary from state to state as some

"In the News" Box 5.1

On May 6, 2014, wilx.com journalist Jason Colthorp published an article entitled "Safe House: Protecting Child Victims." The article discusses an innovative approach to dealing with children who are victims of crime. In order to minimize the harm experienced by the child when he or she is interviewed by criminal justice personnel, many communities have worked to develop centers or homes within which a child victim can feel safe while telling his or her story. The article highlights the Small Talk Children's Assessment Center, which is described as "a place away from the hard chairs and tables of a police interrogation room where kids can explain what happened to them ... once. Not five times to five different people ... once." The article notes that criminal justice officials believe this technique to be both beneficial to the child and to law enforcement and prosecutors' offices. Furthermore, it provides criminal justice personnel an opportunity to unobtrusively hear the story of the child, while also assessing the type of witness the child would make for the case. "Having a trained interviewer also strengthens cases while minimizing the damage to children who are often reliving a nightmare." The concept is akin to a one-stop shop wherein the victim does not have to suffer through multiple interviews and can instead, focus on healing from the victimization.

To read the full article, visit: http://www.wilx.com/topstories/headlines/Safe-House-Protecting-Child-Victims-257961851.html.

religions prohibit treatment by medical professionals. Supervision is necessary to ensure the safety of the child; parents who fail to provide supervision will be guilty of neglect, though the age of the child and their ability to be independent may influence whether a parent is considered neglectful or not. Finally, support may be mandated in those cases where both parents do not reside with or care for the child equally. The family court may require one parent to supplement the income of the parent who may be the primary caretaker, and thus custodial parent, of the child. Failure to provide court-ordered support is an indication that a parent is being neglectful.

Prevalence of Child Abuse

In fiscal year 2015 (July 2014–June 2015), Child Protective Service Agencies across the United States received approximately 4 million referrals alleging child abuse or neglect involving about 7.2 million children overall (US Department of Health and Human Services, Children's Bureau, 2017).

Of those referrals 58.2% were "screened in" for further investigation, while the remaining 41.8% were "screened out," meaning that no further investigation was conducted and those referrals were closed. Of those investigations, it was determined that 683,000 (rounded number) children (about 1 out of 5 referrals) were victims of abuse and/or neglect of some sort, which was a rate of 9.2/1,000 children across the United States. 75.3% of children in those cases suffered from acts of neglect, 17.2% were victims of physical abuse, and 8.4% were victims of sexual abuse (US Department of Health and Human Services, Children's Bureau, 2017). Finkelhor and Jones (2012) report that the rate of sexual abuse has declined significantly from 1992 to 2010 and that this pattern is evident in multiple data sources, which is an encouraging finding (CPS, National Survey of Children Exposed to Violence, National Survey of Family Growth, NCVS). However, the US Department of Health and Human Services estimates that 1,670 children died as a result of abuse and neglect in 2015, with approximately 74.8% of those children being younger than 3 years old, which equates to approximately 4–5 children per day. In sum, though we are seeing some reductions in maltreatment it is clear that there are areas that really need the attention of child victim advocates, namely neglect and homicides.

Characteristics of Victims and Perpetrators

Girls slightly outnumbered boys as the primary victims of child maltreatment, accounting for 50.9% of cases and boys accounting for 48.6% of cases in 2015 (total is not 100% as sex of victim was unknown for just under 1% of victims) (US Department of Health and Human Services, Children's Bureau, 2017). White children accounted for 43.2% of victims, Hispanic children accounted for 23.6% of victims and African American children accounted for 21.4% of all victims. Victims aged 1 or under had the highest rate of victimization in 2014, with approximately 24 out of every 1,000 out of this age group being victimized.

Figure 5.1: Child Maltreatment Case Processing

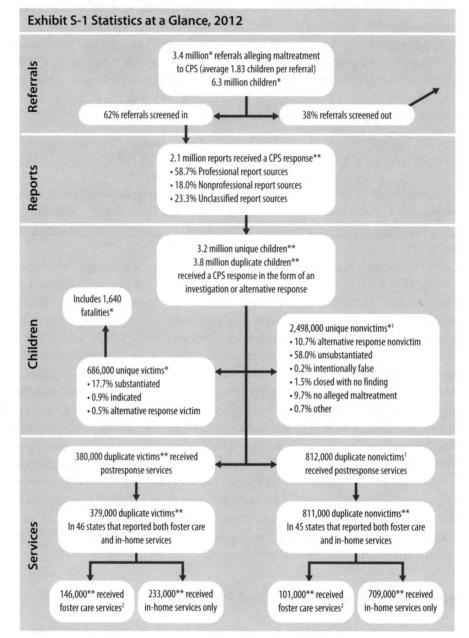

* indicates a nationally estimated number. Please refer to the report *Child Maltreatment 2012* http://www.acf.hhs.gov/programs/cb/research-data-technology/statistics-research/child-maltreatment for information regarding how the estimates were calculated.

** indicates a rounded number.

1. The estimated number of nonvictims was calculated by subtracting the count of estimated victims from the count of estimated children.

2. These children received foster care services and could have received in-home services.

Source: US Department of Health and Human Services, Administration for Children and Families, Administration on Children, Youth and Families, Children's Bureau. (2013). *Child Maltreatment 2012.* Retrieved from http://www.acf.hhs.gov/programs/cb/research—data—technology/statistics—research/child-maltreatment.

Parents accounted for 91.6% of the perpetrators of child abuse and neglect. 40.9% of the perpetrators were mothers acting alone—the highest percentage among all parents.

Mandated Reporters

Since the information that we have on child abuse typically comes from child protective services, which often lies within Departments of Social Services and not police departments, it is important to discuss who typically reports child abuse and neglect. In 1962, physicians, under the leadership of Dr. C. Henry Kempe, wrote an article coining the term battered child syndrome to define the repeated injuries of children that they were seeing come into hospitals and other medical facilities. Shortly thereafter, in response to the article, the Children's Bureau within the United States Department of Health and Human Services created a recommendation for reporting abuse and neglect (National Association of Council for Children, n.d.). Within five years, 44 states had mandatory reporting laws which required that people in certain professions report suspected child maltreatment to an approved agency (CPS, law enforcement, child abuse hotline). Typically, mandated reporters include individuals who work with children in some capacity and/or are responsible for the safety and protection of children on a professional basis. Common professions required to report suspected child maltreatment include: social workers, school personnel (teachers, principals, and other professionals who interact with children in the school setting), medical personnel, mental health professionals, child care workers, medical examiners/coroners, and law enforcement officers (National Association of Council for Children, n.d.). Some states have additional mandated reporting expectations. For instance, 12 states, plus Guam and Puerto Rico, require that individuals who process film must report suspected child maltreatment. Six states require that computer technicians who come across suspicious information while working on a computer must also report that information. In 17 states probation and parole officers are also required to report child maltreatment, while substance abuse counselors are required to report in 14 states. Twelve states also require that individuals who provide activity opportunities to children (camps, youth or recreation centers, etc.) must also report suspicious findings. Not only must teachers working in primary and secondary education report, but 10 states now also require college and university personnel (including athletics staff, volunteers, etc.) to report suspected abuse. As will be discussed later in this chapter, individuals who work with other populations that experience violence, abuse, and neglect may also be called upon to report suspected child maltreatment. In seven states and the District of Columbia, domestic violence workers must report suspected abuse/neglect and the same dynamics exist for animal control or humane officer employees. Probably most notable, in over half of all states, and Guam, clergy are now required to report suspected abuse/neglect. In 18 states and Puerto Rico, one does not have to belong to a specific profession in order for there to be a requirement to report, instead the everyday citizen is required to report suspected child abuse.

In 2015, professionals made up 63.4% of all reports of suspected child maltreatment. Within that group, education personnel were reported as making the largest percentage of reports (18.4%), followed by legal and law enforcement personnel (18.2%), and social service workers (10.9%) (US Department of Health and Human Services, 2017). Nonprofessionals accounted for 18.2% of reports (nonprofessionals are friends, neighbors, family) and "unclassified" accounted for 18.3% (which includes anonymous calls or people who do not have a designated relationship with the party being accused or harmed). Child maltreatment calls are not the only ones that are made to police and other child protection organizations. A decent amount of time and effort is spent in response to calls for assistance for missing children cases.

Missing Children

Prior to the 1980s there were no good indicators for how many children went missing each year, and how many returned home. Additionally, there was no clear definition as to what constituted "missing" in the case of children. It was hard for investigators to compare kids who voluntarily ran away to those who had been taken by a stranger on their way home from school. Due to a number of high-profile stranger kidnappings in the early 1980s, something of a moral panic ensued wherein many believed that children were being kidnapped by strangers at an unprecedented rate (Critcher, 2008). When it was learned that the data on missing children was not consistent, the Office of Juvenile Justice and Delinquency Prevention was mandated to conduct periodic nationwide assessments of the number of children that went missing and were recovered in a year's time. As a result of that mandate the National Incidence Studies of Missing, Abducted, Runaway, and Thrownaway Children (NIS-MART) were undertaken. So far, two NISMART studies have been published and a third is currently in process. In the first NISMART (NISMART-1) by Finkelhor, Hotaling, and Sedlak (1990) the authors created five distinct categories within which all missing children could be counted and put together a comprehensive definition for the term *missing children*. The five categories that were created were: non-family abductions (including stranger kidnappings), parental abductions, runaways, thrownaways, and lost, injured, or otherwise missing children. According to Finkelhor, Hotaling, and Sedlak (1990), a **non-family abduction** occurred when a child was taken into a building or vehicle, or a distance of at least 20 feet away from where they were, or they were taken for over an hour, or the luring away of a child for the purposes of committing another crime (murder, sexual assault, etc.). Within the category of nonfamily abduction fell **stereotypical kidnappings**, which had additional definition properties, including: taken overnight, taken at least 50 miles away, taken by a stranger, was killed or taken to be held permanently by the captor, or was ransomed. **Family abduction** occurred when a parent took a child in violation of a court order or decree or when a parent failed to return a child in the time stipulated in a court order or decree. **Runaways** were defined as children who left home of their own volition and without the permission of a parent and were gone overnight; whereas **thrownaways** were defined as children who were told to leave or left on their own and either were not allowed to come back or for whom the parent did not search, or were abandoned/deserted by caregivers for at least one overnight period. So, thrownaways may have started out as runaways, but given the parental attitude may not have been welcomed back. The last category, **lost, injured or otherwise missing children** included individuals who were gone for a short period of time to overnight, may have sustained an injury which delayed their return, or who didn't fit into the other types of categories (weren't purposefully taken or didn't leave or were forced to leave).

In the NISMART-1, two main numbers were estimated for the incidence of missing children based on either how the family might view the situation (Broad Scope—BS) or how officials collecting reports of the incidents might view the situation (Policy Focal—PF). For non-family abductions, the legal definition was utilized to create the overall definition, with additional characteristics identified for stereotypical kidnappings. The definitions of missing children changed a bit in the NISMART-2 (Sedlak, Finkelhor, Hammer, & Schultz, 2002). First, the researchers defined missing child from two perspectives: (1) "caretaker missing," meaning the child was thought to be missing by the caretaker but no action was taken; and (2) "reported missing," meaning the child was thought to be missing by a caretaker and that caretaker called for assistance in locating the child. Additionally, the five categories changed just slightly. In NISMART-2, runaways and thrownaways were placed into a single category, and a new fifth category was created, that of "missing benign explanation situations." This new category was defined as a situation in which the caretaker became alarmed at the inability to locate the child, they attempted to find the child themselves, and then contacted the local authorities to assist. When the child was found he or she did not turn out to be abducted, kidnapped, was not injured or lost, and did not run away from home. NISMART-1 estimated that the least likely type of missing child fell in the non-family abduction category and the most likely type of missing child fell in the runaway category. A similar pattern was found for NISMART-2, in that non-family abductions accounted for the least amount of missing children and runaway/thrownaway children accounted for the greatest amount.

The type of missing child that is most likely across both NISMART collections so far are those situations where a child voluntarily leaves (runaway), is kicked out or not allowed back in (thrownaway), or is temporarily missing due to miscommunication or slight injury (lost, injured, or otherwise missing; missing benign explanation). Parental abduction is the second least likely type of missing child, and non-family abduction, the type that is focused on in the media, is the least likely.

Table 5A: Comparison of NISMART-1 and NISMART-2 Incidents

Category N1	Incidence	Most at Risk/Most Common	Category N2	Incidence	Most at Risk/Most Common Overall*
Non-Family Abductions (Stereotypical Kidnappings)	LD 3,200–4,600 200–300	Teenagers and girls Blacks and Hispanics highly overrepresented Over 75% sexually assaulted, 85% injured, and a weapon was used by perpetrator	Non-Family Abductions	CM: 33,000 RM: 12,100	Children aged 12 and older were reported as missing significantly more than their younger counterparts (this is largely due to their representation in the runaway/thrownaway category)
Family Abductions	BS: 354,100 PF: 163,200	2- to 11-year-olds taken by fathers	Family Abductions	CM: 117,200 RM: 56,500	Non-White children had significantly higher rates of being reported as missing, though no particular racial/ethnic group stood out more than others
Runaways	BS: 450,700 PF: 133,500	Teenagers Often ran with another person Typically returned within 2 days Living in homes with step-parent-type people	Runaways/Thrownaways	CM: 628,900 RM: 357,600	Male children accounted for a greater percentage of missing children overall (again, this may be largely due to their representation in the runaway/thrownaway category)
Thrownaways	BS: 127,100 PF: 59,200	Older teenagers or under 4 years old Argument often preceded time missing More likely to be victims of violence after they were made to leave			* NISMART-2 did not differentiate children most at risk by category as was done in NISMART-1, so this column is a general statement on which groups appeared to be more at risk based on the data overall.
Lost, Injured or Otherwise Missing	BS: 438,200 PF: 139,100	Children under 4 and children aged 16–17 93% just lost track of time or caregiver and child miscommunicated about time of return and/or location	Lost, Injured or Otherwise Missing	CM: 198,300 RM: 61,900	
			Missing Benign Explanation	CM: 374,700 RM: 340,500	

Sources: Finkelhor, Hotaling, and Sedlak (1990); Sedlak, Finkelhor, Hammer, and Schultz (2002).

Professional Profile 5.1

Child Abuse Prevention

Dr. Robert Jerin
Endicott College

Q: What got you into the field of victimology and/or working with crime victims?

A: I worked with juvenile offenders in the early 1980s and I recognized that most of them had a history of or were currently victims of crime. Additionally, the national report on crime and justice in the US was published and it contained a section on victims of crime which greatly interested me.

Q: What advice do you have for students interested in working with victims and/or becoming victimologists?

A: Go for it, but recognize that the benefits you will receive will be internal and not financial.

Q: What are some challenges to studying crime victims that you have encountered or seen?

A: There are still so many victims who are afraid to come forward and there is still a major problem with the general public understanding the crimes of sexual violence and domestic violence.

Q: What obstacles have you encountered while striving to study crime victims?

A: Being unable to get good data on victims who do not come forward.

Q: What do you feel is the mark you will have left on the field of victimology? What do you want people to see as your mark? At the end of the day, what do you want your "legacy" to be in the field of victimology/victim services?

A: The hundreds of students who never heard of victimology until they took one of my classes and those who took that knowledge and went out into the field of victimology and victim services.

Q: What are some burgeoning issues that you see in the field of victimology?

A: The gaining of recognition of victimology as a discipline and the people who work in the field as skilled professionals because of their academic backgrounds.

Another issue is the sexual victimizations at colleges and universities and in the military; the serious lack of accountability of the administrators and commanders for the victimization and lack of services being provided for them.

Q: What areas within victimology do you think are neglected?

A: DV and its impact on children; sexual violence and its impact on young women.

Adolescents as Victims of Personal and Property Crime

So far we have focused on crime that is perpetrated by adults or older children on children overall, but kids, especially teenagers, are victimized by their peers and siblings as well.

Types of Crime

One in six adolescents (12–17-year-olds) is a victim of property crime, which is a 40% higher risk than adults (Finkelhor & Ormrod, 2000). Finkelhor and Ormrod (2000) suggest that those who are particularly vulnerable include African American adolescents, teens that live in urban areas, and teens in the Western part of the United States. Victimization occurs across the class spectrum, and having a higher income does not protect kids from crime victimization, as most crime occurs in the school setting. Additionally, adolescents in rural areas also experience property victimization, though not as much as those in urban areas. The goods most likely to be stolen include electronic and photo gear, clothing, and luggage (most often backpacks). Fifty-four percent of these crimes occur at school and are typically dealt with in the school setting, as opposed to through law enforcement. When dealt with at school there is a 15% recovery rate, but if a crime is reported to police there is a 76% higher chance of recovery of items. Affluent youth experience 47% more property crime than their lower income peers. The majority of property crimes against adolescents involve items with a value of less than $50. However, the overall impact of that might be just as substantial as a more expensive item taken from an adult because (1) juveniles typically don't have a solid income (or a large income) so it may take them longer to save the money to replace the item(s) stolen, and (2) they will likely not have insurance policies that could help them replace items. If their parents have insurance that could cover property crime, there may be a deductible that the item taken would not meet ($100 deductible, $50 item stolen—insurance won't cover). 21% of crimes happen at or near the home and 40% of violent victimizations happen at the school.

Overall 68% of crimes that happen to adolescents are property crimes and 32% are violent crimes, which is a higher rate of violent crime than adults experience (Snyder & Sickmund, 2006). For instance, teen victims have a robbery rate that is two times that of adults. Younger adolescents are more likely to report the crime to a school authority whereas older adolescents are more likely to involve the police. Interestingly, male and female youth were equally likely to be victims of violent crime (rape/sexual assault, aggravated assault, robbery) in 2010 as reported in the NCVS (White & Lauritsen, 2012). Boys are more likely to report crimes, and most juveniles have an idea as to the perpetrators of their crimes (be they property or violent). Eighty percent of police departments suggested that bicycle theft was the biggest crime affecting juveniles in the NIBRS. Adolescent victimization could have similar effects to workplace violence; since adolescents must attend school they are likely to encounter their perpetrator again and again, and possibly be intimidated by the perpetrator's peers more easily within that environment.

Who Do They Report To?

The juvenile justice system (JJS) itself is not really set up for the support of juvenile victims (Finkelhor, Cross, & Cantor, 2005). Unlike the adult system, juvenile victims can enter the JJ system through CPS reports or law enforcement. For instance, police report that when they are the primary recipient of a crime report dealing with a child or adolescent victim, 71% of the time the victim is 12 years old or older. Fifty-nine percent of calls to police are from the actual victims themselves or family members of those victims and most reports happen when there is an injury, when there are multiple and/or adult offenders, and when a family has had prior contact with law enforcement. Arrests are made in 28–32% of violent crime cases, but only 4% of property crime cases. Alternatively, 74% of victimizations of people under 12 are reported to child protective services and the majority of those calls come from someone other than the actual victim or family of the victim (which makes sense since most victimizations of younger children are committed by family members themselves).

Sibling-on-Sibling Violence

Those of us who have siblings can likely remember any number of verbal arguments that may have occurred (sometimes on a regular basis) and may even recall getting into physical altercations with our siblings. For example, one of the authors consistently fought with her brother over who had control of the remote for the television, and who got the "choice" seat in the living room. It was customary for the seat sitter to get up, place his/her hand on the chair and say "saved" to demonstrate that *no one* else could sit there. If that sibling also had control of the remote, well, that was safe on the "saved" chair as well. On occasion, the non-seat saving sibling would violate the rules and both sit in the chair and "steal" the remote. In these instances, heated arguments as to fairness and humanity could be heard, sometimes with a physical effort to push the violator out of the coveted chair and win back the remote. While no one came out of those arguments with permanent harm, discord occurred. Conflict, and even momentary dislike to an extent, is common among siblings. The arguments and altercations between siblings can help us learn how to successfully (or unsuccessfully) resolve conflict and deal with someone who may not be our absolute favorite person—but who we must engage with on a consistent basis. There comes a point, however, when sibling discord crosses into sibling violence.

Straus, Gelles, and Steinmetz (1980) found that violence among siblings was the most common type of violence among family members that occurred (75.5% versus 15.6% among spouses in the home and 63.5% parent to child violence). Violence was measured on the Conflict Tactics Scale and included low-level behaviors such as pushing, yelling, and threats to more severe forms of violence, such as beating up, and use of a weapon on another. In 48.4% of the occurrences of sibling violence, there were acts of severe violence, compared to 6.1% of severe violence between spouses and 14.2% of violent acts perpetrated by parents toward their children. Straus et al. (1980) reported that sibling violence was considered a normal part of growing up—that it was not perceived as "violence" per se, as we view parent to child violence and spouse to spouse violence. Eriksen and Jensen (2009) found that mild levels of sibling violence occurred within 79.1% of households, while severe violence (consisting of one sibling beating up another, threatening to or actually using a weapon against a sibling) was found in only 14.1% of households. Sibling violence appears to be equally likely across race and socioeconomic status, though there is some evidence to suggest that males may engage in more severe forms of violence with male siblings (Eriksen & Jensen, 2009). Kettrey and Emery (2006) found that unlike intimate partner violence and parent to child violence, most siblings report *mutual* violence perpetration, meaning that both siblings fit into the roles of perpetrator and victim within violence incidents. One of the most interesting aspects of sibling violence is that across the literature there is discussion as to how little sibling violence is labeled as problematic among families (Kettrey & Emery, 2006; Eriksen & Jensen, 2009; Perkins & O'Connor, 2015). Eriksen and Jensen (2009) suggest that to differentiate between the severity of acts we should rely upon the terms set forth by Finkelhor and Hashima in their 2001 piece—identifying the more common, less severe types of sibling aggression as *pandemic victimization*—illustrating that it occurs to most children within their development and *acute victimization*—those acts previously identified as more severe (beating up, using or threatening to use a weapon). They suggest that it is the acute victimization that we need to consider sibling "violence" and for which we need to engage in more research, because of the striking detrimental effects this type of violence may cause. In the child abuse and neglect discourse, it seems that most acts that are considered detrimental to children are characterized in terms of actions (or lack thereof) of the parent or guardian and do not typically focus on sibling-on-sibling violence, though it is more common (Perkins & O'Connor, 2015). The scant amount of literature that does exist suggests that siblings who are victims of sibling violence may demonstrate low levels of self-esteem, loneliness, and depression (Kettrey & Emery, 2006). More discomfort appears to exist when sibling altercations are characterized as bullying, perhaps because that illustrates a malicious type of intent and/or a greater intent to harm. Maybe that is the line people see between "normal" sibling discord and sibling violence (Eriksen & Jensen, 2009). The fact that there is a scant amount of research devoted to it suggests that culturally, we may accept this form of violence to a certain degree; however, more recent research suggests that this is an area that needs to be further investigated as it can have long-term effects on those who engage in and/or experience it (Eriksen & Jensen, 2009; Perkins & O'Connor, 2015).

Intimate Partners as Victims

The term *intimate partner violence* (IPV) refers to "a pattern of abusive behavior that is used by an intimate partner to assert power and control over his or her partner" (Seymour, Gaboury, & DeHart, 2012, p. 2). The terms *domestic violence* and *interpersonal violence* are sometimes used interchangeably with the term intimate partner violence, though some suggest that those terms are more inclusive of family violence as a whole (Seymour et al., 2012). Dating violence also fits within this definition as it involves people in a romantic relationship. Partners include spouses, individuals involved in a romantic relationship but not married, and former spouses and girlfriends/boyfriends. Additionally, IPV includes victims within opposite-sex and same-sex relationships.

Types of Violence

The types of violence perpetrated in IPV include physical, emotional and psychological, economic/financial, and sexual. Other than the addition of economic/financial harm, the types are consistent with what is considered abuse against children. Physical abuse is the use of force to inflict bodily injury, pain, or impairment (Gosselin, 2005). Seymour et al. (2012) suggest that denying medical care is another form of physical abuse as it may result in physical harm of the victim, as well as holding a partner captive, or forcing one's partner to take drugs or drink alcohol against his or her will. Gosselin (2005) suggests that sexual abuse is "nonconsensual sexual contact of any kind" (p. 13), whereas Seymour et al. (2012) state that it also includes attempted coercion of sexual contact without consent. A newer development within this type of abuse has been the inclusion of martial rape as an offense (which became a crime in all 50 states by July of 1993—Gosselin, 2005). Additionally, the use of drugs or alcohol to facilitate sexual contact when it is unwanted, but through which the perpetrator makes the victim compliant through altering his or her mental and physical state, is also considered sexual abuse (Seymour et al., 2012). Psychological and emotional abuse occurs when the victim is in fear of the perpetrator based on intimidation; threats to the partner, children, pets, or others; social isolation from friends, family, work, and other engagements; and tearing the partner down in a manner that affects his or her self-esteem and self-worth (Seymour et al., 2012). When a victim is dependent upon another financially and the person who controls the money does so in a manner that affects the freedom of the victim, it is considered economic/financial abuse. Economic/financial abuse also includes withholding access to money, prohibiting the victim from participating in activities that could provide him or her with an independent stream of funding, and keeping the person from attending school or work (Seymour et al., 2012).

Characteristics of Victims and Offenders and Prevalence of IPV

IPV is an equal opportunity crime, meaning that anyone from any income level, racial background, age, sexual orientation, religion, and gender can be a victim (Seymour et al., 2012). When the victim is a woman, perpetrators are not always deterred from abusing her even if she is pregnant (Gosselin, 2005). Gosselin (2005) states that 1.5 million women are physically or sexually abused every year (citing results from the National Violence Against Women Survey). Truman and Morgan (2016) report that according to the NCVS, 806,050 intimate partners were victims of violent crimes in 2015, with a rate of 3/1,000 per year (up from 2.4/1,000 in 2014). Truman and Morgan (2014) report that for the ten-year period spanning from 2003–2012, IPV accounted for 15% of all violent crime. The main perpetrators of IPV were current or former boyfriends or girlfriends, accounting for 7.8% of violent victimizations overall, whereas spouses and ex-spouses accounted for 6.7% collectively (Truman & Morgan, 2014). Similar to other crime, intimate partner violence dropped precipitously from 1994 to about 2001 from a rate of about 10/1,000 to just over 4/1,000. The rate has stayed in the 3–4/1,000 range from 2001–2012. Females account for the vast majority of both serious violent victimizations (rape, aggravated assault, and robbery) and simple assaults, thus suggesting that females are at greater risk of IPV than males (26.6% for females vs. 5.8% for males in serious violent crime; 33.6% for females vs. 9.4% for males in simple assault) (Truman & Morgan, 2014). Intimate partner violence is more likely to result in injuries (48%) when compared to violence from any other type of "known" perpetrator (immediate family = 37%; other relatives = 36%). Victims of IPV were also more likely than any other known category to suffer a serious injury (gunshot wound, stabbing, broken bones, sexual violence injures, etc.) (11% IPV compared to 4% of both relatives and immediate family) (Truman & Morgan, 2014). The rate of intimate partner violence was highest for females (6.2/1,000 vs. 1.4/1,000 for males), 18–24-year-olds (8.7/1,000 — the next closest was 7.3/1,000 for 25–34-year-olds), victims who identified as two or more races (16.5/1,000 vs. 4.7/1,000 for Blacks, 3.9/1,000 for Whites, 2.8/1,000 for Hispanics, and 2.3/1,000 for other races) and with a marital status of separated (44.7/1,000; next closest was divorced at 11.4/1,000).

The amount of IPV has declined 72% for females and 64% for males from 1994–2011 (Catalano, 2013). Females currently have a 2/1,000 rate of serious violence in an IPV whereas males have a 0.4/1,000 rate. When the IPV is fatal, females are more likely to be killed than males (Catalano, 2013). In 2010, 39% of homicides of females were perpetrated by an intimate partner, whereas 3% of homicides of males were perpetrated by an intimate partner. In raw numbers that equates to approximately 1,183 deaths of females at the hands of her intimate partner and 327 deaths of males at the hands of his intimate partner. When a female victim of repeated abuse kills her partner in order to protect herself from being murdered this is known as **battered woman syndrome**.

Battered Woman Syndrome

According to Gosselin (2005), battered woman syndrome is based on the concept of learned helplessness, whereby the victim believes that there is absolutely nothing that can be done to change her predicament and she must learn to live in a dependent state upon her abuser. Gosselin (2005) states that there are four characteristics that must be met for a woman to claim battered woman syndrome, or battered spouse syndrome, as a defense. First, the abuse victim must believe that the violence against her was her fault; second, she must believe that there is no other person who is accountable for the violence except her; third, she must be living in a state of constant fear for both herself and her children (if applicable); and fourth, she believes that her abuser is always around her, even when he is not physically there. The battered spouse syndrome has also been used in same-sex partner homicides (Gosselin, 2005).

IPV in LGBTQ Relationships

Seymour et al. (2012) report that lesbian, gay, bisexual, transgender, and queer (LGBTQ) victims reported 3,419 incidents of intimate partner violence in 2008, nine of which were homicides. Fifty-one percent of victims of LGBTQ IPV were women, 42% were male victims, and 5% of the victims were transgender. The vast majority of LGBTQ IPV occurred to victims who were 30 or older, which is somewhat older than victims of opposite-sex IPV (highest rate in the 18–24 age range). Taranto (2014) suggests that there are two common myths associated with LGBTQ IPV, (1) that men can't be victims of IPV and women are never the batterers and (2) when a domestic dispute is called in and the couple is a same-sex couple that "mutual battering" always occurs, so there is no true victim or offender because the fighting is equally engaged in by both parties. Taranto (2014) suggests that this misconception by law enforcement has resulted in cases not being taken seriously, charges not being filed, and information on IPV services in the community not given to the victims. Additionally, Taranto (2014) suggests that community programs may not have services for gay males and transgender victims and that civil protection orders may be difficult to acquire from the court system. Additional barriers for LGBTQ IPV victims include (1) not wanting to make the LGBTQ community "look bad," (2) the fear that homophobic and heterosexist attitudes by victim advocacy and criminal justice system staff may result in no, poor, or questionable treatment, (3) the possibility that they will be publicly "coming out" by requesting services, and (4) that there will be a double-stigma associated with them as both LGBTQ and intimate partner violence victim (Taranto, 2014).

The Question on Everyone's Mind: "Why Don't They Leave?"

In probably every class that discusses intimate partner violence, the inevitable question of "why don't they leave?" comes up. For some in the classroom, they may be quite familiar with intimate partner violence, either because they have or are currently experiencing it, know someone who has or is experiencing it, or grew up in a home where it was going on. Conversely, who among us has not had their actions in a relationship questioned by friends and family—even when violence isn't even the issue?! It's somewhat easy to talk about in the safe classroom environment, where we assume we are all rational beings who can approach the subject objectively, but intimate partner violence is not a simple topic.

According to the National Victim Assistance Academy (2000) text for students, IPV relationships start out as blissful and magical as a non-IPV relationship (For the purposes of this chronology, and in recognition of statistics on IPV, the abuser will be referred to as "he" and the victim will be referred to as "she" since that is the most common dynamic—but it must be understood the pronouns could be reversed or could be he/he or she/she.). The soon-to-be victim is wooed and excited at the fact that someone is paying such devoted attention to her. In perceived acts of chivalry, the abuser begins to make decisions for the soon-to-be victim and explains how those types of acts are loving acts. The abuser shows the soon-to-be victim that he is interested in her life as he asks her where she is and where she's going. Instead of seeing these as definite red flags, they can be easily construed as devotion and interest. Everyone has flaws, so the soon-to-be victim chooses to focus on the positive aspects of the abuser's personality and "puts a pin in" the suspicious behaviors, especially as the abuser becomes more demanding. The soon-to-be victim may start noticing how past partners caused the abusers a lot of problems and the abuser fails to be accountable for his behavior in the past relationships and instead blames the faults on the previous partners. Typically, the IPV starts out as psychological and emotional control of the victim where there are emotional consequences when the abuser feels the victim has done something "wrong"— which could be not staying home when instructed. The abuser may play mind games, testing the victim's love and devotion to him, and the victim starts to question herself and tries to "earn back" the love and respect of the abuser. When the abuser perpetrates the first act of physical abuse it is then somewhat easy for the victim to believe that behavior was uncharacteristic and the abuser should be given another chance, especially as he begs for forgiveness. This starts a pattern called the cycle of violence.

Cycle of Violence

Conceptualized as a cycle by Lenore Walker in 1979, the **cycle of violence** has been adapted and updated throughout the years and can be found in various forms publicized by domestic violence organizations on the web. There really is no beginning or end to the cycle of violence, but often relationships begin and evolve through the honeymoon phase, work up to the tension building stage, the violent explosion occurs, and the victim might be convinced to stay upon returning to the honeymoon phase (Walker, 1979). The length of time in each phase or progressing between them is not set in stone. In some relationships there could be years of the honeymoon phase before abuse even begins, in others, the signs of tension building may begin very early. It is important to remember that each victim's experience is unique and might not fit neatly into the model. In the **tension building phase** the batterer may become controlling of the victim's life and may begin threatening the victim. Communication between the two can start to break down, while the victim may try to minimize conflicts that arise and the victim can become withdrawn. Often in this phase the victims describe feeling like they are walking on egg shells to avoid any conflict or incidents with the abuser. When the tension building phase reaches a boiling point, the **violent explosion** or **abusive incident** can occur. The incident may take the form of physical, sexual, or emotional violence, or can occur as a combination. The victim's feelings of helplessness can become compounded if the batterer blames the victim and tells them it's their fault. Following the incident, the **honeymoon phase** begins. The abuser becomes apologetic, may buy gifts or simply become more attentive to the victim. The victim may still feel the outburst was their fault and be willing to accept an apology from the abuser who may promise the abuse will never happen again. The cycle can then continue as the tension builds once again. Over time, the honeymoon phase tends to grow shorter and the tension building phase tends to grow longer. To better understand the different types of abuse perpetrated in concert with the techniques used to coerce a victim to stay in a domestic violence relationship, the Power and Control Wheel was created.

Power and Control Wheel

The **Power and Control Wheel** is a tool that was developed by the Domestic Abuse Intervention Project in 1984 (Domestic Abuse Intervention Project, 2011). It was created as a way to help victims, service providers, and the criminal justice system understand the complex nature of domestic violence. It was developed over a period of time by talking to victims and categorizing their experiences. At the center of the wheel is the power and control the abuser has over the victim. Each of the spokes represents a mechanism of control the abuser may use to keep the victim in an abusive and violent relationship, represented by the outer circle. Each victim experiences abuse in different ways, so too are the mechanisms of abuse utilized by the abuser. For some victims they might occur in isolation, for others they may be experienced in combination with other mechanisms.

Beginning in the upper right is the use of **intimidation**. A batterer may instill fear in the victim through body language including glaring looks, intimidating gestures, and actions. This may also include breaking property, harming pets, or showing the victim a weapon. On the next spoke is **emotional abuse**. This can include put downs by making comments about appearance, humiliation and guilt, or playing mind tricks. Victims may be told they are unattractive, that they'll never find someone else because they are ugly. **Isolation** is the next spoke in the wheel. Isolation can include cutting a victim off from family and friends, even controlling who they speak to at work or in public. This may consist of limiting access to phones, computers, or other media. Next on the wheel is **minimizing, denying, and blaming**. The abuser may try to convince the victim that the abuse isn't that bad, that all relationships are like this, or that the abuse is the victim's own fault. The abuser might remind the victim of the actions or situation preceding the abuse and convince them that they are responsible. **Using children** is the next spoke on the wheel. Children in these relationships are often used as a tool by the abuser to maintain the violence. They might convince the victim to stay in the relationship for the sake of the children, using the children as pawns between them. The abuser might threaten to take the children away from the victim or try and poison the children against them. **Economic abuse** is a spoke on the wheel that is often neglected or overlooked. For batterers money can be a significant way to maintain power and control over victims. Not allowing victims to have jobs contributes to the isolation a victim may feel or taking away a pay check can remove any options a victim may have to get out of an abusive situation. Exercising **male privilege** is another spoke on the wheel. Male privilege can take the form of controlling all of the decisions in a relationship and defining the roles of the relationship, such as forcing a victim to remain in the home. The final spoke in the wheel is **coercion and threats**. The abuser might threaten to harm the victim beyond the abuse, such as leaving the victim alone, reporting the victim to social services, or intimidating the victim to drop any charges if an incident is discovered by the police.

Recognition of the various motivations and tactics of abusers, as well as the overlap among them, can be an important tool for helping victims. Victim service providers can use the wheel to help a victim understand what they have been experiencing and assist them with removing the self-blame and doubt that can keep them in these violent relationships. In addition, the Power and Control Wheel is an important tool for many others to learn about. Friends, family, and even co-workers who are knowledgeable of the wheel may be able to identify the tactics used against the victim and could be the ones to assist a victim in escaping an abusive and violent relationship.

Hopefully it is clear by this point how and why a victim may consider the acts of abuse as things that have to be negotiated and changed, as they seem uncharacteristic of the person she fell in love with, and why she might stay. When the victim does bring up the harmful behavior of the abuser (psychological, physical, or otherwise) the abuser shifts the focus back on the perceived inappropriate behavior of the victim. Because the victim wants a lack of conflict she or he may work to address the issues brought up by the abuser, without seeing that the abuser is being manipulative. She or he will likely experience a great deal of emotional conflict about what is happening to her or him. The abuser may also be working to pull the victim away from friends and family, oftentimes accusing them of interfering in the relationship and making the situation so uncomfortable for the victim that he or she stops engaging with the "outsiders" simply to avoid conflict in the relationship. The purpose of this chronicle is to illustrate that abusive behavior may grow gradually and is hard to reconcile for the person who fell in love with this person who is treating her or him so poorly. By the time the victim realizes he or she must do something to get out of the relationship there may be several obstacles in the way. The victim may be financially dependent on the abuser, he or she may lack the resources and contacts (including friends and family) to be able to leave, there may be children in the relationship and the victim

Figure 5.2: Power and Control Wheel

Source: Domestic Abuse Intervention Project (2011). Wheel Gallery. Retrieved from: http://www.theduluthmodel.org/training/wheels.html, 6/27/14.

may fear that they will be taken away or that they will be harmed if the victim leaves or that a two-parent family is better than a single-parent family. There may also be pets involved, which is another common reason that victims don't leave. The victim may believe, and may have been told repeatedly, that if he or she leaves, the abuser will find him or her ... and there may be threats that the abuser will end the victim's life or the life of someone the victim loves. Studies have shown that one of the most dangerous times in an abusive relationship is when the victim tries to leave. Just page back through to where the statistics on IPV were listed and you'll see that individuals who are listed as "separated" have the highest rate of IPV perpetrated against them. Furthermore, in the NVAA text (2000), it is stated that women who leave have a 75% greater chance of being killed, so the threat of homicide is a real one. Finally, the desire for human companionship is a strong one, and if the abuser pleads with the victim that he or she will change, the companionship desire can be overwhelming because it is natural to *want* that person to change, even if cognitively the victim knows that will never happen. On average, victims attempt to leave the relationship 6–8 times before they maneuver a situation that will ultimately let them stay away

"In the News" Box 5.2

On May 16, 2014, wmur.com published an article entitled "Senate Passes Bill to Protect Pets from Domestic Violence." The brief article discusses the passing of a bill that gave custody of pet and farm animals to victims of domestic violence as an additional component of the protection order awarded through the court system. It was noted in that article that while supporters of the bill believed this would help victims feel like their animals would not come into harm's way, others suggested that the bill was redundant to already existing animal cruelty laws.

To read the full article, visit: http://www.wmur.com/politics/senate-passes-bill-to-protect-pets-from-domestic-violence/26012870#ixzz32HD8knPb.

(Building Futures, n.d.). The reasons are plenty for why a victim would stay even if he or she desperately wanted to leave. So, the answer to "why don't they leave?" is: they do, but it's complicated. Knowing these pressure points that influence victims to stay, however, only helps the criminal justice system and victim advocacy agencies as they can continue to strive to bulldoze over those obstacles to make the path toward leaving clearer.

Because of the association of stalking with intimate partner violence (more specifically, the use of stalking by intimate partner perpetrators as a mechanism of control) it makes sense to discuss this crime in this chapter.

Stalking

According to the NCVC (2014), stalking is a relatively recent issue that has drawn the attention of legislators, the criminal justice system, and victim advocacy agencies alike. Victim advocates and criminal justice personnel were aware of the link between interpersonal violence and stalking long before there were laws that allowed them to act on stalking-type behaviors. According to NCVC (2015, para. 1), **stalking** is "a course of conduct directed at a specific person that would cause a reasonable person to feel fear." The Stalking Resource Center reports that 7.5 million people are stalked annually with women having a greater incidence than men (15% and 6% respectively). Just like domestic violence and sexual assault, most stalking victims knew their perpetrator, because they were either currently or recently dating them. Sixty-one percent of women and 44% of male victims of stalking were stalked by current or former partners. Additionally, 25% of female victims and 32% of male victims were stalked by acquaintances. This means that about 86% of female stalking victims and 75% of male stalking victims knew their stalkers. Forty-six percent of all stalking victims received at least one unwanted contact per week and more than one tenth of all stalking victims are stalked for five years or more. Whereas some may believe

Professional Profile 12.1

Michelle Garcia
National Center for
Victims of Crime
Stalking Resource Center

Q: How did you get involved with working with crime victims? In what capacity do you currently work with victims? Have you ever been engaged in a joint research/ practice project? Please describe.

A: I began as a sexual assault peer educator when I was an undergraduate. In providing sexual assault programming on campus, it was the rare session where I didn't have someone from the audience disclose to me that they were a sexual assault victim/ survivor. From there, I worked in a number of community-based rape crisis programs providing crisis intervention, education/ training, and advocacy services. My first position was a community educator providing programming in schools, then as a legal advocate, which involved working with victims in the criminal justice system, and then as the director of a rape crisis program overseeing all aspects of service provision. Additionally, throughout my career, I have served as a trainer on sexual violence, domestic/dating violence, and sexual harassment.

For the past almost eight years I have been working on the issue of stalking, and how it intersects with domestic and sexual violence. In my current position, I don't work directly with victims, but rather with the various professionals that respond to and directly work with victims.

While I have done work around translating research to practice, I have not engaged in a joint research/practice project. Though not for lack of trying, we just have not gotten the funding we needed for the projects.

Q: What advice do you have for students interested in working with victims?

A: First, be prepared for the fact that doing this work will change how you move through the world. It will affect your relationships, the language you use, the media you consume, and so many other aspects of your life.

Second, connect yourself with a community organization that is providing victim services (e.g., local rape crisis, domestic violence, child abuse, or elder abuse program, or general victim services agency). Volunteer, schedule an informational interview, or attend their programs or events to get a sense of how victim services work and determine if this is really what you would like to do.

Third, develop and maintain healthy boundaries and practice self-care. Healthy boundaries are critical both for victims and service providers. Additionally, burnout, compassion fatigue, and vicarious traumatization are too common among victim advocates/service providers. Practice self-care individually, and encourage any organization you work with to institutionalize self-care.

Q: What are some challenges for working with victims, especially as it relates to dealing with the criminal justice system and/or lawmakers?

A: While there have been significant advancements related to victims' rights and how victimization is addressed in the criminal justice system, there is still room for improvement. First, not every state has codified victims' rights, which in many cases, essentially means victims are treated as witnesses in criminal cases and have no voice in the process. Second, for many (possibly most) victims, they will never get the resolution they seek through the criminal justice system. Many crimes go unreported, fewer are investigated, fewer are prosecuted, and fewer result in a conviction of the offender. A victim seeking validation of their experience or punishment of their offender may be very disappointed with the criminal justice outcomes. Early in my career, someone told me to think of it as a legal system, rather than a justice system. This has stuck with me for decades.

In terms of lawmakers, we should start with the recognition that the legislative process is largely a lengthy and slow-moving process.

Q: What obstacles have you encountered while striving to assist victims? Have the obstacles changed things for the better over the years?

A: In my current position I don't work directly with victims. However, I will note that there are significant challenges that stalking victims specifically face. There are very limited services for victims. Very few communities have dedicated services for stalking victims, meaning victims are left to try and determine where they can access services, whether it is at the local domestic violence, sexual assault, mental health, or general victim services agency.

Q: What do you feel is the mark you will have left on the field of victim services? What do you want people to see as your mark? At the end of the day, what do you want your "legacy" to be in the field of victimology/victim services?

A: My work in this field has focused almost entirely on violence against women and I have had the opportunities to work in the field of and with victims/survivors of sexual violence, domestic/dating violence, and stalking. Because of this, I think I have a unique perspective on the intersections of all of these crimes. I think I would like my legacy to be that I moved forward the conversation that these crimes do not occur in a vacuum, but that they often, if not most often, intersect with each other, and that effective responses to any, has to be inclusive of all.

Q: What are some burgeoning issues that you see in the fields of victimology/victim services?

A: Polyvictimization and the neurobiology of trauma are two issues that are getting increased recognition recently (though neither of these are necessarily burgeoning). The concept of polyvictimization builds upon what I noted above, that often crimes are co-occurring, as well as the fact that many individuals may experience multiple victimizations across their lifespan. The neurobiology of trauma provides a framework for recognizing how victimization affects individuals and can guide responders in more effective responses and services.

Q: Are there groups of victims you think need to be served but are not? Why do you think that way?

A: See my above comment about stalking victims. I think most don't get served. I think there are also marginalized groups (people of color, people with disabilities, children/adolescents, older adults, LGBTQ individuals) who has historically been and continue to be underserved.

stalking to be harmless, consider this next fact: 76% of women who were victims of intimate partner homicide were stalked by their partner and half of the women who were murdered contacted police to report the stalking prior to their deaths (NCVC, 2014). Research has found that when intimate partners stalk their targets (previous or current partners) their violent behavior escalates quickly (NCVC, 2015). Acknowledging stalking behavior as a crime and pursuing it aggressively can clearly lead to decreased deaths for victims stalked by current or former partners.

Elders as Victims

According to Tyiska, Gaboury, Seymour, and Heisler (2012), the older population is larger than it ever has been before, and this trend will continue as the Baby Boomers advance in age over the next two decades. *Older* or *elder* is a funny term, because there is no standard definition of what that means. Some places denote 55 as the time when someone becomes an elder, whereas others indicate that 65 is a better threshold. Needless to say, the term may be relative and contextual, oftentimes based on one's geographic location. The accompanying physical and mental changes that occur with aging can make older adults particularly vulnerable to many different types of criminal activities. While older adults are vulnerable to almost all crimes, just like the rest of the human population, there are particular abuses that might be perpetrated on them specifically because of their advanced age. Additionally, and perhaps akin to crime against teens, because older adults may spend a considerable amount (if not all) of their time in an institution (i.e., senior day care, assisted living, or nursing home) they may be susceptible to abuses that are perpetrated on them from staff within that institution.

"In the News" Box 5.3

On April 27, 2014, Las Vegas *Review-Journal* reporter Yesenia Amaro wrote an article entitled "Elder Abuse Underreported, on Rise in Nevada." The article discusses the fact that, in Nevada over the previous three years, 2011, 2012, and 2013, reports of elder abuse have risen from 5,237 cases in 2011 to 5,562 cases in 2013. Additionally, the percentage of cases that are substantiated (meaning abuse/neglect is validated) has also risen from 22% in 2011 to 28% in 2013. While these percentages may seem somewhat low, Amaro, basing her information on a comment by Tammy Sever, the Las Vegas Elder Protective Services manager, notes that "research has shown that for every case reported five go unreported." Amaro writes that the most common perpetrator in Nevada is someone the victim knows, either the victim's adult children (35%) or spouse/significant other/other relatives (30%) and that the abuse most often occurs to those living at home (82%).

To read the full article, visit: http://www.reviewjournal.com/news/nevada/elder-abuse-underreported-rise-nevada.

Types of Abuse

Similar to child abuse and intimate partner violence, elder abuse consists of many different forms of harm, including physical and sexual abuse, emotional/psychological abuse, financial exploitation (similar to IPV victims), and neglect and/or abandonment (similar to child abuse) (Tyiska et al., 2012). Fraud is another area in which older adults may be especially vulnerable that isn't discussed in child abuse or intimate partner violence. Older adults are vulnerable to fraud because offenders assume they have access to a reserve of cash (in other words a "cache" of cash) that they can access at any time. They may get charged for medical services they never received, they may be talked into investing in a business that doesn't exist or paying for a contracted service they never receive, and they might be manipulated into thinking that a loved one is in need and they must send funds immediately or the loved one could be in great harm. Another form of abuse that may be more specific to elders is institutional abuse (though children and incarcerated individuals are also vulnerable to this as well).

Tyiska et al. (2012) suggest that older adults who become victims of crime are particularly prone to developing more extensive psychological distress during and after the victimization. They may feel bad about themselves for seemingly "letting it happen" and may develop depression, hopelessness, despair, and even PTSD. Individuals who are already suffering from mental illnesses may exhibit greater symptoms and/or regress to a less advanced stage within the illness. When an older person is a victim within an institutional setting, they are at heightened risk for repeated victimization.

Who Perpetrates Abuse?

Caretakers of elders are the most likely perpetrators of elder abuse, in particular the children of the older adult (Gosselin, 2005). Ramsey-Klawsnik (as cited in Gosselin, 2005) created a typology of elder abusers in the late 1970s. The three categories are: (1) the stress-precipitated abuser, (2) the greedy abuser, and (3) the intentional harm perpetrator. The stress-precipitated abuser is one who ends up harming the older person for whom they provide care because they are acting out on the stress and strain of the caregiving duties. It was suggested that this type of abuser might be amenable to therapy to deal more effectively with the stress and strain of caregiving (Gosselin, 2005). The greedy abuser is someone who purposefully exploits and violates the older person for sheer want. The greedy abuser wants to fill his or her own pockets with money and goods of the elders, so he/she just takes it. The intentional harm abuser derives pleasure out of perpetrating harm against the elder and is not truly amenable to change.

According to Gosselin (2005), males and females are both likely to commit acts of elder abuse (as they are equally likely to be caregivers of older adults as well), but some studies suggest that males account for about two-thirds of all elder abuse perpetrators. The vast majority of elder abuse occurs within the victim's home, which technically might be a senior center of some type (Gosselin, 2005). Interestingly, males are more associated with abandonment (83.4%). Almost half of all perpetrators are children of the victims, however, spouses/ex-spouses and others deemed "significant others" are also common perpetrators because intimate partner violence didn't stop at a certain age. Gosselin (2005) notes that after children, spouses account for the next largest percentage of elder abuse perpetrators (19.3%). Other relatives and grandchildren rounded out the perpetrator category and accounted for about 17% of all elder abuse, collectively.

Animals as Victims

Up to this point, we have focused on humans as victims, but many consider animals (especially pets) as members of the family, and research has found that they too are vulnerable to victimization. Early philosophers examined the issue of animal cruelty as both an indication of what those acts could mean for potential human victims, as well as broadening our understanding about the suffering of species other than our own (Arkow & Lockwood, 2013). However, one of the most challenging issues with understanding harm to animals is creating a definition that both recognizes and penalizes harm, but also acknowledges socially acceptable treatment and/or use of animals (food, labor, etc.). There also may not be a consensus about what constitutes cruelty in the eyes of potential perpetrators. For instance, dog-fighting and cock-fighting are socially accepted in some circles within the United States; however, many states have legislation prohibiting these acts. Some religious communities utilize animals for sacrifice in their religious practices and though this is not socially acceptable on a larger scale, those individuals may not be penalized because the United States' Constitution protects certain aspects of religious practices. For the most part, however, all 50 states have enacted legislation that prohibits and penalizes specific harmful acts towards animals and they typically have the following six elements:

1. Specific types of animals that are protected;
2. Specific acts that are not allowed and requirements of care;
3. Mental capability of the offender to understand the act is wrong;
4. Criminal liability defenses;
5. Exemptions from the law (though legal and illegal actions may be the same); and
6. Penalties associated with each offense (Arkow & Lockwood, 2013).

Types of Harm

Ascione and Shapiro (2009) define animal abuse as "[n]on-accidental, socially unacceptable behavior that causes pain, suffering or distress to and/or the death of an animal" (p. 570). An earlier definition included the term "unnecessary" too, as infliction of pain may come in the form of laboratory experiments, labor, food preparation, and order maintenance activities but may come about more by mere happenstance than by intention or knowing allowance of the perpetrator. The term "unnecessary" was taken out in the later definition as the term itself was subjective and problematic (Arkow & Lockwood, 2013). Arkow and Lockwood (2013) suggest that the terms we use to identify harm to animals most commonly include animal cruelty, animal abuse, and neglect — similar terms and behavior that we admonish when they occur against humans. Cruelty applies to the "malicious intent on the part of the perpetrator," while abuse and neglect describe acts of maltreatment or acts of omission whether intended or not by the perpetrator (Arkow & Lockwood, 2013, p. 7). Similar to child maltreatment, Reyes (2013) states that harm to animals can be either "active" or "passive," with active cruelty including acts perpetrated against an animal and passive cruelty being harm that occurs because of the failure of the owner to provide the care and necessities needed for an animal to survive. The more egregious the act (and oftentimes shocking to the sensibilities of humans), the more cruel it is perceived.

Explanations for Harming Animals

Kellert and Felthous (as cited in Merz-Perez & Heide, 2004) describe nine motives for the conduct of animal abuse or animal cruelty, some of which inform us or illustrate parallels for how one might also treat humans.

1. Control (control over an animal, which could escalate into or inform us as to how someone is or could treat humans);
2. Retaliation (striking back at an animal who harmed a human, jealousy for receipt of affection from another human);

3. Acting on a prejudice towards a specific breed;
4. Expressing aggression through the use of an animal (teaching an animal to be aggressive and letting that aggressive animal loose on someone with the intention that harm will occur);
5. Enhancing one's own aggressiveness (utilizing an animal to instill fear in another);
6. Shock value;
7. Retaliation against a person (when a person is angered or hurt by another, or does not like being disobeyed, he or she may harm an animal close to that person to "teach them a lesson" and to make them feel pain as well);
8. Displacement of hostility (may be angry at a human and can't act on it so the human acts out on the animal instead); and
9. Nonspecific sadism (harmful acts perpetrated to experience pleasure).

These motivations suggest that individuals may harm animals for many reasons that may or may not be related to the animal's behavior itself.

Investigation and Incidence of Harm to Animals

Arkow and Lockwood (2013) describe eight categories that are commonly used when law enforcement investigates claims of animal abuse: animal cruelty, animal abuse, neglect, hoarding, animal physical abuse, non-accidental injury, animal sexual abuse, and emotional abuse. Animal cruelty suggests that the act was done deliberately to cause pain and suffering, and which brings pleasure to the perpetrator. This term is most commonly used in statutory language by legislators. Animal abuse is a more recently used term and is modeled after our proscription of harm against children. Abusive acts include knowingly failing to care for an animal in the manner proscribed by law or perpetrating harmful acts that result in maltreatment. Abuse does not require that the act be intentional or that the perpetrator be of sound mind. Neglect suggests the failure of an owner to provide food, water, and shelter for the animal, and/or failure to provide the animal with needed veterinary care, sanitation, and grooming (as needed) regardless of the circumstances. As with harm to children, neglect accounts for the majority of cases brought before animal protection authorities. Hoarding is a heightened form of animal neglect in that an individual collects a large number of animals and cannot provide for them in the manner proscribed by law and/or in a way that provides a safe environment for them. Animal physical abuse includes any act that causes injury and has a wide range of actions, from hitting and kicking to scalding and suffocation. In some states, physically intimidating an animal into submission is also constituted as physical abuse. Non-accidental injury (NAI) is used as an additional description of physical abuse and often suggests repeated acts against an animal. Animal sexual abuse includes any type of sexual contact with an animal involving the rectum, anus, or genitalia. Finally, Arkow and Lockwood (2013) included emotional abuse in their forms of animal abuse, though neither the US nor UK nor Canada have included emotional abuse in their legislation. Emotional abuse

Figure 5.3: Total Animal Abuse Cases 2000–2014 by Type of Abuse

Type of Abuse	Percentage
Burning-Caustic Substance	0.60%
Drowning	0.70%
Hanging	0.70%
Unlawful Trapping/Hunting	0.80%
Other	0.90%
Theft	1.10%
Unlawful Trade/Smuggling	1.20%
Bestiality	1.30%
Choking/Strangulation	1.40%
Kicking/Stomping	1.40%
Poisoning	1.58%
Vehicular	1.80%
Unclassified	1.80%
Burning-Fire/Fireworks	2.10%
Stabbing	2.50%
Throwing	2.50%
Mutilation/Torture	5.50%
Beating	7.00%
Fighting	8.70%
Shooting	11.30%
Hoarding	12.40%
Neglect/Abandonment	32.40%

Source: Pet-Abuse.com; AARDAS project.

of animals is similar to that of humans in which the victim is left in a fragile emotional state due to intimidation, exploitation, coercion, bullying, teasing, and other forms of emotional abuse. As we learn more about the emotional abilities of animals, perhaps this will become a more formalized harm in state legislation.

By now you have a relatively good idea of what is meant by the terms *animal cruelty*, *animal abuse*, and *animal neglect*, so it is important to further describe how much of this takes place. Unlike crimes reported by law enforcement to the FBI and disseminated to us through the UCR, there is no formal governmental database that records instances of harm to animals. However, a nonprofit organization has created a website, Pet-Abuse.com, in which they have created the Animal Abuse Registry Database Administration System (AARDAS) project (Pet-Abuse.com; Reyes, 2013). AARDAS is a compilation of data reporting harm to animals from law enforcement, courts, and the media (Reyes, 2013). The data has been collected since 2000 and illustrates patterns in the types of harm that animals are most at risk of experiencing (Reyes, 2013). Reyes (2013) suggests that the number of cases reported increased consistently from 2000 to 2006 and has dipped and risen ever since. She suggests that we need to be cautious about interpreting these patterns, as incidents of animal cruelty/abuse may not be on the rise, but may be reported more regularly perhaps in response to increased media reports of such events.

"In the News" Box 5.4

On May 19, 2014, newyork.cbslocal.com published an article entitled "Nassau County Legislature Approves Proposal for Animal Abuse Registry." The article discusses a proposal to create an online registry listing names of people who had been convicted of animal abuse. Once a person's name was listed on the registry they would be forbidden to purchase any other animals in Long Island County. According to the article, convicted offenders would have to register within five days and failure to register could "land [them] ... in jail for a year." Nassau County SPCA would maintain the database and the offender's name, photo, and address would be posted so their information could be checked by the distributor or adoption agency.

To read the full article, visit: http://newyork.cbslocal.com/2014/05/19/nassau-county-legislature-approves-proposal-for-animal-abuse-registry/.

Characteristics of Offenses

As of March 6, 2017, Pet-Abuse.com reported 19,464 cases of animal cruelty, abuse, or neglect in the United States from 2000–2015 (Pet-Abuse.com, visited March 6, 2017) (see Figure 5.3).

Neglect/abandonment, hoarding, and shooting accounted for over 50% of all cases in the AARDAS database (N = 17,282). Neglect/abandonment accounted for the vast majority of these cases (32.4%, n = 5,591), followed by hoarding (12.4%, n = 2,148), and shooting (11.3%, n = 1,956). The remaining cases run the gamut of harm from drowning (n = 118 cases) to burning (combined 443 cases) to beating (n = 1,209 cases). Dogs are the most common victims of harm (8,494 cases for non-pit bulls, 2,466 cases of pit bulls specifically), followed at a distance by cats (n = 3,384) and horses (n = 1,643). The most grievous harm that could come to an animal is death. The majority of deaths of animals occurred in hoarding and neglect/abandonment cases, both of which fall within the "passive cruelty" category (Reyes, 2013).

Characteristics of Complainants and Perpetrators

Reyes (2013) reports that for those cases included in the AARDAS, neighbors are the most likely complainants (or reporters of the crimes), accounting for approximately 36% of reports. Owners of the animals accounted for 14% of reports, 10.5% of cases were reported by an unknown party, law enforcement identified 9% of cases (typically when they were responding to calls for harm to humans at the same address), 7% were anonymous reporters, and 11% were "Other." In less than 1% of cases did the perpetrator him or herself report the crime.

Figure 5.4: Animal Abuse Cases with Documented Child or Elder Abuse

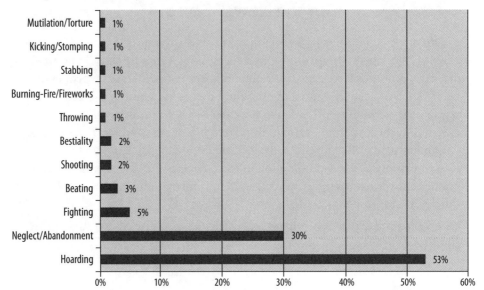

Source: Pet-Abuse.com; AARDAS project.

In AARDAS, over 75% of perpetrators were male and were most often "older" (21% were in 31- to 40-year-old age group). Female perpetrators were most often older as well, with over 25% of female perpetrators reporting to be in the 41 to 50 age group. Most acts of animal cruelty were perpetrated by individuals aged 21 and older (Pet-Abuse.com, visited March 6, 2017). In 63% of cases, the caregiver is the alleged abuser (Pet-Abuse.com, visted March 6, 2017).

The Link

In the last two decades, a great deal of information has been collected acknowledging the existence of a relationship between animal cruelty/abuse, domestic violence, and childhood and/or elder abuse. This relationship is known as "The Link" (American Humane Society, 2004). Oftentimes when individuals respond to a call for service regarding some type of violence, they only have jurisdiction over one or two types of violence, but may not know what to do if they see signs of other types of violence in a household. For instance, when an animal cruelty investigator may come into a home to investigate an allegation of animal cruelty, she may notice that a child or adult in the home is covered in bruises, but because that is not within her jurisdiction may not be able to do anything about it at the time. Conversely, someone who responds to a call regarding child abuse may enter a home and see that there is an animal with cuts and scars, or in need of medical treatment, but because that isn't his area he may not be able to do anything about it or find the time to report it to the proper authorities. To illustrate cases where animal cruelty/abuse investigators encounter child or elder abuse, see Figure 5.4.

Advocates working to educate people about the link state that there is beginning to be a large collection of data supporting the connection between child abuse, intimate partner violence, and animal cruelty (American Humane Society, 2004). It was noted in one study that "85% of women and 63% of children who entered the shelters reported incidents of pet abuse at home" (American Humane Society, 2004, para. 8). As noted in Kellert and Felthous' motivations for animal cruelty, a number of them promote the existence of the link in that children who are abused or aggrieved might abuse an animal to seek revenge on something they can control (as opposed to going up against an older person who may have the authority to punish the child). Recognition of and action related to the link could prevent additional abuse from happening, and/or could get perpetrators and victims the services they need before someone or an animal is killed (American Humane Society, 2005). In sum, there is a great deal of research that illustrates, intentionally or not, the link between two or more forms of abuse/violence against discrete populations. Leaving someone else to respond to the "other" type of harm could have serious consequences.

Summary and Conclusion

Individuals who are in relationships with or dependent upon others in which there is an expectation of compassion, care, and love can be at risk of violence or abuse. Interpersonal violence typically consists of physical abuse, psychological or emotional abuse, and financial harm or exploitation, though children and animals may not be as subject to financial harm. Typically, the perpetrators are caregivers or loved ones, which seems contrary to the nature of the interpersonal relationship. The abuse or violence perpetrated can leave long-lasting effects and can start the path toward generations of abusive and abused families, including animal members of that family. Practitioners working with any of the victims discussed should be sure not to overlook signs of additional types of violence and abuse happening within a home, as that could be a sure indicator that help is needed.

Key Terms

Primary maltreatment

Active maltreatment

Passive maltreatment

Secondary maltreatment

Polyvictimization

Emotional or psychological abuse

Physical abuse

Battered child syndrome

Sexual abuse

Neglect

Non-family abduction

Stereotypical kidnappings

Family abduction

Runaways

Thrownaways

Lost, injured, or otherwise missing children

Battered woman syndrome

Discussion Questions

1. In what ways are the types of harm perpetrated consistent across the four different groups discussed?
2. What is the different between battered child syndrome and battered woman syndrome?
3. What do you think is the connection between types of child abuse and missing children?
4. How is animal cruelty/abuse intertwined into other types of interpersonal or domestic violence? Why is it important to not ignore animal cruelty or abuse?

Websites for Further Information

American Humane Society explores "The Link": http://www.americanhumane.org/interaction/support-the-bond/fact-sheets/animal-abuse-domestic-violence.html.

Pet-Abuse.com: www.pet-abuse.com.

Child, Teen, and Elder Abuse: http://www.victimsofcrime.org/library/crime-information-and-statistics/child-youth-and-teen-victimization.

http://www.nij.gov/topics/crime/child-abuse/impact-on-arrest-victimization.htm.

http://www.victimsofcrime.org/library/crime-information-and-statistics/elder-victimization.

References

American Humane Society. (2004). *The Florida Senate: Interim Project Report 2005-125*. State of Florida: Senate Committee on Criminal Justice.

Arkow, P., & Lockwood, R. (2013). Definitions of animal cruelty, abuse, and neglect. In M. P. Brewster & C. L. Reyes (Eds.), *Animal cruelty: A multidisciplinary approach to understanding* (pp. 3–24). Durham, NC: Carolina Academic Press.

Ascione, F. R., & Shapiro, K. (2009). People and animals, kindness and cruelty: Research directions and policy implications. *Journal of Social Issues, 65*(3), 569–587.

Building Futures. (n.d.). Domestic violence 101. Retrieved from http://www.bfwc.org/pdf/DV%20101.pdf.

Catalano, S. (2013). *Intimate partner violence: Attributes of victimization, 1993–2011*. Washington, DC: US Department of Justice, Office of Justice Programs, Bureau of Justice Statistics. NCJ 243300.

Childhelp.org. (n.d.). National child abuse statistics. Retrieved from http://www.childhelp.org/pages/statistics.

Child Welfare Information Gateway. (2014). *Mandatory reporters of child abuse and neglect*. Washington, DC: US Department of Health and Human Services, Children's Bureau.

Critcher, C. (2008). Moral panic analysis: Past, present and future. *Sociology Compass*, 2, 1127–1144. doi: 10.1111/j.1751-9020.2008.00122.x.

Eriksen, S., & Jensen, V. (2009). A push or a punch: Distinguishing the severity of sibling violence. *Journal of Interpersonal Violence*, 24(1), 183–208.

Finkelhor, D., Cross, T. P., & Cantor, E. N. (2005). How the justice system responds to juvenile victims: A comprehensive model. Washington, DC: US Department of Justice, Office of Justice Programs, Office of Juvenile Justice and Delinquency Prevention. NCJ 210951.

Finkelhor, D., Hotaling, G., & Sedlak, A. (1990). Missing, abducted, runaway, and thrownaway children in America: Final Report: Numbers and Characteristics National Incidence Studies.

Finkelhor, D., & Jones, L. (2012). Have sexual abuse and physical abuse declined since the 1990s? Crimes Against Children Research Center: University of New Hampshire, CV 267.

Finkelhor, D., & Ormrod, R. (2000). Juvenile victims of property crimes. US Department of Justice, Office of Juvenile Justice and Delinquency Prevention. NCJ 210951.

Gaboury, M., Seymour, A., McCown, A., & Modell, S. (2012). Child abuse and neglect. Washington, DC: US Department of Justice, Office of Justice Programs, Office for Victims of Crime, Training and Technical Assistance Center.

Gosselin, D. K. (2005). *Heavy hands: An introduction to the crimes of family violence* (3rd ed.). Upper Saddle River, NJ: Pearson Prentice Hall.

Kettrey, H. H., & Emery, B. C. (2006). The discourse of sibling violence. *Journal of Family Violence*, 21(6), 407–416.

Merz-Perez, L., & Heide, K. (2004). *Animal cruelty: Pathway to violence against people*. Lanham, MD: AltaMira Press.

National Association of Council for Children. (n.d.). Child maltreatment. Retrieved from http://www.naccchildlaw.org/?page=childmaltreatment#.

National Center for Victims of Crime. (n.d.). *Stalking fact sheet*. Stalking Resource Center. Retrieved from http://www.victimsofcrime.org/docs/default-source/src/stalking-fact-sheet-2015_eng.pdf?sfvrsn=2.

National Victim Assistance Academy. (2000). *Chapter 9: Domestic violence*. Washington, DC: US Department of Justice, Office of Justice Programs, Office for Victims of Crime.

Perkins, N. H., & O'Connor M. K. (2015). Commentary: Physical and emotional sibling violence: A necessary role for social work. *Social Work*, 61(1), 91–93.

Pet-Abuse.com, visited March 6, 2017.

Reyes, C. (2013). Statistics and measurement of animal cruelty. In M. P. Brewster & C. L. Reyes (Eds.), *Animal cruelty: A multidisciplinary approach to understanding* (pp. 109–123). Durham, NC: Carolina Academic Press.

Sedlak, A. J., Finkelhor, D., Hammer, H., & Schultz, D. J. (2002). NISMART: National incidence studies of missing, abducted, runaway, and thrownaway children. *OJJDP NISMART Bulletin Series*. US Department of Justice, Office of Juvenile Justice and Delinquency Prevention. NCJ 196465.

Seymour, A., Gaboury, M., & DeHart, D. (2012). Intimate partner violence. Washington, DC: US Department of Justice, Office of Justice Programs, Office for Victims of Crime, Training and Technical Assistance Center.

Snyder, H. N., & Sickmund, M. (2006). *Juvenile offenders and victims: 2006 National Report*. Washington, DC: US Department of Justice, Office of Justice Programs, Office of Juvenile Justice and Delinquency Prevention.

Straus, M. A., Gelles, R. J., & Steinmetz, S. K. (1980). *Behind closed doors: Violence in the American family*. Garden City, NY: Doubleday.

Taranto, A. (2014). Same-sex intimate partner violence: Current barriers to service & future goals for advocacy agencies. Retrieved from http://www.crimeandjustice. org/councilinfo.cfm?pID=60.

Truman, J. L., & Morgan, R. E. (2014). *Nonfatal domestic violence, 2003–2012*. Washington, DC: US Department of Justice, Office of Justice Programs, Office for Victims of Crime. NCJ 244697.

Truman, J. L., & Morgan, R. E. (2016). Criminal victimization, 2015. Washington, DC: US Department of Justice, Office of Justice Programs, Office for Victims of Crime. NCJ 250180.

Tyiska, C., Gaboury, M., Seymour, A., & Heisler, C. (2012). *Elder abuse*. Washington, DC: US Department of Justice, Office of Justice Programs, Office for Victims of Crime, Training and Technical Assistance Center.

US Department of Health and Human Services, Administration for Children and Families, Administration on Children, Youth and Families, Children's Bureau. (2013). *Child maltreatment 2012*. Retrieved from http://www.acf.hhs.gov/programs/ cb/research-data-technology/statistics-research/child-maltreatment.

US Department of Health and Human Services, Administration for Children and Families, Administration on Children, Youth and Families, Children's Bureau. (2017). *Child maltreatment 2015*. Retrieved from http://www.acf.hhs.gov/programs/ cb/research-data-technology/statistics-research/child-maltreatment.

Walker, L. (1979). *The battered woman*. New York, NY: Harper Row.

White, N., & Lauritsen, J. (2012). Violent crime against youth, 1994–2010. US Department of Justice, Office of Justice Programs, Bureau of Justice Statistics, NCJ 240106.

Chapter 6: White-Collar Crimes and Workplace Violence

When we talk about crime or hear about crime on the news the crime that is discussed is typically "street crime"—those crimes that are used as the basis for our overall crime rate. We might assume that these crimes are happening in close proximity and when someone is at home or engaging in a leisure activity of some sort. For the most part the data support these assumptions, but some crime happens within environments we wouldn't necessary expect—the workplace and other organizational environments. For victims of white-collar crimes, locating the source of the victimization is crucial for accurately defining them as such. Individuals, states, and corporations, or some combination thereof, may all commit harms against individuals or groups. The greatest challenge for this population of victims is the *legal* definition of the crimes, and therefore of them as victims. To better understand crime in these contexts we will explore white-collar crimes and workplace violence to identify the challenges that come along with studying these domains.

White-Collar Crime

For criminologists, the history of the term **white-collar crime** is usually traced back to the presidential address made by Edwin H. Sutherland in 1939 at the American Sociological Society meeting in Philadelphia. Referring to "Crimes of the Powerful" or "Elite Deviance," these crimes tended to be committed by individuals of higher social classes than traditional crimes, or what we now call street crimes. As the name implies, white-collar crimes were seen as committed by people working white-collar jobs, often by utilizing their position of employment or their business to an advantage.

Sometimes written off as bad business practices, these crimes were often not viewed as illegal per say. An unrelenting quest for profit and advantage over competitors characterizes capitalism, so while not illegal the actions of these individuals may have exploited people out of their money or caused physical harm to workers or consumers by cutting corners for profit.

Today, the study of white-collar crime has grown dramatically, and the scope of crimes which fall under this category has grown as well. The term **occupational crime** refers to crimes or harms committed by individuals through the course of their employment. This refers to an individual who may embezzle money from an employer, over charge customers and then skim off the top, or use their position in an organization for personal gain. Occupational crimes are one of the few areas of white-collar crime the FBI collects data for, however the data can be misleading because not every instance of these crimes may be categorized as such by criminologists. For 2015, the FBI (Table 43) estimate of arrests for forgery and counterfeiting was 42,436, for fraud there were an estimated 101,556 arrests, and for embezzlement an estimated 12,169 arrests.

Corporate crime refers to crimes or harms committed by corporate entities which benefit the corporation as a whole. While individuals may benefit from these types of crime, the motivation of corporate competitiveness and profit for many distinguish these from occupational crimes. An example of a corporate crime most well-known to the public would be the case of the Ford Pinto (Kramer, 1986). In this case, a series of accidents where Ford Pintos would catch on fire following a rear-end collision drew national attention. During the course of the investigation, it was found that Ford knew about the problems early on, but failed to warn customers and recall the cars. Internal documents from Ford revealed that a cost-benefit analysis of a recall and replacement would be more expensive than paying out civil wrongful death cases if they ever made their way into the courts. This case is an example of how the motivation to maintain the appearance and profits of the corporation was put before the wellbeing of customers and the public. Multiple individuals were involved in the decision making process and the corporation itself was responsible.

Under the broad heading of **governmental crime**, two forms emerge. The first, **political white-collar crime**, refers to individual crimes or harms which may come about in the pursuit of political office or maintenance of such a position. These crimes are viewed as more individual in nature and in the pursuit of one's own goals and aspirations. The second form, **state crime**, refers to illegal or harmful actions carried out by the state or state actors, which fulfill or achieve institutional or organizational goals. Victims of state crime would be:

> individuals or groups of individuals who have experienced economic, cultural, or physical harm, pain, exclusion, or exploitation because of tacit or explicit state actions or policies which violate the law or generally defined human rights (Kauzlarich, Matthews, & Miller, 2001, p. 176).

A contemporary example of a state crime would be Hurricane Katrina in 2005. In this case, the US government had evidence from a simulation called "Hurricane Pam," which showed the levees around New Orleans wouldn't hold if a hurricane of that magnitude hit. While the recommendations to secure up the levees were well known, action was never taken, 1,400 people died, and the lives hundreds of thousands were changed forever (Faust & Kauzlarich, 2008).

Finally, **state-corporate crimes** are those illegal or harmful acts with both government and corporate actors being involved and benefiting from those actions. An example of this type of crime is the explosion of the space shuttle *Challenger* in 1986 (Kramer, 1992). On the morning of the launch, individuals in both government and the private sector discovered that the overnight temperatures on the launch pad had dropped lower than expected and could be problematic for the O-rings on the shuttle. Due to the money already spent on the plans for the launch and the excitement of the first teacher on a shuttle voyage, the launch went ahead as planned, with disastrous consequences.

Definitional Issues

So far, we have been referring to white-collar crimes as *illegal or harmful acts*. This is intentional, as one of the primary characteristics of these crimes was the fact that so many of them weren't (and many still aren't) considered illegal in the criminal sense. Those individuals and groups in positions of power have historically been the same as those who define for the rest of us what is criminal and what is not. As laws and rules for businesses and corporations developed, those entities played a role in shaping the laws they had to follow and resisted the ones which weren't in their interests. As a result, many of the laws governing businesses and corporations were relegated to regulatory law, which could result in fines and penalties if violated. Today, criminologists use a variety of perspectives to define what is studied in the different areas. A legalistic approach follows the model of traditional street crimes by identifying the specific violation with a specific law which has been violated. Particularly for state crimes, international laws, which have been developing in their modern form since the creation of the United Nations in 1945, are used to specify the exact law violated.

An alternative to the legalistic approach, which seeks to address some of the problems and limitations of that approach, is a social harm or human rights approach. This approach, advocated for by scholars such as the Schewendingers (1970) expands the definition of crime. This approach addresses "the problematic way in which crime is defined, the highly political nature of defining harms as crimes (while ignoring equally harmful behaviors)" and therefore enabling "criminologists to focus their efforts not on defining the actions of the state as criminal, but rather cataloging the wide range of state behaviors that are harmful" (Matthews & Kauzlarich, 2007, p. 49). Guidelines for human rights are available to criminologists at the international level through the United Nations, as well as human rights organizations. Thus, a multitude of types of harm can be considered from this perspective, and while human rights don't necessarily have the force of law behind them, they provide a framework by which harms can be judged.

Given the definitional issues raised by criminologists, it is easy to understand how recognizing victimization by the public can be highly problematic. Various forms of white-collar crime may be chalked up to bad business practices, even today. Different forms of consumer fraud or defective products might just be swept under the rug as some form of mistake. As consumers, we may view a recall of a deadly product as a corporation doing the right thing; however, upon deeper investigation the corporation may have known about the defect for a much longer time. They even may have postponed the recall to give themselves time to assess financial or market damage, or hire a marketing agency to do damage control so the impact didn't hurt their bottom line. In the meantime, other individuals were still harmed or killed as a result.

Victims of White-Collar Crime

According to Friedrichs (2004), the financial costs from white-collar crime are hard to estimate. At the low end, white-collar crimes could cost $250 billion dollars a year up to $1 trillion in the US (Schlegel, 2000 in Friedrichs, 2004). Greider (2002 in Friedrichs, 2004) estimated that the single case of Enron alone may have cost $50 billion to the investors and workers who were impacted. According to Reiman (2001), the physical costs from traditional street crimes account for about 18,000 deaths (recall 14,827 estimated homicides in 2012 according to the FBI UCR) and serious injuries impacting 1 million. On the other hand, about 30,000 Americans are killed each year from work-related accidents and diseases and almost 3 million more experience serious physical harm in work-related injuries (Reiman, 2001). In addition, an estimated 12,000 deaths a year are the result of unnecessary medical procedures and another 100,000 die a year from medical mistakes (Reiman, 2001). Often the physical costs are hard to detect, as many individuals may not connect illnesses such as cancer with the illegal dumping of toxic chemicals or fumes from a nearby chemical plant.

Identifying who is more likely to be victimized by white-collar crimes is much harder to pinpoint than victims of traditional crimes. Corporations and states themselves can be victimized by employees or those they serve; individuals as consumers, workers, patients, investors, or just by virtue of the location where they live can become victims. However, due to the imbalance of power Sutherland first identified, those individuals of the lowest status in society, such as the poor, minorities, and women, may experience more victimization than those of higher classes.

Victims of state, corporate, and state-corporate crimes have historically been neglected and their victimization under-theorized. In 2001, six propositions of a victimology of state crime were outlined by Kauzlarich, Matthews, and Miller. These propositions attempt to bring together and explain what has been observed about victims of state crime. The first proposition is that, "victims of state crime tend to be among the least socially powerful actors" (Kauzlarich, Matthews, & Miller, 2001, p. 183). The second proposition is that, "victimizers generally fail to recognize and understand the nature, extent, and harmfulness of institutional policies. If suffering and harm are acknowledged, it is often neutralized within the context of a sense of 'entitlement'" (Kauzlarich et al., 2001, p. 185). The third proposition argues that, "victims of state crime are often blamed for their suffering" (Kauzlarich et al., 2001, p. 186). The fourth proposition explains that, "victims of state crime must generally rely on the victimizer, an associated institution, or civil social movement for redress"

"In the News" Box 6.1

On October 31, 2013, *Huffington Post* reporter Caroline Fairchild published an article entitled "Low-Wage Workers are Robbed More than Banks, Gas Stations and Convenience Stores Combined." The article discusses the illegally withheld wages of minimum-wage employees by their employers. Fairchild writes that "(m)ore than 60 percent of low-wage workers have some pay illegally withheld by their employer each week," which is approximately 15% of their overall pay. Furthermore, Fairchild reports that wage theft resulted in $185 million stolen in 2008, which was "*three times more* than all the money lost in bank, gas-station and convenience-store robberies" (italics in original article). The article states that low-wage workers who recognize that their checks are short typically have no recourse because they either can't afford an attorney to fight their case or the lawyers will turn them down for seemingly small amounts of stolen pay. Miami-Dade County in Florida enacted a law that required employers to pay for the court proceedings related to stolen pay. In a single year, $1.7 million of stolen pay was reclaimed.

To read the full article, visit: http://www.huffingtonpost.com/2013/10/30/low-wage-workers-robbed_n_4178706.html.

(Kauzlarich et al., 2001, p. 186). According to the fifth proposition, "victims of state crime are easy targets for repeated victimization" (Kauzlarich et al., 2001, p. 187). The sixth and final proposition is that, "illegal state policies and practices, while committed by individuals and groups of individuals, are manifestations of the attempt to achieve organizational, bureaucratic, or institutional goals" (Kauzlarich et al., 2001, p. 188).

Victims of the Criminal Justice System

As you should have learned in an introductory criminal justice course, the agents of justice are held to a higher standard of ethical behavior, both on the job and off duty. According to the social contract within which our society operates, we give up a degree of our freedoms in order to enjoy the protections of the agents we deem worthy of administering justice on our behalf. It is no surprise then, that we are particularly outraged when it appears that these freedoms have been violated—when the actions of the agents of justice make little sense to us, and when it appears that we all may not be receiving the same degree of protection. Depending on the section of the United States in which you may live or have lived, you have likely heard about, if not experienced directly or indirectly, an incident with an agent of the justice system that did not go well, and may even have resulted in the death of someone you knew. Relationships between agents of the justice system and the general public have, at times, been strained due to perceived and/or acknowledged abuses by those who are trusted as authorities within the criminal justice system. From police corruption in urban police departments, such as Tammany Hall in New York, wherein people's rights were purposefully denied (voting, etc.) to police shootings of unarmed people, to judges making decisions about the custody of those adjudicated delinquent/found to be criminally guilty based on their own pocket book, to rape/sexual assault of inmates in correctional facilities by correctional staff ... there are numerous examples of situations in which "the people" have been harmed by the actions of criminal justice personnel. We consider these individuals "victims" of the criminal justice system. The term *victims* was placed in quotation marks not to diminish their importance, but because of the unique context within which the term lies. This book has focused, for the most part, on seemingly "innocent" victims, but a discussion of victims of the criminal justice system oftentimes involves acts against individuals who are suspected of or have been found guilty of violating some aspect of our social contract—if not an outright law. The controversies that surround our discussion of victims of the criminal justice system, and for which we see a great deal of debate on what appear to be polarized issues, are (1) whether those who are harmed by agents of the justice system in some way provoked the resulting harm, (2) whether the harm perpetrated was necessary to protect the agents, the community, or the victim him or herself, and (3) whether the harm was perpetrated by a rogue individual or is endemic to the organization to which that person belongs. Additionally, the media wields a great deal of power in deciding what it will present to the public in regard to abuses by the justice system. Is it showing an accurate picture or is it preying upon our reliance on them to tell the story they believe will garner the most viewers/readers? Probably the most notable area reported to us by the media about criminal justice system perpetrated harm is the disproportionate number of police shootings (and killings) of African American males. Over the past several years, police violence against the African American community has made headlines. The shooting death of 18-year-old Michael Brown in Ferguson, Missouri, kicked off a national discussion and debate about the police and the criminal justice system in the United States. Other high-profile deaths at the hands of police include Eric Garner, 43, Walter Scott, 50, Freddie Grey, 25, and 12-year-old Tamir Rice, who was shot only seconds after officers exited their patrol car (Amnesty International USA, 2015). Across the institutions that make up the CJS, we can find victims at the hands of the state actors. The question we need answers to, and quickly, is why are these things happening? While we often hear about police shootings or other incidents being dismissed as a few "bad apples," the widespread, systematic nature of these deaths, and other harms across the institutions of the CJS, may point to a deeper problem within the institutions and nation in which they occur.

Victims of the Police

In 2015, Amnesty International USA released the report *Deadly Force: Police Use of Lethal Force in the United States* and raised serious concerns about human rights violations, including "the right to life, the right to security of person, the right to freedom from discrimination and the right to equal protection of the law" (p. 1). At the international level, human rights laws generally view the taking of a life by the state as a priority protection of citizens throughout the world. When concerning law enforcement specifically, the United Nations Basic Principles on the Use of Force and Firearms by Law Enforcement Officials views the use of force as largely limited to when it is absolutely unavoidable to protect or defend another life, and when less lethal means may not be sufficient (Amnesty International USA, 2015).

In the United States, data on police killings of citizens have been hard to track, largely due to the government's unwillingness to centralize the data. After FBI Director James Comey compared the data they collected on justifiable homicides with information collected on police shootings in the US by the *Washington Post* and *The Guardian*, two news sources, he stated that it was "unacceptable" "embarrassing and ridiculous" that better data was collected by those agencies and not his (Kindy, 2015). In the same news article, Kindy quotes Professor David Klinger of the University of Missouri-St. Louis, a former police officer, as saying

> When agents of the state put bullets downrange in citizens, we need to know about that. In a representative democracy, we need to know about that. We are citizens, not subjects. We also need to understand the circumstances of the shootings, so we spot trends, so we can improve training (Kindy, *Washington Post*, December 8, 2015, National section).

Here's the picture that the statistics that we do have access to actually paint. According to Amnesty International USA (2015) estimates range from 400 people a year to over 1,000 people killed by law enforcement. Research done by the CDC has found that Blacks are disproportionately represented as victims of police killings. For instance, between 1999 and 2013, the percentage of Blacks killed by police (27.6%) was nearly double their representation in the population (13.2%) (Amnesty International USA, 2015). According to *The Guardian*'s project entitled "The Counted: People Killed by Police in the U.S." it was found that 1,146 people died at the hands of or while in custody of police in 2015 (visited March 4, 2017). The raw data shows that 307 people were Black, 13 were Native American, 195 were Hispanic/Latino, 584 were White, 24 were Asian/Pacific Islander, and 23 were other or unknown. While the raw numbers clearly demonstrate that more White people were killed by officers than any other race or ethnicity, it is also important to examine the rate, which standardizes the data so we can compare different races/ethnicities. On a standardized scale of 1,000,000 people, it was found that those raw numbers translated to a rate of 7.49 for Blacks, 5.49 for Native Americans, 3.45 for Hispanics/Latinos, 2.95 for Whites, and 1.34 for Asian/Pacific Islanders. What this means is that Blacks are killed at a higher rate than other races/ethnicities given their representative proportion within the population. Another way to look at this is for every 7.49 Black people killed by or in the custody of law enforcement, 2.95 White people are killed. For that same year, the *Washington Post* reported that "991 people [were] shot dead by police" (visited March 4, 2017). Twenty-six percent of the people were Black (n = 258), 50%

were White (n = 495), 17.4% were Hispanic (n = 172), and 6.6% were other or unknown (n = 66). In the circumstances surrounding these killings it was reported that 730 (73.7%) were in response to an attack in progress, 217 (21.9%) had "other" circumstances, and 44 were undetermined. In the "other" category, an examination of cases listed showed that many incidents arose as the result of a response of an officer to a domestic dispute call, a traffic situation (fleeing, trying to hit officers with a vehicle, pulling a weapon from within a vehicle), calls for assistance with someone acting out behaviorally, oftentimes brandishing a weapon and threatening the lives of others (and/or may have had a mental health issue), situations in which it appears the victim was seeking out "suicide by cop"—a phenomenon in which a person engages officers in a manner that will precipitate deadly force by police (Mohandie, Meloy, & Collings, 2009), and accidents. It is the cases in which those who are killed are unarmed that seem to draw the greatest criticism and pose the most questions. The *Washington Post* reported that 94 of the 991 killed in 2015 were unarmed at the time of their deaths. In that same year, *The Guardian* reported that of the 1,146 killings they researched, 234 (or 20%) of victims were unarmed (see additional raw numbers of victims listed earlier in this paragraph). 30.7% of Native American victims were unarmed, 26% of Black victims were unarmed, 20% of Asian/Pacific Islanders victims were unarmed, 19% of Hispanic/Latino victims were unarmed, and 18% of White victims were unarmed.

Given this information on police killings, in particular the disproportionate rate of killings reported by *The Guardian*, it is important for us to examine if violent altercations with police initially stem from racial bias and stereotyping endemic to our institutions of justice or individual acts of rogue justice agents. In 2015, the Department of Justice (DOJ) investigation into the police and court practices in Ferguson Missouri, found that between 2012 and 2014, "African Americans account for 85% of vehicle stops, 90% of citations, and 93% of arrests made by FPD officers, despite comprising only 67% of Ferguson's population" (p. 4). The DOJ report also found that in documented cases of police use of force, nearly 90% was against African Americans, and in every case of a canine bite the victim was African American. The 2016 DOJ report on policing in Baltimore, Maryland, found similar results; African Americans were disproportionately represented relative to their representation in the population in the areas of stops and searches as pedestrians, as drivers as well as searches of vehicles, and in criminal offences charged, especially in arrests for drug possession.

In many cases of police shootings, officers may only be held accountable in an employment, but not criminal capacity. The investigations into police shootings are generally handled internally by the police department, and, if referred to the local prosecutor, pressures to maintain a working relationship between the two entities rarely lead to criminal prosecution, and even rarer is a conviction (Amnesty International USA, 2015). In addition to the DOJ reports on whole police departments, another indication of the culpability and responsibility of officers and police departments are the civil payouts to victims or their families. Civil cases can have advantages for police departments because they can settle cases with victims and their families and keep the details of cases out of the public view. In many of these cases, the officers may not have been charged, or even acquitted, but civil payouts, in and of themselves, reveal that an individual in some way has been harmed by the entity who is paying. Eric Garner's family, for example, won $5.9 million after he was killed by officers on Staten Island in New York (Feuer, 2016).

In addition to the individual killings by police, many questions have been raised about the militarized police response to the protests which have erupted following many of these shootings, not only in the cities where they occurred, but around the country. Police have responded in full riot gear, confronting many peaceful protesters and using less than lethal means to disperse crowds, such as tear gas, pepper spray, and rubber bullets. Equally concerning to many Americans has been the multi-agency militarized response to the Dakota Access Pipeline (DAPL) in North Dakota, where police used water cannons in freezing temperatures, as well as rubber bullets, against protesters.

Clearly the issue of police-community interactions, especially when they result in the perpetration of harm to individuals, is something that requires deeper investigation and immediate remedies. In a speech at Georgetown University, FBI Director James Comey stated there were a number of "hard truths" that we had to confront in order for us to resolve the fracture that exists between law enforcement and groups that have been mistreated by the agents of justice (see Appendix 1 for the full transcript of Director Comey's speech on race and law enforcement).

Victims of the Courts

Closely related to victims of police violence, are those victims who end up in the courts following harmful or discriminatory police practices, compounded by the actions within the courts. Westervelt and Cook (2010, p. 261) argue that "exonerees are victims of the state" in their article where they apply the victimology of state crime framework, previously discussed, of Kauzlarich, Matthews, and Miller (2001) to wrongful convictions. In these cases, numerous factors come together to result in the wrongful conviction and the harms committed by the state. Police are largely protected by an internal police culture, and an external culture which frequently believes an officer over a suspect based on an ideology that police only go after guilty people (Westervelt & Cook, 2010). In the courtroom, the accused and the prosecutor are not evenly matched, with the accused often putting their life in the hands of an over-burdened, court-appointed attorney, whereas the prosecutor has the full weight, and funding, of the state to throw at a capital case (Westervelt & Cook, 2010). In order to be exonerated, the wrongfully convicted might fight against the same institutional actors and policies that convicted and incarcerated them in the first place.

Once an individual is exonerated, the victimization doesn't end there. Exonerees are rarely compensated by the states who took away their freedom for, on average, between seven and nine years (Westervelt & Cook 2010). Many of these wrongfully convicted individuals must rely on family, friends, or the few non-profits to assist them with restarting their lives. Additionally, the state doesn't automatically expunge their record or fully restore their civil rights; they must have a layer to do that (Westervelt & Cook 2010). This can create barriers to employment and obstacles to the freedoms enjoyed by people who are not formally labelled as criminals. Lack of employment can also impact the ability of an exoneree to access any much needed healthcare or mental health assistance.

The exonerees themselves and their families are not the only victims in the case of wrongful convictions. The primary and secondary victims might experience trauma with the release of an individual. Those victims, if living, or the families of a deceased victim may no longer have the name and face of an "offender" to assign blame for the original crime. Hopefully, as discussed later in this book, a victim's advocate has kept in contact with the victim or their family and kept them informed of the exoneree's attempts to gain their freedom so their release may be less of a shock.

Victims of Corrections

Claims of human rights violations, unjust treatment, and state crimes against the incarcerated in jails and prisons in the Unites States have been made by a variety of organizations. Claims about racial disparities in sentencing, juvenile sentencing to adult facilities, life sentences for non-violent crimes, the ongoing use of the death penalty, jail and prison overcrowding, use of solitary confinement, privatization of prisons, slavery-like labor in prisons, classification and confinement of transgender/ gender non-conforming individuals, lack of health-care, and concerns about the treatment of the elderly all have been raised about US facilities on a widespread and systematic basis (see numerous Amnesty International and Human Rights Watch reports on US prisons).

The specific case of the forced sterilization of female prisoners in California illustrates the state harm committed against inmates in American prisons. According to the California State Auditor Report (2014) 144 women were sterilized between 2005 and 2013 through tubal ligation under circumstances which bring up questions about informed consent and the legality of the procedures. For example, The Center for Investigative Reporting talked with a woman named Kimberly Jeffery who, once she had turned down the suggestion of a tubal ligation at a prenatal check-up, said that Dr. Heinrich again pressured her when she went into labor, after she had been sedated and was already strapped down (Johnson, 2013). The state of California prison medical system had already been under a receivership due to a court order following a claim of "constitutionally inadequate medical care" (California State Auditor Report, 2014 p. 8). Thus, in the case of California, the state was already seen to be violating inmates' rights regarding medical care, but even under the receivership, was unable or unwilling to protect women in custody from being forced into a procedure that would impact the rest of their lives.

Responses to Violence by the Criminal Justice System

A number of social justice and social movement campaigns have started as a result of the highly publicized violence by state actors in the criminal justice system. #BlackLivesMatter was started after the death of 17-year-old Travon Martin and grew into an organization raising awareness about the violence African Americans experience at the hands of the state. Another organization focusing on similar issues is Campaign Zero (visited March 4, 2017). Their policy platform consists of the following:

1. End broken windows policing
2. Community oversight
3. Limit use of force
4. Independently investigate and prosecute
5. Community representation
6. Body cams/film the police
7. Training
8. End for-profit policing
9. Demilitarization
10. Fair police union contracts

Other organizations such as #SayHerName and #BlackTransLivesMatter focus on the violence specific groups experience at the hands of the state. #SayHerName seeks to raise awareness of the violence and deaths of Black women and girls, such as Sandra Bland, 28, who was found dead in a jail cell in Texas (African American Policy Forum, n.d.).

Environmental Crime Victims

Within the realm of corporate and state perpetrated crime lies the specific issue of **environmental crime**. In environmental crime, the victims include humans and non-human entities (to include animals and the natural environment) (Brisman & South, 2012), but are often discussed in terms of the injuries that befall humans based on purposeful acts or omissions that result in harm. Burns and Lynch (as cited in Jarrell & Ozymy, 2012) indicate that though environmental crimes are often considered "victimless" crimes or regulation violations, the deaths, injuries, and illnesses experienced by humans far outweigh deaths, injuries, and illnesses resulting from street crime. White (2009–2010) suggests that environmental victimization includes acts that typically benefit a corporation or state in a financial manner, and usually includes some sort of deceit or regulation violation that results in delayed harm to humans, animals, and the overall ecological system. In the late 1990s, Lynch proposed the term *green criminology* to examine both micro- and macro-level crimes to the environment, perpetrated on the individual level and the larger corporate and state levels (Brisman & South, 2012). Acts which might be deemed "criminal" when perpetrated on the street, are oftentimes addressed more as "regulation violations" when the perpetrator is a corporation or the state, largely due to how those acts are defined by the powers that be in legislation and should be examined within the socio-political context within which they are defined. Therefore, victims of environmental crime may never truly "see their day in *criminal* court" and thus the harm perpetrated is not acknowledged as criminal and the recovery process for these victims may be elongated or hampered completely (Jarrell & Ozymy, 2012).

Environmental crime victims can suffer physical harm, financial harm, and psychological harm, and the acts that occur, though they are addressed more in the civil area (if at all), have the same characteristics as homicide, assault, reckless endangerment, destruction of property, and other crimes typically considered "street crimes." For instance, the April 20, 2010, explosion on the Deepwater Horizon drilling rig owned by British Petroleum resulted in the deaths of 11 people and affected the lives of tens of thousands of people due to the resulting oil spill in the Gulf of Mexico (Jarrell & Ozymy, 2012). Transocean Ltd., the rig's contractor, pled guilty in 2013 to a misdemeanor-level Clean Water Act violation and paid a $1 billion fine, but no one within Transocean Ltd. was held criminally liable (Associated Press, June 4, 2014). In what is called an unprecedented act, the Department of Justice charged BP on a criminal level in the negligent deaths of the workers and obstruction of justice. BP paid a $4.5 billion-dollar criminal fine in relation to the 11 deaths and other charges associated with the explosion and resulting spill, and two BP managers went on trial in January 2014 for 11 counts of involuntary manslaughter (Atkin, January 29, 2014). Another BP executive was charged with obstruction of justice for deleting texts related to the flow rate of the spill and misrepresenting the official amount to the government — so destroying evidence and lying (Krauss & Schwartz, 2012). In another example, 4,000 people were killed instantly in the Union Carbide gas leak in Bhopal, India, in 1984 and an additional 14,000 people lost their lives within several years due to the effects of the poison (Jarrell & Ozymy, 2012), but no person from that corporation was charged with homicide, or even manslaughter.

Jarrell and Ozymy (2012) suggest that cases like the ones referenced above, which capture a great deal of media attention, are not the norm, and thus environmental crime victims in general do not receive any type of attention or recognition for their pain and suffering. Further, they noted that the Crime Victims' Rights Act (CVRA, to be discussed in Chapters 8 and 9) provided safeguards for environmental crime victims to be able to be consulted and heard from prosecutors in cases. However, when a case was brought against BP for a fire and explosion resulting in the death of 15 people and injury of 170 in 2005, the federal courts did not completely abide by the proscriptions in the act and no criminal charges were levied against the company, despite company documentation that BP executives and managers knew about and ignored major safety violations in the plant, which directly resulted in the deaths and injuries of the workers. In another case, *United States v. W.R. Grace & Co.* (2005), it was documented that numerous individuals died as a result of the asbestos they were exposed to in the workplace, but the district court over the trial initially stated that there were no victims as defined under the CVRA. The Ninth Circuit Court ultimately acknowledged the victims, but the company was acquitted of "knowingly" causing harm. In yet another case, *United States v. CITGO*, victims who testified about health issues related to nine years of exposure to toxic emissions from improperly operated oil-water separators in Corpus Christi, TX, were deemed ineligible as victims under the CVRA because the judge ruled that their symptoms could have been the result of old age and/or smoking, despite testimony from scientific and medical experts. The main cause for argument with the CVRA and environmental crime victims is the terminology requiring that a crime victim is someone who is "directly and proximately harmed as a result of a federal offense" (Jarrell & Ozymy, 2012, p. 379). Because identification of a traditional "victim," with immediately identifiable harms, may not often exist in the realm of environmental crime, the courts are loathe to recognize these individuals as true crime victims (Jarrell & Ozymy, 2014). Jarrell and Ozymy (2014) found in an examination of 972 federal environmental crime cases prosecuted in criminal court that only 3% involved identifiable victimizations. Because the effects of environmental crime are oftentimes not immediate, and the victims may not fit the traditional definition of "crime victim," environmental crime victims will likely continue to be neglected in the criminal justice arena.

Workplace Violence

What Is Workplace Violence?

Workplace violence occurs when there is an act or threat by someone to commit physical violence, to intimidate or harass, and/or to engage in other threatening behaviors in the workplace (OSHA, n.d.). The actions of workplace violence perpetrators range from verbal abuse to homicide, affect nearly two million people a year (OSHA, n.d.), and cost the workforce in the United States upwards of $36 billion per year (Romano, Levi-Minzi, Rugala, and Van Hasselt, 2011). More recently, there has been a trend to divide the category into acts occurring in the workplace setting that intend to cause someone physical harm (workplace violence) and acts that intend for psychological or physical harm to occur to a worker (**workplace aggression**) (Piquero, Piquero, Craig, & Clipper, 2013). Baron and Neuman (1996) suggest that the term *workplace aggression* is probably a better term to describe the majority of harmful behaviors perpetrated at the worksite. Since the majority of articles still use the words "workplace violence" that will be the term referred to in this chapter.

Typologies of Workplace Violence

There are four separate categories for workplace violence, focusing attention on the victim-perpetrator relationship (Merchant & Lundell, 2001b). Type I incidents occur when a perpetrator has no prior relationship or dealings with anyone at the worksite; Type II incidents involve perpetrators who receive services from a worksite (receiving service, purchasing service/item, etc.); Type III incidents involve perpetrators who are currently or were formerly employed by the organization and who have a specific intent to act out against the organization; and Type IV incidents involve disputes between an employee and someone in that person's personal life, bringing the violence from outside the workplace into the worksite (Merchant & Lundell, 2001b). The Department of Labor's Occupational Safety & Health Administration (OSHA) classifies the previous typology as such: Type I, violence by strangers; Type II, violence by customers or clients; Type III, violence by co-workers (could be current or former); and Type IV, violence by personal relations (OSHA, n.d.)

Prevalence of Workplace Violence

There is no single database within which acts of workplace violence and aggression are maintained, so presenting a true incidence or prevalence number is difficult. However, from research in the field and collection of information in various forms by government agencies, some trends related to workplace violence and aggression have emerged. Duhart (2001) reported that at the end of the twentieth century, it appeared that there were about 1.7 million acts of workplace violence and aggression happening per year (Duhart, 2001). The vast majority of these acts were simple and aggravated assaults and verbal aggression. Acts of verbal aggression include threats, intimidation, verbal attacks, stalking, bullying, and harassment. Harrell (2011) reported that approximately 572,000 nonfatal violent crimes (robbery, assault, and rape/sexual assault) occurred at the workplace in 2009 alone. Of all violence reported in that year, this accounted for about 15% overall. Though the raw number appears large, in reality the risk of workplace violence is low and incidents are rare.

Piquero et al. (2013) report four major findings related to workplace violence from a review of the literature between 2000 and 2011. First, they noted that incidents of workplace violence and aggression appear to be on the decline. Harrell (2011) reported that four out of every 1,000 employed people were victims of nonfatal workplace violence in 2009 compared to 16 out of every 1,000 employed people in 1993. This basically means for the year 2009, there was a .4% chance that any given person would be a victim of workplace violence. Second, non-physical or psychological acts are more prevalent than physical acts of workplace violence and aggression (see also Baron & Neuman, 1996). Third, in general aggressors are most likely to be the general public, followed by co-workers and then supervisors. Harrell (2011) reported that for both male and female victims, strangers (i.e., the general public) perpetrated the majority of workplace violence acts (52.9% male victims and 40.9% female victims), followed by victims and offenders who were acquainted through work (customers/clients, patients, co-workers/bosses/employees) (25.5% male victims and 31.7% female victims) and then acquaintances (11.7% for male victims, 18.9% for female victims). It should be noted that supervisors were listed as the perpetrators in a very small percentage of cases (1.2% for male victims and 3.3% for female victims). And fourth, certain characteristics, specifically sex and age of victim and occupation of victim, are related to the risk of being victimized either at the workplace or on the job. Males are much more likely to be victims of violent crimes both in and out of the workplace.

However, their risk is greater in the workplace than outside of it. Harrell (2011) reports that in 2009 males accounted for 62.9% of workplace violence victims, compared to 37.1% of females. It also appears that the majority of workplace violence occurs against individuals older than those who are victims of violence outside of the workplace. 82.1% of workplace violence incidents were perpetrated against individuals who were between the ages of 25–64 versus 63.5% of nonworkplace violence incidents between 2005–2009 (Harrell, 2011).

Occupations Most at Risk of Workplace Violence

Whereas workplace violence can happen anywhere, anytime, all occupations do not share the same risk of workplace violence occurring. The factors that seem to increase one's likelihood of the potential for workplace violence include: exchanging money with people, working with volatile and/or unstable people, working alone and/or in isolated areas, working at night, providing alcohol to clients, and working in high-crime areas (Sygnatur & Toscano, 2000).

The occupational categories that show the highest rates of workplace violence include law enforcement (48/1,000), mental health (21/1,000), transportation (12/1,000), and retail sales (8/1,000). Among individual careers law enforcement officers (78/1,000), security guards (65/1,000), and bartenders (80/1,000) have the highest rates of workplace violence among occupations. Given the factors listed previously it is not surprising that these three professions tend to have the highest rates of workplace violence.

Workplace Homicides

The US Bureau of Labor Statistics reported that for 2015, workplace homicides accounted for 18.6% of all fatal occupational injuries, which is about 417 homicides overall. Data from 2012 indicate that approximately 78 people were killed in incidents where there were multiple workplace fatalities; these types of homicides accounted

"In the News" Box 6.2

The term "going postal" was first coined after the August 20, 1986, incident in which Patrick Sherrill, a postman for the Edmond, Oklahoma, post office, shot and killed 14 employees and wounded six others and then committed suicide.

The term gained popularity after additional murders committed by current or former postal employees in 1991 in New Jersey and Michigan, 1993 in Michigan and California, and 2006 in California and Oregon. The US Post Office has strongly attempted to dissuade people from using the term, as workplace homicides perpetrated by postal employees are a relatively rare occurrence, with a rate of 1.48 per 100,000 per year.

Table 6A: Number and Percentage of Workplace Homicides 1992–2015

Year	Number of Homicides/ Number of Workplace Fatalities	Percentage of Workplace Deaths Attributable to Homicide
1992	1,044/6,217	17%
1993	1,074/6,331	17%
1994	1,080/6,632	16%
1995	1,036/6,275	17%
1996	927/6,202	15%
1997	860/6,238	14%
1998	714/6,055	12%
1999	651/6,054	11%
2000*	677/5,920	11%
2001	643/5,915	11%
2002	609/5,534	11%
2003*	632/5,534	11%
2004	559/5,764	10%
2005*	567/5,734	10%
2006	540/5,840	9%
2007*	628*/5,657	11%
2008	526/5,214	10%
2009*	642/4,551	14%
2010	518/4,690	11%
2011	468/4,693	10%
2012*	463/4,383	11%
2013	404/4,585	9%
2014	409/4,821	8.4%
2015*	417/4,836	8.6%

Source: US Bureau of Labor Statistics, US Department of Labor, 2013; updated 2017.
Note: These data do not include fatal work injuries resulting from September 11 terrorist attacks.
   * Years in which a rise in homicides occurred resulting in blips to a steady decline.

for the second largest category of all multiple-fatality incidents in the entire spectrum of workplace deaths. From 1992 to 2015, it appears that workplace homicides have been on a pretty steady decline (see Table 6A).

Some of the most recent comprehensive statistics on workplace homicides exist for the year 2010; the results suggest that there were 518 workplace homicides in that year. The greatest amount of homicides occurred to those in sales occupations (131), protective service occupations (96), and transportation and material moving occupations (78). Most homicides were committed though shootings (401; 80%), with the remainder committed through stabbings (8.1%), hitting/kicking/beating (6.1%), and unknown methods (5.8%). Robbers accounted for the vast majority of workplace homicide perpetrators with approximately 40% of incidents attributable to them in a Bureau of Labor Statistics (2011) analysis of workplace homicides spanning from 1997–2010 (BLS, 2011). Other assailants accounted for about 32% of perpetrators, whereas work associates (former or current co-workers, clients/ customers) accounted for 22% of perpetrators, and relatives or other personal acquaintances accounted for roughly 8.3% of perpetrators. Going back to the typologies of workplace violence victim-offender relationships, this suggests that the majority of homicides fall under Type I offenses — criminal intent motives, followed by Type III perpetrators (current/former co-workers), Type IV — especially for women, and ending with Type II — client/customer.

Whites accounted for just over 50% of all workplace homicides and males accounted for 81.4% of the victims. Interestingly, it appears that the leading cause of death for women in the workplace is homicide. In 2012, homicide accounted for 29% of all deaths of women at the workplace. The age range most at risk for workplace homicide appears to be the 35 to 44 group, with a slight increase in 45- to 54-year-olds in 2010 only.

Two things appear evident from Table 6A: (1) all workplace fatalities (not just homicides) have declined relatively steadily since 1992, and (2) the percentage of deaths accountable to workplace homicide have been on a decline as well (aside from an increase in 2009). Indeed, Harrell (2011) reports that there was a 51% decrease in workplace homicides from 1993–2009. Could this mean that things are being done to make the workplace a safer environment?

Additional Characteristics of Workplace Violence Incidents

The majority of workplace violence victims resisted their offenders in the course of the attack. While they were just as likely as nonworkplace violence victims to engage in nonconfrontational tactics to avoid or stop the offense, they were significantly less likely to threaten or attack the perpetrator without a weapon (Harrell, 2011).

Whereas in nonworkplace violence incidents, perpetrators are often perceived to be under the influence of drugs or alcohol, this does not seem to be the case in workplace violence incidents. In only 24.5% of the cases between 2005 and 2009 the victim believed that the perpetrator was under the influence of a substance, compared to 36.6% of the time in nonworkplace violence incidents (Harrell, 2011). Weapons are relatively unlikely to be used in most nonfatal violent victimizations; however, they were significantly less likely to be used in workplace violence incidents than in their nonworkplace counteractions. Additionally, firearms were much less likely to be used in workplace violence incidents than in nonworkplace violence incidents

(5.2% vs. 10.4% respectively) (Harrell, 2011). The majority of workplace violence victims report no injury (86.7%), but when they do report an injury it is most often a minor one (11.3% minor injury versus 1.3% serious injury) (Harrell, 2011).

Workplace incidents are reported to police just under 50% of the time, which is somewhat similar to nonworkplace incidents. Males are most likely to report an incident which is contrary to nonworkplace violence incidents. Robbery is the most likely type of workplace violence to be reported (76.8%), followed by aggravated assault (64%), simple assault (42.2%) and rape/sexual assault (39.4%). Those that reported the offenses indicated that they chose to report most often because of personal reasons, either they wanted the incident to stop or be prevented from happening (31.1%) or they wanted to prevent future incidents from happening (20.5%). Those that reported for public safety-related reasons most often reported because they didn't want anyone else to suffer the same victimization from that offender (19.9%) and they felt they had a duty to let the police know about the crime (13.7%). People chose not to report most often because it was reported to a different official (38%). Other reasons not to report the crime included that the victim thought the incident was a personal matter (22%) or that the victim thought it wasn't important enough to be reported to the police (24%) (Harrell, 2011).

Causes of Workplace Violence

Some believe that there is a process to workplace violence, wherein violent behavior is often predicated by a perceived provocation or event. Additionally, individuals who perpetrate acts of violence in the workplace start out with non-fatal type behaviors, expressing themselves in what Rugala and Romano (as cited in Romano, Levi-Minzi, Rugala, & Van Hasselt, 2011) term "behaviors of concern," which consist of emotional and psychological behaviors, but not necessarily overt acts of physical violence. These acts include ruminating about an issue in the workplace for a period of time and then acting out. The authors suggest that individuals within a workplace do not typically "snap" or "go postal" and that more subtle behaviors such as ruminating over an issue and unusual writings or drawings may first be seen (see Box 6.2 for a history of the term "going postal").

Special Focus: Law Enforcement Officers Killed and Assaulted in the Line of Duty

One of the most dangerous occupations that exists is that of a law enforcement officer; therefore, a special section will focus on deaths and assaults associated with this particular occupation.

Law Enforcement Officers Feloniously Killed

Over the past ten years, 491 law enforcement officers have lost their lives due to the purposeful, felonious activities of another (see Table 6B). Within those ten years,

Table 6B: Law Enforcement Officers Killed and Assaulted (2006–2015)

Year	Number of Law Enforcement Officers Feloniously Killed	Number of Law Enforcement Officers Accidentally Killed	Number of Law Enforcement Officers Assaulted	Federal Law Enforcement Officers Killed or Assaulted
2006	48	66	58,634	1,273
2007	58	83	59,201	1,650
2008	41	68	58,792	1,349
2009	48	47	57,268	1,808
2010	56	72	53,469	1,886
2011	72	53	54,774	1,689
2012	49	47	52,901	1,858
2013	27	49	50,802	1,774
2014	51	45	48,988	1,410
2015	41	45	50,212	1,336

Source: FBI Uniform Crime Reports, Law Enforcement Officers Killed and Assaulted, 2006–2015.

homicides were most likely committed in the process of arresting someone or in a traffic pursuit or stop (see Table 6C). Suspicious persons/circumstances, unprovoked attacks, tactical situations, and responding to disturbance calls (general and domestic) all led to the deaths of over 50 law enforcement officers for each category. Ambush situations and investigative activities each led to over 20 felonious deaths each; while instances in which an officer was dealing with a prisoner or a person with mental illness, and civil disorders were the least likely events in which a homicide occurred. The year 2011 saw the largest number (72) of homicides of law enforcement officers in the last 10 years, and 2013 saw the lowest number in that decade period (23).

From 2006–2015, the average age of an officer killed in the line of duty was 38 years old and the officers worked between 10–12 years on the force. Males were most likely to be slain and the incident was most likely to occur while on duty and assigned to vehicle patrol. The majority of officers were killed with a firearm (92%) and 33–55% of the time (depending on the year) the perpetrator was only 0–5 feet away from the officer at the time of the shooting. The vast majority (68%) of officers slain on duty were wearing body armor at the time of the incident. Of the 491 officers slain in the 10-year period assessed, 47 (9.5%) were killed **while off duty**, but acting in the capacity of a law enforcement officer. December appeared to be the month with the most recorded officer homicides overall (55/491) and Thursdays and Saturdays appeared to be the most dangerous days for officers over the 10-year period (80 homicides each).

Table 6C: Circumstances Surrounding Homicides of Law Enforcement
Officers by Raw Number (2006–2015)

Year/ Circumstance	2006	2007	2008	2009	2010	2011	2012	2013	2014	2015	Total
Arrest	12	17	9	8	14	10	7	6	4	5	92
Traffic Pursuits/Stops	8	11	8	8	9	14	9	2	8	6	83
Suspicious Person/ Circumstance	6	4	7	4	8	12	8	5	8	8	70
Unprovoked Attack	9	7	5	9	11	6	1	4	1	3	56
Tactical Situation	2	3	7	5	3	13	5	4	4	7	53
Disturbance Calls—General	6	3	1	4	2	5	3	3	10	0	37
Ambush	1	9	1	6	2	2	3	1	7	4	36
Investigative Activity	0	1	2	0	2	4	6	1	5	1	22
Disturbance Calls— Domestic	2	2	0	2	4	5	1	1	1	3	21
Handling, Transporting or Maintaining Custody of Prisoner	1	1	1	2	1	1	3	0	0	2	12
Handling Person with Mental Illness	1	0	0	0	0	0	3	0	3	2	9
Civil Disorder	0	0	0	0	0	0	0	0	0	0	0
Total	48	58	41	48	56	72	49	27	51	41	491

Source: FBI Uniform Crime Reports, Law Enforcement Officers Killed and Assaulted, 2006–2015.

Patterns appear to exist regarding the characteristics of the alleged assailants as well. Characteristics of the alleged assailants were that they were younger than the officers, with the offenders in the 18–24-year-old-age group (29%) accounting for the greatest number of offenders overall, and an average age of offender being between 28 and 31 for the 10-year period. Approximately 97% were male, with an average height of about 5'9"–5'10" and weighing 177–181 pounds. Over the 10-year period about 53% of offenders were White and 41% were Black assailants (289W/222B). Approximately 84% of the alleged assailants overall had prior criminal arrests, with

47% having a prior arrest for a crime of violence. Twenty-five percent of offenders had a prior arrest for assaulting an officer/resisting arrest. Twenty-four percent were under judicial supervision at the time of the homicide, 42% were known to use, deal, or possess a controlled substance (so there was a drug connection), while only 5% were known to have prior mental disorders.

SIDE NOTE: In the previous section, you read about the killing of people by law enforcement and learned about some of the different movements that were created to highlight issues surrounding the disproportionate deaths of certain groups by the criminal justice system. Clearly the issue of police-community relations, and the "hard truths" discussed by FBI Director James Comey (Appendix 1), indicate that the real problem of police-community relations is resulting in unfortunate, unnecessary deaths on both sides of the line. In 2016, we saw the media report on multiple cases of ambush-style killings of law enforcement officers by individuals reportedly responding to the disproportionate killings of African Americans. (It should be noted that representatives from the #Blacklivesmatter movement spoke out against the ambush-style killings of law enforcement officers. (Workneh, 2016)). On November 2, 2016, *USA Today* reported that ambush-style killings increased by 167% in that year alone (2016). In response to the ambush-style killings of Officers Rafael Ramos and Wenjian Liu in Brooklyn, New York, on December 20, 2014, and as a reaction to the #Blacklivesmatter movement, the #Bluelivesmatter movement was created to support the law enforcement community under the scrutiny of the media. The movement also called for the provision of law enforcement officers with lifesaving equipment and training, while also providing assistance to families of officers who are killed in the line of duty (https://bluelivesmatter.blue/organization/).

Law Enforcement Officers Accidentally Killed

Five hundred and seventy-seven law enforcement officers were accidentally killed in the line of duty between 2006 and 2015. Forty-one percent (241) were employed by the city, 32% (187) were employed by the county, 20% (113) were employed by the state, 5% (29) were employed with federal law enforcement agencies, and 1% (7) were employed in US territories (Puerto Rico and the US Virgin Islands). Within the city breakdown, 11% were employed in cities with populations of 250,000 or more persons, 12% were employed by cities with 50,000–249,999 people, 8% were employed by cities with 10,000–49,999 people, and 10% were employed in cities with fewer than 10,000 people. Taken together, it illustrates that one is no less likely to be accidentally killed in one type of place over another.

The vast majority (52%) of accidental killings took place in the South, followed by 21% in the West, 12% in the Northeast, 13% in the Midwest, and 1% in US territories. The two age groups accounting for the largest percentages of accidental killings were 25–30 years old (20%) and 36–40 years old (17.5%). Fifty-seven percent of officers were employed between one and ten years (1–5 years = 32%, 6–10 years = 25%). Finally, about 60% of officers who were accidentally killed were alone at the time of the accident.

"In the News" Box 6.3

From the Officer Down Memorial Page:

Master Police Officer Jeremiah Montgomery Goodson, Jr.

Lumberton Police Department, North Carolina
End of Watch: Tuesday, July 17, 2012

Bio & Incident Details

Age: 32	**Incident Date:** 7/17/2012
Tour: 6 years	**Weapon:** Handgun
Badge #: Not available	**Suspect:** Apprehended
Cause: Gunfire	

Master Police Officer Jeremiah Goodson was shot and killed as he and another officer attempted to arrest a man at a local gas station in the 5000 block of Fayetteville Road.

Officer Goodson, who was off duty, was at the gas station and recognized the subject as being wanted on outstanding warrants for possession of a firearm by a felon and failure to appear in court. He called the police department and notified other officers of the subject's location. Another officer arrived and the two began to approach the car the subject was sitting in. The man opened fire from inside the vehicle, striking Officer Goodson in the chest. The second officer and other responding units took the man into custody.

The 27-year-old ex-convict, who was charged with first degree murder, is being held without bond in the Cumberland County Jail. He was released from prison in 2007 after serving two years and seven months for a felony breaking and entering conviction. Since 2004 he has been convicted of breaking and entering, larceny, receiving stolen property, motor vehicle theft, and possession of a firearm by a felon. The Robeson County District Attorney said he would be seeking the death penalty in this case.

Officer Goodson had served with the Lumberton Police Department for six years. He is survived by his expectant wife, son, daughter, parents, and two siblings.

Read more: http://www.odmp.org/officer/21334-master-police-officer-jeremiah-montgomery-goodson-jr#ixzz34vhwA4P9.

Reprint permission granted.

The vast majority of accidental killings came as the result of automobile accidents (59%) (see Table 6D). The remaining circumstances surrounding the killings included being struck by vehicles (16%), motorcycle accidents (9%), other accidental

Table 6D: Circumstances Surrounding Accidental Killings of Law Enforcement Officers by Raw Number (2006–2015)

Year/Circum-stance	2006	2007	2008	2009	2010	2011	2012	2013	2014	2015	Total
Automobile Accident	38	49	39	34	45	30	23	23	28	29	**338**
Struck by Vehicle	13	12	13	7	11	5	10	9	6	7	**93**
Traffic stop, roadblock, etc.	*4*	*7*	*1*	*3*	*4*	*3*	*2*	*1*	*1*	*2*	*28*
Directing traffic, assisting motorist, etc.	*9*	*5*	*12*	*4*	*7*	*2*	*8*	*8*	*5*	*5*	*65*
Motorcycle Accident	8	6	6	3	7	4	6	4	6	4	**54**
Accidental Shooting	4	4	2	2	3	4	2	2	2	2	**27**
Crossfire, mistaken for subject, firearm mishap	*3*	*4*	*2*	*2*	*1*	*3*	*2*	*2*	*1*	*1*	*21*
Training session	*0*	*0*	*0*	*0*	*1*	*0*	*0*	*0*	*1*	*1*	*3*
Self-inflicted, cleaning mishap	*1*	*0*	*0*	*0*	*1*	*1*	*0*	*0*	*0*	*0*	*3*
Other Accidental	0	6	5	1	3	4	1	4	2	1	**27**
Aircraft Accident	3	3	2	1	2	1	3	1	0	1	**17**
Fall	0	1	0	0	1	2	3	4	0	1	**12**
Drowning	0	2	1	0	0	3	0	2	1	0	**9**
Total	66	83	68	48	72	53	48	49	45	45	577

Source: FBI Uniform Crime Reports, Law Enforcement Officers Killed and Assaulted, 2006–2015.

circumstances (5%), accidental shootings (5%), aircraft accidents (3%), falls (2%), and drowning (1.5%).

Law Enforcement Officers Assaulted

From 2006 to 2015, 556,095 local- and state-level law enforcement officers were assaulted in the line of duty, but the numbers do seem to be declining, from 58,364 in 2009 to 50,212 in 2015 (FBI UCR Law Enforcement Officers Killed or Assaulted, Table 75). Despite the decline, on average about 10% of all officers are assaulted each year, with a general range of 9%–12%. Not all officers who are assaulted suffer from injuries post-incident, however; between 26–28% of officers assaulted report injuries in association with the assault. Most often the injury is the result of personal attack (hands, feet, etc.) and accounts for between 27–30% of injuries, followed by attack with other dangerous weapons, which accounts for about 22–27% of injuries, knives which account for 10–14% of injuries, and lastly, firearms, which account for between 8–11% of injuries. Most assault incidents occurred between midnight and 2 am, which typically accounts for 15–16% of all assaults, followed by 10pm to midnight. The least amount of assaults appears to occur between 6am and 8am and usually accounts for about 2.5% of assaults.

Table 6E illustrates the circumstances under which assaults on officers typically occur. The most dangerous situation for officers is responding to a domestic disturbance. These types of calls account for about one-third of all assaults on officers across the 10-year period of time examined (2006–2015). Two other circumstances that stand out as especially dangerous for officers include attempting arrests, which accounts for about 15% of all assaults, and handling/transporting prisoners, which typically accounts for between 12–14% of assaults. "Other" circumstances also tend to account for a great percentage of assaults on officers, accounting for 14–16% of assaults each year. Traffic pursuits and investigating suspicious persons or situations both tend to account for approximately 10% of assault situations.

The vast majority of officers who were assaulted were in one-officer patrol units (approximately 62–64% over the 10-year period) and the assaults were most likely to be in the form of personal weapons (hands, feet, etc.). Personal weapons accounted for approximately 80% of assaults, whereas the use of firearms and knives were less common (4% and 2% respectively). Other weapons were used in about 14% of assaults overall.

Other Criminal Justice System Assaults and Homicides Due to Workplace Violence

Just as law enforcement officers encounter dangerous persons on a daily basis, so too do other representatives of the criminal justice system, namely in the court system and corrections. Piquero et al. (2013) cited research done by Konda, Reichard, and Tiesman that estimated that about 125,200 correctional officers were treated in medical facilities for injuries incurred on the job. Of those, approximately 38% were the result of assaults and other violent acts (47,576 injuries). Furthermore, there were 113 fatalities of correctional officers from 1999 to 2008, of which 40% (46 fatalities) were due to assaults or violent acts.

In a study by Harris, Kirschner, Rozek, and Weiner (2001) 1,029 judges were surveyed and interviewed about violence experienced on the job. Only 1% reported being physically attacked, but 52% reported that they had received some type of threat of physical harm. They tended to write off the threats as indicating that the perpetrators of the threats were likely just venting.

Table 6E: Circumstances Surrounding Assaults on Officers While on Duty by Percent

Year/Raw Number and Circumstance	2006 58,634	2007 59,201	2008 58,792	2009 57,268	2010 53,469	2011 54,774	2012 52,901	2013 49,851	2014 48,315	2015 50,212
Disturbance Calls	31%	32	32	33	33	33	33	31	31	32
Attempting Arrests	16	15	15	15	15	15	15	16	15	16
Handling Prisoners	12	12.5	12	13	13	13	13	13	13	12
Investigating Suspicious Persons/Circumstances	9.5	9	9	9	9.5	9.5	9.5	9	9	9
Traffic Pursuit/Stop	11	11	10.5	9.5	9	9	8.5	9	8	8
Handling the Mentally Ill	2	2	2	2	2	2.5	2.5	3	3	3
Burglary in Progress	1.5	1.5	1.5	1.5	2	1.5	1.5	1.5	1.5	2
Civil Disorder	1	1	1	1.5	1.5	1.5	1.5	1	1.5	1.5
Robbery in Progress	1	1	1	1	1	1	1	1	1	1
Ambush Situation	.5	.5	.5	.5	.5	.5	.5	.5	.5	.5
Other	15	15	15.5	14	15	15	15	15	16	15

Source: FBI Uniform Crime Reports, Law Enforcement Officers Killed and Assaulted, 2006–2015, adapted from Table 73 each year—rounded to nearest .5.

Addressing Workplace Violence

Prevention

One of the primary ways to reduce workplace violence is for organizations to implement violence prevention plans in their workplaces (Romano et al., 2011). Romano et al. (2011) suggest that workplace violence is not a sudden occurrence; it is something that can be recognized when employees demonstrate behaviors of concern. These behaviors include depression or sadness, irritability and hostility, verbal abuse, hypersensitivity to comments and criticism, coupled with decreased work performance (missing days at work, tardiness, decreased productivity, etc.). These types of behaviors might help to warn someone of a Type III type episode that could occur. Type IV episodes, in which problems in an employee's personal life invade the workplace could be noticed through a worker's negative affect, disruptive phone calls/emails/texts, inability to concentrate, and physical injuries or bruises. Coworkers could also become tardy or miss more work and may experience unplanned and disruptive visits from current or former partners.

Merchant and Lundell (2001a) suggest that prevention should be approached on multiple levels, including environmental, organizational/administrative, and behavioral/interpersonal. On the environmental level, there should be an assessment of entrances and exits, lighting, walkways and stairways, security hardware, and other such controls to discourage motivated offenders from targeting a potential organization. Similar to Romano et al. (2011), Merchant and Lundell (2001a) suggest that programs and policies be put into place, along with practice, to maintain a safe work environment. Finally, Merchant and Lundell (2001a) suggest training staff to recognize possible behavior indicators that could end in violence at the workplace.

When prevention doesn't work, intervention as early as possible is the next step (Romano et al., 2011). It is suggested there be two points at which intervention strategies can be implemented, action points and flash points. **Action points** exist when a coworker notices the behavior of another has changed and that person may be on the path toward committing a violent act within the workplace. The person with the concerning behavior can be taken aside by coworkers and presented an opportunity to vent. If it appears that the coworker is still on the path toward a potential violent act, Romano et al. (2011) suggest notifying supervisors, human resources, an ethics or similar-type hotline, employee assistance program, or security. **Flash points** occur when the workplace violence act is starting to or has taken place. It is at this time that coworkers will only be able to talk about the situation in hindsight and try to recognize a point at which they noticed that something might be off. Once a workplace violence incident has started, it is imperative that employees focus on survival, and realize that they have to take care of themselves as law enforcement may not be able to arrive until after the incident has ended. Romano et al. (2011) suggest that all organizations create, disseminate, and practice strategies for responding to life-threatening workplace violence scenarios (e.g., active shooter and hostage taking) so that if these types of events do occur, employees will have an idea of how to react.

"In the News" Box 6.4

BSO Justified in Workplace Violence Firing, Arbitrator Rules

April 29, 2014

By Brittany Wallman, *Sun Sentinel*

The Broward Sheriff's Office was justified in firing an employee accusing of threatening to kill other BSO employees, an arbitrator ruled.

Zach Flamberg, an information technology employee and gun enthusiast, was fired a year ago after he was accused of making threatening comments about his co-workers.

Flamberg accidentally brought a strip of bullets into the office, and he was accused of joking to a co-worker that one of the bullets was engraved with the name of then-executive officer Donald Prichard.

Though co-workers gave conflicting statements during the BSO investigation, Flamberg also was accused of saying, four days after the movie theater mass-shooting in Aurora, Colo., that the shooter "got it wrong" but he was going to "get it right," and that he had a list of 70 people at BSO he wanted to kill.

Flamberg appealed his termination, but in binding arbitration, Phyllis Almenoff said she didn't believe his story.

"The BSO's version of events is credible," Almenoff's ruling says. "Zachary Flamberg's version of events is not credible."

Almenoff said Flamberg's threats were particularly frightening because he "owns an arsenal of firearms and ammunition, including assault weapons and pistols," and is "capable of carrying out his threats."

Flamberg, 58, has terminal cancer and is without health insurance after the termination, which he likened to a death sentence. He has a pending federal lawsuit against BSO for the termination, but said Tuesday that he can no longer afford to pursue it. He said he was falsely accused.

"I did my best for the community, which is why I joined BSO," Flamberg said, "and if this my fate, then this is my fate. But I stand by my word, and I'm sorry I'm not going to work anymore with some really great people.... I knew I was going to die, but I didn't want to go to my grave with someone destroying my reputation."

http://articles.sun-sentinel.com/2014-04-29/news/fl-bso-flamberg-arbitration-20140429_1_bso-arbitrator-rules-zach-flamberg#.U6CMJXg31_0.email

Reprint permission granted by the *Sun Sentinel*.

Summary and Conclusion

Exploring the topics of white-collar crime and workplace violence illustrate that victimizations can occur in many different domains and are very complicated to deal with both in organizational and the work environments. Some of the issues common to these two topics include who is really "in charge" of investigating these types of acts. Victims of white-collar crimes may take years, if ever, to be identified as victims. The range of harms resulting from these crimes can be difficult to identify and offenders, particularly states and corporations, are hardly ever held accountable for the harms they inflict. For workplace violence, is it the place of employment that is the ultimate authority or is it the criminal justice system? Another issue is the length of time it may take one to recover from these acts. People need to work, so it may be difficult for a victim to figure out how to go back to that environment after a victimization has occurred. These two areas will continue to garner a great deal of attention as these issues are worked out.

Key Terms

White-collar crime

Occupational crime

Corporate crime

Governmental crime

Political white-collar crime

State crime

State-corporate crimes

Environmental crime

Workplace violence

Workplace aggression

Action points

Flash points

Discussion Questions

1. In your own words, define as broadly as possible white-collar crime.
3. Describe the different forms of occupational crimes.
4. Discuss why defining white-collar crimes has been so challenging.
5. Identify and describe the six propositions of a victimology of state crime.
6. What jobs are most dangerous and what can be done to decrease potential harm in those workplaces?

Websites for Further Information

International State Crime Research Center: http://statecrimecenter.com/.

American Society of Criminology, Division on Critical Criminology & Social Justice: http://divisiononcriticalcriminology.com/.

National White-Collar Crime Center: http://www.nw3c.org/.

OSHA: https://www.osha.gov/OshDoc/data_General_Facts/factsheet-workplace-violence.pdf.

CDC, Workplace Violence: http://www.cdc.gov/niosh/topics/violence/.

#BlueLivesMatter. https://bluelivesmatter.blue/organization/.

References

African American Policy Forum. (n.d.) #SayHerName. Retrieved from http://www.aapf.org/sayhername/.

Amnesty International USA. (2015). *Deadly force: Police use of lethal force in the United States.* Retrieved from www.amnestyusa.org/deadlyforce.

Associated Press. (2014, June 4). Court rules BP must pay Clean Water Act fines for Deepwater Horizon spill. Retrieved from http://www.theepochtimes.com/n3/715560-court-rules-bp-must-pay-clean-water-act-fines-for-deepwater-horizon-spill/.

Atkin, E. (2014, January 29). BP rig supervisors must face manslaughter charges for Deepwater Horizon deaths, judge rules. Retrieved from http://thinkprogress.org/climate/2014/01/29/3220691/deepwate-r-death-jury/.

Baron, R. A., & Neuman, J. H. (1996). Workplace violence and workplace aggression: Evidence on their relative frequency and potential causes. *Aggressive Behavior, 22,* 161–173.

Brisman, A., & South, N. (2012). A green-cultural criminology: An exploratory outline. *Crime, Media, Culture, 9*(2), 115–135.

Bureau of Labor Statistics. (2011). *Census of fatal occupational injuries.* US Department of Labor, Bureau of Labor Statistics in cooperation with state, New York City, District of Columbia, and federal agencies. Retrieved from http://www.bls.gov/iif/oshwc/cfoi/work_hom.pdf.

California State Auditor Report. (2014). Sterilization of female inmates: Some inmates were sterilized unlawfully, and safeguards designed to limit occurrences of the procedure failed. Retrieved from www.auditor.ca.gov.

Campaign Zero (visited March 4, 2017). Retrieved from https://www.joincampaign zero.org/#vision.

Department of Justice. (2015). *Investigation of the Ferguson Police Department.*

Department of Justice. (2016). *Investigation of the Baltimore City Police Department.*

Duhart, D. T. (2001). *Violence in the workplace, 1993–1999, National Crime Victimization Survey, Special Report.* Washington, DC: US Department of Justice, Office of Justice Programs, Bureau of Justice Statistics. NCJ 190076.

Faust, K., & Kauzlarich, D. (2008). Hurricane Katrina victimization as a state crime of omission. *Critical Criminology, 16*(2), 85–103.

FBI. (2015a). *Arrests, Table 43.* Retrieved from https://ucr.fbi.gov/crime-in-the-u.s/2015/crime-in-the-u.s.-2015/tables/table-43.

FBI. (2015b). *UCR Law Enforcement Officers Killed or Assaulted, Table 75.* Retrieved from https://ucr.fbi.gov/crime-in-the-u.s/2015/crime-in-the-u.s.-2015/police-employee-data/police-employee-data.

Feuer, A. (2016). In police misconduct lawsuits, potent incentives point to a payout. *New York Times.* Retrieved from https://www.nytimes.com/2016/08/17/nyregion/police-misconduct-lawsuit-settlements.html.

Friedrichs, D. (2004). *Trusted criminals: White collar crime in contemporary society* (2nd ed.). Belmont, CA: Thomson-Wadsworth.

The Guardian (visited March 4, 2017). The counted: People killed by police in the U.S. https://www.theguardian.com/us-news/ng-interactive/2015/jun/01/the-counted-police-killings-us-database.

Harrell, E. (2011). *Workplace violence, 1993–2009, National Crime Victimization Survey and the Census of Fatal Occupational Injuries, Special Report.* Washington, DC: US Department of Justice, Office of Justice Programs, Bureau of Justice Statistics. NCJ 233231.

Harris, D. J., Kirschner, C. L., Rozek, K. K., & Weiner, N. A. (2001). Violence in the judicial workplace: One state's experience. *The Annals of the American Academy of Political and Social Science, 576*(3), 38–53.

Hjelmgaard, K. (2016, November 2). Ambush style killings of police up 167% this year. *USA Today.* Retrieved from http://www.usatoday.com/story/news/nation/2016/11/02/ambush-style-killings-police-up-300/93155124/.

Jarrell, M. L., & Ozymy, J. (2012). Real crime, real victims: Environmental crime victims and the Crime Victims' Rights Act (CVRA). *Crime, Law & Social Change, 58,* 373–389.

Jarrell, M. L., & Ozymy, J. (2014). Few and far between: Understanding the role of the victim in federal environmental crime prosecutions in the United States. *Crime, Law & Social Change, 61*(5), 563–584.

Johnson, C. G. (2013). Female inmates sterilized in California prisons without approval. The Center for Investigative Reporting. Retrieved from http://cironline.org/reports/female-inmates-sterilized-california-prisons-without-approval-4917.

Kauzlarich, D., Matthews, R., & Miller, W. (2001). Toward a victimology of state crime. *Critical Criminology, 10*, 173–194.

Kindy, K. (Dec. 8, 2015). *FBI to sharply expand system for tracking fatal police shootings.* The Washington Post, National Section, https://www.washingtonpost.com/national/fbi-to-sharply-expand-system-for-tracking-fatal-police-shootings/2015/12/08/a60fbc16-9dd4-11e5-bce4-708fe33e3288_story.html?utm_term=.33973c41583e.

Kramer, R. (1986, May). The Pinto prosecutor: An interview with Michael A. Cosentino. Academy of Criminal Justice Sciences White Paper Series. *ACJS Today*, 3–5.

Kramer, R. (1992). The space shuttle Challenger explosion: A case study of state-corporate crime. In K. Schlegel & D. Weisburd (Eds.), *White collar crime reconsidered* (pp. 212–241). Boston: Northeastern University Press.

Krauss, C., & Schwartz, J. (2012, November 15). BP will plead guilty and pay over $4 billion. *The New York Times.* Retrieved from http://www.nytimes.com/2012/11/16/business/global.

Matthews, R. A., & Kauzlarich, D. (2007). State crimes and state harms: A tale of two definitional frameworks. *Crime, Law and Social Change, 48*, 43–55.

Merchant, J. A., & Lundell, J. A. (2001a). *Workplace violence: A report to the nation.* Iowa City, IA: Injury Prevention Resource Center, The University of Iowa.

Merchant, J. A., & Lundell, J. A. (2001b). Workplace violence intervention research workshop, April 5–7, 2000, Washington, DC: Background, rationale, and summary. *American Journal of Preventive Medicine, 20*(2), 135–140.

Mohandie, K., Meloy, J. R., Collins, P. I. (2009). Suicide by cop among officer-involved shooting cases. *Journal of Forensic Sciences, 52*(2), 456–462.

Office of Safety and Health Administration. (n.d.). *Workplace violence.* Retrieved from www.osha.gov/SLTC/workplaceviolence/.

Piquero, N. L., Piquero, A. R., Craig, J. M., & Clipper, S. (2013). Assessing research on workplace violence, 2000–2012. *Aggression and Violent Behavior, 18*, 383–394.

Reiman, J. (2001). *The rich get richer and the poor get prison: Ideology, class, and criminal justice* (6th ed.). Boston: Allyn and Bacon.

Romano, S. J., Levi-Minzi, M. E., Rugala, E. A., & Van Hasselt, V. B. (2011). Workplace violence prevention: Readiness and response. *FBI Law Enforcement Bulletin, 80*(1), 1–10.

Schewendinger, H., & Schewendinger, J. (1970). Defenders of order or guardians of human rights? *Issues in Criminology, 5*, 123–157.

Sygnatur, E. F., & Toscano, G. A. (2000). *Work-related homicides: The facts. Compensation and working conditions.* Office of Safety, Health, and Working Conditions, Bureau of Labor Statistics.

The Washington Post (visited March 4, 2017). Fatal force. https://www.washington post.com/graphics/national/police-shootings-2016/.

Westervelt, S. D. & Cook, K. J. (2010). Framing innocents: The wrongly convicted as victims of state harm. *Crime, Law and Social Change, 53*, 259–275.

White, R. (2009–2010). Environmental victims and resistance to state crime through transnational activism. *Social Justice, 36*(3), 46–60.

Workneh, L. (2016) Don't Blame Black Lives Matter for the Deaths of Dallas Cops. Retrieved from http: www.huffingtonpost.com/entry/dont-blame-black-lives-matter-for-the-deaths-of-dallas-cops_us_577f9409e4b01edea78d6514.

Chapter 7: Hate Crimes and Cybercrime

In some situations, a crime that has already been defined can be conducted with an additional motive or format in mind. Victims of hate crimes and cybercrimes both rely on accurately defining the motive (hate crimes) and/or the mode within which the offense takes place (cybercrimes). In the case of a hate crime, the form of the crime may be similar to traditional crimes like assault, theft, or arson. What makes these crimes distinct from an assault, theft, or arson is that the victim may have been targeted due to a characteristic he or she has, such as race or ethnicity, religious affiliation, sexual orientation, and/or an additional physical characteristic of the primary target of the offender. A key piece of identification of a hate crime relies on ascertaining the motivation of the offender. For victims of cybercrimes, again, a "typical" crime may occur, but the use of the Internet may provide for additional means by which an offender can harm the victim overall. Fraud, child pornography, stalking … these are all crimes in and of themselves, but through the Internet a whole slew of new methods to harm arise.

Hate Crimes

At their core, **hate crimes** or **bias crimes** are separated from other crimes by one very important feature: motive. While they can take a variety of forms, such as murder, assault, and property crime, the motivation of bias or hatred towards the victim due to some perceived or real factor characterizes these crimes as distinct from others. It is important to note that these terms (*hate crimes* and *bias crimes*) have been used interchangeably by both legislatures and academics, but to retain consistency, we will use hate crimes throughout.

During the course of history, groups have struggled against each other for the control of scarce resources and society as a whole. The groups which claimed dominance often were able to maintain control over other groups by identifying some sort of difference based on appearance or religion. This practice of "othering" took many forms throughout history, from slavery to complete elimination of the outside group, a practice today known as genocide.

Our current understanding of hate crimes in the US is the result of the work of the various human rights movements discussed in this book so far. The Civil Rights Movement and the violence perpetrated against Blacks in the Jim Crow era laid the foundation for understanding the problems of prejudice, discrimination, and the role of violence as enforcement of these beliefs. During this period, the focus of bias and hate was largely on race. The locus of types of victims who experience bias based on characteristics was expanded in the 1960s and 1970s due to the Women's Rights Movement and the Gay Rights Movement. Finally, the Victims' Rights Movement crossed many of the barriers between such groups and aided in the establishment of more encompassing hate crime legislation seen today.

History

The first US hate crime law was passed in Wisconsin in 1981 and was based off of an Anti-Defamation League model piece of legislation (ADL Hate Crime Laws, 2012). According to Grattet and Jenness (2001, p. 673), these early models of legislation "included: institutional vandalism (vandalism directed at religious institutions), intimidation (including assault, trespass, vandalism, or harassment), a civil action for both kinds of crime, data collection, and police training law."

According to Shively (2005, p. 2),

> State hate crime statutes differ in terms of: (1) the specific traits legally defined as targets of hate crime motivation; (2) whether and how they address criminal penalties and civil remedies; (3) the range of crimes covered; (4) whether the statutes require data collection, and for what types of crimes; and (5) whether training about hate crime is required for law enforcement personnel.

A variety of approaches are used when constructing hate crime legislation at the state level. One strategy is to create penalty enhancements for hate crime offenders (Shively, 2005). Penalty enhancements add additional time to a traditional sentence because of the motivation based on prejudice. Another strategy is to define new offenses as hate crimes. As Shively (2005) points out, this may not technically be accurate. According to Shively (2005, p. 26), some states may only be redefining already existing crimes and enhancing penalties, making these strategies "functionally equivalent."

In 1990 the Hate Crime Statistics Act was passed by Congress and in 1994 the FBI released the first batch of supplemental hate crime data reporting on data collected from 1992 with the annual UCR. The original language stated that "the Attorney

General shall acquire data, for each calendar year, about crimes that manifest evidence of prejudice based on race, religion, sexual orientation, or ethnicity" (FBI, 2012). In 1994, Congress passed the Violent Crime Control and Law Enforcement Act, which added "disability" to the FBI's definition for reporting (Shively, 2005). This act also included the Hate Crime Sentencing Enhancement Act, which provided for sentencing enhancements for hate crimes committed on federal lands, and in 1995 was also implemented by the US Sentencing Commission. Other federal legislation on hate crimes have included the 1994 and 1998 Violence Against Women Act and the Church Arson Prevention Act of 1994 (Shively, 2005).

Two seemingly unrelated events in 1998 expanded the definitions and scope of previous hate crime legislation. On June 7, 1998, James Byrd Jr., an African American, was severely beaten, chained by his ankles to the back of a pickup truck and dragged, still conscious, for three miles. James' murderers, three white supremacists, were caught and two received the death penalty, while one was sentenced to life in prison. A few months later, on October 7, 1998, Matthew Shepard, who was gay, was abducted by two men and driven to an isolated area. The men tied Matt to a fence, assaulted him, beat him, and left him for dead. He was later found, still alive, but died as a result of his injuries on October 12. Both of these crimes shocked the national consciousness and led to an expansion in hate crime legislation, both in Texas, where Byrd's death occurred, and also at the federal level.

In 2009, following the passage of the Matthew Shepard and James Byrd, Jr. Hate Crime Prevention Act, the FBI's definition was expanded to include "gender and gender identity" (FBI, 2015, About Hate Crime Statistics). In addition to expanding the definition, the Hate Crime Prevention Act allows for expanded federal jurisdiction over hate crimes in situations where "state or local officials (1) were unable or unwilling to prosecute, (2) favored federal prosecution, or (3) prosecuted, but the investigation's or trial's results failed to satisfy the federal interest to combat hate crimes" (Congressional Research Service Report for Congress 2010, Summary). The definition for a hate crime that the FBI operates under is based off the definition provided by Congress, which states "crimes that manifest evidence of prejudice based on race, gender and gender identity, religion, disability, sexual orientation, or ethnicity, including where appropriate the crimes of murder, non-negligent manslaughter, forcible rape, aggravated assault, simple assault, intimidation, arson and distruction, damage or vandalism of property" (FBI, 2015, Hate Crime Statistics Act).

Data and Research

Data on hate crimes are presented by the FBI in a separate report from the *Annual Crime in the United States* report. The data is reported as two different types of incidents; a "single-bias incident is defined as an incident which one or more offense types are motivated by the same bias," whereas a "multiple-bias incident is defined as an incident in which more than one offense type occurs and at least two offense types are motivated by different biases" (FBI). In 2015, the FBI reported on 5,850 total incidents, comprised of 6,885 offenses with 7,173 victims and 5,493 known offenders (Hate Crime Statistics, Table 1). Of those incidents, the majority (3,310) of single-bias incidents were racially, ethnically, or ancestry-based, with 1,745 incidents characterized as anti-Black, 613 incidents anti-White, and the remaining incidents dispersed among other racial and ethnic groups. This category has changed from 2014, when ethnicity, defined only as anti-Hispanic or Latino, and anti-not Hispanic or Latino was a separate category representing 648 incidents (FBI, 2014, Hate Crime Statistics, Table 1).

Religious bias made up the second largest category of bias crimes with 1,244 incidents (FBI, 2015, Hate Crime Statistics, Table 1). Anti-Jewish crimes accounted for the largest number of religious bias incidents (664) followed by anti-Islamic (257), both of which were increases from 2014 (FBI, 2015, Hate Crime Statistics, Table 1). The next largest incident group consisted of biases based on sexual orientation (1,053) with most incidents being anti-gay (male 664), followed by anti-lesbian, gay, bisexual, or transgender as a mixed group (203), and anti-lesbian (136), with the remaining divided among anti-heterosexual (19) and anti-bisexual (31) (FBI, 2015, Hate Crime Statistics, Table 1). Included in the 2015 statistics are hate crimes based on gender and gender identity, categories which were added in 2013. In the category of gender, a total of 23 incidents were reported, with 7 being anti-male and 16 anti-female (FBI 2015 Hate Crime Statistics, Table 1). Gender identity represented higher numbers than for gender with a total of 114 incidents (FBI, 2015, Hate Crime Statistics, Table 1). Of those, 73 were anti-transgender and 41 were anti-gender non-conforming.

The types of hate crimes committed are divided among crimes against persons (3,646 incidents) and crimes against property (2,338 incidents) (FBI, 2015, Hate Crime Statistics, Table 2). The largest number of incidents involved what can be described as destruction, damage, and vandalism (1,698), with the next highest being intimidation (1,495), followed by simple assaults (1,436), (FBI, 2015, Hate Crime Statistics, Table 2). In 2015, eight incidents involved murder and non-negligent manslaughter, totaling eighteen victims with nine known offenders (FBI, Hate Crime Statistics, Table 2).

The National Crime Victimization Survey has been collecting hate crime data since 2003. According to the Bureau of Justice Statistics, the "NCVS measures crimes perceived by victims to be motivated by an offender's bias against them for belonging to or being associated with a group largely identified by these characteristics" (BJS Special Report, 2013). A 2013 Bureau of Justice Statistics report based on NCVS data covers hate crime victimization from 2003–2011. The report found that an estimated 259,700 hate crime victimizations occurred from 2007 to 2011 and included both nonfatal violent crimes and property crimes associated with bias. Of these crimes, victims reported that offenders were motivated by perceived religious bias in 21% of cases and racial bias in 54% of victimizations.

Across the whole study period, from 2003–2011, men were more likely to experience hate crime victimizations than women, individuals under 18 years old were more likely to be victimized than those over 18, and people with income under $25,000 per year were most likely to be victimized. In contrast to the FBI data, for the 2003–2006 timeframe, Hispanic Americans experienced the highest rates of violent hate crime victimization (1.4/1,000) followed by Whites (0.8/1,000) and Black/African Americans (0.5/1,000). However, data from the 2007–2011 timeframe more closely resembles the FBI data, where Hispanic Americans and Black/African Americans experienced the same rates (1.0/1,000), followed by Whites (0.9/1,000).

The total percentage of violent hate crimes increased from 2003–2006 (84%) to 2007–2011 (92%), while property hate crimes decreased over the same timeframe (15% to 8%). In 25% of the violent victimizations counted as hate crimes the offender used a weapon resulting in injuries to the victim 17% of the time. In terms of location, nearly a third (27%) of violent victimizations from hate crimes happened in the vicinity of the victim's home. Additionally, 24% occurred in public places, 22% at schools, and 16% of violent hate crime victimizations occurred in commercial locations.

Both the overall reporting of hate crimes by victims to the police (46% down to 35%) and those that resulted in arrests (10% down to 4%) declined between the comparable study periods of 2003–2006 and 2007–2011. When asked why they hadn't reported to the police, 35% responded in 2003–2006 and 23% in 2007–2011 that they "dealt with it another way" or that they felt it was a "private or personal matter." Victims who reported that "they believed that police could not or would not help" increased from 2003–2006 to 2007–2011 (14% to 24%). "Fear of reprisal or getting the offender in trouble" increased as a reason for not reporting from 9% in 2003–2006 to 15% in 2007–2011.

The NCVS also collects and reports data on schools through the BJS. The report *Indicators of School Crime and Safety: 2012* found that 9% of 12–18-year-olds had been targeted by hate-related words in school during 2011. This number is down from 12% in 2001, but consistent with the survey conducted in 2009. Students were also asked about seeing hate-related graffiti in their schools. In 1999, 36% percent of students reported hate-related graffiti and the number fell to 28% in 2011. Students were asked generally about hate-related language and the findings show 11% of Black students, 10% of Hispanic students, 9% of Asian students and 8% of White students reported being targeted with hate-related words. When asked about hate-related language associated with race, 7% of Black, Asian, and Hispanic students reported being called a negative word based on their race, followed by 8% of students of other races and only 2% of Whites reporting experiencing hate-related language used against them. In addition, the study found students were also targeted by hate-related words based on religion (1.4%), disability (1.2%), gender (1.4%), and sexual orientation (1.3%).

Motivation

Levin and McDevitt (2001, cited in Shively, 2005, p. 71) identify four areas of offender motivation:

> *Thrill-seeking offenders* are motivated by the desire for excitement and power, and often go outside their "turf" and spontaneously vandalize property or attack members of groups they consider to be inferior to them (as well as vulnerable).

"In the News" Box 7.1

On April 15, 2014, Reuters.com reporter Carey Gillam published an article entitled "White Supremacist Charged with Murder in Kansas Shootings." The article discusses charges filed against Frazier Glenn Cross (a.k.a. Glenn Miller) for the murders of three people outside two different Jewish facilities. The article suggests that Cross was a high-ranking former KKK member who has spoken out about exterminating Jews for years. Cross was charged at the state level with one count of capital murder for the deaths of a 14-year-old and his grandfather and one count of premeditated murder for the killing of Terri LaManno; at the time of the article federal hate crimes charges were also possible. While none of the victims were Jewish themselves, they were engaged in activities at Jewish facilities (a Jewish community center and a retirement home). Kansas is a death-penalty state and the prosecutor was keeping that possibility open, but had not yet decided if he was going to pursue a death sentence.

To read the full article, visit: http://www.reuters.com/article/2014/04/15/us-usa-kansas-shooting-idUSBREA3C0MX20140415.

Defensive offenders are motivated by feeling a need to protect their turf or resources under conditions they consider to be threatening.
Retaliatory offenders are inspired by a desire to avenge a perceived insult or assault on their group.
Mission offenders see themselves as "crusaders" on a mission to eliminate groups they perceive to be inferior or evil.

The motivations for hate crimes will vary by offender. Childhood experiences and socialization can shape individual motivations for committing hate crimes. However, individuals and groups are embedded in the larger social context. Messages about "othering" of different groups are communicated through societal institutions and as well as governments. Therefore, while identifying the motivations on an individual level is useful, as a society we must continue to identify the hate and biases in the larger social structures. As a whole, we must all work towards a better understanding and acceptance of difference and diversity in the world.

Criticisms

Critics of hate crime legislation argue that these laws violate the First Amendment's guarantee of freedom of speech. These critics believe that hate crime laws criminalize the thoughts in an individual's head and prohibit the expression of those thoughts through their speech. However, the courts have found that legislation which specifies intimidation or harassment are in reference to language which include "direct threats" (Grattet & Jenness, 2001, p.682). In other words, "a speech act must qualify as a 'true threat,' an established standard that requires demonstration that a speaker has both the intent and the capacity to carry out the threat" (Grattet & Jenness, 2001, p. 682). Furthermore, opponents of hate crime legislation have attempted to argue that their political and ideological viewpoints are being criminalized by hate crime laws. Again, the courts have taken up this issue and expanded the understanding of hate crime laws. According to Grattet and Jenness (2001) the courts have interpreted the "because of" language in hate crime legislation and connected it to antidiscrimination laws. For example, in *Dobbins v. State* (1992) the court ruled:

> It does not matter why a woman is treated differently and a man, a black differently than a white, a Catholic differently than a Jew; it matters only that they are. So also with section 775.085 [Florida's hate crime statute]. It doesn't matter that Dobbins hated Jewish people or why he hated them; it only mattered that he discriminated against Daly by beating him because he was Jewish (in Grattet & Jenness, 2001, p. 684).

This interpretation shifts the motivation from what is inside the head of a person to the focus on the selection of the victim based on their characteristics and connects to the actions of the offender against that victim.

Another problem that has arisen with understanding and identifying victims of hate crimes is that these crimes are based off of the perception of the offender that the victim is a member of or displays characteristics of a protected category, even if the victim is not actually associated with that group. For example, following the terrorist attacks of 9/11, Americans' lack of understanding of cultural, ethnic and religious diversity around the globe created a climate where retaliations for the attack against businesses of perceived Muslims resulted in the actual targeting of individuals from India who practice Hinduism or the Sikhism religions. Another example is the increased reports of bullying in schools against kids who are perceived to be gay based off their clothes or mannerisms, when in fact those children don't identify as gay.

Addressing Hate Crimes

In 1998 a summit was held with the International Association of Chiefs of Police to discuss the issues surrounding hate crimes and to develop ways to address the problem. According to the Bureau of Justice Assistance report *Addressing Hate Crimes* (2000), three key recommendations emerged:

- Provide broad-based training for police officers at three levels: first responders, investigators, and managers.
- Introduce training for prosecutors.
- Assign responsibility for responding to hate crimes to one officer or one unit in the law enforcement agency.

From these recommendations, a variety of police officer trainings and strategies have been implemented. In 1998, the DOJ began training law enforcement officers on the skills needed to identify and investigate hate crimes, as well as provide refresher trainings. In addition, Roll Call videos and pocket-sized guides to remind officers of the information learned in those trainings were provided on a regular basis. To assist with the training of prosecutors, the American Prosecutors Research Institute created a 100-page guide intended to help prosecutors navigate hate crime prosecutions. In addition to addressing legislation and prior case examples, the guide is intended to help standardize the treatment of hate crimes in prosecutor's offices around the country.

The Anti-Defamation League has created some programs to address the problems of hate crimes which specifically target juvenile offenders. Offered in a nine-week program, the ADL created "The Juvenile Diversion Program: Learning about Differences" to teach juveniles about issues related to hate crimes, such as racism, as well as the history of civil rights and hate crimes in the US and abroad. The philosophy behind such training is that "juvenile civil rights offenders are more likely than their adult counterparts to act out of ignorance rather than deeply ingrained attitudes" (ADL, 2012, p. 11).

The Global Context

The Holocaust, committed by the Nazis in Germany during WWII, is one of the most striking examples of bias and hate crimes, amounting to crimes against humanity, war crimes, and genocide. While most well-known for targeting Jews, Hitler and his army also targeted gays as well as the disabled. In his quest to form the most perfect race, any group deemed "defective" were eliminated under the laws of the Nazi Party (Yeadon & Hawkins, 2008). Hitler and the Nazis are not the only examples of genocide in recent history. Prior to Hitler, the Ottoman Empire was accused of killing over 1 million ethnic Armenians, and Assyrians as well as Greeks, starting around 1915 and ending around 1923 (United to End Genocide). More recently, genocides have continued in the 1990s and 2000s. In the early 1990s, Yugoslavia broke apart and many ethnic groups struggled to gain power in the region. Serbs, Croats, and Bosnian Muslims all fought for control in the region, a conflict that left 96,000 people dead and led to the formation of the International Criminal Tribunal for Yugoslavia by the UN in 1993 (United to End Genocide). As the 1990s progressed, conflict in Africa grew and in Rwanda, the ethnic conflict between Tutsi and Hutus resulted in the deaths of an estimated 800,000 to 1 million (United to End Genocide). Following the genocide in Rwanda, the UN formed the International Criminal Tribunal for Rwanda to investigate and prosecute those responsible. In 2003, genocide once again erupted in Africa, this time in the Darfur region of Sudan, resulting in the deaths of nearly 300,000 people (United to End Genocide). The case of Darfur has been taken up for prosecution by the International Criminal Court. In the Middle East today, conflicts along religious and sectarian lines continue in Israel and Palestine, as well as across the borders of Syria and Iraq.

These more recent genocides have resulted in new understandings and terms about the ways ethnic cleansing have been carried out. While rape as a strategy or a tactic of war has been around for centuries (see Brownmiller, 1975), the term *genocidal rape* has more recently been used to describe the sexual violence which has been characteristic of more recent conflicts (Barstow, 2000). These types of conflicts tend to "employ organized rape as a means of humiliating the enemy and destroying family life" (Barstow, 2000, p. 3). Mass rape has been used to destroy or control an ethnic group by the spoiling of lineage through forced impregnation. Mass rape, "when it is combined with a deliberate policy of forced impregnation, as by the Serbs in Bosnia and the Hutus in Rwanda, […] aims at the destruction of an ethnic group" (Barstow, 2000, p. 45). Mass rape "becomes a technique of genocide: to so defile the enemy's women that they will no longer be considered as future mothers for their own people" (Barstow, 2000, p. 45). The identification and naming of "genocidal rape" is another example of the ways new populations of victims and forms of victimization continue to be identified in the world today.

Around the world today the targeting of individuals and groups based on race, religion, ethnicity, gender, sexual orientation, and disability continues outside of conflict situations. The UN estimates that in seventy-eight countries around the world sexual orientation and gender expression are criminalized, with seven countries maintaining laws where being gay is punishable by death (UNAIDS, 2013). So long as governments and social institutions, such as religions, continue to promote prejudice and discrimination, we will continue to see hate and bias crimes committed against individuals or groups.

Cybercrime

What Is Cybercrime?

According to the National Crime Prevention Council (2012), a **cybercrime** is "a crime committed or facilitated via the Internet" (p. 1). Crimes can range from downloading illegal music files or movies to fraud to child pornography distributed over the Internet to hacking into a computer for the purpose of detecting and sharing secrets of corporations or governments. The potential for crime via the Internet is seemingly endless and new categories of crime continue to pop up. Three areas that appear to be most common, and most talked about in the media, are fraud committed via the Internet, child pornography over the Internet, and identity theft.

Fraud

In May of 2000 the Federal Bureau of Investigation and the National White-Collar Crime Center created a partnership to deal with Internet-related crime. This new agency was called the Internet Fraud Complaint Center, later changed to the Internet Crime Complaint Center (IC3). The IC3 accepts complaints of Internet fraud from the United States and other countries and helps to both investigate the crimes and compile information on the crimes themselves so a working database of specific types of cybercrime can be tabulated.

In 2015, the IC3 reported the receipt of 288,012 cybercrime complaints with 127,145 of those complaints reporting a monetary loss totaling $1,070,711,522 (broken down to $8,241 average loss per complainant reporting a loss) (IC3, 2015). Males and females appear to be equally susceptible to cybercrimes with males accounting for 52.91% of the complaints and women accounting for 47.09% of complaints. Young adults and children (those under age 20) appear to be the least likely victims, whereas persons 20–39 account for 38% of complaints and persons 40–59 account for 41%. Persons aged 60 and over account for approximately 18% of all complaints. The most frequently reported frauds via cybercrime include auto fraud, FBI impersonation e-mail scam, hit man scam, scareware/ransomware, real estate fraud, and romance frauds (see Table 7A).

Table 7A: Cybercrime Fraud Complaints, 2015

Complaint	Number of Complaints	Loss Associated with Complaint
Non-Payment/Non-Delivery	67,375	$121,329,122
419/Overpayment	30,855	$49,217,119
Identity Theft	21,949	$57,294,589
Auction	21,510	$18,906,416
Other	19,963	$56,153,977
Personal Data Breach	19,632	$43,477,526
Employment	18,758	$33,890,824
Extortion	17,804	$14,799,705
Credit Card Fraud	17,172	$41,503,502
Phishing/Vishing/Smishing/Pharming	16,594	$8,174,316
Advanced Fee	16,445	$50,721,226
Harassment/Threats of Violence	14,812	$13,126,123
Confidence Fraud/Romance Scam	12,509	$203,390,531
Government Impersonation	11,832	$12,090,159
Real Estate/Rental	11,562	$41,417,647
Lottery/Sweepstakes	5,324	$19,365,223
Malware/Scareware	3,294	$2,912,628
Corporate Data Breach	2,499	$38,890,824
Ransomware	2,453	$1,620,814
IPR/Copyright and Counterfeit	1,931	$7,230,803
Crimes Against Children	1,348	$97,584
Charity	411	$1,230,812
Gambling	131	$955,360

Source: IC3, 2015 Annual Report. Adapted from tables on pages 15, 16 and 17.
Note: This table does not include all cybercrime complaints received by IC3.

Recently, the IC3 broadened the categories within which they collected information on cybercrimes to better represent the types of incidents being reported to their agency. These crimes occur to both private individuals and businesses. It appears that the reconceptualization of offenses focuses on a few different areas: (1) demand/request/receipt of money through manipulation, false representation, fake/faulty product purchase, and/or by threat; (2) identity theft; (3) intent to steal information or property through gaining access to personal or business information; or (4) other. In the first category there are a number of schemes that involve an individual or business being contacted and asked for money, told they owe money, or the victim is requested to assist in the transfer of money, typically from or to somewhere abroad. For example, in 419/overpayment schemes people are asked to transfer, receive, and/or send money to another entity for which they can retain a portion of the money in the transaction (IC3, 2015). An advanced fee scam occurs when someone pays money for receipt of services or a product, but receives little to nothing of what they expected. Auction fraud occurs when someone participates in an online auction and the resulting transaction is fraudulent or fails to occur. A charity offense occurs when someone is deceived into believing they are donating to a legitimate charity which in fact does not exist. For example, numerous websites were developed soliciting donations for Hurricane Katrina victims. In these cases, donations were never received by the disaster victims; instead the website creator kept all donations for him/herself (see Box 7.1 on Hurricane Katrina scams). Other instances include auto fraud, real estate fraud, credit card fraud, lottery scams, and other. In these instances, an item(s) may be purchased and an exchange of funds occurs, but the buyer may never receive the merchandise requested and may have great difficulty getting in contact with the "seller." See Table 7A for a breakdown of cybercrimes reported to the IC3.

Intimidation/extortion scams occur in a variety of ways. One method is for a person to receive either an email or telephone call alerting the person to malware detected on their computers. The perpetrator indicates that for a price they can fix the problem, but they must act immediately. Another common method, called payday loan scams, occurs when individuals are contacted by companies saying that they are debt collectors and that the individual is delinquent in their payments to resolve the debt. The perpetrators refuse to give the victim information related to the origination of the debt but demand payment immediately. In some cases the perpetrators imitate law enforcement agents and inform the victim that there is a warrant out for the victim. One more scam of this type is the "grandparent scam" in which fraudsters call grandparents alleging to be the person's grandchild. The fraudster says they are in a foreign country and have no money and need help immediately. They often act distressed in their phone calls and may even state that they are US embassy representatives calling on behalf of the grandchild (IC3, 2013).

Hit man scams occur when a victim receives an email from someone indicating that he or she has been hired to kill the victim. The fraudster says that they will not follow through with the contract if the victim can pay a certain amount to call off the contract. Women appear to be victims at a 2:1 ratio to men (IC3, 2013).

Box 7.1 Beware Hurricane Katrina Relief Scams

FBI Cyber Exec Warns of Online Schemers Exploiting the Tragedy

09/14/05

Days before Hurricane Katrina slammed into the Gulf Coast of the US, fraudsters began registering Katrina-related websites hoping to profit from an anticipated outpouring of charitable donations for storm victims. How prevalent are these fraud schemes? What are we doing to stop them? How can you safely make donations online? For the answers to these questions and more we talked with our top cyber exec, Louis M. Reigel.

Q: How widespread are Katrina-related online frauds?

Mr. Reigel: There are more than 4,000 Katrina-related websites registered now, more than four times the number we saw just last week. Many of them may be legitimate, but fraudulent ones are popping up faster than we can pound them down. We're seeing more scams now than we saw after the Southeast Asian tsunami last December. The complaints started rolling in just a few days after Katrina made landfall. As of this morning, we've received hundreds of Katrina-related complaints from people all over the country.

Q: What types of frauds are you seeing?

Mr. Reigel: Websites that spoof those of legitimate charitable organizations to steal people's credit card numbers, bank account information, Social Security numbers, and other personal information. Phishing e-mails, or spam, with links that redirect your web browser to those spoofed sites. E-mails that trick people into opening virus-laden attachments under the guise that they're opening photos of the hurricane damage. You name it—we're discovering new tactics every day.

Q. What are we doing to stop these schemes?

Mr. Reigel: We're working several cases right now based on the complaints we've received and from investigating the fraudulent sites themselves. We're working very closely with the American Red Cross, which has been a primary target of these frauds, to identify sites that are spoofing their site. Through our Legats, we're working with our foreign counterparts to track down people who are running these scams from Eastern Europe, Asia, and elsewhere. We've also partnered with the Justice Department, Federal Trade Commission, and other government agencies to form the Hurricane Katrina Fraud Task Force, led by Assistant Attorney General Alice Fisher, which is addressing all of the frauds that have—unfortunately—resulted from the hurricane.

Q: How can people make sure the donations they make online are actually reaching the intended recipients?

Mr. Reigel: Be cautious in your giving. Don't respond to any unsolicited incoming e-mails requesting donations, even if they look like they're coming from reputable charitable organizations. Reputable charities don't use spam to solicit donations. To make sure your donation is going to a legitimate, U.S.-based non-profit organization, type the charity's web address directly into your web browser. Be very leery of emails with attachments, even if they're from someone you know. And if you think you've been victimized by one of these scams, file a complaint with the Internet Crime Complaint Center.

Resources: E-Scams & Warnings

Source: https://archives.fbi.gov/archives/news/stories/2005/september/katrina_scams091405.

Reprint permission granted per public information.

Scareware/ransomware scams occur when a victim receives a pop-up alert stating that there is a virus on the computer and that the victim can purchase software to fix the problems. In some instances a pop-up appears stating there has been a violation of US federal law and that the victim's IP address was identified as one that visited child pornography sites. The victim is told to pay a fine to the US Department of Justice for the violation. These types of complaints come from males more than females on a bit more than a 2:1 ratio and can also fall within the category of government impersonation scams (IC3, 2013).

Similar to auto fraud scams, real estate scams focus on trying to sell someone something without actually having a product to sell. Typically these types of frauds include rental properties, timeshare marketing scams, and loan modification scams. The rental property scams occur when individuals re-post information about legitimate rental properties from other sites and insist that all communication must take place over e-mail and payment must be completed using a wire transfer for first and last month's rent. Timeshare marketing scams occur when timeshare owners are contacted by fake companies who promise to sell or rent their properties for them. They require a fee to conduct the transactions but there is no real buyer for the timeshare. The victims may also be contacted by a "fraud recovery specialist" who validates that a fraud occurred and asks for a fee to help resolve the fraud and recover the fee paid initially. Loan modification scams occur when a homeowner receives a notification about an opportunity to adjust the home loan and requires a fee for processing and closing costs (akin to a refinancing). The fraudsters also instruct the homeowner to cease paying the mortgage company. When the fraud is identified, the homeowner has lost the money paid in fees and is often behind on the mortgage they had difficulty managing in the first place (IC3, 2013).

Confidence/romance scams occur almost equally to males and females, with females reporting them slightly more often. The fraudsters establish online relationships with people and after "wooing" them with gifts and companionship they ask for money, stating that they need financial help and they ask the victims to receive and ship packages to/from overseas (IC3, 2013). The IC3 states that along with the financial harm that comes from this type of a scam, there are mental/emotional harms as well because the victim has become invested in what they believe is a true relationship.

Other cybercrimes include threats via the computer against a person or his/her loved ones, child pornography, transferring contraband via the Internet, copyright or trademark infringement, money laundering, cyberbullying, cyber terrorism, human trafficking, online gambling, hacking, and criminal mischief. Identity theft is also often associated with cybercrime as personal bank information may be stolen from someone via the Internet and/or may be used by another to purchase items over the Internet.

Identity Theft

In 2012, 7% of persons 16 years and older were victims of identity theft in the United States (Harrell & Langton, 2013). Most of these incidents (85%) involved the use of an existing bank account or credit card. Others had their information stolen to create new accounts. Financial and emotional distress is often experienced by victims of identity theft. Slightly over one-third of victims reported both emotional distress and financial loss. Harrell and Langton (2013) report that 14% of identity theft victims experienced financial losses of $1 or more and half reported losses of less than $100. For those victims who could resolve their identity theft issues, about half resolved them within one day, whereas about 29% of those who had personal information stolen in addition to or in lieu of financial information spent a month or more seeking a resolution to their situation. Total losses, including direct and indirect originations, totaled about $24.7 billion overall.

The majority of identity theft victims do not know the person who stole their identity and do not know how their identity was stolen in the first place. Individuals who had their personal information stolen were more likely to experience credit-related problems (12% versus approximately 1% of existing account victims), problems with debt collectors (17% versus 2% of existing account victims), and banking problems (7% versus 2% of existing account victims). Only about 10% of identity theft victims reported the crime to police. Within the category of identity theft, victims who had personal information stolen and a new account opened in their name were most likely to contact the police (accounted for 40% and 22% of reports to police). This seems to make sense given that they appear to experience more difficulties with recovering after the identity theft than those who had their accounts broken into.

Some acts are deemed cybercrimes when they are crimes in and of themselves, but are conducted with the use of computers and/or the Internet as a new format or means by which to transmit and/or receive information. Two crimes receiving a great deal of attention are cyberstalking and child pornography on the Internet.

Cyberstalking

According to Reyns, Henson, and Fisher (2016), "cyberstalking occurs when a victim is repeatedly pursued or monitored by a stalker using digital technologies" (p. 149). As with stalking (discussed in Chapter 5), the behaviors can include harassment, unwanted contact, and statements indicating that one's actions are being watched/monitored and for which the victim develops a distinct level of fear. Reyns et al. (2016) note that various studies have found that between 30–40% of college students surveyed indicated they believed they were cyberstalked at some point in their lives. With the advent of multiple social media sites, it is becoming easier for a stalker to "follow" someone online, and to harass and/or insist on communication with a victim. One need only watch someone's Facebook page, Instagram account, Twitter account, SnapChat, etc. to see what someone may be doing at any moment in time. Reyns et al. (2016) found that individuals who added strangers to their social network accounts had a 2.5 times greater likelihood of being stalked in cyberspace. Additionally, they found that people who indicated that they had peers who were coded as "deviant," meaning that they were more likely to potentially engage in stalking-type behaviors, also reported higher levels of actual cyberstalking. Spitzberg and Hoobler (2002) suggest that cyberstalking can stand alone or may be used as an additional method of stalking. For instance:

> Stalking is a problem that affects millions of people and causes them great stress and diminishment of quality of life. Stalkers and obsessive pursuers clearly incorporate any means that facilitate their pursuit, and one of the increasingly available means of intrusion is the advent of cyberspace technologies (p. 75).

Child Pornography on/via the Internet

Child pornography involves the production, distribution, and downloading of images related to the sexual exploitation of minors (Wortley & Smallbone, 2012). Production of child pornography includes the creation of images that will be displayed and/or sold, whereas, distribution of child pornography, specifically on the Internet, involves uploading and distributing pornographic images, and downloading child pornography involves accessing images off of the Internet. Wortley and Smallbone (2012) suggest that on any given day there are over one million pornographic child images available on the Internet with a growth of over 200 new images added per day. A problem with developing a true estimate of the amount of images available on the Internet is that many sites are only available briefly, so they're hard to track. Additionally, the sites may be "hidden" and incredibly difficult to locate.

In terms of official complaints filed, according to the 2011 Annual Report for the Office of Juvenile Justice and Delinquency Prevention there were over 40,000 complaints of child sexual exploitation received by the 61 joint task forces in the Internet Crimes Against Children Task Force Program across the United States (OJJDP, 2012). (The

Internet Crimes Against Children (ICAC) Task Force Program is a collaboration between over 2,000 federal, state, and local law enforcement and prosecutorial agencies from across the United States.) From those complaints, approximately 5,700 people were arrested, 45,000 computers underwent forensic examinations for materials related to child sexual exploitation, and more than 9,800 cases were referred to other law enforcement agencies (OJJDP, 2012).

As you read in Chapter 2, there are pros and cons of the Uniform Crime Reports (UCR). Some of the cons have attempted to be addressed in the National Incident-Based Reporting System (NIBRS). In 2004, Finkelhor and Ormrod published a report attempting to determine measurements of child pornography in 2000 using the NIBRS database. At the time, only 14% of law enforcement agencies reported information to the FBI NIBRS program, as the predominant reporting system was the UCR. Though the information has the limitation of representing a small proportion of the country, the findings of their investigation are worthwhile to report. Finkelhor and Ormrod (2004) note distinctions between a few different types of pornography involving children and juveniles. **Child exploitation pornography** involves the possession or distribution of pornography that depicts underage juveniles. **Juvenile victim pornography** includes using pornography to seduce a child and/or producing child pornography. Finally, **pornography with juvenile involvement** encompasses the prior two actions together. Approximately 2,469 incidents of pornography were reported to local and state law enforcement agencies in 2000. Twenty-seven percent (or approximately 667 incidents) of those were incidents with juvenile involvement. Child exploitation pornography accounted for 23% overall and juvenile victim pornography accounted for 4% overall. Of those, only 7% of juvenile victim pornography and 13% of child exploitation pornography involved the use of a computer. Given the information discussed so far, it seems likely that the 40,000 complaints received by the ICAC Task Force program were dealing with child exploitation pornography, but there is a long way to go to get a more clear understanding of the issue at hand. Indeed, there is an even longer way to go to keep up with the technology and craftiness evidenced by the perpetrators of these acts.

The Center for Problem-Oriented Policing compiled a report to law enforcement on how to root out and address child pornography on the web (Wortley & Smallbone, 2012) and described eight commonly used methods of distribution. One of the major methods of distributing child pornography is newsgroups. In newsgroups there is a forum for participants to discuss their interest and to post child porn images. These are akin to discussion groups on the World Wide Web and there is typically an administrator who runs the site. Users take the risk of getting caught through tracking by their credit cards, which are used to pay for access to the site. E-groups and web pages/websites exist that provide opportunities in which members can exchange or purchase child porn images. These methods may be linked with legal adult pornography sites, making them more difficult to detect. Bulletin board systems (BBS) and chat rooms are additional methods by which interested parties may become aware of child pornography sites. Because of the open nature of these particular sites on the Internet, they are more easily infiltrated and/or monitored by undercover police. E-mails are another risky way to distribute materials because of the potential for undercover police to participate and catch perpetrators. However, e-mail is a known method for sharing images and grooming potential victims as well. Peer to Peer networks (P2P) are closed networks in which trading of images occurs, but in a supposedly more secure forum. Web cams offer the ability of child porn viewers to request particular activities in a live fashion.

Who Is Involved in the Production, Distribution, and Viewing of Child Pornography?

Wortley and Smallbone (2012) report that prior to the Internet about one-fifth to one-third of individuals arrested for child pornography had also engaged in actual hands-on sexual abuse of children (roughly 20–33%). With the advent of the Internet, it becomes much easier to view pornographic images, however. Alternatively, research has found that only about 10% of persons convicted of sexual abuse of children also collect Internet child pornography. Just as in other categories of crime, the perpetrators come from all walks of life, but may be more likely to be White, male, in the age range of 26–40 and may use the Internet excessively, to the point of disrupting their daily lives. A number of different typologies of online child pornographers exist. The COPS office suggests that there are three main categories of Internet child pornography users: recreational users, at-risk users, and sexual compulsives. **Recreational users** tend to visit the sites out of curiosity, on impulse, and only for the short-term. **At-risk users** are those that have an interest in child pornography, but may not have engaged in seeking out images were it not for the Internet. Finally, **sexual compulsives** are those who actively seek out child pornography and have a very strong interest in children as sexual objects. Krone (2004), an Australian researcher, created a typology of offenders based on a continuum of the seriousness of the offending behavior itself, which ranges from indirect abuse of children to direct abuse. Those in the **indirect abuse** categories include browsers, private fantasizers, trawlers, non-secure collectors, and secure collectors. **Browsers** are individuals who might stumble across child porn and decide it's interesting enough to keep. **Private fantasizers** are those who create images by morphing images together to satisfy their desires about sex with a child. A **trawler** is someone who seeks child pornography through available, or open, browsers. This individual is not as savvy as others as they typically do not employ security strategies. **Non-secure collectors** are those who visit distribution sites (chat rooms, etc.) that do not typically employ security barriers. **Secure collectors** are those who do belong to groups where high security protocols are used and they may spend an inordinate amount of time collecting a huge amount of images, including rare and high-risk prizes. Those in the **direct abuse** categories include groomers, physical abusers, producers, and distributors. Oftentimes, the only way that the abuse may be detected is if the child tells someone about it. A **groomer** is one who seeks out children for the purpose of developing relationships with them. This type of individual may collect pornographic images of the children he/she wants to be in a relationship with. **Physical abusers** are those who actively sexually abuse children who they may or may not have met online. They may record images of themselves with their victims, thus producing child pornography. **Producers** are those who record children being sexually abused so that they can give it to interested parties. They may also coerce children into submitting pornographic images of themselves as well. Finally, **distributors** are those who provide child pornographic images to anyone and solely have a financial interest in the abuse.

What Are the Effects of Child Pornography on the Victims?

Wortley and Smallbone (2012) suggest that victims of child pornography most often know the perpetrators of their victimization and are victimized on many levels, including sexual, physical, social, and psychological. The first victimization comes when they are abused and those images are recorded, but each time one of those images is accessed they are victimized again. Physical pain and sexual abuse occurs when the act is taking place. Additionally, victims report that they lose their appetites, have frequent headaches, and experience an inability to sleep. Psychologically, victims have reported being fearful and anxious and feeling emotionally isolated. When a victim knows the perpetrator, there is also the compulsion to be obedient to the adult figure who they trusted, along with a sense of loyalty resulting in not reporting the crime. Along with this comes a sense of shame that they feel about themselves, which is akin to what other sexual assault victims experience as discussed in Chapter 4. Oftentimes, the long-term effects include the exacerbation of the psychological distress experienced as child victims and lead to adulthood hopelessness, despair, and worthlessness. This translates also into difficulty cultivating and maintaining healthy relationships with other adults, both emotionally and sexually, which could be considered a social harm. Additionally, the child pornography victims could be recognized in public—even years later, thereby attracting attention from people who may wish to engage in (or view) acts with them in person or cultivate a relationship with them.

Cybercrime on the International Level

It is not possible to discuss cybercrime without addressing it from a global perspective. Victims and perpetrators of cybercrime incidents do not have to, and often do not, reside within the same legal jurisdiction, not to mention in the same country. As an example, the recent hacking of Target that affected victims in the United States and was committed by perpetrators believed to be living in Russia and the Ukraine illustrates that victims can live in countries other than that in which the perpetrators are believed to be living in (Coldewey, 2014). This creates a very complicated case, both jurisdiction- and investigation-wise. It is estimated that over 40 million people had their credit or debit card information stolen and that about 70 million people were also affected by the security breach (some of whom may be in the original 40 million), but where did the actual crimes "take place" (Yang & Jayakumar, 2014)?

The United Nations Office on Drugs and Crime has published two recent reports investigating cybercrime at the international level, in 2010 and more recently in 2013. In the 2010 report (United Nations Office on Drugs and Crime, 2010) the UN identified that there were over 1.5 billion users of the Internet spanning 233 countries. This is a huge and diverse population to "police" in a global manner.

The 2010 report focused on identity theft and child pornography. The report suggests that cybercrime is accessible to the individual-level criminal and organized crime alike for three main reasons. First, the technology to perpetrate cybercrime is easily accessible and easy-to-use, allowing both sophisticated hackers and people with a general knowledge of computers the ease of installing software used in cybercrimes. Second, more and more Internet users, in both developing and industrialized countries, have increased both the victim and predator pools. And lastly, there is a growing use of automation in cybercrime attacks, allowing for more attacks to happen in a single operation. This last point is important in that it suggests that to be successful at their scheme, perpetrators need only a few "hits" on millions of attacks and they can also steal small, seemingly undetectable amounts, on large amounts of people when they attack incredibly large numbers of victims.

Global Identity Theft

The 2010 UN report suggests that identity-related frauds were the most common type of fraud perpetrated on the international level. The three techniques used most often in acquiring identity information include **phishing**—convincing someone to divulge their personal information to another, **malware**—unintentionally installing software that transmits personal information to another, and **hacking**—illegally gaining access by breaking into computer systems that house peoples' personal information.

The report indicates that it is very difficult to pinpoint where the perpetrators reside. For instance, in May of 2009 the United States was found to host 54% of phishing sites, with the remaining localities as follows: Sweden—7%, China—6%, Canada—4%, UK—3%, Germany—3%, and Other 23%. However, two months later, in July of 2009, there was a dramatic shift among hosting countries: US—42%, Sweden—46% (a huge jump from 7% only two months prior), Canada—4%, China—2%, UK and Germany—1% each, and Other—5%. This example alone illustrates that detection and prevention efforts of international policing groups may be extraordinarily difficult.

Some reports suggest that there is a great deal of intra-country victimization, as the United States appears to be the leading source for stolen credit card information and US citizens appear to be the most likely victims. The UN report highlights the fact that there simply isn't a lot of information out there investigating the issue of identity theft to provide a true illustration of the problem on a global level.

Global Child Pornography

An estimate of how many global perpetrators or purchasers of child pornography exist is difficult to assess. One estimate cited in the 2010 UN report included between 75,000 and 390,000 consumers of a single company offering credit card services for over 5,000 child pornography sites. The perpetrators were located across the globe. Prosecutions of those in possession of child pornography are relatively low. In the UK there were 116 child prostitution/pornography offenses recorded in 2008–2009. In Canada, 1,408 people were charged with possession in 2008. The US referred 2,539 suspects for prosecution in 2006.

One question addressed by the 2010 UN report was whether child pornography was produced on the amateur-level (individuals creating images for their peer group) or commercial-level (images produced for purposes of a business-type enterprise). Though it is difficult to estimate the ratio of amateur to commercial, it was reported that peer-to-peer (or amateur) exchanges were more popular. A UK study, cited within the UN report, suggests that whereas in 2005 and 2006 there seemed to be an almost equal amount of amateur and commercial child pornography circulating the Internet, commercial domains started to dominate in 2007 and 2008. A similar study conducted by a group called Cybertip.ca in Canada, found that in 2009 only about 13% of sites were commercial across a number of countries, including Russia, Canada, France, the US, Germany, Spain, and the UK. Interestingly, the UK had the highest percentage of commercial sites (21%), which may confirm what was beginning to be found in 2007 and 2008 in the UK report itself. The type of child pornography shown on both commercial and amateur sites appears to be very similar, with both sites showing predominantly modeling-type images with sexualized posing of the victims. However, the non-commercial sites were more likely to show sexual assaults (approximately 38% of non-commercial sites versus 30% of commercial sites).

The UN report also investigated the ages of victims. They noted that the Cybertip.ca study found that the majority of victims were under the age of 8, though commercial sites were more likely to show the younger children than non-commercial sites. The UK study cited in the UN report noted that 69% of the victims appeared to be younger than 10, with 24% of the victims appearing to be less than 7 years old. Girls were the primary victims on both sites with upwards of 83% of images overall.

Similar to the discussion about how images are distributed, the majority of child pornography distributed on a global level appeared to be through newsgroups (usenet groups) and bulletin boards. Globally, the vast majority of victims appear to be White girls from developing nations, more specifically from Eastern Bloc countries in Europe, including the Russian Federation, Ukraine, the Republic of Moldova, and Belarus. The perpetrators are people the victims knew, and who were often in a caretaker role to the victim.

Summary

Victims of hate crimes and cybercrimes both face challenges in accurate identification of their victimization, as well as remedies for those experiences. Victims of hate crimes may not be correctly identified if police or prosecutors don't pursue their cases as such. Identifying a clear motivation in some cases may be difficult, and particularly if the victim doesn't fit within the identified protected classes or were targeted for a perceived, rather than actual, characteristic. Cybercrime victimizations may never be addressed given challenges with establishing jurisdiction and identifying perpetrators in the digital world. Victims within both crime groups may never experience the justice they deserve simply because of the difficulties that exist in developing strong cases against the perpetrators.

Key Terms

Hate crimes

Bias crimes

Child exploitation pornography

Juvenile victim pornography

Pornography with juvenile involvement

Indirect abuse

Browsers

Private fantasizers

Trawler

Secure collectors

Non-secure collectors

Direct abuse

Groomer

Physical abusers

Producers

Distributors

Phishing

Malware

Hacking

Discussion Questions

1. Define hate crimes. What populations qualify as victims under current laws and how are the different groups differentially at risk? What populations are excluded or may be added in the future?
2. What is the issue with jurisdiction and cybercrime and how can we work to resolve this issue, for the benefit of cybercrime victims?
3. Hate crimes and cybercrime are global issues—what can be done on a global level to create responses and prevention plans to deal with these crimes?

Websites for Further Information

National Crime Prevention Council: http://www.ncpc.org/topics/hate-crime.

Partners Against Hate: http:// www.partnersagainsthate.org/.

Campus Pride Stop The Hate: http:// www.campuspride.org/ stop—the-hate/.

For more information on Matthew Shepard: http:// www.matthewshepard.org/.

Internet crime complain center: https://www.ic3.gov/default.aspx.

Internet scam warnings: http:// www.scamwarners.com/.

References

Coldewey, D. (2014, January 16). Target breach takes shape: Hints at malware and hackers. *NBC News*. Retrieved from NBCNews.com.

FBI. (2015a). *About Hate Crime Statistics*. Retrieved from https://ucr.fbi.gov/hate-crime/2015/resource-pages/abouthatecrime-final.

FBI. (2015b). *Hate Crime Statistics, Table 1 and 2*. Retrieved from https://ucr.fbi.gov/hate-crime/2015/tables-and-data-declarations/1tabledatadecpdf.

FBI. (2015c). *Hate Crime Statistics Act*. Retrieved from https://ucr.fbi.gov/hate-crime/2015/resource-pages/hatecrimestatisticsact_final.

Finkelhor, D., & Ormrod, R. (2000). *Juvenile victims of property crimes*. US Department of Justice, Office of Juvenile Justice and Delinquency Prevention. NCJ 210951.

Grattet, R., & Jenness, V. (2001). The birth and maturation of hate crime policy in the United States. *The American Behavioral Scientist, 45*(4), 668–696.

Harrell, E., & Langton, L. (2013). *Victims of identity theft, 2012*. Washington, DC: US Department of Justice, Office of Justice Programs, Bureau of Justice Statistics. NCJ 243779.

Internet Crime Complaint Center. (2013). *2013 Internet Crime Report*. Retrieved from http://www.ic3.gov/media/annualreport/2013_IC3Report.pdf.

Internet Crime Complaint Center. (2016). *2015 Internet Crime Report*. Retrieved from http://www.ic3.gov/media/annualreport/2015_IC3Report.pdf.

Krone, T. (2004, July). A typology of online child pornography offending. *Trends & Issues in Crime and Criminal Justice, 279*. Australian Institute of Criminology: Australian Government.

National Crime Prevention Council. (2012). *Cybercrimes*. Arlington, VA: Bureau of Justice Assistance.

Office of Juvenile Justice and Delinquency Prevention. (2012). *How OJJDP is working for youth justice and safety, 2011 Annual Report*. Washington, DC: US Department of Justice, Office of Justice Programs, Office of Juvenile Justice and Delinquency Prevention. NCJ 238638.

Reyns, B. W., Henson, B., & Fisher, B. S. (2016). Guardians of the cyber galaxy: An empirical and theoretical analysis of the guardianship concept from routine activity theory as it applies to online forms of victimization. *Journal of Contemporary Criminal Justice, 32*(2), 148–168.

Schewendinger, H., & Schewendinger, J. (1970). Defenders of order or guardians of human rights? *Issues in Criminology, 5*, 123–157.

Shively, M. (2005). *Study of literature and legislation on hate crime in America.* Prepared for the National Institute of Justice.

UNAIDS. (2013). Towards a free and equal world. Retrieved from http:// www.unaids. org/en/resources/infographics/20140108freeequal/.

United Nations Office on Drugs and Crime. (2010). *Cybercrime.* Retrieved from www. unodc.org/documents/data—and-analysis/tocta/10.Cybercrime.pdf Originally created 06-16-2010.

Wortley, R., & Smallbone, S. (2012). Guide No. 41: Child pornography on the Internet. Problem-Specific Guides Series, Problem-Oriented Guides for Police. Washington, DC: Center for Problem-Oriented Policing, Inc.

Yang, J. L., & Jayakumar, A. (2014, January 10). Target says up to 70 million more customers were hit by December data breach. *The Washington Post.* Retrieved from http://www.washingtonpost.com.

Yeadon, G., & Hawkins, J. (2008). The Nazi hydra in America: Suppressed history of a century. Joshua Tree, CA: Progressive Press.

SECTION III

Victims' Rights

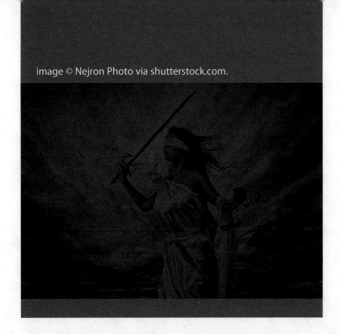

Chapter 8: An Overview of Victims' Rights

As you read in Chapter 1, the role of the victim in the criminal justice process has evolved over the ages, from a totally victim-centered system to one in which victims were a small part of the process in a defendant-centered system (Trulson, 2005). To review, early "primitive" societies codified the need for offenders to repay victims for harms perpetrated against them. These codifications were seen as necessary as the handling of crimes in earlier societies often led to blood-feuds and the failure to achieve fair justice, thereby exacerbating and extending the harms alleged to have occurred in the first place (Morgan, 1987). These repayments could take the place of or be done in concert with retributive physical sanctions for crimes as well. The focus of these codes, however, was to lead to the recovery of the victim without the risk of "outside-the-law" retribution (Tobolowsky, 2001). Things changed dramatically for victims in early Western civilizations in the eleventh century, when monarchs and governments became more involved in dealing with the harms perpetrated among their subjects (Tobolowsky, 2001). Crimes committed became crimes against the crown or state, rather than the victim, and punishment was doled out by the government. One of the main repercussions of this was that fines and restitution that would have gone to the victim now went to the government instead, so if a victim wanted any type of financial recompense he or she had to seek it in civil court.

Theoretical investigations into why someone "becomes a victim" started as early as the 1940s, but a real focus on how victims are treated by the many entities that provide services to them and what rights they themselves have in relation to the criminal incident that occurred didn't begin until the 1960s, with momentum really beginning in the 1970s and 1980s (Tobolowsky, 2001). After more than 40 years of increased evaluation of victims' needs and issues, the pendulum can be seen to be slowly shifting back towards a more victim-inclusive criminal justice process where legislation exists that provides victims with rights mimicking those endemic to earlier victim-centered systems. This chapter will explore the history of the Victims' Rights Movement and examine the impact on the state level of the 1982 President's Task Force on Victims of Crime to improve treatment and rights of victims. Chapter 9 will highlight important pieces of influential legislation at the federal and state levels to once again codify rights for crime victims.

The Victims' Rights Movement

Most agree that the Victims' Rights Movement was borne out of a confluence of social movements, academic and media attention, political responses to crime, and the valiant efforts of victims and survivors themselves (Tobolowsky, 2001; Young & Stein, 2004). The three main social movements that influenced the Victims' Rights Movement were the Civil Rights Movement, the Women's Movement, and the Law and Order Movement.

Social Movements

The **Civil Rights Movement** highlighted the need for equal justice, meaning justice not just for the powerful and majority class, but to all victims of crime (Davis, 2005). Barlow and Barlow (2001) highlight this need as they describe the "underpolicing" that occurred in African American communities, wherein African American victims of crime were not afforded the same level of assistance by law enforcement in response to calls for service. As far back as the time of slavery and Reconstruction, African Americans were not always seen as "victims" of crime because of their status in American society. For instance, what would logically be looked upon as rape had it happened to a White woman was not seen as rape of a Black woman simply because she was seen to be either (1) property or (2) sexually promiscuous and/or available (West, 2004). Over time, unequal application of law was rampant by law enforcement and the courts as responses to calls for service were often lengthy or didn't occur, and penalties for those who victimized African Americans were not equivalent to those for offenders of White victims (Barlow & Barlow, 2001). For these reasons, the Civil Rights Movement was integral in influencing the Victims' Rights Movement to address equality for all.

At around the same time period of the Civil Rights Movement, the United States saw a surge in its crime rate. The **Law and Order Movement** was a response by political conservatives in the late 1960s and early 1970s to address the increasing crime rate of the times. Essentially, they argued for more justice for victims in the form of stricter penalties and lengthier sentences for convicted offenders as both punishment and as general deterrence to the country as a whole. Some of the policies espoused under the Law and Order Movement that sought to improve the situation for victims included proposals to deny bail so that those accused of crimes would not be out and able to further harm the victim, to abolish the exclusionary rule so that all evidence collected could be used to prosecute the alleged offender, mandatory sentencing to ensure that alleged offenders got the punishment they deserved, and elimination of parole to ensure that offenders served their entire sentence for the full punishment effect that was initially ordered (Tobolowsky, 2001). Some of these policies came into fruition, but others were thought to go too far and to perhaps violate rights of defendants that were guaranteed in the US Constitution. The Law and Order Movement sought to provide "peace of mind" to victims through addressing crime, and criminals, with a strong hand, and policies exist today that exemplify this movement (truth-in-sentencing laws, abolition of parole in some states, mandatory sentencing guidelines, etc.).

The **Women's Movement** was undoubtedly central to the development of the Victims' Movement, both in the United States and Great Britain (Young & Stein, 2004). The issues of sexual assault and domestic violence had traditionally been dealt with poorly by the criminal justice system. Sexual assault and rape victims were often discredited or disbelieved by law enforcement and were forced to take polygraphs to demonstrate that they were not lying (Houser & Dworkin, 2009). Domestic violence victims (predominantly female) were told that the offenses against them should be dealt with as a family issue, not a criminal justice issue (Davis, 2005). Women took to the streets and demanded that the views surrounding sexual assault and domestic violence change. Women who were victimized themselves often provided great momentum to the movement as they shared their experiences with the criminal justice system (Young & Stein, 2004; Davis, 2005). As a result of the Women's Movement, we saw the first victim advocacy/service agencies emerge in the early 1970s. The country's first rape crisis center was founded in 1971 in San Francisco, California. The Bay Area Women Against Rape (BAWAR) was created by a group of women, including a mother of a rape victim, in response to the treatment of a teenage rape victim by criminal justice and hospital personnel. Shortly thereafter, two more victim assistance programs were established in St. Louis, Missouri (Aid for Victims of Crime) and Washington, DC (D.C. Rape Crisis Center) (Davis, 2005; Office for Victims of Crime, 2014). The Women's Movement highlighted the need to deal differently with the crimes of sexual assault and domestic violence, particularly against women, and started the hands-on, grassroots efforts of women to provide assistance to victims of these crimes. They lobbied for sexual assault/rape and domestic violence to be dealt with more severely within criminal statutes and they have expanded our understanding of the victims of these crimes.

Academia

In the world of academia, the field of victimology gained more followers after World War II in Europe as people sought to understand the dynamics of the victim-offender relationship (Young & Stein, 2004). The early victimologists that you read about in Chapter 1 focused on the shared responsibility of victims in the crimes that happened to them. Therefore, the early focus on victims failed to understand the effect of the crime from the victim's perspective, but instead looked at how to "fix" this group of affected people. In a sense, this is similar to what was happening in the overall process, whereby states acted as proxies for victims and the harm done to a victim was considered a "social harm." In both arenas, victims were not included in the conversation and instead were considered a component in a problematic situation. In the 1960s, as the crime rate was increasing, researchers started to look at crime victims and the effects of crime a bit differently. Of particular importance was the work of Stephen Schaefer, who wrote a seminal book on shared responsibility for crime between the victim and the offender (Young & Stein, 2004). Prior to that work, in the early 1960s, Schaefer conducted a study on the criminal-offender relationship in violent crimes for the US Department of Health, Education, and Welfare in part to examine the high crime wave that occurred at the time. What he discovered was that rates of victimization were even higher than the official crime rates suggested. His work also showed that many of those who chose not to report crimes to the police did so out of a general distrust of the system. This work honed the focus within victimology on the effects of crime on the victim, as well as, victim discontent with the system. Therefore, the evolution of victimology took a great leap forward after we started conducting surveys measuring victimization, as the true picture was perceived to be much greater than just "shared responsibility" for crime by crime victims (Young & Stein, 2004).

Media Attention

In the 1960s, news reports of crimes started to highlight information about the victims of crimes as opposed to just reporting on the offenders or the crime incidents themselves (Dignan, 2005). A primary purpose of this tactic was to illustrate the impact of the crime on the victim, something that hadn't been focused on previous to this time. Therefore, it is important to note that media helped to bring the plight of crime victims to the forefront of society's attention in the overall discussion of crime. In Chapter 10, we will discuss the more recent discussion about the impact of the media on crime victims' ability to recover, but in terms of being a catalyst in the Victims' Rights Movement, it is safe to say that the media's focus on the plight of crime victims in news reports helped to bring attention to a previously invisible population.

Presidential and Political Influence

In response to the crime wave of the 1960s, President Lyndon Johnson established the President's Commission on Law Enforcement and Administration of Justice to assess how to address the increase in crime. Out of this commission came the first national victimization survey, conducted in the United States in 1966. For the first time, there was strong evidence that crime victimization was far higher than was recorded in official statistics presented by law enforcement. Additionally, the commission's report based on the study identified that victims did not report crime due to a general distrust of the criminal justice system, and that victims had specific needs that weren't being addressed, specifically the need for financial assistance after a crime and the need for services to assist them in their recovery. Furthermore, it was recommended that victims play a greater role in the criminal justice process (Tobolowsky, 2001). The commission also highlighted the need to provide financial assistance to victims, separate from restitution, which at the time was largely unused as a penalty by the court system. This recommendation seemed to follow the evolving standards of other nations as well, mirrored after work by Margery Fry, an English penal reformer, who first suggested it in the 1950s, leading to implementation of a crime victim compensation program in New Zealand in 1963 and Great Britain in 1964 (Dignan, 2005). (Victim compensation will be discussed in greater detail in Chapter 10.)

Another program created in the 1960s that had a great deal of influence on victims' rights was the Law Enforcement Assistance Administration (LEAA). The goal of this entity was to fund projects that could prevent crime or reduce its effects. Some of the programs that gained financial support from the LEAA were victim witness assistance programs in local-level prosecutor and law enforcement offices. These offices were integral to meeting the goal of providing victims with information about the criminal justice process and to aid victims in their recovery from crime. As discussed previously, at the same time, grassroots efforts started to take formation and local-level projects were created to provide assistance to specific groups of victims, for instance victims of sexual assault and domestic violence (Tobolowsky, 2001).

Without a doubt, President Ronald Reagan is responsible for two of the most impactful developments in our recognition of victims' needs and understanding of victims' issues. In 1981, President Reagan established the first National Crime Victims' Rights Week, a recognition that continues to this day in which activists, advocates, criminal justice and other practitioners, academics, and victims and survivors publically devote time, statements, and activities to empowering victims and celebrating the growth in the victim services and rights fields.

Whereas some saw the National Crime Victims' Rights Week establishment as merely symbolic, though important, President Reagan's second act demonstrated his commitment to understanding and improving the impact of crime on victims. On April 23, 1982, President Reagan issued Executive Order 12360, which established the President's Task Force on Victims of Crime, a nine-person panel who investigated the "current state" of victimology and victims' issues (Hook & Seymour, 2004). The members of the committee, led by Hon. Lois Haight (see profile this chapter), reviewed existing research in victimology and victimization, held cross-country hearings with professionals who provided services to and worked with victims, and spoke with victims themselves. Many in the victims' rights field believe this report was a significant turning point in the victim assistance field (Hook & Seymour, 2004). The task force members were particularly shocked at the level of secondary victimization, or revictimization, that seemed to be occurring. (**Revictimization** occurs when the crime victim feels harmed by his/her interaction with criminal justice personnel who are charged with serving and protecting the victim.)

Professional Profile 8.1

Judge Lois Haight Herrington

California Superior Court Judge

Q: What got you into the field of victimology and/or working with crime victims?

A: I first started working with victims of crime when I was a deputy District Attorney in Oakland, California (1975–1981). I realized how terrible victims were treated and blamed by almost everyone. I actually had a case that I tried and got a conviction and the victim came to court with me at the sentencing date ...

The judge recognized her and ordered her out of the court because he felt she was trying to influence or intimidate him in his decision. I responded "who would be more interested in the sentence than the person who had been raped"? The judge became furious and ordered us both out of court or face contempt of court.

Not only were most victims not allowed to write or speak in court about the impact of the crime on them and their family, they were not told when the court dates were to be held for bail hearing, plea bargains, trial setting, or sentencing. No one inquired of the victim when setting a trial date regarding their availability. The most egregious and most insulting of all was the constant blame on the victim for their victimization that came from everywhere: law enforcement, hospitals, doctors, nurses, victims, [and] employers when the victim needed time off to testify; friends and family even often blamed the victim.

When we moved to Washington, DC, in 1981, I was asked to chair the President's Task Force on Victims of Crime. This task force was a labor of love. I could actually verify with victims testifying throughout the United States that the poor treatment of victims and witnesses was universal and had to be changed.

When we presented the report to then President Reagan, he asked that I become Assistant Attorney General and implement the recommendations that were in the report. One of the first things I did was set up an Office for Victims of Crime in the US Department of Justice. I appointed the first director and then the office gained such prestige that it became an Attorney General appointment; and I believe even a presidential appointment for some of the time.

I have been a superior court judge in California for the past 20 years and have been the presiding judge for the juvenile court. I now see victims from a slightly different perspective. Victims of juvenile crime are no less harmed if the perpetrator was an adult or minor and many times have a lot more problems just from the fact that they were vulnerable and victimized by a young person. I also see many cases of child abuse where child victims have been severely injured and/or sexually abused by their parents. The word "molested" is often a euphemism for what is "rape" in the adult world. These children are often not even recognized as being victims of crime as if being beaten, burned, or molested is different if the actions were done by a parent or guardian.

Q: What advice do you have for students interested in working with victims and/or becoming victimologists?

A: The advice I have for students would be to look carefully at not just what is in the law, but is it being followed in fact. I would definitely sit in the courtroom for some cases, talk to victims who had to testify, and find out what help if any they were offered.

Q: What are some challenges to studying crime victims that you have encountered or seen?

A: The challenges are too many to enumerate. Making actual changes to a system with its attitudes and prejudices that has been in place for 100 years is very difficult. It takes a lot of patience and information sharing and understanding.

Q: What obstacles have you encountered while striving to study crime victims?

A: The biggest changes I have seen in assisting victims have come from their treatment by law enforcement. I believe they have made great strides in understanding and assisting victims of crime. Many have had excellent training and as one police officer stated to me "helping people is why I became a police officer" and victims definitely need help.

I think judges need a lot more training and understanding of victims' needs and fears and time availability. The prosecutors also need more training to be sensitive to victims' needs and not just getting their case finished. One example is that often when a victim has testified in a horrific case and they walk off the stand, the prosecutor doesn't even acknowledge them as they walk by them out of the courtroom; no "thank you for your time and effort" or anything, just on to the next witness.

Q: What do you feel is the mark you will have left on the field of victimology? What do you want people to see as your mark? At the end of the day, what do you want your "legacy" to be in the field of victimology/victim services?

A: I would leave this to others to judge or determine but I can say that I do care about victims. I was able to serve along with others at a time of transition for a legal system that served only judges, lawyers, and defendants. The victims were considered to on the same level as a piece of cold evidence. That has changed to a large degree over the last 25–30 years. It makes me proud to have been a part of that rebalancing of the system. I believe we helped some lawyers and judges and others to find their way again.

Q: What are some burgeoning issues that you see in the field of victimology?

A: Certainly a big issue is enforcement of the rights of victims. Just because it is statute does not mean it is followed in practice and what remedies do the victims have?

Q: What areas within victimology do you think are neglected?

A: The dependency court child victims need a lot of help that is not being provided.

The Final Report of the 1982 President's Task Force included 68 recommendations for improvement when working with crime victims and addressed many different factions, including:

> 1) The federal and state executive, legislative, and judicial branches; 2) criminal justice service agencies, including the police, prosecutors, and parole authorities; and 3) other professionals involved in crime victim service delivery, such as health care personnel, clergy, lawyers, educators, mental health care providers, and relevant private sector personnel (Tobolowsky, 2001, p. 9).

The tone of the report suggested that there needed to be more attention paid to providing "victim-friendly" services, including an expansion of overall services and a focus on how victims were treated by criminal justice and related victim service personnel. The task force advocated for the implementation of state victim compensation programs and the requirement of restitution in all cases in which a victim experienced financial loss, unless there was a compelling reason not to do so. Similar to the Law and Order Movement, the task force suggested that the exclusionary rule be abolished, suspects be detained (incarcerated) prior to trial, sentencing guidelines be imposed to thwart judicial discretion on cases, and parole be abolished (Tobolowsky, 2001). The task force also suggested that the Sixth Amendment within the Bill of Rights of the US Constitution be amended to include a statement about the victims' inclusion in judicial proceedings related to their cases. A great deal of attention was paid to addressing the lack of notification victims' appeared to be receiving in relation to court proceedings, and the lack of input victims were allowed to have in cases that affected them.

Hook and Seymour (2004) indicate that the members were unanimous in their findings, which suggested that (1) the criminal justice system routinely revictimized victims, (2) there was an imbalance of rights between defendants and victims, with defendants benefitting from a great many rights and victims few to none, and (3) victims were poorly treated more often than was initially imagined. The impact of the 1982 President's Task Force has been quite far-reaching. For the most part, policies and programs have been created to address most of the 68 recommendations, with the exception of the constitutional amendment. State victims' bills of rights have been passed in over thirty states (to be discussed below), with the remainder of states implementing some type of legislation addressing victim services and victims' rights (Tobolowsky, Gaboury, Jackson, & Blackburn, 2010). Numerous developments, including the establishment of the Office for Victims of Crime and the Victims of Crime Act of 1984, came out of the President's task force recommendations as well and will be discussed a bit later in this chapter. It is clear that the 1982 President's Task Force on Victims of Crime has had a major impact on how crime victims are treated and the report continues to impact the field to this day.

Politicians in the federal and state legislatures also had a hand in bringing attention to victims' rights. Tobolowsky et al. (2010) report that there are "currently over 27,000 federal and state statutes that directly or indirectly affect crime victim rights and interests" (p. 11). Mostly notably there have been numerous bills written and sponsored by politicians using a victim's name to advocate for changes in law based on gaps that become obvious after the media shines light on notable cases. Almost everyone is familiar with Megan's Law and Amber Alert; these are the most notable examples of these types of laws. The good thing about these laws is that in many instances they do indeed address gaps or loopholes in laws that weren't previously considered. There is a downside, however, when a victim's name is used to advocate for a law but it is merely symbolic and there is no true meat to the law and/or the politician is doing it for (1) personal gain, or (2) to pressure other politicians into voting for a bill (that may have other things in it) as opposed to appearing as if they are "anti-victim" or soft on crime.

Victims' Bills of Rights

The most current information suggests that there are 33 states with victims' bills of rights within their state constitutions and the remainder of states have passed some type of crime victims' rights legislation (NCVLI, 2011). Wisconsin was the first state to enact a crime victims' bill of rights in 1980 and the most recent enactments occurred in 1998 (see Table 8A).

Though each state has variations in their victims' bill of rights, most states have the following protections and guidelines:

- The right to be treated with fairness, respect, and dignity;
- The right to information;
- The right to notification of criminal justice proceedings;
- The right to be present at criminal justice proceedings;
- The right to be heard at criminal justice proceedings;
- The right to protection;
- The right to privacy; and
- The right to financial recompense for losses suffered. (Tobolowsky et al., 2010)

Table 8A: State Enactments of Crime Victims' Bills of Rights

Year of Enactment	State(s)
1980	Wisconsin
1982	California
1986	Rhode Island
1988	Florida; Michigan
1989	Texas; Washington
1990	Arizona
1991	New Jersey
1992	Colorado; Illinois; Kansas; Missouri; New Mexico
1994	Alabama; Alaska; Idaho; Maryland; Ohio; Utah
1996	Connecticut; Indiana; Nebraska; Nevada; North Carolina; Oklahoma; South Carolina; Virginia
1998	Louisiana; Mississippi; Montana; Tennessee
1999	Oregon (originally enacted in 1996, repealed in 1998, reenacted in 1999)

Source: 2014 NCVRW Resource Guide.

The right to be treated with fairness, respect, and dignity is a guideline for criminal justice personnel when dealing with crime victims. The purpose of this right is to help to eliminate the revictimization that was highlighted in the president's task force report from 1982. It does not require that the criminal justice system neglect evidence, contradictions, or gut feelings, but instead it suggests that victims not be treated in a manner that would wound them further, giving them the benefit of the doubt that their claims are honest.

The right to information is meant to address the lack of knowledge crime victims have about the criminal justice process and the rights and services that might be available to them to help them through the process and to recover from the incident.

A main finding of the President's Task Force on Victims of Crime in 1982 was that victims were not being told about criminal justice proceedings taking place. Additionally, victims were not being notified about case conclusions and sentences of offenders as well. The task force recommended that victims be notified of *all* criminal justice proceedings. This right ensures that victims are aware of when proceedings are occurring so they can plan out if and how they will attend. Some states have enacted automated notification systems that enable victims to provide the system with their contact information and the information of the defendant/offender so they can receive notice of any proceedings and/or changes in custody (to be discussed further in Chapter 10).

The task force heard from crime victims that oftentimes they were not allowed into the courtroom to attend criminal justice proceedings. Defense attorneys often employed tactics that disallowed victims from coming into the courtroom. The right to be present eliminates the ability of defense attorneys from being able to bar victims from the courtroom for any reason.

Victims are also often afforded the right to be heard at criminal justice proceedings. Typically, victims will provide a victim impact statement to the agency responsible for putting together the presentence investigation report. This statement is in written form and is included in the pre-sentence investigation report that is presented to the judge. One of the critiques of victim impact statements is that they are requested early in the process and might not address the full spectrum of harm a victim will experience. When victim impact statements are allowed to be presented can also vary from state to state. Some victim impact statements are only allowed to be presented after a sentence has been determined. In this sense, the victim impact statement may be more of a symbolic act than an element to be considered by a jury or a judge, but it can have a cathartic effect for victims as it allows them to tell the offender and the jury/judge how the crime has impacted them.

The right to protection has been afforded to crime victims as a result of victims being forced to inhabit the same space as the defendant throughout a criminal justice proceeding. Some of the testimony that the president's task force heard included comments from victims about having to share the same physical space with the defendant and being harassed by the defendant or defendant's family. This right entitles victims to protection from intimidation and harassment from the defendant or defendant's family/friends, but also allows for some physical separation between them so that the victim does not have to relive the incident.

The right to privacy provides victims with the security that their personal information will not be provided to parties who do not have a reasonable expectation to have it.

The right to financial recompense provides victims with the security that if they experienced financial losses or financial hardships, part of the punishment for the offender will include restitution to help the victims recover from the loss. In addition, if the crime is a personal crime, the victim may be eligible for crime victim compensation if he/she meets the eligibility criteria for the state. Trulson (2005) suggests that deeming some crimes more worthy of assistance than others is a bit of a slap in the face. He notes that victims will evaluate the situation from their own perspective and may believe that what happened to them is just as traumatic as what happened to another victim, but according to the state, one victim's experience may be eligible for assistance while another's is not. This is a compelling issue that should be investigated further.

It is a huge step for states to incorporate victims' bills of rights into their state constitutions, but what happens when those rights are violated? Tobolowsky (2001) suggests that the biggest problem with crime victims' rights as proscribed in state legislation is that there are specific prohibitions against victims citing any claim of action for a violation of their rights or requesting an alteration in the outcome of the proceeding. Additionally, some states have written into their amendments that the offender cannot use the violation of victims' rights as a cause for relief. In the grand scheme, it appears that most states prohibit victims from seeking specific types of redress when their rights are violated, though many states do include remedies for at least some types of violations.

Victim Assistance Organizations and Victimology Societies

Since the 1970s there has been a tremendous amount of growth in national organizations whose purposes are to provide information to victims and victims service providers, to advocate on behalf of victims in both legal arenas and for legislation, and to provide services to victims themselves. Many of these organizations were started by primary or secondary victims themselves in response to the lack of assistance available to them in their time of need and the desire to help others like them. The following chronology comes from the 2014 National Crime Victims' Rights Week Resource Guide as well as other sources.

In 1975/1976, the **National Organization for Victim Assistance (NOVA)** was created; it was co-founded by Dr. John Dussich and Dr. Marlene Young, noting the development of the first national victim assistance in the United States (Young and Stein, 2004). Young and Stein (2004) note that the organization was the outgrowth of ideas propagated at the first national conference on victim assistance held in Ft. Lauderdale, Florida, in 1973 and that the goals of the organization were to promote and provide opportunities for networking and training for those working with victims.

In 1977 the **National Association of Crime Victim Compensation Boards** was created by the 22 states that operated compensation programs. The purpose was to create a network of compensation programs to improve services so that victims are given the assistance they need to cope with the costs of crime (National Crime Victims' Rights Week Resource Guide, 2014).

The **Protect the Innocent** organization was created in Indiana in 1977 as well, by a number of individuals, including Betty Jane Spencer who was left for dead after being attacked in her home and witnessing her four sons being murdered (Hook & Seymour, 2004). The purpose of the organization was to change the laws in Indiana to improve rights for victims.

In 1978 two organizations espousing the convictions of the Women's Movement entered the spectrum. The **National Coalition Against Sexual Assault (NCASA)** was formed to provide guidance to the rape crisis centers that were growing throughout the country. The **National Coalition Against Domestic Violence (NCADV)** was founded by over 100 battered women's advocates across the country with the goals of getting formal criminal justice recognition of domestic violence as a crime and persuasion to deal with these acts as criminal and not personal matters. Similar to the National Coalition Against Sexual Assault, the NCADV sought to also provide guidance and support to the growing women's shelters, hotlines, and advocacy agencies dealing with domestic violence (Davis, 2005).

The **Parents of Murdered Children, Inc. (POMC)** organization was also created in 1978 in Cincinnati, Ohio, by the parents of a woman who was murdered by her ex-boyfriend. The organization continues as a self-help organization established for the purpose of providing support to people who have lost someone to murder. As of 2015 the organization has just over 45 chapters and holds an annual conference each year that provides support, networking, and information on legal processes (Parents of Murdered Children, visited June 22, 2017).

The **Crime Victims' Legal Advocacy Institute, Inc., (renamed The Victims' Assistance Legal Organization, or VALOR in 1981)** was established in 1979 to advocate for the rights of crime victims in both civil and criminal justice systems.

The **World Society of Victimology**, an international organization focused on advancing research, service, education, victims' rights, and awareness of victims on a global spectrum was formally created in Munster, Germany, in 1979 (Dussich, 2006). Today the organization has affiliations with victimology associations in 26 different countries and routinely provides recommendations on a global scale, including to the United Nations Crime Congress (World Society of Victimology, visited March 4, 2017).

In 1980, Candy Lightner and Cindi Lamb co-founded **Mothers Against Drunk Driving** after Lightner's daughter was killed and Lamb's infant daughter became a quadriplegic by repeat drunk driving offenders. The purpose of the organization is to provide support to victims and survivors, to educate the public on the effects of drunk driving, and to lobby for legislation related to drunk driving (Hook & Seymour, 2004).

In 1983, in response to the President's Task Force on Victims of Crime report, the **Office for Victims of Crime (OVC)** was created within the US Department of Justice. OVC was formally established in an amendment to the 1984 VOCA Act. The OVC is the organization that administers the Crime Victims Fund, which exists to fund federal and state victim compensation programs, training and technical assistance, and funding for victim assistance programs. It is also a repository of information for practitioners, researchers, and crime victims, with an information portal that can lead victims to services available in their own communities.

In 1984, after much lobbying by John Walsh (father of Adam Walsh and host of *America's Most Wanted*) the **National Center for Missing and Exploited Children (NCMEC)** was created as the nation's primary resource agency for missing children. The agency was designed after the Adam Walsh Outreach Center for Missing Children set up in Florida to aid in the recovery of Adam Walsh after he was kidnapped. The purpose of this agency is to provide case management, advocacy, and information to law enforcement agencies and parents in an effort to find and recover missing children, address child sexual exploitation, and enhance the safety of children in the United States (DeValve, 2008; 2014 NCVRW Resource Guide). Additionally, the agency has a peer support component of parents of missing children named Team HOPE, which provides support and guidance to families of missing and sexually exploited children (Team Hope, visited June 22, 2017).

In 1985, the **National Victim Center** was founded in honor of Sunny Von Bulow with the purpose of both advocating on behalf of victims and providing education

"In the News" Box 8.1

On December 8, 2008, *New York Times* reporter Yolanne Almanzar published an article entitled "27 Years Later, Case Is Closed in Slaying of Abducted Child." The article discusses the case of Adam Walsh, son of victims' rights advocate and host of *America's Most Wanted* and *The Hunt*, John Walsh. After 27 years, police in Hollywood, Florida, finally closed the case, naming Ottis Toole as the murderer of Adam Walsh. According to the article, the chief of police in Hollywood, Florida, noted regret that the case was not closed earlier, given the amount of evidence they had against Mr. Toole while he was still alive. The article goes on to discuss the important contributions John and Revé Walsh have made to the victims' rights field, including creation of the National Center for Missing and Exploited Children, as well as the Missing Children's Act in 1982.

To read the full article, visit: http://www.nytimes.com/2008/12/17/us/17adam. html?_r=0.

to practitioners and the general public about the effects of crime. The name of the center was changed to the **National Center for Victims of Crime** in 1998. More recently, the center has created a new Stalking Resource Center, and is invested in addressing the issues of DNA backlogs and financial abuse of the elderly (personal communication with Kath Cummins, NCVC, February 3, 2014). In addition to being a leading information clearinghouse and advocacy center, NCVC was asked by victims and family members to partner with them to establish the National Compassion Fund, which solicits donations for victims of mass violence, of which 100% of those donations are distributed to victims of crime incidents such as the Aurora Theater shooting, the Ft. Hood shooting, the Pulse nightclub shooting in Orlando, and most recently, the Las Vegas shooting (National Center for Victims of Crime, National Compassion Fund, visited June 22, 2017 & October 26, 2017).

In 1987, **Security on Campus, Inc. (SOC)** (now the Clery Center for Security on Campus) was established by the parents of Jeanne Clery, a student at Lehigh University who was raped and murdered by her ex-boyfriend. An important piece of federal legislation was borne out of this organization, known as the "Clery Act," in which universities must report specific types of crime to the campus community, or a specific segment of the campus community, in a timely manner following an occurrence. Additionally, the act requires that universities include three years' worth of statistics in their reports, including efforts by the university to improve safety and prevent dating violence, sexual assault, and stalking. There are four categories of crimes that need reporting—criminal offenses (including Part I Index crimes excluding larceny-theft), hate crimes, Violence Against Women Act (VAWA) offenses, and arrests and referrals for disciplinary action (Clery Center, Clery Act Requirements, visited June

Professional Profile 8.2

Aurelia Sands Belle
Executive Director, Durham
Crisis Response Center

Q: How did you get involved with working with crime victims? How did your role evolve in victims services (i.e., started out as victim advocate, became executive director of an agency, etc.)? In what capacity do you currently work with victims? Have you ever been engaged in a joint research/ practice project? Please describe.

A: Upon the recommendation of my college professor, I began working at the Grady Rape Crisis Center in Atlanta, GA. Prior to that time, I worked at a children's home and had a peripheral understanding of sexual assault. Within in three years, I was asked to establish services in Atlanta for all crime victims, thus the Victim Witness Assistance Program (VWAP) began, where I served as the first executive director. VWAP was initially located in police headquarters and was eventually relocated to the municipal court, and thereby more convenient to victims and their families. As this was the founding years of the victim assistance field, we worked hard to successfully impact and change the mindsets of law enforcement, the court system, and the legislature. I had the privilege of working to establish the first laws around victim compensation, victims' rights, representation of victims on state boards/councils, and numerous other types of laws relevant to victims.

Since residing in North Carolina, I served as director of Rape Crisis Volunteers of Cumberland County and interim director for the NC Coalition Against Sexual Assault. Currently, I am the executive director of Durham Crisis Response Center (DCRC) in Durham, NC. DCRC provides comprehensive services to victims of domestic and sexual violence.

I have worked on a number of small research projects with students at the graduate and undergraduate levels.

Q: What advice do you have for students interested in working with victims?

A: Working with victims of crime can be extremely challenging, yet rewarding. Students will have to consider their personal goals and reasons for coming into the field. Oftentimes, survivors want to "give back" but find direct services overwhelming. I would remind students that help can come in many forms so consider support services, but always have a heart for the voice of victims. Avoid becoming cavalier, or judgmental. Know that you are not going into this field for monetary gain or other self-aggrandizement. Often, lives hang in the balance and it takes those who are a concerned and want to truly make a difference.

Most victim services programs are either community-based or system-based. The latter takes on the essence or beliefs of that office (i.e., police, sheriff, prosecutor, corrections) and the advocate must adhere to that agency's beliefs, even when they seem to override or be insensitive to the voices of victims.

Community-based programs are generally nonprofits with more latitude and their services are not contingent upon cooperation with systems. The victim advocacy movement began as a community ground swell and such programs continue to exude that same spirit. While independent, they have learned to work effectively with system-based advocates on behalf of victims.

For direct services, I believe a human service degree such as counseling, social work, psychology, or a similar degree would be the most beneficial. These fields clearly express an interest in working directly with clients.

Many survivors want to work in this field, but until they have reached a level of healing I do not recommend it. This work can trigger issues and concerns that unless addressed, might be harmful to those served and certainly those who wish to help. Vicarious trauma can also result from hearing tragic stories over and over. Students have to develop a constitution and an outlet for dealing with this work. It certainly is not for the faint of heart, but is exceptionally rewarding!

Q: What are some challenges for working with victims, especially as it relates to dealing with the criminal justice system and/or lawmakers?

A: Although things have improved and we are making strides, many of the challenges we were faced with in early years continue to plague us. This is especially true as we consider sexual assault. Their behaviors—pro or con—are still scrutinized and they are often the butt of victim-blaming. This is reflected in recent nationally publicized sexual assault cases (i.e., Sandusky, Steubenville, and military rapes).

The greater difficulty lies in the perceptions of legislators. Recently, agencies were informed that North Carolina was considering phasing out funding to existing programs after a specified period of time. Some administrators believe that victim programs should receive support locally and not through the state. Although this sounds good it is an incorrect assumption. First, many local entities do not have the resources to adequately support these programs. Secondly, dedicated funds have been allocated through the federal and state governments to provide these services without reference to time-limits. Finally, if such constraints are put in place it would serve to undermine the rights and needs of crime victims, while offering similar/same services to offenders.

Over the last year we have heard astounding comments from legislators and other leaders about sexual violence, in particular:

- Rep. Lawrence E. Lockman, Maine — (in reference to abortion) He also asked why rape should be illegal if abortion is to be allowed, saying, "At least the rapist's pursuit of sexual freedom doesn't (in most cases) result in anyone's death."
- Rep. Todd Akin, Missouri — (in reference to abortion) "It seems to me, from what I understand from doctors, that's really rare," Mr. Akin said of pregnancies from rape. "If it's a legitimate rape, the female body has ways to try to shut that whole thing down. But let's assume that maybe that didn't work or something: I think there should be some punishment, but the punishment ought to be of the rapist, and not attacking the child."
- Montana District Judge G. Todd sentenced a former teacher for raping a 14-year-old to one month in jail. When Baugh delivered the sentence that reduced the man's possible 20-year sentence, he determined the victim was "older than her chronological age" and was "as much in control of the situation" as the teacher. The victim took her life a few days before her 17th birthday, while the case was still pending. Her mother told the court that the rape was a "major factor" in her suicide.
- A judge in Alabama has ruled that a man convicted of raping a 14-year-old on three occasions will get no jail time. Instead, Limestone County Circuit Judge James Woodroof reduced the rapist's 10- and 20-year prison sentences to two years in a program for nonviolent criminals and three years on probation. He will also pay a $2,000 fine.

Interestingly enough, these men seem to link rape with abortion.

Another systemic challenge is accurately tracking sex offenders and others who perpetrate violence against women and children. So often these offenders are not properly charged and their patterns of abuse are not identified. If they arrested or even brought to court the charges are pled down and deviant behavior patterns are not properly tagged and followed.

Q: What obstacles have you encountered while striving to assist victims? Have the obstacles to providing good service to victims changed over the years?

A: External obstacles include systems that are supposed to help actually end up hurting victims. Victims have gone to the hospital for a forensic examination where they were re-traumatized. For years, they had to pay for the examination. Nurses spoke harshly, questioned their stories, and embarrassed them in the waiting area ("We have a lady in waiting room saying she is a rape victim"). They were made to wait hours (and this still happens today) for a nurse willing to do the exam and now for a SANE to come in. Although there have been improvements, in many parts of our state victims of sexual assault have to travel exceptional distances for help. While animal shelters exist in almost every county, similar programming is not available for women and children.

One of the biggest struggles continues to be overcoming the culture of abuse and violence against women and how that translates in the community (including communities of faith) and criminal justice system. Victims of domestic violence can be asked to leave their apartments because of violence, even though there are statues against it. Unless she seeks help and is told otherwise, she feels compelled to leave her home.

One of the other primary obstacles is adequate funding. Efforts are underway to reduce the cap on VOCA and to divert funds designated for victim services. In North Carolina programs are being advised to look for funding from other sources in the future because the focus will be on other issues such as stopping gang violence and drugs. Both contribute to victimization.

Q: What do you feel is the mark you will have left on the field of victim services? What do you want people to see as your mark? At the end of the day, what do you want your "legacy" to be in the field of victimology/victim services?

A: My mark should be that I helped—what I did made the difference in someone's life. My mark should be that I opened someone else's eye to the need to care. My mark should be that I left someone else to carry the baton. I cherish the fact that I see interns and volunteers establish their careers in the field.

Q: What are some burgeoning issues that you see in the fields of victimology/ victim services?

A: Greater access to services. Increased respect for victim service providers and a continuing need is for addressing stronger system collaborations without territorial fear.

Q: Are there groups of victims you think need to be served but are not? Why do you think that way?

A: I recently spoke with a survivor whose offender was exonerated and another where the perpetrator will be released without supervision (he will have completed his prison sentence).

22, 2017. The organization has evolved to improve campus safety through training of university personnel on how to best prevent victimization and respond to victims. Additionally, it provides tools for schools to assess their policies for compliance with the Clery Act and other federal legislation related to crime occurring to students both on and off campus and/or on public property surrounding the campus, thereby impacting the safety of those attending, working, or living on the campus environment. A primary goal of the organization remains raising awareness about crime and victimization on college campuses across the nation (National Sexual Violence Resource Center, visited June 22, 2017).

In 1988, collaboration among the University of Delaware, the National Association of State Units on Aging, and the American Public Welfare Association led to the establishment of the **National Center on Elder Abuse**. This organization provides information and statistics to the public on the burgeoning issue of elder abuse.

In 1999, the **National Crime Victim Bar Association** was formed by NCVC. The purpose of this association is to promote justice in the civil realm for victims of crime.

To address the growing problem of cybercrime, the **Internet Crime Complaint Center** was created in 2000 as a collaboration between the Federal Bureau of Investigation and the National White Collar Crime Center. The purpose of the center is to collect information from individuals who believe they have been victims of cybercrime perpetrated fraud and to refer those cases out to law enforcement in the various regions as applicable. They also compile annual reports illustrating the amount of cybercrime fraud that is perpetrated and the characteristics of the victims of these offenses.

In 2002, the **National Association of VOCA Assistance Administrators (NAVAA)** was established. The purpose of the organization is to provide technical support to agencies who receive VOCA funding with training and technical assistance.

In 2003, the **American Society of Victimology** was established as a forum for academics and practitioners to discuss all topics related to victimology. The creation of this new group was done in partnership with the already established World Society of Victimology. A conference takes place every year.

In 2014, the **It's On Us movement** emerged to combat campus sexual assault nationwide. It asks people to pledge that they recognize sexual assault, they will identify dangerous/vulnerable environments in which it could occur, they intervene when they see a situation occurring that could lead to sexual assault, and to create a world in which we are no longer at risk of this crime. It has garnered a great deal of support from both organizations on and pertaining to campus life and is advocated for by many notable people in the entertainment community (It's On Us Movement, visited June 22, 2017).

Summary and Conclusions

A great deal of growth has occurred in the Victims' Rights Movement in the past 40 years. National organizations have been created to collect information and data; to act as clearinghouses for victims, practitioners, and academics; and to provide assistance to victims of all crimes. Additionally, given the influence of social movements, the media, politicians, and academia, there have been great strides made in securing rights for victims that lead to better opportunities for sensitive and effective treatment for victims in the long run. Victimology and victims services have truly started to be seen as partners at the table of criminology and criminal justice, and though there is more work to be done, looking back it is clear that a great deal has been accomplished in the last four decades.

Key Terms

Civil Rights Movement of 1964
Law and Order Movement
Women's Movement
Revictimization
National Organization for Victim Assistance (NOVA)
National Association of Crime Victim Compensation Boards
Protect the Innocent
National Coalition Against Sexual Assault (NCASA)
National Coalition Against Domestic Violence (NCADV)
Parents of Murdered Children, Inc. (POMC)
Crime Victims' Legal Advocacy Institute, Inc., (renamed The Victims'

Assistance Legal Organization, or VALOR)
World Society of Victimology
Mothers Against Drunk Driving
Office for Victims of Crime (OVC)
National Center for Missing and Exploited Children (NCMEC)
National Victim Center
National Center for Victims of Crime
Security on Campus, Inc. (SOC)
National Center on Elder Abuse
National Crime Victim Bar Association
Internet Crime Complaint Center
National Association of VOCA Assistance Administrators (NAVAA)
American Society of Victimology
It's On Us movement

Discussion Questions

1. Given what you have learned thus far, what rights are still missing and/or what groups of victims do not have national organizations devoted to their safety and well-being?
2. Do you think there will ever be an amendment to the US Constitution addressing victims' rights? Why or why not?
3. What common right within state victims' bill of rights do you think is the most important and why?

Websites for Further Information

NCVC, Victims Rights: http://www.victimsofcrime.org/help-for-crime-victims/get-help-bulletins-for-crime-victims/victims'-rights.

National Crime Victims Law Institute: www.ncvli.org.

OVC, Overview of Victims' Rights: http://www.ovc.gov/rights/overview_rights.html.

References

Barlow, D. E., & Barlow, M. H. (2001). *Police in a multicultural society: An American story.* Long Grove, IL: Waveland Press, Inc.

Clery Center, Clery Act Requirements, https://clerycenter.org/policy-resources/the-clery-act, visited June 22, 2017.

Davis, J. T. (2005, spring/summer). The grassroots beginnings of the victims' rights movement. *NCVLI News.* Retrieved from www.ncvli.org.

DeValve, E. Q. (2008). For Adam: The John Walsh story. In J. Bumgarner, *Icons of crime fighting: Relentless pursuers of justice* (Vol. 2), (pp. 421–436). Westport, CT: Greenwood Press.

Dignan, J. (2005). *Understanding victims and restorative justice.* New York, NY: Open University Press/McGraw Hill.

Dussich, J. P. J. (2006). *Victimology—Past, present and future.* In S. Cornell, Resource Material Series, No. 70, (pp. 116–129). NCJ 219628.

Hook, M., & Seymour, A. (2004). *A retrospective of the 1982 President's Task Force on Victims of Crime: A component of the Office for Victims of Crime oral history project.* Washington, DC: Department of Justice, Office of Justice Programs, Office for Victims of Crime.

Houser, K., & Dworkin, E. (2009). *The use of truth-telling devices in sexual assault investigations.* National Sexual Violence Resource Center: Critical Issues, National SART Tookit.

It's On Us Movement (visited June 22, 2017). http://www.itsonus.org/.

Morgan, A. (1987). Criminal law—Victims' rights: Remembering the "forgotten person" in the criminal justice system. *Marquette Law Review, 70,* 572–597.

National Association of Crime Victim Compensation Boards. (n.d.). Crime victim compensation—An overview. Retrieved from http://www.nacvcb.org/index.asp?bid=14.

National Center for Victims of Crime, www.victimsofcrime.org (visited June 22, 2017 & October 26, 2017).

National Compassion Fund, FAQ, https://nationalcompassionfund.org/faq (visited June 22, 2017.

National Crime Victim Law Institute (NCVLI). (2011). History of victims' rights. Retrieved from https://law.lclark.edu/centers/national_crime_victim_law_institute/about_ncvli/history_of_victims_rights/.

National Crime Victims' Rights Week Resource Guide (2014). Section 5: Landmarks in Victims' Rights & Services: An Historical Overview. National Center for Victims of Crime.

National Sexual Violence Resource Center. Clery Center for Security on Campus. http://www.nsvrc.org/organizations/98 (visited June 22, 2017).

Office for Victims of Crime. (2014). Chapter 5: Landmarks in victims' rights & services: An historical overview. In Office for Victims of Crime, 2014 NCVRW Resource Guide, 30 years: Restoring the balance. Washington, DC: US Department of Justice, Office of Justice Programs, Office for Victims of Crime. Retrieved from http://ovc.ncjrs.gov/ncvrw2014/.

Oregon Department of Justice, Crime Victims' Rights Division. (2014). Crime victims' rights. Retrieved from http://www.doj.state.or.us/victims/pages/rights_enforcement_task_force.aspx.

Parents of Murdered Children.(visited June 22, 2017). Retrieved from http://www.pomc.org/chapters.html.

Security on Campus, Inc. Campus Sexual Assault Victims' Bill of Rights. Retrieved from http://dsa.csupomona.edu/vpwrc/files/campus_sexual_assault_bill_of_rights_7546.pdf, June 22, 2017.

Team HOPE. Retrieved from http://www.missingkids.com/, June 22, 2017.

Tobolowsky, P. M. (2001). *Crime victim rights and remedies.* Durham, NC: Carolina Academic Press.

Tobolowsky, P. M., Gaboury, M. T., Jackson, A. L., & Blackburn, A. G. (2010). *Crime victim rights and remedies* (2nd ed.). Durham, NC: Carolina Academic Press.

Trulson, C. (2005). Victims' rights and services: Eligibility, exclusion, and victim worth. *Criminal Justice Policy Review, 4*(2), 399–414.

West, T. C. (2004). *African Americans.* In M. D. Smith (Ed.), *Encyclopedia of Rape* (pp. 6–7). Westport, CT: Greenwood Press.

World Society of Victimology. Retrieved from http://www.worldsocietyofvictimology.org/about.html. Visited June 22, 2017.

Young, M. D., & Stein, J. (2004). *The history of the crime victims' movement in the United States: A component of the Office for Victims of Crime oral history project.* Washington, DC: US Department of Justice, Office of Justice Programs, Office for Victims of Crime.

Chapter 9: Federal Victims' Rights Legislation

Evolution of Victims' Rights and Assistance through Legislation

Overview

Morgan (1987) suggests that victims' rights legislation tends to fall within three broad categories: (1) financial assistance to victims, (2) victims' rights as proscribed in both federal and state legislation, and (3) services and benefits to specific classes of victims, such as children, battered women, and rape/sexual assault victims. These three categories cover a broad spectrum of rights, and as you'll see, these rights took some time to be secured. For some, particularly those advocating for a constitutional amendment at the federal level, the wait continues. The information highlighted below illustrates the evolution of federal crime victim legislation and state-sponsored or supported victim assistance programming in the United States, with some additional discussion about important events outside of the US. The information provided here was compiled by and disseminated in the 2014 National Crime Victims' Rights Week Resource Guide, as well as some additional resources.

1960s: First Steps

Initial forays into victim legislation appear to have been in the area of victim compensation legislation. In 1965, California established the first crime victim compensation program in the country. By the end of the 1960s, five more victim compensation programs were established in New York, Hawaii, Massachusetts, Maryland, and the US Virgin Islands. The same pattern exists for outside of the United States, as New Zealand and Great Britain passed similar victim compensation legislation in the 1960s as well.

1970s: Gaining Momentum in Victim Activism

The 1970s saw a lot of important firsts in the area of victim activism and victim advocacy. As discussed previously, the first rape crisis centers and battered women shelters were established in the early 1970s on the coasts and in the heartland of the United States. The first official National Crime Survey (later to be named the National Crime Victimization Survey) was administered and the first official results were disseminated in 1973. In 1974, the Law Enforcement Assistance Administration (LEAA) funded the very first victim/witness program in nine district attorney's offices across the United States. Additionally, the first law enforcement-based victim assistance programs were created in Florida and Indiana. Also in 1974 we saw the passing of the **Child Abuse Prevention and Treatment Act**, the first piece of victim-related legislation passed by Congress. The act created the National Center on Child Abuse and Neglect and was created as an information clearinghouse, a technical assistance center, and a place where information about best practices could be collected and shared. In 1975, the first "Victims' Rights Week" was organized by the Philadelphia District Attorney's Office and the first national victim assistance organization was created, the National Organization for Victim Assistance (NOVA).

When it comes to the issue of domestic abuse/battering, 1976 was a big year of firsts. The National Organization for Women called for research on and funding to address the issue of battering of women. The first national conference on battering was held in Milwaukee, Wisconsin, the first telephone hotline for battered women was established in St. Paul, Minnesota, and in Pasadena, California, the first battered women's shelters were established. Also in California in 1976, we saw the first uses of victim impact statements being included in presentence investigation reports by Chief Probation Officer James Rowland.

By 1977, 22 states had victim compensation programs and were eager to share information among themselves as to best practices, so they created the National Association of Crime Victim Compensation Boards. Also in that year, Oregon enacted the first mandatory arrest law for domestic violence cases. Shortly thereafter, in 1978, Minnesota began to allow warrantless arrests for domestic assaults regardless of whether a protection order had been issued.

1980s: Recognition and Growth

The 1980s brought about a great deal of recognition and growth in the area of victims' rights and advocacy. This was the decade in which some of the most impactful pieces of legislation were enacted in the history of victims' rights.

In 1980, the organization Mothers Against Drunk Driving (MADD) was founded with two chapters opening in California and Maryland. Relatedly, the first victim impact panel discussing the impact of drunk driving was sponsored by a local organization named Remove Intoxicated Drivers (RID) in Oswego County, New York. Wisconsin established the first Crime Victims' Bill of Rights and the NCADV established its first National Day of Unity to honor the lives of battered women who died, celebrate the lives of those who have survived domestic violence, and to acknowledge the great work done by victim advocates in the domestic violence field. Congress also passed an important piece of legislation that year when they enacted the **Parental Kidnapping Prevention Act of 1980**. This act made it criminal for a non-custodial parent to take a child away from the custodial parent.

As previously discussed, President Ronald Reagan dedicated the first Crime Victims' Rights Week in April of 1981 and the Attorney General's Task Force on Violence Crime recommended to the president that an in-depth study be conducted exploring victims' needs. The tragic kidnapping and murder of six-year-old Adam Walsh also occurred in 1981, which led to a campaign to educate the public about missing children and establish better laws to protect children from abduction.

It is no surprise, then, that in 1982 Congress passed the **Missing Children's Act of 1982** to ensure that information on missing children was promptly entered into the National Crime Information Center (NCIC) maintained by the FBI. The **Victim and Witness Protection Act (VWPA) of 1982** was also enacted and thus provided clarity and guidance for how federal crime victims and witnesses should be treated. This act had a large impact on victims' rights and addressed a number of different areas that had become concerning to persons working with victims. The VWPA was meant to be a model to state and local governmental agencies as well, as the majority of violent crime was dealt with in those jurisdictions. Morgan (1987) states that there were six main provisions of the VWPA: (1) inclusion of victim impact statements in presentence investigation reports prepared for federal judges; (2) protection against intimidation for both witnesses and victims (previous law had protections for witnesses only); (3) mandatory restitution orders for victims by the court and if not ordered, a statement explaining why they chose not to do so; (4) accountability of the federal government for premature releases and escapes of felons and ability of victims to seek redress if a person was harmed by an offender prematurely released or escaped; (5) guidelines for government agents on how to best treat victims, with the suggested implementation of a Victims' Bill of Rights to codify the treatment that victims should receive; and (6) set guidelines that prohibited offenders from gaining financially from the telling of his/her crime.

In terms of information gathering about crime victims, 1982 was a big year, as this was the year that President Reagan appointed the nine-person Task Force on Victims of Crime that provided strong recommendations for states and local areas to follow to improve services to victims. Smaller in scope, but no less important, California amended its constitution to establish a constitutional right to victim compensation for crime victims. Though there were some great steps forward, there was also one large step back in the fight for victims' rights. Congress decided to abolish the Law Enforcement Assistance Administration, which led to the closing of numerous victim assistance programs. Perhaps this is the first time that we see the important link between words (legislation) and action (funding associated with new legislation) and the devastation that commences when that link is broken.

Some important growth in the areas of policing and court treatment of crime victims occurred in 1983. The US Attorney General established a task force on family violence and held hearings across America to explore the issue. He also issued a set of guidelines that outlined how government agents should work to provide the best service to crime victims. The International Association of Chiefs of Police (IACP) committed solid resources to understanding the needs of crime victims in terms of law enforcement interactions with them and IACP adopted a Crime Victims' Bill of Rights for their organization. The First National Conference of the Judiciary took place in Nevada wherein it developed recommendations for how judges could best serve the needs of crime victims. We also see the first attempt to address a "one-size-fits-all" approach to working with crime victims when Wisconsin passed the first Victim and Witness Bill of Rights for children. Probably one of the most notable accomplishments in 1983 was the creation of the Office for Victims of Crime within the US Department of Justice. The purpose of the organization was to implement the recommendations, as well as they could, of the 1982 President's Task Force on Victims of Crime. The organization's goals were to become a national clearinghouse of information, provide training on how best to work with victims, and to delve into creating legislation protecting victims' rights.

We saw assistance to victims grow exponentially in 1984 with the passage of the **Victims of Crime Act (VOCA)**. VOCA established the Crime Victims Fund, which was a fund that would provide state compensation to personal crime victims, training for those working with victims, and funding for victim assistance programs all from collections of offender fines, penalties, and bail bond forfeitures. The Crime Victims Fund has grown from $68 million in its first year (1984) to almost $3 billion in 2012 and is administered by the Office for Victims of Crime (2013 NCVRW Resource Guide). The **Justice Assistance Act of 1984** established the Office of Justice Programs and brought together various clearinghouses established to understand crime, including the Office for Victims of Crime. The **Family Violence Prevention and Services Act of 1984** set aside money for domestic violence victim advocacy programs. Remembering that criminal justice agents themselves can become victims of crime, the **Concerns of Police Survivors (COPS)** group was organized in Washington, DC, in 1984 to address issues of those killed in the line of duty. In another part of the criminal justice system, the Federal Bureau of Prisons created the first victim/witness notification system, alerting victims to the custody status of offenders. In the academic realm, California State University, Fresno established the first Victim Services Certificate Program across the country.

In 1985, the National Victim Center (later named the National Center for Victims of Crime) was established to provide education and training on victims' issues. In the global arena, the United Nations General Assembly adopted a declaration that created a guideline for victim services reform at local and national levels. The guide was called the **Declaration of Basic Principles of Justice for Victims of Crime and Abuse of Power**. The intersection between social service and public health occurred when the US Surgeon General issued a report stating that domestic violence was a major public health problem.

1986 is the first year in which the Office for Victims of Crime awarded grants to programs providing victim assistance and victim compensation. Additionally, VOCA was amended to supply funding specifically for child abuse investigation and prosecution. An earmarked $10 million was set aside just for child abuse from the Crime Victims Fund (later this was amended to $20 million). 1986 also marks the first year in which there was a formal discussion on pursuing a constitutional amendment on victims' rights at the federal level.

In the next year, 1987, the discussion about a federal constitutional amendment grew stronger with the establishment of the National Victims' Constitutional Amendment Network (NVCAN) at a meeting hosted by NCVC. This group would have a great impact on state-level constitutional amendments as well. Whereas in 1983 we saw a large national policing organization start to explore victims' rights and treatment of victims by law enforcement, in 1987 the American Correctional Association created its own Task Force on Victims of Crime. For the first time ever, the NCADV established a national toll-free hotline for victims of domestic violence and October was officially designated as National Domestic Violence Awareness Month. Once again, despite much growth, there is a note of disappointment in 1987 when the US Supreme Court ruled that victim impact statements were unconstitutional in the sentencing phase of capital trials as only offender information should be considered at that stage (*Booth v. Maryland*).

In 1988, there was a greater focus on special populations within crime victims. The OVC set aside special funds to address victimization in Indian Country, specifically on-reservation crimes, where laws and culture were integrated to address victimization to those native populations. There was also a focus on victimization of elders through the establishment of the National Center on Elder Abuse. In the courts, another significant case occurred. In *State v. Ciskie* the court allowed for the use of an expert witness to testify about an adult rape victim's behavior and mental state post offenses and we, as a country, started to address the issue of rape within intimate relationships. In the legislature, the **Drunk Driving Prevention Act** passed, which increased the legal drinking age to 21. Though the Office for Victims of Crime was initially established in 1983, amendments to VOCA legislatively established the office as a formalized organization in 1988. Additional amendments to VOCA, spurred on by MADD and POMC, added a funding focus for previously underserved victim populations. OVC also created a fund for federal victims of crime, titled the Federal Emergency Fund.

The 1980s was a significant decade of growth in the area of victims' rights and victim assistance. The 1982 President's Task Force on Victims of Crime, the passing of VWRA and VOCA, the creation of national-level organizations created for the purpose of addressing victims' needs, and dedicated efforts by major organizations representing each sector of the criminal justice system made it clear that a **paradigm shift** (an event in which the overarching belief structure changes and a new belief structure takes over) had occurred in regards to how victims were to be treated by agents of the government at all levels.

1990s: Depth and Maturation

The 1980s was a decade of immense growth in victim legislation, victim assistance programs, and case law. It was also a decade in which we started to see the impact of funding problems for programs that had a strong impact on criminal justice and victims' issues. Having some major pieces of legislation for victims accomplished (notably VWRA and VOCA) and the establishment of strong national victim assistance organizations (notably OVC and NCVC, with the continuation of NOVA), the 1990s was a time when we could focus on honing in on issues perhaps not previously addressed and/or found to be in need of attention. In 1990, Congress passed the **Hate Crime Statistics Act**, which required agencies to collect data on the number of hate crimes and the motivation surrounding those crimes for the purpose of better understanding at risk groups and the impact of hate crime. On college campuses, the **Clery Act of 1990** was established, honoring the hard work of the parents of Jeanne Clery and Security on Campus, Inc. This act required institutions that received federal funding to report all murders, rapes, robberies, and select other crimes that occurred on campuses and/or may involve college students. To better serve child victims and witnesses, Congress passed the **Victims of Child Abuse Act**, with the intent to make the criminal justice process less traumatic for child abuse victims. Along the same lines, we saw the first comprehensive study of missing children. The National Incidence Study on Missing, Abducted, Runaway and Thrownaway Children in America (NISMART) was conducted to provide more evidence-based estimates of the number of missing children cases in the United States. Though proscribed in law before, the **National Child Search Assistance Act of 1990** required law enforcement to utilize the FBI's NCIC system to enter cases of missing children and unidentified persons so law enforcement across the country could have real-time access to that information. The **Victims' Rights and Restitution Act of 1990** codified specific services that victims should have access to in the federal system. At the behest of MADD, Congress passed a law that prohibited drunk drivers and other offenders from filing for bankruptcy in order to get out of paying restitution or fines ordered by the either the criminal or civil court systems.

In 1991, the **federal crime victims' amendment** was introduced for consideration by the US Congress for the first time. In California, the first academic victimology program in the country was approved. Additionally, the NCVC disseminated its report on public opinion about crime victimization, the first of its kind. In case law, the US Supreme Court did a reversal on its opinion about victim impact statements and their impact in a capital trial. In *Payne v. Tennessee*, it was ruled that a victim impact statement describing the impact of the death of the loved one *could* be introduced at the sentencing phase in a trial and was not a violation of the Eighth Amendment. The updated Attorney General Guidelines for Victim and Witness Assistance incorporated recommendations from state-level Victims' Bill of Rights, and Federal Victims of Child Abuse Act and Victim and Witness Protection Act. Similar to the ACA response to crime victims years earlier, the American Probation and Parole Association established a committee to explore the needs of crime victims from a community corrections perspective. In a step back, the US Supreme Court stated that New York's notoriety-for-profit statute was unconstitutional and overly broad in *Simon & Schuster v. New York Crime Victims Board.* This meant that offenders would be able to profit from publications related to the crime they commit. In a very progressive move, the Washington State Legislature enacted the first Address Confidentiality Program for victims of domestic violence, rape/sexual assault, and stalking and allowed for their motor vehicle and voter registration information to be kept confidential.

In 1992, the Association of Paroling Authorities International established a committee exploring victims' needs from a parole perspective, similar to what the American Probation and Parole Association did in 1991. The pattern was clear that in a five-year span the corrections component of the criminal justice system was making a concerted effort to address issues victims of crime encountered when dealing with the different branches of the correctional system. In 1992, we also saw continued growth in the area of violence against women. The NCVC published a report titled "Rape in America," which was a groundbreaking report on the incidence of rape, including date rape, report levels to police, the toll of the crime on the victims, and the impact of media disclosure of identifying victim information. Massachusetts passed a landmark bill that required judges to check a domestic violence registry when handling cases to assess if these were new or repeat offenses and to deal with them accordingly. Twenty-eight states passed anti-stalking laws, bringing legislative attention to yet another intimate-level crime that had been ignored for far too long. Congress passed the **Battered Women's Testimony Act,** which urged states to utilize expert witnesses in cases involving battered women. In the same year, Congress reauthorized the Higher Education Bill, implementing a new piece of legislation within it titled the **Campus Sexual Assault Victims' Bill of Rights.** This act required that institutions of higher education notify sexual assault victims as to their rights and alert them to the option of reporting the crime to the local law enforcement authorities as well (National Institute of Justice, visited June 22, 2017). If colleges and universities fail to do this they could be fined up to $27,500 per offense. On the hate crime front, some might suggest that a step back was taken in 1992 when the US Supreme Court ruled that a local ordinance in St. Paul, Minnesota, prohibiting the display of symbols that could incite anger or the like was a violation of the First Amendment's protection of free speech.

A number of new pieces of legislation were enacted at the federal level in 1993 to further specific foci of the Victims' Rights Movement. The **Child Sexual Abuse Registry Act** was passed, which established a repository of information on child sexual abuse offenders. Additionally, President Clinton enacted the **"Brady Bill,"** legislation that required a waiting period when attempting to purchase a gun. NCVC developed and implemented **INFOLINK**—a hotline that provided victim advocacy to victims of all crimes. This was an important creation as many services available to victims were focused on women and children, so providing a service to victims of all crimes was something long overdue. By the end of 1993, all 50 states and the District of Columbia had adopted anti-stalking laws, an accomplishment achieved within two years!

In 1994, an important piece of legislation was signed into law by President Clinton. The **Violent Crime Control and Law Enforcement Act** included within it the **Violence Against Women Act (VAWA)**, which allocated over $1 billion dollars in funding to address violence against women; it enhanced the funding provisions within VOCA, increased sentences for drunk drivers who had children in their cars at the time of the offense, and established the **National Child Abuse Sex Offender Registry**—likely in response to the repository of information created the previous year. The ACA released its report on juvenile crime victims, a groundbreaking piece that highlighted ways to improve treatment of victims within the juvenile justice system. On the state level, Kentucky instituted the first automated network which would inform victims of the status of offenders in their cases. Finally, the OVC launched the Community Crisis Response program, which assisted victims in communities where multiple violent crimes had taken place.

In 1995, there were a number of important, non-legislative-type developments that occurred. The first comprehensive report on fraud was completed, which suggested that $40 billion was lost to fraud every year. The revised Attorney General Guidelines for Victim and Witness Assistance increased accountability of federal criminal justice officials when dealing with crime victims, including the inclusion of victim treatment in performance evaluations and the suggestion that annual reports include best practices with victims. The National Victim Constitutional Amendment Network (NVCAN) suggested language for a federal constitutional amendment and the first National Victim Assistance Academy was held in Washington, DC, a format that was adopted by many states and funded with federal funding to improve treatment for crime victims.

In 1996, there was a lot of activity surrounding the federal victims' rights constitutional amendment. It was introduced to both the Senate and House of Representatives with strong bipartisan support, and it was supported by both US Attorney General Janet Reno and President Clinton, but *it didn't get passed*. On a more positive note, a number of new acts were ratified. **Megan's Law**, otherwise known as the **Community Notification Act**, amended the Child Sexual Abuse Registry law by requiring that communities be notified about sex offenders in their neighborhoods. Two significant acts voted in during 1996 focused on terrorism. The **Antiterrorism and Effective Death Penalty Act** was instituted in 1996 and outlined a number of recommendations for victims: (1) funds were allocated to combat terrorism, (2) restitution was made mandatory for all federal violent crimes, and (3) victims of terrorist acts became eligible for compensation, including members of the military. Under this act, mandatory restitution was also ordered to victims of fraud, highlighting the financial harm this type of crime creates. In the same token, VOCA was amended to revise its definition of "crime victim" so that victims of financial crime were now included under that definition. The **Church Arson Prevention Act** was created to address the increase in arsons perpetrated against religious institutions around the nation. The **Drug-Induced Rape Prevention Act** was enacted in response to growing knowledge about techniques utilized by rapist to perpetrate drug-facilitated rape and sexual assault.

In 1997, the **Victims' Rights Clarification Act** was instituted to clarify the guidelines by which victims could attend and appear at trial for capital and non-capital cases during the sentencing phase of the process. Because the federal victims' rights constitutional amendment did not pass in 1996 it was reintroduced to the 105th Congress in 1997. Hearings were conducted to address the provisions of the proposed amendment by both the House and Senate judiciary committees. Attorney Janet Reno once again provided her support for the bill, but it once again did not pass. The federal government enacted an anti-stalking law in the **National Defense Authorization Act of 1997**. OVC released a study examining the implementation of recommendations made in the 1982 President's Task Force Report on Victims of Crime (15 years previously). An additional 250 recommendations were proposed by the group for better assisting victims in the twenty-first century.

In 1998, a revised version of a federal victims' rights constitutional amendment was introduced to the Senate. Despite the Senate Judiciary Committee approving it, the resolution went no further in Congress. An amendment to the Higher Education Act provided grant funding for violence against women to be addressed on college campuses. The link between sexual assault and drinking was made in this revision as well. A focus on sex crimes perpetrated against children was also a highlight of 1998. The **Child Protection and Sexual Predatory Punishment Act of 1998** increased sentences for sex crimes against children and included those crimes that were perpetrated across interstates and over the Internet. Continued focus on populations that previously did not receive special attention was a theme in 1998 with the adoption of both the **Crime Victims with Disabilities Awareness Act** and **Identity Theft and Deterrence Act of 1998**. In both of these acts, the collection of information on these crimes was ordered, and assistance was required as part of the Identity Theft Act. The OVC created a new position to focus on citizens of the United States who were victimized while outside of the United States.

In 1999, the federal victims' rights constitutional amendment was once again brought before Congress ... and failed to be enacted. The OVC continued with its National Victim Assistance Academies and funded a number of State Victim Assistance Academies as well. NCVC created a National Crime Victim Bar Association to assist crime victims in pursuit of civil justice.

The 1990s was a time when the United States could rely on and adjust previously enacted legislation for victims and begin to focus on those groups that became identified as special populations needing additional legislation to better assist them.

2000s: Expanded Commitment to Victims' Rights

The first decade of the new millennium focused steadily on victims of terrorism, human trafficking, women and children, and fraud. Despite numerous attempts in the 1990s, a federal constitutional amendment was not enacted, but in 2004 an act was ratified by President George W. Bush that provided the same protections. This was a huge step in victims' rights, though some still maintained that the amendment is still needed (Tobolowsky, Gaboury, Jackson, & Blackburn, 2010). Landmark studies were accomplished in this decade and our understanding of the impact of different types of crime on many different populations of crime victims was expanded. A record amount of money was deposited into the Crime Victims' Fund, but at the same time, victim services agencies across the country were struggling to survive because of lack of funding (NCVC, n.d.). Still, the 2000s so far have enhanced our understanding of and assistance to crime victims and the trend appears to be to focus on bringing even more previously underserved victim populations into the fold.

In 2000, Congress changed the legal blood alcohol concentration level to 0.08 and tied receipt of federal highway funding to states' compliance with changing their laws. VAWA was reauthorized through 2005 with stalking and Internet-related violence against women added to the act. In order to better understand cyber-fraud, the Internet Crime Complaint Center was created. The federal victims' rights amendment was once again introduced to Congress and was addressed by the full Senate for the first time. Support for the measure appeared to be waning and the co-sponsors of the bill withdrew it for further consideration. The **Trafficking Victims Protection Act of 2000** was enacted, focusing more attention on human trafficking and greater penalties against traffickers. Victims were legislated benefits similar to other crime victims.

In 2001, the attacks on September 11th occurred and the government responded by enacting legislation to further assist victims of terrorism on probably the largest scale to date. The **Air Transportation Safety and System Stabilization Act** created a specific victim compensation program for victims of September 11th. A large pool of funding was set aside to assist survivors of victims with damages that were typically only seen in civil court (lifetime earnings, pain and suffering, loss of enjoyment of life, etc.). Additionally, the **USA Patriot Act of 2001** was adopted, which not only gave a bit more freedom in investigations to law enforcement and intelligence agencies, but it also amended VOCA to provide larger percentages of compensation to states and to fund evaluation and compliance projects as well. The **Child Abuse Prevention and Enforcement Act** and **Jennifer's Law** increased the mandatory amount of funding from the Crime Victims Fund for children from $10 million to $20 million. Jennifer's Law had an even larger impact on providing funds that would assist law enforcement agencies to input full information about unidentified crime victims into the NCIC.

In 2002, President George W. Bush publicly stated his support for a federal Crime Victims' Rights Amendment, but it was not adopted in that year. The National Association of VOCA Assistance Administrators was created to provide states technical assistance with their VOCA grants. Congress provided $20 million to assist agencies that work with trafficking victims and by the end of the year all 50 states, Puerto Rico, the US Virgin Islands, and Guam had victim compensation programs. The OVC established the Helping Outreach Programs to Expand grant program and awarded grants under this program for the first time. This grant assisted agencies with relatively small operating budgets to try to expand their services, especially to underserved populations. A conference was held on missing and exploited children, sponsored by the White House, and the NCVC and National Council on Crime and Delinquency released a landmark report on juvenile victims of crime, highlighting the disproportionate amount of teenagers (12–19 years old) who were crime victims.

In 2003, the Senate Judiciary Committee once again passed a victims' rights constitutional amendment, but it did not move forward that year. Congress made the

Professional Profile 9.1

John Gillis

Chief of Maricopa County
Victim Services Division

Q: How did you get involved with working with crime victims? In what capacity do you currently work with victims? Have you ever been engaged in a joint research/practice project? Please describe.

A: In 1979 I was a sergeant with the Los Angeles Police Department when my daughter, Louarna Gillis, was murdered by a gang member who wanted to move up in the gang hierarchy. He became an important member of the gang world because he had murdered the daughter of a cop. Through the months and years after Louarna was murdered I frequently came in contact with other people whose children, siblings, relatives, and others, had closely connected people who were victims of homicide. The family, friends, and relatives all seemed to have questions and issues about their case and how the case was handled by law enforcement. I was able to answer many of their questions and at times could put them in touch with their investigator. I soon became active with Parents of Murdered Children and subsequently co-founded several other organizations that worked with crime victims.

Q: What advice do you have for students interested in working with victims?

A: Many students are not well prepared for the emotionality, time constraints, frustrations with the justice system, intensity of victim reactions, lack of resources, and political agendas that are involved with victim services. First and foremost, students should attempt to volunteer or intern with an agency that serves crime victims. That may be crisis response with local law enforcement, domestic violence shelters, rape crisis agencies, shelters for abused and/or neglected children, or prosecutor or court-based advocacy and includes advocacy with the adult and juvenile probation systems. In addition, background knowledge is critical: understanding how the brain works—emotion versus reaction, human growth and development; victimology; the processes involved with the criminal justice system; and the criminal acts. Students must appreciate and develop strong communication skills, the ability to demonstrate empathy, commitment, assertiveness, accountability, and the true capacity of caring that crime victims deserve.

Q: What are some challenges of working with victims, especially as it relates to dealing with the criminal justice system and/or lawmakers?

A: Working with victims is, in itself, challenging, and providing that service constrained by the inconsistencies and idiosyncrasies of the criminal justice system compounds that challenge. From law enforcement through the court system, treatment of and services to victims vary among agencies and individuals, depending upon commitment, finances, election results, and/or current interpretation of law. Though a standard of care for crime victims should be the norm, service may begin with a flip of the coin to determine which officer interviews the victim at the scene of a crime. Legislatively, the champion of new legislation may crusade for personal reasons rather than the good of the public and may, in its latent function, be detrimental to crime victims. Inconsistency must not be allowed to continue thwarting excellence in service to crime victims.

Q: What obstacles have you encountered while striving to assist victims? Have the obstacles to providing good service to victims changed over the years?

A: One of the biggest obstacles, as a crime victim, is most people believe victims are looking for compensation when, in fact, victimization is far more complicated than that. When a life is taken, or someone is seriously injured by a perpetrator, money will not take away the pain and suffering endured by the victims and next of kin. The victim looks to the criminal justice system to apprehend the offender and ensure that the offender is held accountable. The criminal justice looks at the victim as a piece of evidence whose only purpose is to aid in a successful conviction. As a result, the victim often has no desire to participate in court proceedings and opts to get back to their daily routines. This leaves the criminal free to continue the criminality and victimization. Although there have been some improvements throughout the years, there's a long way to go!

Q: What do you feel is the mark you will have left on the field of victim services? What do you want people to see as your mark? At the end of the day, what do you want your "legacy" to be in the field of victimology/victim services?

A: I would like to think I have made some kind of impact in the field of victim services, but that will not be known till I am long gone from this world. If at that time I have left everything on the field, then scholars and pundits will decide if there was enough left on the field to establish a legacy.

Q: What are some burgeoning issues that you see in the fields of victimology/victim services?

A: Crime victims have no protection under the United States Constitution. Many attempts have been made to move a bill through Congress for a constitutional amendment that would give victims a standing in the US Constitution, but Congress is reluctant to give victims any constitutional rights. The proposed amendment would give the victim a right to be present at any hearing or proceeding where the defendant has a right to be present. It would give the victim a right to be heard at sentencing and the right to be notified if the defendant is released or escapes. The victim would be entitled to a speedy trial, which is privilege the defendant enjoys. The victim would also have a right to restitution.

The rights of the defendant are fully protected by the Constitution and are mentioned more than twenty times in the document; on the other hand, victims are mentioned zero times.

Q: Are there groups of victims you think need to be served but are not? Why do you think that way?

A: One has only to visit a community of immigrants to be made aware of an underserved population. Be it their own cultural background that encourages underreporting or rejection of services or their exclusion from the majority population, fewer immigrants seem to be receiving services. Being served as a crime victim in the United States should be dependent upon being a victim, not a person's country of origin or immigrant status. A criminal act reverberates and can, eventually, impact a whole community—how we serve victims can prove to be a far greater force in the unification and healing process of that community.

Office of Violence Against Women its own independent office under the US Department of Justice. The **PROTECT Act of 2003** (i.e., **AMBER Alert**) was enacted, which created a system alerting law enforcement and the community to kidnapped children situations. The American Society of Victimology was established and held their first meeting, in partnership with the World Society of Victimology. The **Prison Rape Elimination Act of 2003** was enacted to address rape and sexual assault in the correctional system. January was established as National Stalking Awareness Month by Congress. The **Fair and Accurate Credit Transactions Act of 2003** was established to protect identity theft victims and to assist them in recouping their financial losses. Finally, President Bush signed the **Trafficking Victims Protection Reauthorization Act**, which strengthened the previous TVPA and helped to clarify the guidelines so it was easier for victims to navigate through the system and to receive assistance.

2004 was an important year for victims' rights as this was the year that the **Justice for All Act** was enacted, including the **Scott Campbell, Stephanie Roper, Wendy Preston, Louarna Gillis, and Nile Lynn Crime Victims Rights' Act**. This act provided for rights in the areas previously proposed in a federal victims' rights constitutional amendment and was very similar to state victims' bills of rights in its proscription of expectations from criminal justice personnel. This act also allowed for victims to seek redress when they believed their rights had been violated, something that was not always seen in state victims' bills of rights. The implementation of this act was thought

"In the News" Box 9.1

On February 15, 2013, Rock Center reporters, Mario Garcia, Kristen Powers, and Jessica Hopper, published an article entitled "Prosecutor Leads Effort to Test Long-Abandoned Rape Kits, Brings Justice to Victims." The article discusses the discovery of 11,303 untested rape kits in a former police storage warehouse in Wayne County, Michigan. All of the kits had been collected on women and men who reported that they were raped or sexually assaulted, but none had been sent for DNA testing to identify the perpetrator. Prosecutor Kym Worthy wrote a grant to get funding to test the rape kits, which has resulted in the identification of 21 serial killers, and some heart-breaking results—such as the identification of a rapist who subsequently murdered three women after the rape kit was collected on an earlier victim. The article illustrates the difficulty of labeling the criminal justice system a "system," as the prosecutor's office and police department were clearly at odds regarding the rape kits. Due to the testing of the kits, however, the article reports that at least one case had some positive resolution. Audrey Polk was raped at night in February 1997 while her children were in bed with her. She immediately went to the hospital and reported the attack to police. Fourteen years later she received news that as a result of the grant to test the kits, her perpetrator had been found, was charged and convicted, and sentenced to a long stint in prison.

To read the full article, visit: http://rockcenter.nbcnews.com/_news/2013/02/ 15/15848051-prosecutor-leads-effort-to-test-long-abandoned-rape-kits-brings- justice-to-victims?lite.

to supplant the need for a federal constitutional amendment of the same nature. The Justice for All Act also allocated funding for DNA-related programs in order to increase the processing of DNA samples for more speedy case processing. The NCVC produced a report that examined state compensation programs across the 50 states and provided recommendations for improving those programs.

In 2005, the US Department of Justice created a national sex offender registry that was considered to be incredibly user friendly for victims. A website portal was created that allowed victims to search nationwide in a single search. The US Department of Justice also created the office of the Victims' Rights Ombudsman wherein victims could receive assistance when alleging that their rights have been violated. The US House of Representatives formed the first Victims' Rights Caucus to better understand the needs of crime victims outside of the political arena. In 2005, we started to see action by the US Department of Defense to better serve and understand sexual assault of military personnel serving in the US Armed Forces.

In 2006 Congress and President Bush enacted the **Violence Against Women and Department of Justice Reauthorization Act of 2005**. This act continued VAWA and committed to protecting women and children from violent acts. Another reauthorization that took place was the **Trafficking Victims Protection Reauthorization Act of 2005**. Through this act, not only were foreign-born trafficking victims protected, but there was a new focus on domestic trafficking as well. The **Adam Walsh Child Protection and Safety Act of 2006** was signed into law, which expanded the scope and reach for child sexual crime prosecutions. In a similar vein, the Project Safe Childhood program was launched to help end Internet-based child sexual exploitation. Continuing the discourse on the use of victim impact statements, the U.S. Court of Appeals for the Ninth Circuit decided in *Kenna v. U.S. District Court for Central District of California* that victim impact statements could be heard in a case where there were multiple victims, as a component of the 2004 Crime Victims' Rights Act. Additionally, a sentence determined in a court where a victim was denied his or her right to speak could be remanded to a new sentencing phase so the victim would have an opportunity to speak. In the **International Terrorism Victim Expense Reimbursement Program (ITVERP)** American victims of international terrorism became eligible to receive compensation related to the acts that took place while abroad. Finally, the **Older Americans Act Reauthorization** was signed in by President Bush, expanding assistance and support for elder abuse and older victims of crime.

In 2007, we saw the president and US Congress acknowledge the needs of identity theft victims and murder victims in the President's Identity Theft Task Force and Congress' National Remembrance Day establishment on September 25th.

In 2008, perhaps in response to the findings of the President's Identity Theft Task Force, President Bush signed into law the **Identity Theft Enhanced and Restitution Act** providing courts the ability to award restitution to cybercrime victims for not only their losses due to identity theft, but also restitution toward the money and time they spent trying to clear their names. The OVC focused attention on victims of mentally ill offenders by disseminating two guides on the rights of victims in these cases and the role of the courts when dealing with these types of offenders. Additionally, OVC produced a guide for victims of crimes while abroad. The Government Accountability Office (GAO) produced a report suggesting improvements to the Crime Victims' Rights Act so that victims might be better informed and able to reap the benefits of the act. There was a bit of a focus on youth in 2008 as well. Congress passed the **Reconnecting Homeless Youth Act of 2008** to assist in finding shelter for homeless youth and preventing the sexual abuse of this population. Additionally, President Bush signed legislation creating a National Strategy on Child Exploitation Prevention and Interdiction to assist in cyber-pornography detection and prosecution for child pornography.

In 2009, the Bureau of Justice Statistics provided the first comprehensive report on stalking in the United States, suggesting that 3.4 million people reported being stalked in the last year. President Barack Obama signed the **American Recovery and Reinvestment Act of 2009**, which provided additional money for victim assistance and compensation and a focus on domestic violence victims. The month of April was designated as National Sexual Assault Awareness Month and was celebrated for the first time. The **Fraud Enforcement and Recovery Act of 2009** was signed into law to address mortgage and securities fraud. This act also created the Financial Crisis Inquiry Commission to investigate the reason for the economic and financial crisis that was going on at the time. Three additional paramount investigations were set up in 2009—the Financial Fraud Investigation Task Force was created to understand fraud by lending institutions, the Bureau of Justice Statistics presented its first ever report on crime victims with disabilities and informed us that people with disabilities were one and a half times more at risk of victimization than the rest of the citizenry, and the Office of Juvenile Justice and Delinquency Prevention conducted the most comprehensive investigation to date into childhood exposure to violence. Hate crimes were once again focused upon with the passing of the **Matthew Shepard and James Byrd, Jr. Hate Crimes Prevention Act**. This expanded the definition of hate crimes to include discrimination based on sexual orientation, gender or gender identity, and hate crimes committed by and against juveniles.

In 2009, the Oregon Department of Justice proposed a piece of landmark legislation, Oregon Senate Bill 233, which was later enacted by the Oregon Legislature, in which crime victims could uphold their state constitutional rights in a court of law. If a victim in Oregon felt that there was a violation of his/her Victims' Bill of Rights he/she could file a claim in court to allege the violation. Some of the rights that became automatic to victims in Oregon included: the right to notification of rights, the right to attend any open hearing, the right to have a personal representative with them through the process, the ability to speak at hearing, protection from personal information getting to a defendant, the freedom from having to speak to a private investigator or defense attorney for the defendant, prompt restitution, and the right to a copy of the court transcripts (NCVRW Resource Guide, 2014).

2010s: The Future — What's Next?

In the current decade of the twenty-first century, it appears that the focus remains on financial crime and children, and expands to include crime victims in the military, crime on reservations, and crime related to current events—including victimizations that occur on cruise ships.

In 2010, StopFraud.gov was created by the Financial Fraud Enforcement Task Force, which is an informational website in which people can learn methods of protecting themselves against fraud and on which they can report fraud. Congress reinvigorated its Project Safe Childhood by releasing its first National Strategy for Child Exploitation Prevention and Interdiction guide. The **Tribal Law and Order Act** improved public safety and assistance to victims on reservations, and the **Cruise Vessel Security and Safety Act of 2010** ensured that there was proper monitoring of activities on cruise ships to record victimizations when they happened and required victimizations to be reported to authorities as well. The **Coast Guard Authorization Act of 2010** required that the Coast Guard present Congress with a report about sexual assaults occurring to or committed by members of the US Coast Guard.

In 2011, President Obama proclaimed January as National Stalking Awareness Month. Two acts were created to address sexual assault in the military. The **Skelton National Defense Authorization Act for Fiscal Year 2011** and the **National Defense**

Authorization Act for Fiscal Year 2012 include guidelines both strengthening the military's response to sexual assault and preventing and responding to sexual assault in the military. In the year of the tenth anniversary of 9/11, President Obama signed into law the **James Zadroga 9/11 Health and Compensation Act,** allowing for those exposed to harmful chemical agents in the clean-up of 9/11 to be eligible for compensation. The OVC set out on its Vision 21 initiative, a campaign to improve services to victims in the new millennium.

In 2012, Congress passed and the president signed into law new legislation that will take away the need for the OVC director to be confirmed by the Senate. Most notably, the FBI changed its definition of rape for the UCR to include any gender for the victim or perpetrator and to acknowledge the capacity of the victim when he/she is incapable of giving consent due to age or mental or physical incapacity (including being drugged or under the influence of drugs or alcohol).

In 2013, the OVC published the Vision 21 final report, focusing on improving treatment to crime victims in the field. President Obama signed in the VAWA 2013 Reauthorization Act, which increased protections to LGBTQ victims of violence, as well as American Indian victims and young adults and teens. It also expanded the ability of American Indian tribes to investigate, prosecute, and sentence American Indian domestic violence perpetrators. Also within the VAWA 2013 Reauthorization was the **SAFER Act,** which listed a deadline by which labs must have protocols established to deal with the DNA backlogs for sexual assault evidence kits. The VAWA 2013 Reauthorization also expanded the Trafficking Victims Protection Act Reauthorization by making it a crime to destroy, conceal, or withhold someone's passport for more than 48 hours for the purpose of smuggling them into a country or controlling them. A great stride was taken for victims of sexual assault in the military when a directive was sent out indicating that immediate action was needed to improve treatment and prevention of sexual assault, to provide power to commanders to reassign accused service members elsewhere, and to provide victims the ability to have input in post-trial court martial actions. Finally, 2013 saw the authorization of the **Campus Sexual Violence Elimination Act (Campus SaVE Act)** as an amendment to the Clery Act and further extension of the Higher Education Act of 1965, which provided a great deal of guidance and directives on addressing sexual violence on campuses. Included within this act was the provision that colleges and universities must provide education to their students, staff, and faculty about safe dating and prevention of domestic and sexual violence, as well as stalking, and procedures by which universities must function when dealing with cases of domestic and/or sexual violence and stalking (NCVRW Resource Guide, 2014).

In 2014, we saw continued expansion of reforms to how the military dealt with sexual assault with the National Defense Authorization Act. In this act, requirements for dealing with sexual assault in the court setting were stated, as well as, providing opportunities for victims to remain in the military without suffering repercussions for reporting the offense. The White House also focused on initiatives to receive better reporting on child abduction and child abuse laws with specific directives to the US Attorney General on compiling information about these crimes. The **Sean and David**

Goldman International Child Abduction Prevention and Return Act of 2014 requires an annual report from the Secretary of State on how the US works with other nations to record and address international child abduction.

Human trafficking is a clear focus for 2015, with the signing into law of the **Justice for Victims of Trafficking Act**, establishing the Domestic Trafficking Victims' Fund and the creation of the US Advisory Council on Human Trafficking. This act provides funding for training of law enforcement, medical personnel, and others who work with trafficking victims, including child pornography production. Attention was brought to an oft-forgotten group of victims—male victims of violence. 2015 saw the creation of the **Supporting Male Survivors of Violence Demonstration Initiative**, a partnership between OVC and the Office of Juvenile Justice and Delinquency Prevention. This initiative seeks to provide trauma-informed care to male victims of violence; young men of color are a specific focus of this particular initiative as they are disproportionately dominant in this population. Additional provisions are put in place to assist male victims of sexual violence and to provide more services to male victims. Additionally, the Department of Housing and Urban Development is brought into the discussion on maintaining and providing appropriate shelter for victims of domestic violence.

In 2016, there was a great focus on expanding services to victims in Native American communities, and providing funding to decrease domestic violence homicides, overall. It seems that the most recent uses of funding and reauthorization or newly implemented acts are now focusing on improving existing services and pinpointing specific populations that may have been neglected in the past. This is a sign of progress in the victim services field as it demonstrates a belief in the programs that are available and a continued effort to reach out to all victims across the land.

Summary and Conclusions

Given the current political climate, including the divisiveness witnessed during and after the 2016 presidential election, where it seems that Democrats and Republicans have difficulty agreeing on many things, it is gratifying to see such bipartisan support for victims' rights. The first steps towards securing rights in the 1960s and 1970s really laid the groundwork for some of the most impactful pieces of victims' rights legislation ever seen in the 1980s. VWPA and VOCA have truly made the world a different place for crime victims and finally validated their place at the criminal justice table. The continued growth in specific areas, violence against women, violence against children and elders, cybercrime and identity theft, terrorism, and many more areas has shown how the collective efforts of victim activism, advocacy, politics, and academia can truly bring about change. Though some continue to fight for a federal constitutional amendment, the 2004 Crime Victims' Rights Act was a big step towards ensuring victims' rights were respected. The strength of the organizations that have been created for victims and the momentum in the field of victimology will surely grow as we continue to fight for and monitor the evolution of victims' rights in the future.

Key Terms

Missing Children's Act of 1982

Victim and Witness Protection Act (VWPA) of 1982

Victims of Crime Act

Paradigm shift

Hate Crime Statistics Act

Clery Act of 1990

Victims of Child Abuse Act

National Child Search Assistance Act of 1990

Victims' Rights and Restitution Act of 1990

Federal Crime Victims' Amendment

Campus Sexual Assault Victims' Bill of Rights

Child Sexual Abuse Registry Act

Brady Bill

INFOLINK

Violent Crime Control and Law Enforcement Act

Violence Against Women Act

National Child Abuse Sex Offender Registry

Megan's Law or Community Notification Act

Antiterrorism and Effective Death Penalty Act

Church Arson Prevention Act

Drug-Induced Rape Prevention Act

Victims' Rights Clarification Act

National Defense Authorization Act of 1997

Child Protection and Sexual Predatory Punishment Act of 1998

Crime Victims with Disabilities Awareness Act

Identity Theft and Deterrence Act of 1998

Trafficking Victims Protection Act of 2000

Air Transportation Safety and System Stabilization Act

USA Patriot Act of 2001

Child Abuse Prevention and Enforcement Act

Jennifer's Law

PROTECT Act of 2003 (AMBER Alert)

Prison Rape Elimination Act of 2003

Fair and Accurate Credit Transactions Act of 2003

Trafficking Victims Protection Reauthorization Act

Justice for All Act

Scott Campbell, Stephanie Roper, Wendy Preston, Louarna Gillis, and Nile Lynn Crime Victims Rights' Act

Violence Against Women and Department of Justice Reauthorization Act of 2005

Adam Walsh Child Protection and Safety Act of 2006

International Terrorism Victim Expense Reimbursement Program (ITVERP)

Older Americans Act Reauthorization

Identity Theft Enhanced and Restitution Act

Reconnecting Homeless Youth Act of 2008

American Recovery and Reinvestment Act of 2009

Matthew Shepard and James Byrd, Jr. Hate Crimes Prevention Act

Tribal Law and Order Act

Cruise Vessel Security and Safety Act of 2010

Coast Guard Authorization Act of 2010

Skelton National Defense Authorization Act for Fiscal Year 2011

National Defense Authorization Act for Fiscal Year 2012

James Zadroga 9/11 Health and Compensation Act

SAFER Act

Campus Sexual Violence Elimination Act (Campus SaVE Act)

Sean and David Goldman International Child Abduction Prevention and Return Act of 2014

Justice for Victims of Trafficking Act, Supporting Male Survivors of Violence Demonstration Initiative

Discussion Questions

1. In terms of overall impact, which do you think was greater, the Victim-Witness Protection Act or the Victims of Crime Act of 1984?
2. Do you think the 2004 Crimes Victims' Rights Act does the same as a federal constitutional amendment would? Why or why not?
3. When bills are named after specific victims, do you think they are easier to get passed by the legislature? Why or why not?

Websites for Further Information

Oral History of the Victims' Rights Movement: http://vroh.uakron.edu/index.php (The Oral History of the Victims' Rights Movement is a must view.).

Victims' Rights: http://www.cvhr.org/about/the-victims-rights-movement/.

References

Morgan, A. (1987). Criminal law—Victims' rights: Remembering the "forgotten person" in the criminal justice system. *Marquette Law Review, 70*, 572–597.

National Institute of Justice. *Campus Sexual Assault Victims' Bill of Rights*. Retrieved from https://www.nij.gov/topics/crime/rape-sexual-violence/campus/Pages/laws.aspx (visited June 22, 2017).

NCVC. (n.d.). *VOCA funding: Victim advocates speak out*. Retrieved from http://nnedv.org/downloads/Policy/VOCA_SurveyResults.pdf.

Office for Victims of Crime. (2014). Chapter 5: Landmarks in victims' rights & services: An historical overview. In Office for Victims of Crime, *2014 NCVRW Resource Guide: Strength, resilience, justice*. Washington, DC: US Department of Justice, Office of Justice Programs, Office for Victims of Crime. Retrieved from http://ovc.ncjrs.gov/ncvrw2014/.

Office for Victims of Crime. (2017). Landmarks in victims' rights & services: An historical overview. In Office for Victims of Crime, *2017 NCVRW Resource Guide, 30 years: Restoring the balance*. Washington, DC: US Department of Justice, Office of Justice Programs, Office for Victims of Crime. Retrieved from https://ovc.ncjrs.gov/ncvrw2017/.

Oregon Department of Justice, Crime Victims' Rights Division. (2014). Crime victims' rights. Retrieved from http://www.doj.state.or.us/victims/pages/rights_enforcement_task_force.aspx.

Tobolowsky, P. M., Gaboury, M. T., Jackson, A. L., & Blackburn, A. G. (2010). *Crime victim rights and remedies* (2nd ed.). Durham, NC: Carolina Academic Press.

Working with Victims and Next Steps

Chapter 10: Crime Victims and the Criminal Justice System

Criminal justice programs across the country focus their courses on understanding the motivations behind crime (be they individual-level, societal, critical, etc.), discussing specific types of crimes and understanding the system itself, all for the purpose of decreasing crime in general. Many programs have adopted coursework in victimology, but typically those are in the realm of elective offerings. So where does an understanding of victims come into play? It seems intuitive to think that crime victims are the primary client of police services, but when we look at the duties of law enforcement, particularly in the US, the limited studies that do exist on the topic suggest that just about 44–64% of their time is spent responding to calls for service from crime victims (Wilson & Weiss, 2012). Police have other duties related to order maintenance, responding to calls that are not related to crimes in progress or crimes committed, prevention, community relations, and so forth. All of these duties can help to decrease the amount of crime and fear of crime that citizens may experience, but this illustrates that victims are not the only consumers of police services. In the court system, victims may be the primary consumers of victim-witness legal assistant/liaison services, but not the actual prosecutor's time themselves. In corrections, clearly the focus of personnel is on the offender and the interactions with victims will be limited, especially for institutional corrections personnel.

We know from examining reported crime to police, victim surveys, and self-report surveys that about 50% of crime is reported to police. For instance, in 2015, through a comparison of the UCR to the NCVS it appeared that 47% of violent victimizations were reported to police, with 55% of serious violent victimizations (robbery, aggravated assault) reported (Truman & Morgan, 2016). There was a decline in the amount of property crime reported, per NCVS respondents. Only about 35% of property crimes were reported to police in 2015 (Truman & Morgan, 2016). Truman and Morgan (2016) state that reporting rates for property crimes fluctuated from 34–40% from 2003–2015. From 2014 to 2015, both violent crime and property crimes experienced a decreased reporting rate to police. In those instances, victims typically have some type of explanation for why they report the crime or not. Additionally, based on previous experiences with criminal justice personnel, victims may have an understanding about how they believe they will be treated, how their cases will or should be handled, and how they will be treated by criminal justice agents. This chapter will focus on the interactions, both positive and negative, between victims and the agents of the criminal justice system. As we review these interactions we will also discuss the different types of activities that victims should expect to engage in (in general) with each different component of the system, based on both general criminal case process and crime victims' bills of rights.

Before we begin our investigation into the interactions between victims and criminal justice personnel, it is important to consider what types of reasons a victim might have for choosing to report a crime officially.

Why Do They Report?

Though reasons may vary based on the type of offense that occurred, some of the most common reasons include: to prevent future violence, to stop the offender, to protect others, and to recover property (Hart & Rennison, 2003). Some characteristics of the offender, victim, and incident itself also lead to higher rates of reporting than others. When females were the victims of the crime it was more likely to be reported and if the victim was an older person it also had a higher rate of reporting. If the offender appeared to be under the influence of drugs or alcohol and if the offender was armed with a weapon there was a higher rate of reporting. If the victim suffered an injury, especially if it was a gunshot wound, there was a higher likelihood of reporting. Reporting rates tend to vary by the type of crime as well, as some crimes are more likely to be reported than others, for various reasons. The highest reported crime is homicide, but not all homicides are investigated by police. For instance, in 2010, the Centers for Disease Control reported 16,259 deaths due to homicide, but in that same year the UCR only reported 14,748 murders/manslaughters, which accounts for approximately 91% of homicides reported in the CDC Vital Health Statistics Report (Murphy, Xu, & Kochanek, 2013; FBI, 2010). There are a number of reasons why the CDC number may be different than the UCR number. For instance, some homicides are not included in the UCR statistics, such as justifiable homicides, executions, and accidents that lead to death, whereas the CDC bases its information off of what is listed on death certificates. Additionally, the UCR is based off of the charge that is recorded by law enforcement, which could mean that a homicide is not

Table 10A: Victimization Reported to the Police by Percent — Rounded Up

Type of Crime/Year	2003	2011	2012	2015
Motor Vehicle Theft	77%	83%	79%	69%
Robbery	64%	66%	56%	62%
Domestic Violence	57%	59%	55%	58%
Rape/Sexual Assault	56%	27%	28%	33%
Aggravated Assault	56%	67%	62%	62%
Burglary	54%	52%	55%	51%
Assault — Simple	43%	43%	40%	42%
Theft	31%	30%	26%	29%

Sources: Truman, Langton, and Planty (2013) — Criminal Victimization, 2012; Truman and Morgan (2016) — Criminal Victimization, 2015.

charged as a homicide, but a lesser offense instead. Take the case of deaths due to drunk driving. In some states this type of death is considered a homicide, but in others it may be considered something else. For instance, South Carolina, Rhode Island, and Montana have statutes related to fatalities due to drunk driving not listed as manslaughter or homicide. In Montana, the statute governing deaths due to drunk driving is Reckless Driving Resulting in Death, which may not be included in the homicide statistics for that state (National Conference of State Legislators, n.d.). According to Truman, Langton, and Planty (2013) and Truman and Morgan (2016), in an analysis of reports to police stated by NCVS respondents for 2003, 2011, 2012, and 2015 it appears that there is a consistent pattern as to those crimes that are reported most and reported least. Table 10A illustrates the reporting rates for 2003, 2011, 2012, and 2015.

It appears that motor vehicle theft is the most often reported crime, with over 75% of victims reporting to police (all years except 2015), and theft is consistently the lowest reported crime with typically less than one third of theft victims reporting to police. Rape/sexual assault appears to be the least often reported violent crime, with about one-third of victims reporting on average, despite a two-year high of 56% reporting to police. Aggravated assault and robbery also appear to have some significant shifts across the years as well, though most other crimes tend to stay relatively consistent. One additional pattern found with NCVS data is that individuals who are injured have a higher tendency to report the crime, so perhaps that contributes to the fluctuations for aggravated assault over the years. Figures 10.1a and b illustrate reporting patterns over a 20-year period for violent and household victimizations, as reported in the NCVS. These figures provide an additional illustration of the shifts in reporting across time and crime.

Figure 10.1: Percent of Violent Crimes Reported, 1993–2012, NCVS, NVAT

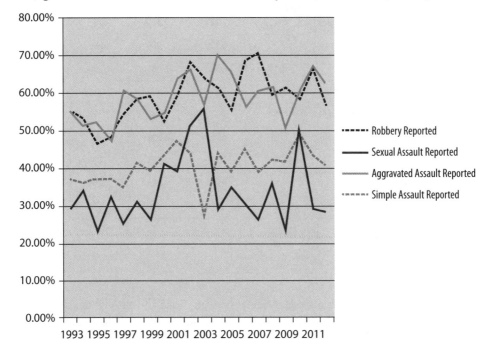

Who Reports to the Police?

It is important to remember that the primary target may not be the only one to report the crime; a family member or loved one, neighbor, or witness to the crime may call for assistance as well. Hart and Rennison (2003) found that NCVS respondents who were the primary victim were the most likely person to report a crime, typically accounting for between 50–60% of reports, followed by "someone else," which was a generic term for a witness/bystander, acquaintance, or family member and accounted for 10–20% of reports, followed by household members (who had a higher rate of reporting when someone they knew was sexually assaulted), an official who was not the police, the police at the scene, and other. For violent crime, females (47%) are more likely to report crime to police than males (40%), Black victims (49%) are more likely to report crime to police than White victims (42%), Asian victims (40%), and victims of Hispanic origin (44%). However, American Indian victims are most likely to report to police when the crime is rape/sexual assault and simple assault (47% versus 31% for White victims, 35% for Black victims, 16% for Asian victims, and 28% for victims of Hispanic origin).

Why Don't They Report?

The primary reasons crime victims choose not to report are: the victimization was dealt with in a different way — usually entails reporting the crime to another official of some sort (34%), the victimization was deemed not important enough to report (18%), the victim didn't believe the police could or would try to help (18%), and the fear of reprisal from the offender or the preference not to get the offender in trouble (13%) (Langton, Berzofsky, Krebs, & Smiley-McDonald, 2012).

Langton, Berzofsky, Krebs, and Smiley-McDonald (2012) conducted an analysis of NCVS data related to why victims do not report from 1994–2010 and some significant trends appear to be taking place. It appears that property crime and simple assault are significantly more likely to be reported to police now versus the mid-1990s. From 2005–2010 alone, the percentage of victims who chose not to report violent crime because of the perceived reaction of the police tripled from approximately 4% to 12%. The main reason behind this was because the victims believed the police would not think the victimization was important enough to address. Whereas in 1994 it was more likely for a victim to not report to police because he/she didn't believe the crime was important enough (21%) versus a police-related reason (10%), in 2010 that trend seems to have flipped with more victims failing to report violent victimizations for a police-related reason (20%) versus not thinking the crime as important enough (15%). The type of crime that occurred also seemed to affect why someone might choose not to report. For violent crime, victims chose not to report most often because it was dealt with some other way (usually a report to another authority figure) (34%), whereas for property crime victims the most likely reason for not reporting was because they didn't think the police could or would do anything about it (36%). Victims of rape/sexual assault (28%) and aggravated assault (22%) had the highest levels of fear that the offender might retaliate and/or were afraid to get the offender in trouble. For assault victims, both aggravated and simple, the most common reason they did not report was because it was dealt with another way. For robbery, personal larceny, burglary, motor vehicle theft, and theft the most common reason to not report was because the victim believed the police could or would not help. One trend that seems rather intuitive is that the greater degree of threat or fearful maneuvering by the offender, the less likelihood the victim would report and they would fail to report because of that fear. For instance, victims who sustained serious injury, as well as rape/sexual assault victims without injury, failed to report because of fear of reprisal (50% and 28%, respectively). When a firearm was used as the weapon in an offense, victims most often stated they did not report due to fear of reprisal (37%). When a victim was injured and a weapon was present, the reason they gave for not reporting was most often also fear of reprisal (40%). When compared to victims where no weapon was used and/or when there was no sustained injury even with the presence of a weapon, these victims chose to deal with the crime in another manner versus reporting it to the police.

What seems clear from this information is that victims may report, but not necessarily to the police, and oftentimes they do not report simply because they are afraid or they do not want to get the offender in trouble. However, the increasing numbers of victims failing to report because they believe the police could not or would not do anything about it requires us to examine the relationship between police and victims to see if there is anything concrete that may have contributed to the rise in this belief.

Victims and the Police

The significance of law enforcement's role in responding to crime victims cannot be overemphasized. Law enforcement officers interact more often with crime victims than other professionals in the criminal justice system. The way that victims are treated by dispatchers, the first officers arriving at the scene of the crime, and detectives investigating the case shapes their expectations of how they will be treated throughout the justice process (Office for Victims of Crime, 1998).

Police interact with victims in the following ways: initial response to call for service, depositions/statements/interviews, evidence collection, and case status updates. They also provide victims information on victims' rights and services in the community and refer them to the victim advocate within law enforcement agencies, if one exists. In order to truly assess interactions between victims and police, it is important to know what victims want or need from police in the first place. As you learned in Chapter 3, victims have three major needs that law enforcement officers should address (Woods, 2010). First, victims need to feel safe. This can be accomplished by a police officer making a point of introducing himself or herself to the victim and explaining his or her role and reassuring the victim that she or he is safe. Words aren't the only thing can reassure a victim, body language, tone of voice, eye contact, and other modes of active listening can contribute to feelings that one is in a safe place. Officers should make a point to ask victims if they have any medical needs, finding out if there is someone that can be called to come provide support, ask if there are any special needs or accommodations they might need, and start giving "power" back to the victim by asking them if it is ok to ask them questions and/or move to a different location to ask questions. It is also important that officers give victims their contact information, in writing, and provide them with written documentation about services that are available to them. Victims may not remember a lot of what is being told to them immediately following a victimization (as the body responds to trauma and chemical excretion in the brain) which is why written information is imperative.

Second, victims need to be able to express their emotions. As discussed previously, there is no single reaction to crime, people may express "negative" like emotions, sadness, anger, confusion, or frustration, or "positive" emotions, like laughter or smiling, or simply display no emotional reaction to the victimization at all. Allowing victims to express their emotions without judgment and questions is what victims need from law enforcement. Victims may also need to get their "story" off their chests, so providing them the opportunity to talk without cutting them off or asking them to finish up quickly allows for that to happen. Reassuring them that whatever emotion they're exhibiting is common or "normal" and helping to counter self-blame are also ways to provide support to a victim. Asking open-ended questions can help a victim to express him or herself and talking with them as opposed to just taking a report can show that they are important and worthy of attention and support.

Finally, victims need information and to know "what comes next." As discussed in Chapter 3, most victims do not have any experience with or personal knowledge of the criminal justice system, so they may have questions about how they will be involved in the investigation, what their rights are as victims, when they can expect to hear from someone about progress in the case, what resources might exist to assist with medical care and/or property damage, and if they can expect to be contacted by the media. Providing victims with this information can help them in preparing for the days immediately following the victimization and can put them on a positive path toward recovery. Victims may need to know why an officer is asking the questions he or she is asking and how that will be used in the investigation. Additionally, victims may need to be forewarned about follow-up interviews from both the police and prosecutor's offices. If the victimization requires some type of a medical exam, it is important to inform the victim what should be expected from that exam, especially if it might be painful (such as the rape kit, which requires that hairs be pulled from both the top of the head and the pubic region). There should be no surprises to victims about what information will be available to both the public and the media, so they are not shocked if they see their victimization written up in the paper. Woods (2010) suggests that it is also important to alert victims to the psychological reactions to crime, such as depression, loss of memory or inability to concentrate, and other manifestations that may follow a victimization. Victims may also need to be told what they need to do next and should be asked if they have any questions.

It is clear that the interaction between the crime victim and law enforcement officer is instrumental and important and that failure to attend to those three basic needs may result in the lack of cooperation from a victim, creation of distrust of the police, and may hamper the recovery of the victim overall. DeValve (2004) reports that levels of victim satisfaction related to police rely on three main areas: (1) validation or belief by police (or the lack of judgment or criticism in their report) and overall treatment, (2) information, and (3) inclusion in the process.

Skogan (2005) reports that much of the research on citizen and victim satisfaction of police suggest that victims are less satisfied with police than non-victims overall. Victims who were treated courteously, were informed of the status of their cases, and were referred to community resources had higher satisfaction levels, more akin to non-victims. In his analysis of the International Crime Victim Survey, van Dijk (2003) found that 75% of first-time victims and 63.5% of repeat victims in developed countries were satisfied with the police handling of cases. When they reported dissatisfaction it was because they believed the police did not do enough or were not interested in their cases. DeValve (2004) reports that satisfaction levels of victims were more often based upon how they were treated by police, rather than on the overall outcome of the case.

In the follow-up report to the President's Task Force on Victims of Crime (discussed in Chapter 8) an examination was conducted on how well law enforcement agencies across the country were responding to the main recommendations for improving services to crime victims (Office for Victims of Crime, 1998). The main critiques were that law enforcement needed to provide more training on victim sensitivity and awareness of victims' issues, that there needed to be more prompt return of property used in a case, that communication between law enforcement and victims needed to be more consistent, and that reports of intimidation or harassment by victims and witnesses needed to be investigated more seriously. They concluded their report with additional recommendations that suggest that while progress might have been made in the 15 years after the task force report, much more needed to be done. They reiterated the need for sensitivity and awareness training to occur and suggested that this training be given to dispatchers as well as law enforcement officers. They emphasized the need for law enforcement agencies to either create victim assistance positions within their departments or become more knowledgeable about services available in their communities that provided assistance to victims. They emphasized the need for victims to be made aware of their rights, including how they should be involved in the process. Finally, they highlighted the strong need for communication to be improved, especially as to giving victims case status updates (even when there wasn't anything new to report). Shapland (2000) reports that the issue is no longer *what* is needed to increase satisfaction of victims, indeed they understand that they need to improve upon providing information, consultation, and support, but HOW to go about building those mechanisms into the police culture and *who* will provide those needs.

Kennedy and Sacco (1998) suggest that one area of dissatisfaction expressed by victims in their interactions with police is with the way in which victims are treated by police. If there is the impression that a victim is not believed, was responsible for the crime (stated explicitly or implicitly by law enforcement), or is an "unworthy" of attention by law enforcement, the victim could experience something called **secondary victimization** or **revictimization**, whereby the victim feels retraumatized by the criminal justice agent. This can be especially exacerbated if there is an already tense relationship between police and a victim from a group that feels it has been treated unjustly by law enforcement in the past and for which much distrust exists.

Another area of contention between victims and law enforcement lies in the area of communication. There is no standard policy regarding how often law enforcement must communicate with victims about their cases, so it is often left up to the individual officer to establish his or her own practice of victim update. In some cases, victims have reported that they received monthly phone calls from the investigators on their cases, even when there was nothing new to report (OVC Video Series: Criminal Justice Professionals). Victims reported that this at least provided them with the comfort that they were not forgotten (or in the case of homicide survivors, that the case of their loved one was not forgotten). In other instances, victims have reported that they have been admonished for calling and "pestering" officers and told that when the officers have new information they will call (DeValve, 2004). In these cases, victims are left with a feeling of helplessness and experience secondary victimization, which gets in the way of recovering from the victimization overall.

Posick and Policastro (2014) found that an important indicator of victim satisfaction with police is confidence level of the victim in the police overall. They examined the effect of emotional distress on satisfaction levels of victims and found that individuals who exhibited higher levels of emotional distress to their victimization were more likely to report the crime to police, but overall were dissatisfied with the police response, unless they had pre-existing high levels of confidence in the police and their function in society. In this same study, they found that victims who were physically injured reported higher levels of satisfaction with police and they suggested that this might be because the victims felt legitimized in the eyes of the police and thus felt they were taken more seriously. Conversely, victims who knew their perpetrators and/or had been victimized before (especially in the case of interpersonal violence) had higher levels of dissatisfaction of police, perhaps because they did not feel validated by police as to the seriousness of their cases.

Tewksbury and West (2001) found in their analysis of the Louisville, Kentucky, police department that victims were generally satisfied with their interactions with police, especially in the way they felt they were treated by police (in a courteous and respectful manner) (81% of victims ranked officers at an 8 or above on a 10-point scale). Seventy-eight percent of victims in that study reported they with highly satisfied with the overall interaction with police. Approximately 77% reported high levels of satisfaction with the amount of concern they felt was showed by the officers and 73.5% reported high levels of satisfaction with the level of helpfulness they felt officers provided.

Victims and the Courts

Approximately 90% of cases that move beyond the law enforcement component of the criminal justice system never "go to trial" (Erez & Roberts, 2013), but the victim may still be involved in the judicial process in some ways. Since the writing of the Declaration of Independence, the state has been formally referred to as the "victim" in a criminal case, so the state acts as a "proxy" for the actual victim (Trulson, 2005). The victim is most often involved in the process as a witness and provider of information (Erez & Roberts, 2013). Most state victims' bills of rights require that victims be heard by prosecutor's offices as it relates to the type of charge they would like pursued and the punishment they would like to see doled out. However, the prosecutor is not required to abide by the wishes of the victim. It's an interesting conundrum: the state is reliant upon the victim to be forthcoming with information about the crime so the state can prosecute the offender, but the victim has no real say in the actual outcome and no recourse if they don't feel that justice has been done. Some suggest that victims are starting to earn more rights that give credence to their claims and recourse when they feel their rights have been violated (Erez & Roberts, 2013), known as the "third wave of victims' rights" and as was discussed in Chapter 8.

Erez and Roberts (2013) purport that victims' satisfaction with the court system is often dependent on three things: (1) the degree to which they felt heard by the prosecutor and were both involved in and informed of important proceedings throughout the process, (2) that "justice" was doled out, which may include financial recompense when appropriate and/or recognition and validation of the claim of harm that they reported, and (3) an admission of guilt and/or statement of apology by the offender. Earlier research by DeValve (2004) noted that there were five areas within which victims had concerns about their treatment by the court system, which align with the Erez and Roberts' (2013) findings: (1) lack of information and input into cases, (2) lack of notification about proceedings, (3) victims' rights versus defendants' rights, (4) information about and ability to present a victim impact statement, and (5) information about and assistance with filing for victim compensation (will be discussed in the section on victims and corrections). Additionally, victims are often subject to underhanded tactics of the defense attorney that may adversely affect them and color their opinion about the overall court process.

Shapland (2000) reports that victims often felt as if their input was not welcome or invited by prosecutors' offices and that they were often not told about court dates or decisions that had been made about their case, particularly in the cases of plea-bargaining. In addition, there was a history of failing to notify victims when court dates had been postponed (Reiff, 1979). This means that a victim may have taken off of work or arranged for care of a dependent and travelled to the court house only to find out the case was not being heard that day. Not only does this create emotional harm, but financial harm could also be experienced as the person may be out a day's wages and/or may be paying for day care services that aren't necessary. Even when a victim is informed about a court proceeding this does not ensure that he or she will be able to sit in court on that particular day. Under the **rule of witnesses** (Tobolowsky, Gaboury, Jackson, & Blackburn, 2010) if there is a concern that the presence of the victim may influence the treatment of the defendant the judge may exclude the victim and/or the victim's family members from the courtroom in order to protect the rights of the defendant (Tobolowsky et al., 2010). If the defense attorney can make an argument that the victim or victim's family and friends testimony would be affected by testimony being given on a specific day he or she can request that the victim not be allowed to be present for that day's testimony (Tobolowsky et al., 2010). **Rules of exception** exist to the rule of witnesses, but the exceptions were provided to those that were considered *essential* to the process, which victims and victims' friends and family were not. Taking it one step further, a defense attorney can also list the victim and/or victim's friends and family as potential witnesses to keep them out of the courtroom, even if there is no intention to call them to testify at any time (Tobolowsky et al., 2010). However, Tobolowsky, et al. (2010) point out that the recommendation of the New Directions study was that the court (judge or defense attorney) must present a truly compelling reason why a victim or a victim's family or friends should not be present in the courtroom and unless a compelling reason was presented, the victim and his or her support must be allowed in. What this demonstrates is that the rights often stipulated in state victims' bills of rights may be secondary to the rights afforded defendants in the US Constitution, and there are loopholes that allow for shady treatment by defense attorneys that could result in revictimization at the court level. Two other primary criticisms of defense attorneys that victims report are the ability of the defense attorney to request continuances to delay the case, and the form of questioning a defense attorney might conduct with the goal of discrediting the victim on the stand. Defense attorneys may use the strategy of delaying the case to weaken the memories of victims and witnesses so that the case becomes less solid for a prosecutor and/or to weaken the resolve of victims, with the intention of getting them to withdraw their participation and assistance because of the time that is required in the process. When a case does go to trial, a defense attorney may try to discredit the victim through his or her line of questioning by suggesting that he or she was either responsible for the victimization happening or that the victim's character is questionable and thus is not deserving of consideration by the court. In some cases, defense attorneys are specifically prohibited from besmirching the reputation of the victim in order to defend their clients. For instance, states have enacted **rape shield laws** that prohibit defense attorneys from bringing up a victim's sexual past if it has no bearing on the case at hand. If the case is before a jury, there may be some on the jury who would be put off by a rape victim having a sexual history that included many partners or seemingly "non-traditional" sexual practices. This may color the jury members' perceptions about the victim and call into question whether this person brought the victimization on in the first place.

The president's task force and the New Directions investigations both also suggested that there be separate waiting areas for victims and defendants during the legal process, as victims and witnesses were often complaining that they were being harassed or intimidated by the defendant or defendant's friends or family while they were sitting at court. Consider this: in the hallways of court houses, while waiting to testify, victims, witnesses, and the defendant's supporters may all be in the same area with limited (or perhaps no) security around to provide protection or order. As a result of the recommendations, many states have created separate waiting areas and have also developed or enhanced legislation dealing with harassment or intimidation of victims or witnesses (Office for Victims of Crime, 1998).

One way a victim can have his or her voice heard is through the submission of a **Victim impact statement (VIS)**. The VIS allows the victim to tell the court how the crime has impacted him or her in psychological, physical, social, and financial ways and may also include a listing of all costs the victim has been assessed to respond to the crime. Some of the critiques of victim impact statements include that they are typically requested early on in the justice process and may not represent the full impact of the crime on the victim. For instance, in many cases victim impact statements are submitted within the first six months following a crime, therefore, there may not be the opportunity to report any additional costs incurred (medical costs, loss of work, child care, etc.). Additionally, victims cannot always foresee all the challenges they will undergo as a result of the crime at the time that they write the statement. One area of controversy surrounding VISs is the amount of impact they may have on the outcome of the case. In other words, there is a fear that juries and/or judges may be

Professional Profile 10.1

Dr. Thomas Underwood
Washburn University

Q: What got you into the field of victimology and/or working with crime victims?

A: As an adult educator, my areas of interest in the development of professional development reflected my prior experience in the areas of criminal justice, social services, and mental health. Discussions with Washburn University faculty and administrators from the areas of human services, criminal justice, social work, psychology, and legal studies as to how the university can and should address issues of violence and victimization led to the development of workshops and other professional offerings related to victimization. Due to these offerings, Washburn was approached by the Office for Victims of Crime (OVC) to serve as the Midwest host site for the National Victim Assistance Academy. The involvement with OVC and other prominent organizations and academic institutions enhanced my interest in victimology/victim services, which further increased my professional work.

Q: What advice do you have for students interested in working with victims and/or becoming victimologists?

A: Service in the field requires more than passion and empathy; it requires professional knowledge and complex skills.

Q: What are some challenges to studying crime victims that you have encountered or seen?

A: Bias is an inherent challenge, as these issues generally solicit very strong emotions or opinions.

Q: What obstacles have you encountered while striving to study crime victims?

A: "Turf" and "silos" can be a significant obstacle in studying crime victim issues. Service organizations may not share goals or may be protective of their services to the extent that they are not willing to engage in collaborations with other programs. Further, organizations are often very suspicious of academic institutions.

Q: What do you feel is the mark you will have left on the field of victimology? What do you want people to see as your mark? At the end of the day, what do you want your "legacy" to be in the field of victimology/victim services?

A: I think people will recognize my efforts in promoting the professionalization of the field. This is evidenced through the courses offered, consultations, research, and professional writings.

Q: What are some burgeoning issues that you see in the field of victimology?

A: Areas that have received recent attention and should be a major area of focus include victims with disabilities and victimization and substance abuse.

The professionalization of the field as received only very limited attention. It remains to be seen if the field will continue to emerge as a full-fledged profession, or will maintain is status as an ancillary service.

Q: What areas within victimology do you think are neglected?

A: As a society we tend to have preferred victim areas, that is, victimization that tends to get attention (and service) when it affects a certain group or is a certain type of offense. This perpetuates the notion that victimization is a unique circumstance. As such, we can offer special programs that receive limited funding and have limited access to quality professionals. Or we study certain groups of people without generalization to the whole.

Just as our healthcare, education, and criminal justice system as social institutions are intended to serve society as a whole, the study of victimization and services provided need to do the same.

swayed on an emotional level because of the impact statement and fail to assess the case on the legal merits only. Secondary victims may also present victim impact statements in cases where the primary victim was killed. Those that support the inclusion of VISs in the criminal justice process suggest that it gives victims the recognition they deserve and is an illustration of treating them with dignity and respect, as proscribed in most victims' bills of rights (Erez & Roberts, 2013). They further suggest that it puts a face to the "true" victim in the case and does not allow for the judge, attorneys, and jury to neutralize the importance of the case. It has been noted that it is also serves a therapeutic component whereby the ability to address the court and participate in the process may psychologically help the victim on the road to recovery. Opponents of VISs suggest that they may lead to disparate sentencing practices as some juries or judges may be particularly moved by them, whereas others may not, therefore offenders with similar crimes and other circumstances may be treated differently (Erez & Roberts, 2013). It is further suggested that victims are not a recognized party in the adversarial legal systems that dominate the United States, England, Wales, and Canada, so including them in the process fundamentally changes the legal system from an adversarial one to a continental legal system as might be found in many European countries and which puts the burden on the defendant. Two additional critiques of VISs are that they may give the victim false hope as their

"In the News" Box 10.1

On May 20, 2014, lakeconews.com reporter Elizabeth Larson published an article entitled "Judge Hands Down Six-Year Sentence in Fatal 2013 Clearlake Stabbing." The article discusses the judgment imposed in a case in which an argument led to the killing of one neighbor by another. The offender was sentenced to six years in prison for voluntary manslaughter in the stabbing death of his neighbor after an argument about where a boat was parked in between the two properties; a charge that was reduced from murder and a possible lifetime sentence. The family asked the victim/witness advocate to read their victim impact statement into the record, reflecting the devastation the loss of their son has had on family and friends.

To read the full article, visit: http://www.lakeconews.com/index.php?option= com_content&view=article&id=36841:judge-hands-down-six-year-sentence- in-fatal-2013-clearlake-stabbing&catid=1:latest&Itemid=197.

wishes may be unrealistic in the sentencing scheme and thus victims may feel let down if the judge determines a sentence lower than what the victim wishes. Alternatively, some victims may be traumatized by the process of putting together the victim impact statement because they either don't want the offender to have that knowledge about the degree of harm that was perpetrated and/or they do not want to feel responsible for the sentence of the offender. When a victim impact statement is not taken seriously, this could result in the victim feeling revictimized by the criminal justice system in the VIS process and for many different reasons. Additionally, research has found little impact on actual sentences when VISs are presented in court. Furthermore, the fear that including victims more thoroughly in the criminal justice process would slow down the court system has also not come to fruition. Finally, victim satisfaction rates appear to increase for the most part when VISs are included in the process, though there are also greater reports of disappointment when victims' wishes are not met (Erez & Roberts, 2013).

Overall, the improvements that have been made in prosecutors' offices and the attention that has been given to victims through state victims' bills of rights have created a more inclusive environment for victims, which has resulted in greater levels of satisfaction and decreased levels of revictimization, despite the overall outcome of the court case (DeValve, 2004).

Victims and Corrections

In contrast to dealings with law enforcement and court personnel where the needs they have are typically directly met by personnel within those offices, when victims interact with corrections agents (institutional, probation/parole, other) it is normally related to the offender. The main expectations that victims have for corrections personnel include: (1) information, (2) protection, (3) to be heard, and (4) restitution (Howley, 2012).

The needs for information, protection, and to be heard are related to the movements and changes of status of inmates. Most state victims' bills of rights state that victims have a right to know when an offender is moved from a facility for any reason (going to court, transfer to new facility, etc.), going to be in the community (furlough, work release duty), has escaped, or is being released (Howley, 2012). Additionally, victims may have the right to be told where the released offender is going to be living and in one state (Michigan) if he or she has been granted a legal name change. Victims in Illinois even have the right to be given a recent picture of the inmate. This information may be important for the victim so he or she can be prepared to see the offender back in the community and/or to change his or her own situation, perhaps including moving to a different jurisdiction. Howley (2012) reports that victims in many states also have the right to have the contact information for the agent or agency that will supervise the offender once released. In essence, victims may need these different pieces of information in order to protect themselves from additional acts by the offender. For instance, offenders may be prohibited from contact with victims and as such may have this as a condition of probation or parole. If a victim is contacted in those instances he or she would have the ability to contact the offender's supervisory agent to inform him or her of the violation. Prior to a release from a confined facility, victims have the right to provide input in parole proceedings and/or other supervised release opportunities. This right to be heard provides victims with the opportunity to discuss the continued impact of the crime and to voice concerns about their safety if or when the offender is released, which could be important information when establishing conditions for release and/or parole guidelines for offenders (Howley, 2012).

Many states have created automated information and notification systems that provide victims with information regarding the whereabouts of an incarcerated offender at any time (VINElink, n.d.). In fact, 47 of the 50 states are networked into the national **Victim Information and Notification Everyday (VINE)** system either in full or in part. The VINE system requires that victims provide VINE staff with their correct contact information so an automatic notice will be generated to them when the status of an inmate is about to change. Additionally, victims may simply call the 1-800 number associated with that state's VINE system to check on the current whereabouts of the offender. Some states have retained the VINE acronym within their official state automated system name (e.g., Virginia) whereas others may call it something different (e.g., North Carolina, NC SAVAN: North Carolina Statewide Automated Victim Assistance and Notification). This may offer great comfort to victims if they know they can check on the status of the offender whenever they need and so they can prepare for the imminent release of an offender on a specific date (or be alerted to an escape, as well). In addition to protection and reports of probation/parole condition violation, supervisory agent contact information may also be

"In the News" Box 10.2

On April 23, 2014, *USA Today* reporter Richard Wolf published an article entitled "Justices Limit Restitution to Victims by Child Porn Users." The article discusses how restitution to a victim of child pornography should be doled out among the offenders found guilty of downloading her images. The article reports that the US Supreme Court ruled that a "common sense" approach needed to be taken when ordering restitution to a victim. In the case under review, a victim's images of her being raped and filmed between the ages of 8 and 9 were downloaded over 3,200 times. The victim found out about the proliferation of images available on the Internet at age 17 and has had difficulty functioning ever since. According to Wolf, the victim's lawyers have estimated that psychotherapy and lost wages due to an inability to work as a result of the posted images total to approximately $3.4 million dollars over her expected lifetime. To date, Wolf reports that 182 cases have been successful and $1.7 million has been ordered in restitution. The issue before the US Supreme Court was to determine how much was reasonable to order upon a single offender. While some justices argued that it was "impossible to approximate [his] share of the crime" and thus no restitution should be ordered per the current writing of the law, other Justices noted that if that reason was justified then victims would receive no restitution simply because there were too many offenders.

To read the full article, visit: http://www.usatoday.com/story/news/nation/2014/04/23/supreme-court-child-pornography-restitution/6182319/.

important for those victims for whom restitution was ordered, as the agent or agency may likely be the one collecting and distributing the restitution.

Restitution is court-ordered payment by an offender to the victim for harm incurred in the victimization (NCVC, Restitution, 2004). The President's Task Force on Victims of Crime required that all victims be awarded restitution unless a judge could provide a compelling reason not to (Tobolowsky, 2001), but in reality this mandatory sentence of restitution occurs in only about one third of all states (NCVC, Restitution, 2004). Restitution can cover any expense incurred by the victim as a result of the crime, including medical or counseling costs, criminal justice process costs, lost or damaged property costs, crime-scene clean up, and insurance deductibles (as applicable). Typically, restitution will be awarded for tangible losses, things for which the victim can provide documentation as to the expense of the harm incurred. Courts may order full or partial restitution, often dependent on the ability of the offender to pay (NCVC, Restitution, 2004). There is some controversy about this consideration as the victim may be just as economically disadvantaged as the offender, so consideration of the offender's financial situation, but not the victim's, is an additional type of revictimization the victim may suffer.

Another controversy surrounding restitution is if and how the victim receives it. Most often, the state probation and parole (community corrections) agency is tasked with collecting and distributing restitution. In some cases, restitution may be collected from prison work programs while the offender is incarcerated; however, the pay rate for inmates is exceedingly low, therefore the amount of restitution that can be expected from these types of programs is minimal. A 2011 NCVC study entitled "Making Restitution Real" reported that the vast majority of victims do not receive any restitution both for "street crime" type offenses and "white-collar crime" offenses. The NCVC study provided a few examples to back up their claims: only 12% of restitution ordered in 2007 had been collected by Maryland's Division of Parole and Probation by December of the following year, over 90% of Texas offenders discharged from parole from 2003– 2008 still owed restitution to their victims, and outstanding amounts in the millions of dollars range went unpaid in Pennsylvania, Arizona, and Nevada. McLean and Thompson (2007) suggest that victims are often competing with two powerful financial obligations that offenders may have that severely impacts an offender's ability to pay the restitution ordered by the court. The first competing obligation is criminal justice system costs, namely supervision fees and court fees. Many states depend on offender fees to cover a substantial proportion of their operating costs. For instance, the Travis County, Texas, Probation Department relies on probation fees for 46% of its overall budget (which was $18.3 million in 2006). The second obligation is child support, which according to federal law can be garnished directly from the wages of the offender (up to 65% of overall wages). McLean and Thompson (2007) report that policy is often not helpful in determining how a probation or parole officer should disseminate the fees it collects. Some policies prioritize criminal justice system costs above all others, whereas other states' policies prioritize restitution first. The collection of restitution is also complicated by the difficulty ex-cons have in finding and retaining employment, especially post-incarceration. This may lead an offender to engaging in criminal activity once again, which could lead to a new charge and/or reincarceration. Additionally, failure to pay back restitution can lead to revocation of probation, which means the individual will end up incarcerated and thus unable to secure employment, which would help to pay back the restitution. Some states have provided opportunities for the length of the probation or parole sentence to be extended until restitution has been collected in full and other states have even converted the criminal court-ordered restitution to civil judgments, to ensure that there is some accountability agent on the offender to continue payment of restitution (OVC, 2002). One final compounding issue regarding restitution is that some offenders may not be old enough to secure legal employment. Victims of juvenile offenders under the age of 16 may have great difficulty receiving court-ordered restitution unless the juvenile receives assistance from an adult.

Additional Modes of Repaying Victims

When discussing the treatment of victims by members of the criminal justice system, the fact that the crime has been reported to authorities is a given. Much of the information provided in this chapter has dealt with a victim reporting a crime and a suspect being arrested, charged, and possibly convicted and the attendant responsibilities of the formal criminal justice system is making sure victims' needs are met. However, victims may also receive assistance from state governments even if no suspect has been arrested for a case. Specifically, a victim can receive government assistance in the form of victim compensation, if they meet the case characteristics common to state victim compensation boards.

Crime Victim Compensation

Crime victim compensation is a program funded through the Victims of Crime Act of 1984, in which offenders' fines, forfeited bonds, forfeitures of profits from crimes, special assessments, and gifts/donations/bequests by private parties are the sole sources of revenue (OVC, 2013). At the federal level, money that is appropriated from the fund to the states is all offender or private party-based. At the state level, funds may be set aside from the state legislature, which may include taxpayer dollars but will also come from offender fines and forfeitures.

Only victims of violent crime are eligible for crime victim compensation, therefore the vast majority of victims will not be able to apply for assistance through this channel. Typically, the costs associated with violent crime are greater than those associated with property crime, on average, as they may also include substantial medical, ophthalmological, and dental expenses, funeral or burial expenses, counseling costs, forensic examination costs, crime scene cleanup, and general support (OVC, 2013). Most states will cover the medical/health-related expenses, counseling costs, funeral or burial expenses, and lost wages; however, some states also cover financial counseling, travel to/from court and/or medical assistance, relocation expenses, and crime scene cleanup (NCVC, 2003). The National Center for Victims of Crime, in its Crime Victim Compensation Overview (2003), notes that both primary and secondary victims are eligible to apply for crime victim compensation. More specifically, the direct target of the crime (primary victim) or the survivors of a homicide victim, or family of sexual assault, child abuse, or domestic violence victims (secondary). In order to be eligible to apply for crime victim compensation a victim must have (1) reported the crime to police, typically within a specific period of time (varies by state, with exceptions granted for child victimization, incapacitated victims, and other circumstances determined by the states), (2) willingly cooperate with the police and prosecution in the processing of the cases, and (3) may be considered ineligible for assistance if they became a victim in the commission of an illegal act or serious misconduct (i.e., a burglar breaks into a house and is shot, necessitating medical assistance; prostitute becomes an assault victim from a "john"). (4) The application for compensation must be submitted in the period of time specified by the state. And victim compensation is a **payment of last resort**, meaning that all other avenues of financial assistance must be exhausted before victim compensation will be considered and awarded. In most victim compensation applications, applicants will be required to specify if they are receiving funds from private or public insurance, Workers' Compensation, or restitution as ordered by the court in a criminal proceeding.

States vary as to how much compensation a victim may be entitled to, with a range from $10,000 to $100,000, with limits for specific claims, such as funeral expenses and counseling sessions. Victim advocates within the criminal justice system and at victim advocacy agencies may assist victims with putting together the application and should make all eligible victims aware of the funds.

Civil Court

When a victim seeks redress for pain and suffering experienced because of crime or wrongful death that is not met by restitution, he or she may seek to take the offender to civil court, the primary purpose of which is to seek a financial settlement from the offender to assist in expenses the victim feels were caused by the crime. The benefits in taking an offender to civil court are that costs for which there are no "receipts" can be covered and the standard of evidence is more easy to prove, as civil courts rely on a preponderance of the evidence to demonstrate culpability whereas criminal courts rely on evidence beyond a reasonable doubt. Additionally, a jury may award a substantial amount for pain and suffering that could greatly assist the victim in recovering from the crime. The drawbacks are that the judgment for the victim is not a given and he or she must bear the burden of the costs of the process, which may be costly, particularly if culpability of the defendant is not found (Karmen, 2013).

Direct Victim Services within the Criminal Justice System

Law enforcement officers, paralegals, attorneys, and probation and parole officers all work with victims as a component of their jobs within the criminal justice system. However, there are positions that exist within policing, courts, corrections, and state government that provide opportunities for public servants to work directly, and primarily, with crime victims. Both prior to, but also in large response to the President's Task Force on Victims of Crime (1982) recommendations, many agencies have created victim assistance positions throughout the criminal justice system to better serve crime victims. In police departments, victim advocate positions are typically civilian (or non-sworn officer positions) in which the advocates provide victims with information about services available to them, information about next steps in the criminal justice process, rights that have been proscribed through legislation, and may help them file the paperwork for victim compensation (previously discussed).

Professional Profile 10.2

Bettye Renee Carter
Victim-Witness Assistant for
Cumberland County's N.C.
District Attorney's Office,
Judicial District 12

Q: How did you get involved with working with crime victims? How did your role evolve in victims' services (i.e., started out as victim advocate, became executive director of an agency, etc.)? In what capacity do you currently work with victims? Have you ever been engaged in a joint research/practice project? Please describe.

A: My career in victim services began immediately after graduation from college, where I was introduced to the fight for victim's rights which was evolving in North Carolina. I was privileged to meet and work with two women who changed my life forever. Peggy Strong who was the first victim-witness assistant for Cumberland County's District Attorney's Office and one of a handful in the state, and Lynn Minnick, one of the founders on the North Carolina Victim Assistance Network. Their determination to give a voice to the victims of violent crimes and their loved ones inspired me to want to do the same. Over the years I have seen my position evolve from three victim-assistants who handled all victim issues (violent and nonviolent), prepared various court orders and motions, arranged for travel and lodging for witnesses, and maintained statistical data, all while assisting the district attorneys with trial preparation. Now there are approximately 10 victim-witness legal assistants who handle these tasks, allowing me to concentrate on more advocacy, community training and prevention, and agency collaboration. Currently I am the head of Victim Services in the district attorney's office and I work primarily with homicide families and the victims of adult and child rapes and sexual assaults as well as felony child abuse.

Q: What advice do you have for students interested in working with victims?

A: Students interested in working with victims should ask themselves in which capacity are they best suited to serve. Meaning which area of victimology are they interested in (i.e., domestic violence, sexual assault, child abuse and neglect, homicide, human trafficking) and in what type of agency (profit or nonprofit, local or US courts, government agencies, law enforcement, corrections, or on a global level). It is important to understand the victim population you are interested in, because each area of victimization brings its own complexities. It is equally important to find your niche. Are you best suited to the hands-on, emotional, touchy-feely component, community training and prevention, investigation, crisis on-call intervention services, or research and development? Volunteering in their area of interest will help them to determine if they truly have a passion for this area.

Q: What are some challenges for working with victims, especially as it relates to dealing with the criminal justice system and/or lawmakers?

A: Victims are often as complex as the criminal justice system they enter. They bring with them their beliefs, their culture, their environment, and their strengths and weaknesses as well as their dysfunction to a one-size-fits-all system of justice and punishment. Breaking down a wall of misconceptions and fears is usually the first issue I encounter, followed by helping them to understand the excessive time it can take to bring a case to trial. Having said that, it is also my job to introduce and personalize that victim and family to the prosecutor who spends the majority of their time preparing for their cases. When expectations of the criminal justice system are not met, victims can feel as if they have been re-victimized. Bridging the gap towards a healthy respect for the victim's rights and the prosecutor's duty to the state to provide justice can be the greatest challenge of all, but one of the best ways of eliminating re-victimization.

Q: What obstacles have you encountered while striving to assist victims? Have the obstacles to providing good service to victims changed over the years?

A: Many of the obstacles that I have encountered over the years involved lack of resources and budget constraints. Staff shortages and nonexistent resources often made it difficult to give the level of care I as a service provider wanted to give. Though the volume of cases involving victim services has increased greatly over the years, the Administrative Office of the Courts has worked diligently to provide resources and adequate staff to keep pace. This has allowed our office to meet the needs of specific victim populations with compassion and professionalism. Other issues, such as judgmental attitudes and stereotypical ideologies from victims towards the court system, and at times frustration from attorneys towards victims, often presented and still present obstacles and barriers to assisting victims and their families through the court process. Unfortunately, at times I still have to fight this battle.

Q: What do you feel is the mark you will have left on the field of victim services? What do you want people to see as your mark? At the end of the day, what do you want your "legacy" to be in the field of victimology/victim services?

A: As a victim-witness assistant and advocate within the district attorney's office, the mark that I would have left is that I upheld and furthered the legal rights of crime victims going through the court process and that I taught those coming behind me that there are real solutions to every problem They just don't always come laid out in a manual or a book. The heart's ability to care deeply, usually creates the commitment to find solutions and go the extra mile.

So at the end of the day, I want my legacy in the field of victimology and victim services to be that, I valued and respected each victim God sent my way and they knew that I had listened with my heart and tried to ease the chaos in their lives.

Q: What are some burgeoning issues that you see in the fields of victimology/ victim services?

A: As new victim populations emerge, the field of victimology will find itself expanding to include and address their specific issues. Mental health issues create victims and defendants. Solutions to this increasing demographic are becoming more and more difficult to address with budget cuts and the influx of homeless war vets and military personnel with PTSD and traumatic brain injuries. Another burgeoning issue includes human trafficking, which is probably one of the most serious threats to teens and young adults today. More education and prevention campaigns need to be launched on all levels.

Q: Are there groups of victims you think need to be served but are not? Why do you think that way?

A: Not current victims but more so the *potential* victims of human trafficking. If we could educate middle and high school kids to the dangers, we could prevent this horrendous crime from happening to many.

Law enforcement victim advocates also may be a point of contact for victims if they are unable to reach the officer or detective responsible for investigating their case.

Most district attorney's offices employ victim witness liaisons or victim witness legal assistants who are charged with providing victims information on the court process, listening to them and finding out their needs as they relate to the victimization, informing them of their rights and of services available to them, and perhaps most importantly, providing them with notification about when hearings will take place dealing with "their" case. They are also supposed to inform victims when there is going to be a delay in the case, so that the victim does not come to the courthouse only to find out that the case is not being heard that day.

Within the Department of Corrections in most states are crime victim assistance units that are responsible for notifying victims of changes in status of the offenders in their cases, to coordinate victim-offender mediation (as applicable), can alert victims to services within their communities, and to provide safety planning along with those community resources for the victim. Additionally, for offenders who have victimization histories themselves, the crime victim assistance units within state Department of Corrections can link inmates/offenders with services within prisons or jails and/or link offenders with community resources to assist them with their victimization histories.

Professional Profile 10.3

Tarra Collins
Victim-Witness Legal Assistant
for Alamance County,
N.C. District Attorney's Office,
Judicial District 15a

Q: How did you get involved with working with crime victims? In what capacity do you currently work with victims? Have you ever participated in a joint research/ practice project? Please describe.

A: In 2005, I was hired as a paralegal in a busy family law firm. Our work consisted of divorces, child custody, and equitable distribution. Now and again I would find that one of our clients or the client's spouse was party to a criminal case in addition to our civil case. If I needed to know the status of one of our client's criminal cases I would visit the district attorney's office to speak with an assistant district attorney or victim-witness/legal assistant (VWLA). Over time I became friends with one of the VWLAs and was able to pick her brain about the work she did. I became fascinated and started looking for jobs at surrounding district attorney's offices. In 2007, I was hired as a VWLA for North Carolina's 15a Prosecutorial District working with victims of felony crimes.

Q: What advice do you have for students interested in working with victims?

A: Working with victims of crime is taxing, but it is rewarding. My two mantras are "there is no room for ego" and "never judge." In my experience in an office with prosecutors focused on jury trials, the work that VWLAs do often goes overlooked and unpraised. I don't say this to chastise the prosecutors—it's just the nature of the job. Prosecutors must focus on the law and procedures, and the VWLAs must focus on the victim. I say "never judge" because some of your victims may be people you don't like or might live a lifestyle that you don't agree with, but they need services all the same.

Q: What are some challenges for working with victims, especially as it relates to dealing with the criminal justice system and/or lawmakers?

A: Time. In North Carolina, a felony must go through a second test of probable cause after arrest which we call grand jury. Preparing a proposed indictment for grand jury to sign can be time consuming because a prosecutor must receive and review the investigative report from law enforcement, receive and review any laboratory results from the crime lab, discover all documents to the defense, and then assess that the legal language is correct from the warrant for grand jury's review. If it is a complex case like a rape or murder the process takes even longer. Once a case is indicted the defendant is re-arraigned in superior court and given a least one superior court administrative date to see if the defense attorney and prosecutor can negotiate an appropriate plea arrangement. If no plea arrangement is drafted then the case is put on a trial calendar at least one month out from the administrative date. Getting on a trial calendar is just half the battle, as this begins the defense's motions for continuances, motions to suppress, etc. My biggest challenge is always making sure the victim understands why it takes so long to reach a disposition in a felony and reassure that victim that we are taking their case seriously and doing everything we can to move it forward.

Q: What obstacles have you encountered while striving to assist victims? Have things changed for the better?

A: Funds are very low for victim reimbursement. If a family lost a family member to a murder the survivors can apply to North Carolina Crime Victim's Compensation for reimbursement for funeral expenses. If a victim is injured in an assault or a vehicle crime that victim can also ask for reimbursement for medical bills rising out of the crime from North Carolina Crime Victim's Compensation. Victim's comp does not pay for property damage or fraud and does not cover future medical expenses like counseling or medications. Your ability to file for victim's compensation expires after two years. This means if a suspect is not charged within two years that victim cannot recover from victim's comp.

At the trial level, the conference of district attorneys will pay for travel, lodging, and subsistence for one day and one night. This means that a victim (who we ask to be present for the entirety of the trial) has to find another way to pay for the rest of the time spent in the courtroom. North Carolina's Victim Assistant Network (NCVAN) has a subsistence program that can reimburse a victim for hotel and food but the victim has to pay up front for his or her arrangements. VWLAs in our office often buy meals for victims and witnesses, because they don't have any money. If I have victim or witness arriving at the airport I drive from Graham to Raleigh to pick them up and then drop them off when the trial is over.

Q: What do you feel is the mark you will have left on the field of victim services? What do you want people to see as your mark? At the end of the day, what do you want your "legacy" to be in the field of victimology/victim services?

A: I hope that victims walk away from my office feeling like we advocated as much as we possibly could for them. I always explain that our service to victims doesn't stop when the trial is over. I often check up with victims a couple of times a year just to see how they are doing. A lot of times victims keep in touch with me through Facebook or the occasional phone call.

Q: What are some burgeoning issues that you see in the fields of victimology/ victim services?

A: My passion right now is our Elder Protection Initiative. This a multidisciplinary approach to educating, preventing, reporting, and prosecuting cases of elder abuse. The district attorney's office actually goes into the community to different civic groups and gives a presentation on what elder abuse is and how we can all help prevent it. My office works with local law enforcement and DSS in handling these cases. Our next step is to establish elder abuse identification training for first responders that may initially get called to a home for one complaint like domestic violence but upon arrival realizes there is an elder in the home that could be the victim of neglect.

Q: Are there groups of victims you think need to be served but are not? Why do you think that way?

A: I think we could do a better job of protecting women from human trafficking. I'd like to see an initiative in my county that brings awareness to the folks about the prevalence of the exploitation of poor minority women in our community.

Each state employs victim compensation case workers who are responsible for determining eligibility and award amounts of victim compensation for victims of violent crime. Typically, these positions are housed within the overarching state Department of Justice or Public Safety (terms may vary depending on the state).

Summary and Conclusions

Both the 1982 President's Task Force on Victims of Crime and the New Directions study that came out 15 years later highlighted some important areas within which criminal justice personnel needed to strive to improve so victims experienced less revictimization and more satisfaction with case processing within the criminal justice system. Research on victims suggests that they need to be treated with compassion and without judgment, to be given information, and to be able to express themselves. Rights have been established to provide for these desires, and there have been improvements overall in the treatment of victims by criminal justice personnel, but the lack of communication and information persist perhaps more than they should, having had 30 years or more since the initial report came out. Perhaps continued improvement in those areas will increase reporting rates of victims, thereby eliminating one of the reasons victims choose not to report—namely that they don't think the police will do anything about it. One area that needs greater focus is on how to improve collection of restitution. Some innovative ideas are being offered by practitioners, but most victims are still getting the short end of the stick when it comes to repayment. In Chapter 12 you will read about some innovative collaborations between criminal justice and victim advocacy personnel that might help to improve treatment and increase the satisfaction victims have with the overall criminal justice system.

Key Terms

Secondary victimization or
   revictimization
Rule of witnesses
Rules of exception
Rape shield laws
Victim impact statement (VIS)

Victim Information and Notification
   Everyday (VINE)
Restitution
Crime victim compensation
Payment of last resort

Discussion Questions

1. If a victim does not provide his or her updated contact information to the VINE system in his or her state, does that person have a right to be upset if they learn through other channels that the offender is out on the streets?
2. Should defense attorneys and judges be allowed to bar victims and witnesses from the courtroom? Why or why not?
3. Should victim compensation be a payment of last resort or be automatic for tangible costs associated with eligible crimes?
4. Should victim compensation be limited to personal crime victims? What is your rationale for your response?

Website for Further Information

Victims and the Criminal Justice System: http://www.victimsofcrime.org/help-for-crime-victims/get-help-bulletins-for-crime-victims/the-criminal-justice-system.

References

DeValve, E. Q. (2004). Through the victims' eyes: Towards a grounded theory of the victimization experience. Sam Houston State University, ProQuest, UMI Dissertations Publishing. 3143578.

Erez, E., & Roberts, J. (2013). Victim participation in the criminal justice system. In R. Davis, A. Lurigio, & S. Herman (Eds.), *Victims of crime* (4th ed.), (pp. 251–270). London: Sage Publications.

FBI. (2010). Crime in the U.S. *Homicide.* Retrieved from http://www.fbi.gov/about-us/cjis/ucr/crime-in-the-u.s/2010/crime-in-the-u.s.-2010.

Hart, T. C., & Rennison, C. (2003). *Reporting crime to the police, 1992–2000,* Special Report, Washington, DC: US Department of Justice, Office of Justice Programs, Bureau of Justice Statistics. NCJ-195710.

Howley, S. S. (2012). *Crime victims and offender reentry.* Voice of the Victim, a perspectives spotlight issue. *Perspectives: The Journal of the American Probation and Parole Association,* 18–27.

Karmen, A. (2013). *Crime victims: An introduction to victimology* (8th ed.). Belmont, CA: Cengage Publishing.

Kennedy, L. W., & Sacco, V. F. (1998). *Crime victims in context.* Los Angeles, CA: Roxbury Publishing.

Langton, L., Berzofsky, M., Krebs, C., & Smiley-McDonald, H. (2012). *Victimizations not reported to the police, 2006–2010,* National Crime Victimization Survey, Special Report. Washington, DC: US Department of Justice, Office of Justice Programs, Bureau of Justice Statistics. NCJ 238536.

McLean, R. L., & Thompson, M. D. (2007). *Repaying debts.* New York, NY: Council of State Governments Justice Center.

Murphy, S. L., Xu, J., & Kochanek, K. D. (2013). Deaths: Final data for 2010. *National Vital Statistics Reports, 61*(4), 1–118.

National Center for Victims of Crime (NCVC). (2003). Crime victim compensation. *Help Bulletin.* Retrieved from http://www.victimsofcrime.org/help-for-crime-victims/get-help-bulletins-for-crime-victims.

National Center for Victims of Crime (NCVC). (2004). Restitution. *Help Bulletin.* Retrieved from http://www.victimsofcrime.org/help-for-crime-victims/get-help-bulletins-for-crime-victims.

National Center for Victims of Crime (NCVC). (2011). *Making restitution real: Five case studies on improving restitution collection.* Washington, DC: US Department of Justice, Office of Justice Programs.

National Conference of State Legislators. (n.d.). *Sanctions for drunk driving accidents resulting in serious injuries or and/or death.* Retrieved from http://www.ncsl.org/documents/transportation/drunkdrivesanctions.pdf.

Office for Victims of Crime (OVC). (1998). *New directions from the field: Victims' rights and services for the 21st century.* Washington, DC: US Department of Justice, Office of Justice Programs.

Office for Victims of Crime (OVC). (2002, November). *Restitution: Making it work. Legal Series Bulletin #5.* Washington, DC: US Department of Justice, Office of Justice Programs. NCJ 189193.

Office for Victims of Crime (OVC). (2013). Crime victims fund fact sheet. Washington, DC: US Department of Justice, Office of Justice Programs. Retrieved from http://www.ovc.gov/pubs/crimevictimsfundfs/intro.html#PrimarySources.

Posick, C., & Policastro, C. Victim injury, emotional distress, and satisfaction with the police: Evidence for a victim-centered, emotionally-based police response. *Journal of the Institute of Justice & International Studies, 13,* 185–196.

Reiff, R. (1979). *The invisible victim: The criminal justice system's forgotten responsibility.* New York, NY: Basic Books, Inc.

Shapland, J. (2000). Victims and criminal justice: Creating responsible criminal justice agencies. In A. Crawford & J. Goodey (Eds.), *Integrating a victim perspective within criminal justice: International debates* (pp. 147–164). Aldershot, UK: Ashgate.

Skogan, W. G. (2005). Citizen satisfaction with police encounters. *Police Quarterly, 8*(3), 298–321.

Tewksbury, R., & West, A. (2001). Crime victims' satisfaction with police services: An assessment in one urban community. *The Justice Professional, 14*(4), 271–285.

Tobolowsky, P. M., Gaboury, M. T., Jackson, A. L., & Blackburn, A. G. (2010). *Crime victim rights and remedies* (2nd ed.). Durham, NC: Carolina Academic Press.

Trulson, C. (2005). Victims' rights and services: Eligibility, exclusion, and victim worth. *Criminal Justice Policy Review, 4*(2), 399–414.

Truman, J., Langton, L., & Planty, M. (2013). *Criminal victimization, 2012.* Washington, DC: US Department of Justice. NCJ 243389.

van Dijk, J. J. M. (2003). Attitudes of victims and repeat victims toward the police: Results of the International Crime Victims Survey. *Crime Prevention Studies, 12,* 27–52.

VINELINK. (n.d.). Retrieved from https://www.vinelink.com/vinelink/initMap.do.

Wilson, J. M., & Weiss, A. (2012). A performance based approach to police staffing and allocation. US Department of Justice, Office of Community Oriented Policing Services.

Woods, T. O. (2010). *First response to victims of crime, Guidebook.* Washington, DC: US Department of Justice, Office of Justice Programs, Office for Victims of Crime. NCJ 231171.

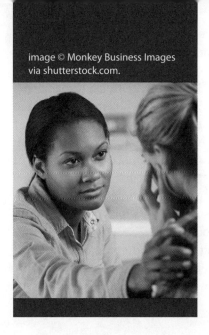

image © Monkey Business Images
via shutterstock.com.

Chapter 11: Working with Victims — Victim Advocacy Outside of the Criminal Justice System

In Chapter 10, we focused on the services provided by the criminal justice system and other government entities. There are additional entities and individuals who assist victims as well, who operate within many different organizations with the primary goal of providing direct services to crime victims. For the most part these organizations are created with a purpose to provide services to a specific group of victims, be they women, children, homicide survivors, or others with a primary goal of assisting crime victims in the recovery process. This chapter will focus on the history of victim advocacy, what services are provided for victims, who tends to use these services, and the effects of these services on the recovery of victims overall.

History of Victim Advocacy

During the 1960s and 1970s a number of social movements contributed to grassroots efforts to focus specific attention on social problems that appeared to be gaining attention at the time (Zweig & Yahner, 2013). The Civil Rights Movement, the Women's Movement, the Law and Order Movement, and the Children's Movement all identified that segments of the population were experiencing victimizations with a paucity of coordinated response by the government (including the criminal justice system) and the private sector. This led to activists and advocates taking things into their own hands and creating services for the people they felt were being ignored by more formal organizations. According to Zweig and Yahner (2013), in the 1970s the United States and Britain saw the creation of the first women's domestic violence shelters and advocacy agencies and rape crisis centers, often staffed solely or predominantly by volunteers. In the 1980s, additional organizations were created to focus attention on murdered children (e.g., Parents of Murdered Children) and homicide survivors of victims of drunk-driving fatalities (e.g., Mothers Against Drunk Driving). Federal legislation (discussed in Chapters 8 and 9) led to the creation of national victim assistance organizations, and pockets of funding to support the efforts of the grassroots agencies and the work of advocates to educate policymakers have opened doors for the recognition of additional crime victim populations, including victims of human trafficking, illegal immigrants, stalking victims, identity theft victims, cybercrime victims, prisoners who are victims of rape, and many more.

What Is a Victim Advocate?

According to the National Center for Victims of Crime (2008) a **victim advocate** is someone who is trained to provide support to victims. In most cases a victim advocacy agency will provide information; give emotional support; assist victims in creating safety plans for themselves and finding shelter and transportation; accompany victims to law enforcement interviews, court, parole hearings, and other criminal justice functions as necessary; intervene on behalf of victims with creditors, landlords, and employers; provide victims with referrals to additional services (and may even arrange initial appointments); help to arrange funerals; and notify victims of status changes

"In the News" Box 11.1

On April 29, 2014, Ocala.com staff writer, April Warren, published an article entitled "Help in Times of Trial: Victim Advocates Navigate the System." The article discusses the role of victim/witness advocates in the state of Florida. The article notes that many components of the criminal justice system are hiring victim advocates to provide more compassionate and focused attention on victims. Most victim/witness advocates are found in the court system, but law enforcement has its fair share of victim advocates as well. According to the article, victim/witness advocates are involved in misdemeanor and felony cases and provide victims with information on community resources, updates on court dates, companionship during interviews and court processes, and help to prepare them for testifying and getting to know the general environment of the court. The bond is so strong between the victim/witness advocate and victims that "[m]any advocates still hear from victims whose cases have long concluded."

To read the full article, visit: http://www.ocala.com/article/20140429/ARTICLES/140429660?p=4&tc=pg.

of inmates. Someone working in a victim advocacy agency may also provide education on victimization prevention, victimization recognition, and working with crime victims to schools, criminal justice professionals, medical professionals, clergy, neighborhood groups, businesses and other groups requesting information. Additionally, some victim advocates work to change legislation and garner recognition for victims and the services they need. Clearly, the job of a victim advocate is varied and advocates must retain or be able to access a great deal of information in order to best assist crime victims.

As mentioned in Chapter 10, each facet of the criminal justice system has created specific victim assistance positions within them, though all criminal justice agencies do not employ victim advocates, particularly if the agencies are relatively small. Victim advocacy agencies can be non-profit, private, or public and an agency may be staffed by paid staff and/or volunteers. In the non-profit sector, you most often see victim advocacy agencies focused on violence against women (stand-alone—meaning singular topic—rape crisis centers, domestic violence centers, and shelters, or duo-focus—meaning a combined rape crisis/domestic violence advocacy agency, human trafficking, stalking), child abuse (child advocacy centers, etc.), homicide survivors (Parents of Murdered Children, Compassionate Friends), and animals (American Society for the Prevention of Cruelty to Animals, People for the Ethical Treatment of Animals, etc.).

Some centers, such as the **Crime Victim Advocacy Center of St. Louis** (http://www.supportvictims.org/) and the **Victims Outreach Information Center** (VOICe, http://www.voiceforvictims.com/index.html), provide information, counseling, and other advocacy services to victims of all crime and there is a growing movement to merge victim advocacy agencies into "one-stop shops" or "family justice centers" to better

Figure 11.1: Victim Outreach Information Center (VOICe), Butler, Pennsylvania
http://www.voiceforvictims.com/ourservices.html

Our Services

Victim Outreach Intervention Center (VOICe) is a non-profit systems change organization that provides free and confidential services to individuals and families who are survivors of crime. VOICe works within our community to bring about social change and provide survivors with the ability to take control of their lives.

We support survivors of:

- Domestic violence
- Rape or sexual assault
- Violent crimes including simple or aggravated assault
- Child sexual assault
- Adult survivors of sexual abuse or incest
- Stalking
- Sexual harassment
- Attempted homicide or families of homicide victims
- Terroristic threats
- Burglary
- Robbery

assist the victim, or families experiencing multiple types of victimization, with all their needs as they relate to the victimization and recovery (to be discussed later in this chapter). In sum, it can be said that there are some core areas within which victim advocates provide service: (1) information and education, (2) direct advocacy, (3) accompaniment/companionship, (4) emotional support, and (5) safety assessment and crisis intervention. These services are provided via 24-hour crisis lines, individual and group counseling (including support groups), educational workshops and presentations at public meetings, website publications/brochures/handouts, self-defense workshops, accompaniment to legal proceedings and/or interviews with criminal justice personnel, emergency room accompaniment/companionship, and one-on-one case management-type sessions. In the next section, we will address each of the different types of services in the five main areas.

Information and Education

Victims may be very unfamiliar with the criminal justice system and may simply need information on next steps and who to contact within the system itself. They may need information on services that are available to them, their rights as crime victims, and on what they need to do to report a crime. Educational workshops are provided to a variety of audiences oftentimes to inform individuals about what it means to be a crime victim, what constitutes victimization, how to stop or prevent victimization, and how to work with crime victims. Information can be provided through conversations and through written formats (e.g., pamphlets, postcards, newspaper columns, websites, other publications).

Direct Advocacy

Direct advocacy includes any service provided to victims that will assist them with planning, logistics, housing, finances (including providing assistance with filing for victim compensation when eligible), transportation, finding caregivers, referrals to other agencies, and other case management-type activities (Zweig & Yahner, 2013). Direct advocacy activities encompass things that will help the victim with next steps toward recovery, but don't typically include the provision of counseling or emotional support directly. Zweig and Yahner (2013) also mention the use of cell phone provision, which is a program that is seen in agencies that are often focused on ameliorating violence against women. In these cases, victims are provided with cell phones for which they can call emergency services, victim advocacy, and other pertinent places/persons to help reestablish their lives. Typically, these phones are provided on a limited time basis to help the victim get back on her or his feet.

Accompaniment and Companionship

Victims may need accompaniment and/or companionship in both medical and legal systems. For instance, rape crisis centers generally provide emergency room companionship for victims who are being physically examined by medical staff following a sexual assault or rape. In these cases, advocates can help explain the process of a rape kit, can provide emotional support during the process, can try to get some assistance for the victim from medical personnel (for instance, if a long period of time has gone by and the victim is still in the exam room the advocate can ask when she might be released and/or what is next in the process), can help the victim determine a safety plan for when he or she leaves the hospital, and can work with the victim to make sure he or she returns to a safe environment. Legal advocacy can include accompanying and/or transporting (or securing transportation for) the victim to attend court hearings, to attend interviews with law enforcement and the prosecutor's office, and provide general information about next steps and legal rights with the criminal justice system. A nongovernmental victim advocate may not have access to as much information as a criminal justice system victim advocate, who may also be able to provide the victim with a secure waiting area at the legal proceeding and may have more access to the detective's or prosecutor's case files in which case they may have more information they can provide to victims, in addition to the emotional support of staying with them through the proceedings (Zweig & Yahner, 2013).

Emotional Support

Emotional support comes in many shapes and forms in victim advocacy agencies, including 24-hour crisis hotlines, individual counseling (with a licensed therapist or social worker), group counseling, and support groups (both general and therapeutic) (NCVC, 2008). Yassen and Glass (1984) suggest that for survivors of sexual assault, different types of emotional support may be necessary at different stages following the assault. For instance, in the first stage they may need more one-on-one to help them understand their reaction to and start the recovery process following the sexual assault. In stage two they have progressed emotionally to a point where they feel they are able to return to their previous routines and may choose not to seek emotional support from outside agencies. However, in the final stage, stage three, they may encounter situations or people that trigger memories about the sexual assault and may need to seek out assistance with emotional support, but may not feel the need for individual counseling as the only option.

Safety Assessment and Crisis Intervention

Zweig and Yahner (2013) suggest that victims may need both long- and short-term guidance as it relates to safety and security. Some of the assistance that is offered can be in the form of crime prevention, such as discussing the physical environment and assessing a household and other physical settings for proper locks and security (cameras, alarm systems, and other security measures), discussing ways to prevent future revictimization from both strangers and familiars, and perhaps even moving to a new location. Participation in self-defense workshops can be an additional component in this area as some rape crisis, domestic violence, and women's centers provide opportunities for these programs, often at a considerably reduced fee or free of charge. Additionally, Shoemyer (2009) suggests that some states provide opportunities for participation in an address confidentiality program, which allows for victims (particularly in cases of domestic violence and stalking) to utilize a substitute address for government, personal, and mailing uses while protecting the actual residential

Professional Profile 11.1

Cindy Linquist Yadav

Q: How did you get involved with working with crime victims? In what capacity do you currently work with victims? Have you ever participated in a joint research/ practice project? Please describe.

A: For as long as I can remember, I always loved helping people. I was always that friend that people came to when they needed a listening ear, or some advice about something. My childhood was traumatic for me; I was in and out of group homes, and had a couple of suicide attempts. Some of the events that took place during that time were so traumatic for me that I have blocked them out completely, or I have difficulty remembering the sequence of events. I remember the feelings of helplessness, unworthiness, and my anger at the world and at God (if there was one).

When I was 19, I joined AmeriCorps. I went to work in a police department, and my job was working with domestic violence victims. That was my first real exposure to working with crime victims, and I realized that it was my passion. It was during this time that I had the sudden realization that the experiences and feelings that I went through as a teenager were actually a gift; I could identify with some of the feelings that victims felt and it helped me know what to say, since I had no one to say those words to me when I felt those feelings.

A few years later, I learned about Sam Houston State University, which was the only school in the country with a victim studies degree. As soon as I went to visit, I knew it was meant to be. I picked up my life from upstate New York and moved to Huntsville, Texas. While I was there, I met a teacher that really impacted my life; she became my mentor. She and I formed an organization called the Crime Victims Services Alliance, a group for students interested in working with crime victims.

My role never really evolved into anything else; I loved what I did as a victim advocate. However, I did work with volunteers who also had a passion for working with victims. Currently, I am not working in the field of victim services, due to the lack of positions available.

Q: What advice do you have for students interested in working with victims?

A: One of the problems that I faced is that this is a very narrow field; employment opportunities can be few and far between, depending on the area that you are looking in. As a student, the best thing that you can do to help your career is to network. Get to know people in the field; they might be the key to getting a good position when you get out of school. Volunteer work is also a good way to get your foot in the door. Get recommendation letters from everyone that you work with and bring them in a portfolio to interviews. This way, you will leave them with a lasting impression of you.

Q: What are some challenges for working with victims, especially as it relates to dealing with the criminal justice system and/or lawmakers?

A: I think the biggest challenge for me was working with criminal justice professionals that were burned out, or were not at all interested in doing what's best for the victim or the victim's family. Even something as simple as informing them of what to expect while going through the criminal justice process, which can be overwhelming and difficult to understand. Also, if you work with a nonprofit, sometimes the criminal justice professionals would already have preconceived notions about you and the organization that you represent.

Q: What obstacles have you encountered while striving to assist victims? Have the obstacles changed things for the better over the years?

A: As stated above, the main obstacle that I faced was difficulty with the criminal justice system itself. I think that they have gotten better in recent years; I think the key to this is awareness. I feel that it is not just about the criminal anymore; now there is new focus on the victim. Some examples of this might be the formation of the Crime Victims' Compensation Fund or the option for the victim to speak at sentencing (victim impact statement).

Q: What do you feel is the mark you will have left on the field of victim services? What do you want people to see as your mark? At the end of the day, what do you want your "legacy" to be in the field of victimology/victim services?

A: My hope is that I made an impact on each of the lives of the victims that I worked with; that they felt like someone was listening and helping them through what is probably the worst thing that any person can experience. I want to be remembered as one of the many voices of change as well; I would like to think that I was able to help the officials in the criminal justice system realize that victims were not just a number but a real person who is living a nightmare.

Q: What are some burgeoning issues that you see in the fields of victimology/ victim services?

A: I am seeing that the awareness of victim services is increasing, but the funding and availability of services are not. It is not enough to just become aware of victims' needs; we have to be able to do something about it. It seems that the human service field is always the first to lose funding of existing services or not having the funding in the first place to create much needed support systems.

Another issue that I see a lot of is the reluctance to "get involved." People are so mindful of not interfering with other people's issues that they neglect to report things that they know are wrong. I think that we really need to change that mentality in our society. We have the potential to save so many lives by being the voice for someone who feels like they don't have one of their own.

Q: Are there groups of victims you think need to be served but are not? Why do you think that way?

A: I think that bullying has been a long underserved population that is finally getting some media attention. People dismiss it as children are just children, or they tell the victim that they have to "toughen up," Research has shown that bullying can lead to many long-term problems such as low self-esteem and PTSD. Unfortunately, it has led to many children committing suicide, some as young as preteens.

Another area where I feel services are lacking is immigrants, especially immigrant women when it comes to domestic violence. Sometimes they come here with their husbands and feel trapped—they have no money; they have no family here, and feel alone and isolated and they sometimes are unable to speak the language. In addition to that, I also think that immigrant workers who come here with the promise of a better life are often misled. They feel as though they have no one to help them or they feel like they have no place to go.

address at which the victim resides. This helps to protect the victim from the perpetrator finding her using traditional public records requests. Zweig and Yahner (2013) suggest that survivors of homicide may have additional needs, such as crime scene clean-up and assistance with notifying others of the homicide. This is particularly noteworthy as illustrated in the OVC Video Series "Voices of Victims: Financial Considerations." In this video, one mother recounts how she and her husband had to drive her son's car back home after police released it from evidence in his homicide case. The son was murdered in the car and the driver's seat and dashboard was covered in her son's blood. Working with a victim advocate to have the advocate coordinate clean-up of this type of a situation would have eliminated that traumatic experience of this particular family.

Child and Older Adult Victims

As you learned in Chapter 5, there are separate organizations that exist to investigate claims of harm to children and older adults (or elders) that may be official channels (often through county- or state-level Departments of Health and Human Services/ Social Services) but not necessarily criminal (i.e., Child Protective Services and Adult Protective Services). These agencies refer those clients that they have deemed to have suffered from some type of abuse or neglect to services that can assist them.

Child Advocacy Centers

Child advocacy centers (CAC) are organizations that provide care after sexual or physical abuse or neglect has been determined by Child Protective Services staff (National Children's Alliance, visited March 4, 2017). To minimize the trauma experienced by children when they are asked to repeat what happened multiple times, CACs put together multidisciplinary teams (MDT) who meet to interview and investigate the abuse or neglect in a singular or minimal settings. At that point an assessment is made as to what services the child may need to assist in recovery and the family is referred to professionals in the field who have specific training on how to best serve child abuse and neglect victims. CACs also offer training to various audiences to prevent, recognize, and help others to assist children they believe to be at risk for child abuse or neglect (National Children's Alliance, visited March 4, 2017).

Guardian ad Litem

The Guardian ad Litem program is a government sponsored program in which a court advocate is assigned to a child who has been removed from the home due to physical or sexual abuse or neglect. The advocate meets with the child and collects information from additional sources (supervised visitation case worker, foster parents, and school) to determine what is in the best interest of the child in terms of placement and reconciliation with the family (Guardian ad Litem Program, visited June 22, 2017).

Exposure to Domestic Violence — Shelter Services

Zweig and Yahner (2013) indicate that some shelters are including child advocacy activities for children living within them. The services are focused on assessing and improving the child's physical and mental health, helping to promote safety and security, and helping children to deal with the exposure to violence that they experienced. Additionally, the services help to prevent the cycle of violence from continuing into the children's own victimization or abusive behavior.

Challenges for Elder Domestic Violence Victims

One dynamic that has been highlighted when researching elder abuse is that domestic violence responses (services and shelters) are not necessarily set up to attend to the needs of older domestic violence victims (Payne, 2008). Payne (2008) suggests that domestic violence shelters may not be set up to deal with the different health-related issues of older DV victims and that support groups may focus more on issues for younger victims (dealing with younger children, etc.) and not on how the violence affects victims at older ages.

Utilization of Victim Advocacy Services

Langton (2011) reports that approximately 9% of victims of violent crime utilized victim services on average from 1993–2009. Truman and Morgan (2016) confirm that there has been no significant change in victim service utilization as measured by the NCVS through 2015. When examining serious violent crime (rape/sexual assault, aggravated assault, robbery) there appears to be a bit of a higher utilization percentage with an overall range from 1996–2015 of 8%–19%, with the most recent data recording approximately 9% of victims using victim advocacy services (Truman & Morgan, 2016). Perhaps the greater percentage of utilization in violent victimization is directly related to sexual assault/rape victims reporting as they have higher rates of victim service utilization than other victims of violent crime (Langton, 2011). For instance, in 2015, 18.8% of rape/sexual assault victims, 14% of aggravated assault victims, 11.6% of robbery victims and 6% of simple assault victims indicated that they did use victim services to aid in recovery from the crime (NCVS, Victimization Analysis Tool, completed March 1, 2017). In the same time period, victims of property crime also reported little use of victim services (between 1–7% annually). While the percentage is small, it is important to realize that the raw number of victims who received victim services is substantial. For example, in 2015, 454,358 victims of violent crime and 237,339 victims of property reported using victim services (NCVS, Victimization Analysis Tool, completed March 1, 2017). Langton (2011) found that victims who reported receiving services were more likely to do so from a public service agency rather than a private service agency (so, perhaps criminal justice and other governmental organizations versus nonprofit organizations). Langton (2011) reports that victims of domestic violence and sexual assault were among the largest groups of victims to utilize victim services (roughly 23% and 20% respectively).

A greater proportion of victims who reported crime through official channels were also seen to use victim services (14% vs. 4% respectively) (Langton, 2011), which suggests that perhaps knowledge of programs may also influence utilization of programs in the first place. Sims, Yost, and Abbott (2005) found that many victims in their study did not know that victim services existed (47%), and if they were aware of agencies that provided assistance they didn't know the scope of services that were offered. It seems clear that information about the availability of victim services is something that needs to be addressed, though there are likely some barriers to "getting the word out" that will be discussed a bit later. Of note, about half of the victims in the Sims et al. (2005) study suggested they could rely on family and friends, themselves, or didn't really need assistance in recovering from the crime.

Impact of Family and Friends

Concurrent with the Sims et al. (2005) study, Davis and Ullman (2013) suggest that most victims do not use victim services because they rely on family, friends, and neighbors to provide them with the assistance they need to cope with and recover from victimizations. It also makes sense that since about only 50% of crime is reported to police, victims may not be aware of programs that exist and may believe they must only rely on their families and other social support networks to assist them. The perceptions of friends, family, and others of the crime victim can strongly contribute to the overall recovery of victims. Davis and Ullman (2013) note that individuals who are supported and perceived positively by friends, family, and others are aided in their recoveries, whereas negative perceptions of victims (blame, disbelief, etc.) tended to result in greater negative affect in crime victims, which hampered their ability to recover. Williams (1999) suggests that survivors of homicide victims may experience avoidance or desistance of aid as time goes by as support and patience of friends and family tends to wane. An OVC publication (1998) suggested that family and friends may also try to distance themselves from the victims as a defense mechanism, illustrating that there was something different about the victim that made them vulnerable. Distancing themselves can allow friends and family members to feel safe in their "Just World Philosophy" cocoon, but the drawback is that victims feel abandoned, burdensome, and depressed. The happy news is that for the most part, friends and family come through. The unhappy news is that if they do withdraw from victims, and victims are unaware of other programs that are available to them, this could result in a more difficult and lengthier recovery time post-victimization.

Overall Effectiveness of Victim Advocacy Services

At this point, it is important to assess how effective victim services truly are—are they helping victims, as is their primary goal? Perhaps the best way to evaluate if victim services are effective is to examine the five main goals of the services to assess victim satisfaction with each.

Information and Direct Advocacy

In Lyon, Lane, and Menard's (2008) study of domestic violence shelter residents, 85% reported increased knowledge about community resources as a result of their interaction with the agency. Information would enable them to survive and continue recovery once they moved outside of the shelter, into a more permanent location on their own. Approximately 57% of respondents in Wasco et al.'s (2004) evaluation of rape crisis hotline and brief advocacy services stated that the assistance they received provided them with a lot more information than they had. An additional 17% (for an approximate total of 74%) suggested that they gained somewhat more information through their hotline calls and advocacy experiences.

Emotional Support

Bennett, Riger, Schewe, Howard, and Wasco (2004) found that domestic violence victims who utilized counseling-type services experienced growth in their coping skills, self-efficacy, overall support, and decision-making abilities. Wasco et al. (2004) found similar results for victims of rape, most notably that rape victims who utilized the hotline and/or counseling-type activities from a victim advocacy agency reported greater coping skills, support, and decision-making abilities. Lyon, Lane, and Menard (2008) found strong levels of emotional support reported by domestic violence shelter residents in their analysis, with 92% reporting more confidence in their futures, 90% expressing confidence in their ability to make decisions, 89% indicating they felt they could ask someone for help if necessary, and 86% reporting they felt comfortable talking with someone about their troubles. Additionally, for women who had children in the shelter, 77% reported that their children learned how to express their own feelings without having to simultaneously express violence while doing so. 100% of the 13 men surveyed in the Lyon, Lane, and Menard (2008) study who utilized the shelter stated that they wanted emotional support and respect when they entered the shelter and felt like they had received it by the time they were leaving. From these three studies alone, it appears that victim services agencies are rather successful at providing emotional support.

Safety Assessment and Crisis Intervention

Zweig and Yahner (2013) suggest that safety is best understood as the reduction of repeat victimizations and overall feelings of safety. In their review of seven different studies addressing feelings of safety in domestic violence and human trafficking victims it appeared that those that utilized victim advocacy services did experience fewer repeat victimizations and greater feelings of safety overall. Lyon, Lane, and Menard (2008) reported that in a multi-state assessment of shelter victims, 91% of female respondents and 100% of male respondents reported that the shelter assisted them with creating a plan of safety for themselves.

Victims and Other Personnel

Crime victims may need assistance from service providers outside of the criminal justice system and victim advocacy agencies. They may need medical assistance, may seek out counseling on their own, or may seek guidance from someone within their religious organization. Macy, Giattina, Sangster, Crosby, and Montijo (2009) suggest that service providers in these areas may not necessarily have the training they need or trauma-informed programs to work with crime victims and can inadvertently exacerbate the traumatic effects of the crime (see also Campbell, Greeson, Bybee, & Neal, 2013).

Medical Services

When a victim of crime experiences a physical injury it may be necessary to seek out medical treatment depending on the severity of the injury. Gunshot and stab wounds, arriving at the emergency room near death, treating broken bones, internal bleeding, and conducting forensic evidence collection exams are all examples of the types of cases medical personnel might engage in on a daily basis that brings them into contact with crime victims. An analysis using the NCVS Victimization Analysis Tool (NCVS VAT) results indicated that in 2015 approximately 48% of victims of violent crimes who were injured sought medical treatment for their injuries. In 2015, 49% of rape/sexual assault victims sought medical treatment for their injuries. Injured robbery victims had a similar pattern with about 48% of victims using medical treatment. Alternatively, aggravated assault victims with injuries sought medical treatment about

Professional Profile 11.2

Kelly Anderson
Executive Director of the
Dane County Rape Crisis Center,
Madison, WI

Q: How did you get involved with working with crime victims? In what capacity do you currently work with victims? Have you ever participated in a joint research project? Please describe.

A: About 1987, my university started the Sexual Assault Awareness & Prevention Center and recruited volunteers for a brand new crisis line. I knew nothing about the issue of sexual violence, but as a psychology major who wanted to help people I signed up. The training was phenomenal, and that experience transformed my world view as well as my career path. After college I began working in non-profits and volunteering with women's issues. In 1994, I combined those passions with a job at the (Washington) DC Rape Crisis Center, and in 2003 I moved to Madison, WI, to be the executive director of the rape crisis center here. As ED, my role is to ensure that staff and volunteers have the resources to do their jobs well—focusing primarily on management, grants, media, personnel, and community partners like SANE & SART, although I do still answer crisis line calls or work directly with clients facing challenges with systems or our services. From working directly on the crisis line to supervising advocates and counselors, I've been privileged to hear the experiences of survivors, and I'm committed to channeling their voices and representing their perspective in the community.

Q: What advice do you have for students interested in working with victims?

A: My advice for those wanting to work with "victims" is to think twice. First, because victims are just people—people who happened to have a crime committed against them. Victim status is not inherently noble; crime victims can be just as frustrating and difficult as any other human being. We've worked with rape victims who were angry, drunk, high, numb, resentful, sarcastic, withdrawn—and of course, many who were grateful and appreciative.

Second, because too many people are drawn to working with victims as a way to address their own issues or needs. Victim empowerment is about helping survivors identify their best options and assert their own right to make decisions—it's not about "saving" someone or fixing things for them. If you're working with victims in order to feel needed, or because you haven't resolved your own trauma experience, you're not going to be able to be fully present with the person in front of you. It's essential to be able to recognize that s/he is not you, but instead an individual with his/her own experiences and needs.

The job is not just about empathy or caring. It's essential to develop the skills and knowledge to be of use. Self-awareness and incredibly strong boundaries are essential to work effectively in direct contact with victims/survivors. Those who realize that they care too much to keep a professional distance—or who feel overwhelmed after doing the work for a while—can still contribute in ways other than direct services. The need can seem overwhelming, and we need folks to advocate, educate, research, and engage in this issue.

Q: What are some challenges for working with victims and the criminal justice system?

A: The criminal justice system is a fairly blunt tool for addressing an issue as sensitive and complex as sexual violence. The majority of sexual assault victims (60%–90%) never report the crime, and acquaintance assaults (85% or more of sexual assaults) are unlikely to be successfully prosecuted. Juries still doubt victims' testimony, often because the perpetrators don't fit stereotypes of rapists; district attorneys are often reluctant to pursue prosecution that may not be successful; and law enforcement may anticipate that reluctance and never refer cases to the DA. At each of these stages, victims may hear something along the lines of "I believe you, but we just can't prove it"—which is not as supportive as it's intended to be, since it basically means "We don't think the jury will believe you and so we're dropping your case."

With the advent of DNA, this crime is now most frequently an issue of consent; the alleged perpetrator doesn't have to prove s/he had consent, but rather the victim is required to prove beyond a reasonable doubt that s/he did not consent ... which is extremely difficult.

Victims who do report may find that the legal processes drag out (often as an intentional strategy by defense attorneys) and delay their ability to heal and move on. Spending months—or longer—dreading testifying in a system where your rapist has the benefit of the doubt can exacerbate the harm.

In addressing sexual assault in particular, we are still confronting the myths about rape that pervade our culture. Without input from victim advocates, these myths and misunderstandings can lead well-intentioned legislators to craft harmful laws. While the legal frameworks addressing sexual violence have greatly expanded over the last 40 years, the system's ability to respond, and to hold perpetrators accountable, has not kept pace with the laws.

Q: What obstacles have you encountered while striving to assist victims? Have the obstacles to providing good service to victims changed over the years?

A: One huge obstacle in helping rape victims in their recovery is still the societal pressure toward self-blame and shame, which can be incredibly debilitating and prevent victims from accessing the support they need to recover. The shame and blame that victims feel—and the lack of support from the community—

leads to the further silencing of victims and the continued lack of public awareness, which then perpetuate the feelings of self-blame. There is so much more awareness now of sexual violence than ever before, and yet most of the time our society still does a terrible job of responding appropriately and supporting victims.

Q: What do you feel is the mark you will have left on the field of victim services? What do you want people to see as your mark? At the end of the day, what do you want your "legacy" to be in the field of victimology/victim services?

A: It's been such a privilege to spend my professional life with organizations that have assisted many thousands of victims in the immediate aftermath of this trauma and throughout their recovery. Part of my contribution has been a willingness to face ugliness and still hold out hope for recovery and change, to sit with people in pain and believe they can find their way, with help. Like anyone, I pretty much fall short of my ideals every single day—but my hope would be that I've promoted compassion and empathy while helping to maintain the ethical and professional standards of the sexual assault services field. My priority is to ensure a social justice framework that helps to balance the social services aspect of this work with the imperative of ending sexual violence and inequity.

Ultimately, of course, it's not about me. If I hadn't been here to do this work, someone else would have. Because I chose to see the need, and to pursue the skills that would let me contribute, I've had the honor of being able to contribute in a way that's meaningful to me.

Q: What are some burgeoning issues that you see in the fields of victimology/ victim services?

A: Emerging issues include an increased awareness of the needs of victims who are members of traditionally marginalized and oppressed groups (people of color, LGBTQI, and people with disabilities, for example). The general public and mental health professionals have become more aware of trauma, although a deeper understanding of the impact is still needed. As the field expands, the developing professionalization can create issues in maintaining a victim-centered approach.

Specifically, in the area of sexual assault victim services, the incredibly low level of reporting to law enforcement makes it imperative that we ensure access to services for non-reporting victims as well as those engaged with the legal system. Culturally, a major issue is how to translate the increased general awareness of sexual violence, including child sexual abuse and acquaintance assault, into support for victims and accountability for perpetrators.

Q: Are there groups of victims you think need to be served but are not? Why do you think that way?

A: The majority of sexual assault victims never report the crime; many never tell anyone and never receive help in their recovery. Within traditionally marginalized and oppressed communities, there are many factors that can prevent victims from accessing resources. Accessibility, language, and cultural barriers need to be proactively addressed, and service providers need to create meaningful partnerships with culturally specific organizations to ensure victims can access appropriate support services.

Victims with AODA or mental health issues often face difficulty in accessing services, as do the elderly and people with disabilities—while these individuals are extremely vulnerable to being targeted for sexual violence. Prison rape is being addressed more directly than in previous generations, but appropriate services are still not generally available for these victims. And male victims—particularly adult men—are among the least likely to seek sexual assault services or self-identify as a survivor of sexual violence.

With an issue that affects so many individuals across our entire society, the need for outreach and accessible, appropriate services can feel limitless. We have the opportunity to continue to expand our understanding of victims, and our efficacy in supporting their recovery.

59% of the time, while 42% of simple assault injured victims reported using medical services overall. The difference is likely predicated on the fact that aggravated assault victims may be wounded by weapons as opposed to "fisticuffs" alone. Clearly, crime victims who are injured seek out treatment from medical personnel. The majority of studies examining treatment of crime victims by medical staff often surround domestic violence and sexual assault, though there are a number of studies that assess overall numbers of violent crime victims and characteristics of those cases. Typically, however, when talking about the interaction between medical staff and victims, the discussion is focused on interpersonal violence and sexual violence. As a result, the following discussion will focus on interactions, challenges, and remedies dealing with providing specific types of crime victims effective services in medical facilities.

As you've learned, victimization can impact a person physically and psychologically, so whereas someone may come into the emergency room seeking treatment for a broken arm, medical staff need to be on the lookout for indicators that the injury may have been the result of a criminal incident and need to be mindful about how they're asking questions and what types of information and/or advice they are seeking. Phelan, Hamberger, Ambuel, and Wolff (2009) suggested that doctors routinely fail to screen for and identify indicators of interpersonal violence. In one case they discuss, a woman stopped talking medication for hyperthyroidism, which resulted in a trip to the Emergency Department (ED) for her because of an elevated heart rate. She had called in a refill for her prescription but was prohibited from picking it up by her abusive husband. When the Emergency Department physician conducted a physical exam on the patient he noticed linear bruises down her back. When asked, she disclosed that her husband routinely beat her on the back and abdomen area and submitted that she came to the ED without his knowledge—an act for which she was fearful she would be beaten. The authors suggest that advice on taking care of oneself is routinely given in a medical context, so it is an ideal location for assessing if injuries are related to victimization and a place at which victims can hear about services available to them.

In some cases, victims are forthcoming about what has happened to them from the start. Rape victims, for instance, often seek medical treatment both to deal with injuries and for the purpose of evidence collection. In those instances, the victimization is out in the open so it may be more comfortable for medical staff to ask questions related to the incident and how it may have resulted in specific injuries. Unfortunately, the line of questioning is not always appropriate or sensitively approached. For example, Campbell (2005) reports that approximately 58% of rape victims felt distressed and harmed after their treatment by medical personnel for the rape/sexual assault. Additionally, Campbell (2005) suggests that research studies investigating the types of medical issues discussed with crime victims varied and was relatively inconsistent. Medical staff should be discussing the prospect of pregnancy and emergency contraception and sexually transmitted diseases with victims of rape, however only about one third of women receive information on STDs and under 50% receive information about pregnancy and emergency contraception. Campbell (2005) suggests that reports of dissatisfaction with medical staff were higher for those who didn't receive information about pregnancy or sexually transmitted diseases. Because medical staff may be the only service provider that rape victims come into contact with, it is important for them to provide information about psychological and advocacy services in the community to assist the victim in his or her recovery. Campbell (2005) found in her study that the vast majority of rape victims did not receive this type of information from medical staff. Additionally, Campbell (2005) reports that victims were distressed when doctors asked if they had responded sexually to the penetration, if they had a previous sexual encounter with that person, why they were with the perpetrator, and if they fought back or said no. Some of these questions may be pertinent for a legal investigation but may not be appropriate in the medical context. Maier (2008) stated that rape victim advocates also witnessed victims being revictimized by medical staff. In Maier's study (2008) advocates noted that doctors and nurses shrugged off questions the victims asked and in some cases outwardly told the victim that they did not believe them and they were going to refuse to treat them. On the bright side, only about one third of advocates reported seeing this type of behavior, so the majority of advocates reported a lack of revictimization by medical staff.

Unfortunately, statistics are not collected consistently in emergency rooms and doctors' offices that help us to track how many patients seek medical assistance for crime-related problems. For instance, in an assessment of domestic violence service utilization in four counties in North Carolina, DeValve (unpublished, 2008) found that in the four counties under investigation only one of them collected data on victims that utilized the emergency room for treatment related to domestic violence, and in that case there was a motivated nurse who collected the data on her own, without direction from medical administrators of the hospital. Indeed, the largest hospital in the study, which served two of the counties within the study, did not have any protocol in place to record which victims came in for crime-related injuries. There are caveats to this — medical staff are mandatory reporters of child abuse and neglect, so those cases will be reported, but may not be maintained within their own databases. Similarly, sexual assault evidence collection kits are completed in emergency rooms so there may be a record of that, but it may not be readily available. To address these issues, Maier (2012) states that emergency rooms created the Sexual Assault Nurse Examiner role in the 1970s. In the 1990s there was a great deal of growth in the number of SANE nurses to address the inadequacies leading to revictimization of rape victims by medical staff (Littel, 2001). These programs provided training to nurses on how to collect evidence, inform rape victims of medical conditions they might encounter and protocols for dealing with those issues, as well as how to talk with a rape victim sensitively while still collecting the information pertinent for the exam. The intensive training that nurses undertook culminated in certification as a Sexual Assault Nurse Examiner (SANE).

Sexual Assault Nurse Examiners (SANE)

SANE nurses are trained in the legal requirements for evidence collection and in how best to attend to rape victims so revictimization does not occur. The SANE program has helped to reduce or eliminate a number of problems that sexual assault victims encountered; for instance, victims were often required to wait in Emergency Room waiting areas for long periods of time because medical staff did not see their injuries as all that severe. Littel (2001) reports that with the advent of the SANE program, rape/sexual assault victims are now promptly taken to a secure room where they will have privacy and will be attended to promptly. Another issue that has been addressed through the SANE program is that medical staff were often not trained in evidentiary collection, so they could easily have failed to collect everything needed and may have contaminated evidence through their collection. Some doctors reported that they were hesitant to collect evidence as they knew it might require them to testify in court and that their qualifications and ability to collect evidence would be brought up in court (Littel, 2001). SANE nurses are versed in the "chain of evidence" and necessity to follow a specific protocol in evidence collection, which might ensure a stronger case and a higher likelihood of prosecution and conviction down the road. Finally, prior to the implementation of the SANE program, victims reported that they often felt blamed for what happened to them and/or disbelieved that they were victims at all. Whereas this type of action has not gone away completely, SANE nurses are trained in how to talk with rape victims and the detrimental effects that the victim might experience if she or he believes the medical staff do not believe their story (Littel, 2001).

Psychological Services

Victims of crime are at risk of adverse psychological conditions as a result of the trauma suffered from the criminal incident. Both personal and property crime victims show evidence of psychological harm from situational depression to more impactful diagnoses, such as post-traumatic stress disorder (DeValve, 2004). The psychological

Professional Profile 11.3

Katherine Adkinson

Sexual Assault Nurse Examiner-
Adolescents and Adults (SANE-A)

Q: How did you get involved with working with crime victims? In what capacity do you currently work with victims? Have you ever participated in a joint research/practice project? Please describe.

A: I first became involved with crime victims through my job as a registered nurse in the Emergency Department. I worked at a community hospital (Level II, Trauma Center) where I was seeing victims of sexual assault multiple times in a 12-hour shift. There was a dire need for a Sexual Assault Nurse Examiner (SANE) for night shift, as there was only one SANE on day shift. We were a 72-bed Emergency Department with only one skilled nurse for the patients whose primary complaint was sexual assault. I was so shocked and saddened by this that I began studying immediately so that I could obtain my SANE certification for the state I was living in. I am currently certified through the International Association of Forensic Nursing (IAFN) to practice as a SANE-A (Adolescent/Adult). I have also served as a fact witness in a sexual assault criminal trial for the United States military.

Q: What advice do you have for students interested in working with victims?

A: My advice for students interested in working with victims: Make sure you have adequate emotional support at home, through your job, etc. No matter how hard you try, at some point you will take the images of these victims and their anguish home with you. Some cases are just memorable to nurses for one reason or another. It's how you interpret and process your stress with regard to these victims than can make or break a victim advocate.

Q: What are some challenges for working with victims, especially as it relates to dealing with the criminal justice system and/or lawmakers?

A: Some challenges when working with victims are helping them understand that they can trust the criminal justice system. Often, I'm the first responder to the victim. It's part of my job to make the patient feel safe and to earn their trust. For instance, they trust me when I say they can trust the criminal justice system with regard to making a statement/report about what happened to them. However, when the patient goes to file a police report and instead, is interrogated rather than interviewed, they not only lose trust in the criminal justice system, they have also relinquished any trust that they initially invested in me. In that moment, they have been victimized for a second and third time.

Q: What obstacles have you encountered while striving to assist victims? Have the obstacles changed things for the better over the years?

A: One of the biggest obstacles for me when working with victims is providing adequate teaching and resources for patients without medical insurance. This is a struggle even when the patient has insurance. For instance, HIV prophylaxis medications are $1,400 out of pocket, without insurance. When starting out as a SANE nurse I was able to give prophylaxis medications for most STDs, except the one STD victims were most afraid of. Most of the STD prophylaxis medications are a one-time dose of antibiotics provided in the Emergency Department. Unfortunately, there is no one-time dose for HIV prophylaxis. Instead, it's a 28-day treatment regimen that costs more than the average monthly mortgage/rent payment for these patients. Through networking with my peers, however, I found a company that will provide the medication free of charge for my low-income patients. This was simply not an option at my ER two years ago because no one knew that such services were available, much less how to look for them.

Q: What do you feel is the mark you will have left on the field of victim services? What do you want people to see as your mark? At the end of the day, what do you want your "legacy" to be in the field of victimology/victim services?

A: The mark I want to leave on the field of victim services is one that empowers those that follow in my path of nursing. I've been told, "No," and "We just don't have the funds for that," so many times when advocating for my patients and the much-needed resources they deserve. For those interested in pursuing this field, don't take no for an answer. Don't let the lack of money and the naysayers get in the way of what is right for your patients. Cultivate a passion for networking, so that you're part of a community committed to campaigning for those who deserve a higher standard of care than they are receiving.

Q: What are some burgeoning issues that you see in the fields of victimology/victim services?

A: Some burgeoning issues in the fields of victimology/victim services: Unskilled nurses required to provide care to and collect evidence from the victims of sexual assault, and how those nurses feel about what is expected of them in providing medical care to victims of sexual assault. People don't realize that Sexual Assault Nurse Examiners are not victim advocates. Rather, they are patient advocates that can provide victim assistance resources.

Q: Are there groups of victims you think need to be served but are not? Why do you think that way?

A: Groups of victims that need to be served but are not are teenagers in the Southern states. There's absolutely no adequate, dynamic, honest teaching about where to go, what to do, and who to talk to if you are the victim of sexual assault in the Southern states.

effects of crime can last well beyond the first few days after the incident and certain groups of victims seem to be particularly at risk of developing psychological disorders (Jennings, Gover, & Piquero, 2011). Victims experiencing these negative emotions and who suffer from mental illness as a result of the crime often are referred to counseling to assist in their recovery and for treatment of the mental illnesses. Macy et al. (2009) and Campbell et al. (2013) suggest that though mental health practitioners may be well versed in treating individuals suffering from mental health issues, they may not have the specific skills need to work with clients suffering from a traumatic event, specifically as that trauma relates to a criminal victimization.

There is no doubt that when mental health counseling is done right, the results can be powerful (Bennett et al., 2004; Wasco et al., 2004; Lyon, Lane, & Menard, 2008). In fact, many victims report that counseling helped them in the recovery process following their victimizations and they reported fewer negative feelings months after the victimization compared to those that did not participate in counseling-type assistance post-incident (Bennett et al., 2004; Wasco et al., 2004; Lyon, Lane, & Menard, 2008). The issue, for victim advocates at least, is that mental health professionals may approach treatment for the crime victim differently than what is thought to be helpful for crime victims (Jennings, Gover, & Piquero, 2011). Jennings, Gover, and Piquero (2011) suggest this is the result of being trained differently, but that with cross-training and collaborations, mental health professionals could become an even greater resource for victims of crime.

Religious Counseling

Some victims do not want the assistance of the criminal justice agency or other social service personnel when recovering from victimization. In the last decade, there has been an effort by faith-based organizations to provide assistance to crime-affected persons, including offenders, victims, and at-risk youth. To that end, it is important for clergy members to be able to understand the unique issues a crime victim may face, particularly when the perpetrator is a family member (as in the case of interpersonal violence, child abuse, and elder abuse) or is a well-known member of the community (oftentimes also with a strong religious tie). Additionally, religious proscriptions toward appropriate dating behavior, including premarital sex, may be an issue that a clergy person has to be sensitive to if a person discloses that she or he was a victim of a sex crime. Sheldon and Parent (2002) report that many sexual assault victims do not disclose victimizations to clergy persons, with one of the reasons being the clergyperson's attitude toward the crime or victim. In particular, the more conservative values held by the clergyperson, the more likely he or she will buy into rape myths suggesting that there was something wrong with the rape victim or that the rape victim deserves the blame for the assault. Perhaps the fear that clergy will judge the rape victim, particularly if the victim attends a conservative congregation, is an important factor in choosing not to speak with clergy about the victimization.

Kaukinen, Meyer, and Akers (2013) reported that approximately 9% of the women in their study sought social support from their clergy members for issues of interpersonal violence. None of the male intimate partner violence victims sought assistance from clergy, though the sample was small so the finding may not be representative of male IPV victims overall. Barnett (2001) suggests that many battered women may first turn to their religious leaders (Christian, Muslim, Jewish, etc.) for assistance in leaving a domestic violence situation, but when the organization espouses conservative notions of a woman's role in the family the victims may be discouraged from leaving.

Sharpe (2013) found that for African American survivors of homicide victims faith-based practices were commonly relied upon for assistance in the bereavement process and in finding meaning in the loss to help cope with the tragedy. Both private spiritual practicing (praying to God and connecting with the deceased through prayer on one's own) and participation in public faith-based practices were methods of coping utilized by African American homicide survivors.

The Office for Victims of Crime put together a video on faith-based responses to crime victims in 2008 and highlighted some progressive movements in the faith communities to assist crime victims. Programs highlighted included Christian groups working with domestic violence victims, children who were victims of abuse, human trafficking victims, and crime victims within poor communities who needed assistance with general support and companionship after the crimes, multi-denominational groups who formed after 9/11 to provide support to women victims of battering, police chaplains who work with crime victims to help recover from the criminal incident, and American Indian tribal communities in which the spiritual traditions are relied upon for healing from crime. These are encouraging illustrations as the majority of victims rely on friends, family, and other forms of support from within their social sphere to assist them with crime. Faith-based leaders will continue to be contacted by crime victims for assistance and there are clear examples of where the support they provide brings solace to a victim (Sharpe, 2013; OVC, 2008). What remains clear, however, is that for some victims of crime the interactions may be more harmful than helpful, so efforts to train faith-based leaders in how to respond to requests for support will likely be helpful.

Challenges Faced by Victim Advocacy Agencies

Sims et al. (2005) suggest there are three main challenges faced by victim advocacy agencies if they want to increase their client base and garner higher satisfaction rates. First, they suggest that victim advocacy agencies are going to need to do a better job marketing their agencies and educating the public about what services they offer. One complication with this is that victim advocacy agencies typically rely on a grant funding to sustain a large proportion of their budgets. Many grants (be they public or private) do not allow for agencies to write in a budget line for marketing, and in some grants this is strictly prohibited. This means that the agencies may need to rely on donations and other unrestricted (can be used for anything) funds to support advertisements, but this may not be practical as oftentimes the unrestricted money may be used for general operating expenses that aren't covered by the grants or are simply a means of keeping the agency operating overall (Sobota, 2014). Second, they suggest that they will need to listen more acutely to what victims actually need and broaden their programs to include those services, and perhaps dismiss others. This can be done through surveys of victims to assess what those who are using other services might also need and by seeking out victims who do not choose to use an agency's resources and finding out why. Finally, they indicate that the agencies need to have larger staffs to be able to assist all the victims that do need them and to be sure that the staff who are employed have the proper education, training, and skills needed to best serve victims overall. This is probably a grand wish of all victim advocacy agencies, but funding severely limits what agencies can do, particularly when agencies are competing against each other for scarce resources. Victim advocacy agencies grew on the backs of grassroots volunteers and still today rely heavily on volunteers for a great deal of their direct services (especially to staff the 24-hour crisis line, emergency room accompaniment, and support groups) (Hellman & House, 2006). Currently there is not a great deal of research that investigates the roles of volunteers in victim advocacy agencies, but this should be an area that is focused on, especially as economic times continue to affect the abilities of advocacy agencies in retaining staff and even staying open.

Not only may victims encounter diverse agencies and services on their post-victimization journey, they may also have to deal with being viewed by others in the community, either because they are familiar with the victim and they are aware that he or she is a crime victim or because attention has been focused on the victim by the media.

Victims and the Media

Studying and understanding victimization in relation to the media is an important area of victimology. Victims are portrayed in the media through a variety of contexts and forms. We often encounter victims on a daily basis from the news media. "If it bleeds it leads!" is a tag line often associated with the ways the news media reports on crimes. The accused offenders are typically highlighted in such news pieces, but victims are also often discussed. First and foremost, the identification of victims in the media can lead to a variety of consequences such as re-victimization of primary victims and secondary victimization of family members and friends. The race to be the first to report on crimes and other events where there are victims can lead to misinformation, if names or the status of victims are not reported correctly. In 2010, a coal mine in West Virginia collapsed, trapping miners underground. As CNN was reporting live, Anderson Cooper got word and reported on air while standing with several family members of the trapped miners that all of the miners had been found alive; however, this was inaccurate and the remaining miners had all been killed in the incident (cnn.com). News outlets need to be cautious with their reporting, and we often hear statements that names of victims will be released following notification of family members.

The news media are also responsible for what is left out of their reporting. While some cases are sensationalized, others are down played or ignored by the news. A variety of research has shown racial and gender bias in reporting on missing women (Stillman, 2007) and children (Min & Feaster, 2010). The bias in reporting serves to minimalize the crimes and victimization among certain populations, while exaggerate the risks and vulnerabilities of other populations. Another example is the minimal reporting of sexual violence against boys or men. In large part, these areas have been relegated to only prison rapes (for men) and the Catholic Church sex scandal (for boys), even though men and boys are victims of sexual violence in a variety of contexts the same way women are.

High-profile cases may result in news media camped out on lawns or in driveways of victims and their families, causing unwanted and unneeded attention, often at some of the most difficult times in people's lives. For example, following the shooting at Sandy Hook Elementary School, the news media camped out in the town, trying to speak with anyone and everyone who could even have been remotely touched by the events of that day. It has become more and more common for families of victims to issue statements and requests for privacy from the media.

Some forms of victimization, such as child abuse, neglect, or sexual violence, call for the protection of victim identities from the press for their protection; however, unethical journalists may disregard such policies and others may investigate the victims as possible offenders. The way the news media characterizes an individual victim can have potential negative consequences for a trial, particularly with a jury. In addition, broad generalizations and stereotypes about victims portrayed in the news media may also impact the way the consumers of media think and behave when they sit on a jury with certain types of victims. For example, myths and stereotypes of rape victims abound in our society, so a jury who buys into these stereotypes may find an offender not guilty, not based on the case in front of them, but because of those commonly held and media reinforced beliefs.

Beyond the news media, entertainment in many forms contributes to the myths and stereotypes about victims and victimization. Movies, television shows, and even music inform society's views about victims and impact everything from how juries view victims to how family members and friends respond to victimizations. Even first responders and service providers are not immune from falling for myths and stereotypes about victims.

Social media has also been an important avenue for victims. Many advocacy groups and victims service providers use social media such as Facebook or Twitter to gain support for victims. It may be used to draw attention to an overlooked form of victimization or as a call to action. For example, several hundred young girls were kidnapped from a boarding school in Nigeria in April 2014. There was very little international media attention until a coordinated social media campaign #bringbackourgirls brought the issue to the forefront and the international community began to take action. Advocacy groups and service providers may also use social media to raise money for their organizations. In more rare cases, social media may bring attention to a victim who hasn't gone to the authorities, as happened in the Steubenville Rape case. In this case, the night-long rapes of an unresponsive, intoxicated high school female were documented and posted by her perpetrators on Facebook and Twitter. The role of social media in this case lead to national outrage and discussion of sexual violence.

Summary and Conclusions

Many people are involved in the recovery process for crime victims. Victim advocates grew out of movements focusing on specific types of victims and thus programs available to victims are, for the most part, segregated. We are starting to see a shift, as you'll read in Chapter 12, with the creation of more inclusive victim service agencies. The real problem of funding for victim service organizations can limit the effectiveness of an agency, no matter how passionate the personnel are about working with victims. Though it appears that victim advocacy is quite effective at assisting victims through their recovery processes, it is important to continue training those who are not familiar with the effects of victimization so as to reduce revictimization of victims overall. It is also important that media demonstrate sensitivity for victims too, so that the journey toward recovery can be more successful.

Key Terms

Victim advocate
Sexual Assault Nurse Examiner (SANE)

Discussion Questions

1. What groups of crime victims benefit most from victim advocacy services? Why do you think that is?
2. How can individuals not traditionally trained in trauma as it relates to crime victimization improve their skills when working with victims?
3. How can the SANE program inform other non-victim advocacy agencies on how to work with crime victims?
4. What are all the different groups that victims will encounter that can support or hamper their recovery process?

Websites for Further Information

National Children's Alliance: http://www.nationalchildrensalliance.org/.

SANE-SART: http://www.sane-sart.com/.

International Forensic Nurses Association: http://www.forensicnurses.org/.

References

Barnett, O. W. (2001). Why battered women do not leave, Part 2: External inhibiting factors—Social support and internal inhibiting factors. *Trauma, Violence & Abuse, 2*(1), 3–35.

Bennett, L., Riger, S., Schewe, P., Howard, A., & Wasco, S. (2004). Effectiveness of hotline, advocacy, counseling, and shelter services for victims of domestic violence: A statewide evaluation. *Journal of Interpersonal Violence, 19*(7), 815–829.

Campbell, R. (2005). What really happened? A validation study of rape survivors' help-seeking experiences with the legal and medical systems. *Violence and Victims, 20*(1), 55–68.

Campbell, R., Greeson, M., Bybee, D., & Neal, J. W. (2013). *Sexual assault response team (SART) implementation and collaborative process: What works best for the criminal justice system? Final Report.* Washington, DC: US Department of Justice.

cnn.com (visited Oct. 3, 2017) Anderson Cooper 360 Degrees. Aired January 4, 2006, 22:00 ET. (transcripts cnn.com/TRANSCRIPTS/0601/04/acd.01.html).

Davis, R. C., & Ullman, S. E. (2013). The key contributions of family, friends, and neighbors. In R. C. Davis, A. J. Lurigio, & S. Herman (Eds.), *Victims of crime* (4th ed.), (pp. 233–250). Thousand Oaks, CA: Sage Publications.

DeValve, E. Q. (2008). *Domestic violence prevalence, service availability, and service utilization among adult household members in Black and Latino households in Cumberland, Harnett, Hoke, and Robeson counties, North Carolina: A report to county administrators and non-governmental organizations.* Unpublished report prepared for The Research Center for Health Disparities at Fayetteville State University.

Guardian ad Litem Program, North Carolina Judicial Department, Administrative Office of the Courts. Retrieved from http://www.nccourts.org/Citizens/GAL/Default.asp, June 22, 2017.

Hellman, C. M., & House, D. (2006). Volunteers serving victims of sexual assault. *The Journal of Social Psychology, 146*(1), 117–123.

Jennings, W. G., Gover, A., & Piquero, A. R. (2011). Integrating the American criminal justice and mental health service systems to focus on victimization. *International Journal of Offender Therapy & Comparative Criminology, 55*, 1272–1290.

Kaukinen, C. E., Meyer, S., & Akers, C. (2013). Status compatibility and help-seeking behaviors among female intimate partner violence victims. *Journal of Interpersonal Violence, 28*(3), 577–601.

Langton, L. (2011). *Use of victim service agencies by victims of serious violent crime, 1993–2009,* Special Report. Washington, DC: US Department of Justice, Office of Justice Program, Bureau of Justice Statistics. NCJ 234212.

Littel, K. (2001). *Sexual assault nurse examiner (SANE) programs: Improving the community response to sexual assault victims.* OVC Bulletin. Washington, DC: US Department of Justice, Office of Justice Programs, Office for Victims of Crime. NCJ 186366.

Lyon, E., Lane, S., & Menard, A. (2008). *Meeting survivors' needs: A multi-state study of domestic violence shelter experiences. Final Report — Executive Summary.* Washington, DC: US Department of Justice, Office of Justice Programs, National Institute of Justice.

Macy, R. J., Giattina, M., Sangster, T. H., Crosby, C., & Montijo, N. J. (2009). Domestic violence and sexual assault services: Inside the black box. *Aggression and Violent Behavior, 14,* 359–373.

Maier, S. L. (2008). "I have heard horrible stories …" Rape victim advocates' perceptions of the revictimization of rape victims by the police and medical system. *Violence Against Women, 14*(7), 786–808.

Maier, S. (2012). Sexual assault nurse examiners' perceptions of their relationship with doctors, rape victim advocates, police, and prosecutors. *Journal of Interpersonal Violence, 27*(7), 1314–1340.

Min, S. J., & Feaster, J. C. (2010). Missing children in national news coverage: Racial and gender representations of missing children cases in national television news. *Communication Research Reports, 27,* 206–216.

National Center for Victims of Crime. (2008). What is a victim advocate? Retrieved from http://www.victimsofcrime.org/help-for-crime-victims/get-help-bulletings-for-crime-victims.

National Children's Alliance. Retrieved from http://www.nationalchildrensalliance.org/, visited March 4, 2017.

Office for Victims of Crime. (1998). *New directions from the field: Victims' rights and services for the 21st century.* Washington, DC: US Department of Justice, Office of Justice Programs.

Office for Victims of Crime. (2006). *Voices of victims: Financial considerations.* Department of Justice, Office of Justice Programs. NCJ 213806.

Payne, B. (2008). Training adult protective services workers about domestic violence: Training needs and strategies. *Violence Against Women, 14*(10), 1199–1213.

Phelan, M. B., Hamberger, L. K., Ambuel, B., & Wolff, M. (2009). Screening for intimate partner violence in the health care setting. *Family & Intimate Partner Violence Quarterly,* 327–360.

Sharpe, T. L. (2013). Understanding the sociocultural context of coping for African American family members of homicide victims: A conceptual model. *Trauma, Violence, & Abuse, 16*(1), 48–59. doi: 10.1177/1524838013515760.

Sheldon, J. P., & Parent, S. L. (2002). Clergy's attitudes and attributions of blame toward female rape victims. *Violence Against Women, 8*(2), 233–256.

Shoemyer, W. (2009). Address confidentiality programs: Helping victims of abuse feel safe at home. *American Journal of Family Law, 22*(4), 214–216.

Sims, B., Yost, B., & Abbott, C. (2005). Use and nonuse of victim services programs: Implications from a statewide survey of crime victims. *Criminology & Public Policy, 4*(2), 361–384.

Sobota, E. (2014, January 28). Doing business with the government: Administrative challenges faced by nonprofits. *Nonprofit Quarterly*, Retrieved from https://nonprofitquarterly.org/management/23589-doing-business-with-the-government-administrative-challenges-faced-by-nonprofits.html.

Stillman, S. (2007). The missing white girl syndrome: Disappeared women and media activism. *Gender and Development, 15*(3), 491–502.

Truman, J. L. & Morgan, R. E. (2016). *Criminal victimization, 2015.* Washington, DC: US Department of Justice, Office of Justice Programs, Bureau of Justice Statistics.

Wasco, S. M., Campbell, R., Howard, A., Mason, G. E., Staggs, S. L., Schewe, P. A., & Riger, S. (2004). A statewide evaluation of services provided to rape survivors. *Journal of Interpersonal Violence, 19*(2), 252–263.

Williams, B. (1999). *Working with victims of crime: Policies, politics and practice.* London, UK: Jessica Kingsley Publishers, Ltd.

Yassen, J., & Glass, L. (1984). Sexual assault survivors groups: A feminist practice perspective. *Social Work, 29*(3), 252–257.

Zweig, J., & Yahner, J. (2013). Providing services to victims of crime. In R. C. Davis, A. J. Lurigio, & S. Herman (Eds.), *Victims of crime* (4th ed.), (pp. 325–348). Thousand Oaks, CA: Sage Publications, Inc.

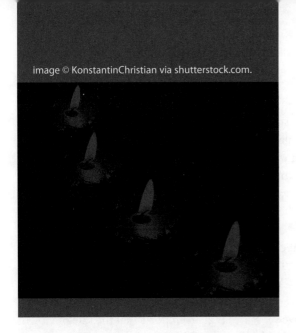

image © KonstantinChristian via shutterstock.com.

Chapter 12: Burgeoning Issues and the Future

At this point, you have learned about how we study victimization, the major patterns and trends associated with crimes used to determine the crime rates in the United States and other countries, some theoretical and descriptive information about crime victims and their perpetrators, specific types of crime, victims' rights, and working with victims in both the public and private sectors. Victimology itself is still a relatively young science and as such we continue to discover groups and types of victimization that we have either ignored in the past or that we are newly realizing need our attention. This chapter will focus on areas within victimology and victim services that have recently been recognized as needing greater attention by both researchers and practitioners.

Working with Special and/or Underserved Populations of Victims

The Office of Victims of Crime, the National Center for Victims of Crime, and the National Organization of Victim Assistance provide information on and training related to best practices in the service of crime victims. A review of the publications they post on their websites illustrate that they include information from both research and practice realms to identify what is working and who still needs our help. These organizations provide us with an informational map of what we need to know to be up-to-date on standards of care for victims of crime. To that end, the following topics have been given special attention and are some of the more current foci of research and service improvement in the last 5–10 years.

Victims with Disabilities

Though scarce in its appearance, some early research on crime against persons with disabilities suggested that this population was between 4 and 10 times more likely to be a victim of a crime, and children with disabilities were approximately twice as likely to be victims of physical and/or sexual abuse (Tyiska, 1998). In the latter half of the 2000s the Bureau of Justice Statistics started reporting statistics on crimes perpetrated against victims with disabilities, collected through the National Crime Victimization Survey (and thus limited to victims 12 years old and up). Harrell (2014) reports that in 2012, 1.3 million nonfatal violent crimes were perpetrated against persons who had disabilities (this includes rape, sexual assault, robbery, aggravated assault, and simple assault). Similar to reports in the NCVS for people without disabilities, violent crimes against persons with disabilities increased significantly from 2010 to 2012 (from 742,800 to 1,346,900 violent crimes respectively). Harrell (2014) reports that the rate of violent victimization was higher for people with disabilities than those without, 34.2/1,000 to 22.7/1,000 in 2012. In every age group for which data was collected, persons with disabilities had higher rates of victimization than those without (see Table 12A).

Table 12A illustrates that persons with disabilities between the ages of 12 and 64 had between two and a half and three times higher likelihoods of being victims of violent crime than persons without disabilities. Of violent victimizations against persons with disabilities, 38% were serious violent victimizations (rape/sexual assault, robbery, and aggravated assault), whereas only 29% of violent victimizations for persons without disabilities were of the same variety. Persons with cognitive disabilities had the highest rate of violent victimizations, consistently from 2009–2012, and they had rates that were approximately one and a half to two times greater than persons with other types of disabilities. Persons with hearing and vision disabilities had the

Table 12A: Rate of Victimization for People with Disabilities and People without Disabilities (2012)

Age of Victim	Rate per 1,000 Persons with Disabilities	Rate per 1,000 Persons without Disabilities
Total	34.2	22.7
12–15 years old (almost 3x higher)	122.5	42.7
16–19 years old (2.5x higher)	101.8	40.7
20–24 (almost 2.75x higher)	100.6	36.6
25–34 (almost 3x higher)	82.6	27.9
35–49 (almost 2.75x higher)	61.0	22.1
50–64 (approx. 2.5x higher)	27.9	11.2
65 or older	5.9	4.6

Source: Harrell, E. (2014). Crime against persons with disabilities, 2009–2012, Statistical Tables.

lowest rates of victimization consistently across the four years. Perhaps this has to do with the perpetrator's perception that victims with cognitive disabilities will be more likely to be ignored or disbelieved, or that the victim may not understand that what occurred was either wrong or criminal (Tyiska, 1998).

In 1998, the National Organization for Victim Assistance coordinated a symposium to address the issue of victimization against persons with disabilities. Representatives attended from the fields of victim assistance, disability advocacy, and the research arena to discuss a topic that before that date had not been discussed in such an open forum (Tyiska, 1998). The disability advocates reported that crimes against persons with disabilities often went unreported to police, that those that did get reported often were not prosecuted, and for the small percentage that worked with victim advocates it was evident that the advocates did not have adequate training or services available to assist them (Tyiska, 1998). Common obstacles that were reported for crime victims with disabilities included: isolation, limited accessibility, underreporting of the crime, and limited advocacy. Tyiska (1998) reports that persons with disabilities are often segregated in some form or fashion and may not have information about services that are available to victims of crime. Additionally, there may be both physical and attitudinal accessibility issues, as the victim advocacy agencies and criminal justice agencies may not all be outfitted to accommodate persons with disabilities and their demeanor may not be welcoming. Victims with disabilities may choose not to report the crime to police because of shame and guilt (similar to victims without disabilities), lack of understanding about the criminal justice system, barriers surrounding mobility and communication, and/or the perpetrator may be the primary caregiver of the victim, putting the victim in a very precarious and uncertain situation. It was reported that even when victims with disabilities did report the crimes, there were often questions about the reliability of the information presented and prejudicial assumptions about the ability of the victim to testify in court. In the OVC video series "Voices of Victims: Criminal Justice Professionals" (2006) a segment was included that illustrated the danger of revictimization that crime victims with disabilities can face. One woman who reported the crime to police was deaf and requested a sign language interpreter to provide assistance to her so she could tell the officers what had happened. She recounts that the officer asked if she could "just write it down," but she was not comfortable with that because her hands were shaking so tremendously. At that point, she did not feel that her needs were being acknowledged and there was a startling lack of patience and sensitivity to her situation.

Persons with disabling conditions may be especially vulnerable to victimizations as they may lack the ability to fight or flee, and/or may not have the ability to identify the offender or call for help (Tyiska, 1998). The NOVA symposium resulted in the identification of a number of unique issues that victim assistance agencies were tasked to address as they sought to improve their overall services to all victims of crime. First, it was important to address that crime victims with disabilities had unique issues: persons with disabilities may have similar reasons for being reticent to report a crime to police, with an additional reason being that they may be dependent on a caregiver for their livelihood (hence, if the caregiver is the perpetrator the report will substantially alter their situations); crime victims who become disabled as a result of the crime may have additional strains and stresses as they attempt to deal with both the victimization and the recent disability at the same time; and in cases of domestic violence, if the victim has a disability it may be more difficult for him or her to secure custody in family court if he or she attempts to leave the violent situation (Tyiska, 1998). Finally, it was noted that "disability" was not a one-size-fits-all type of a situation and that there were many different types of disabilities that must be accommodated if agencies want to include all crime victims under their umbrella of services. In order for victim service providers to become more fully functioning agencies, it was recommended that they address the physical accommodations of their facilities to make sure they are accessible to all crime victims and that they utilize (perhaps purchase) technology that may assist in their service to victims with disabilities (i.e., TTY phones for victims who may be deaf or hard-of-hearing; ramps and elevators that can accommodate wheelchairs so victims may get to places where services are occurring, etc.). Additionally, it was recommended that criminal justice and victim advocacy personnel receive specific training on how to serve crime victims with disabilities. Finally, it was suggested that direct services take note of the unique aspects of crimes against persons with disabilities, noting specifically the potential for retaliation and/or returning a victim to a hostile and abusive environment because of a caregiver situation.

In a 2008 series produced by the Office for Victims of Crime, entitled "Promising Practices in Serving Crime Victims with Disabilities" the OVC notes that there are significant challenges still present in serving crime victims with disabilities. Specifically, there is a lack of "authoritative" research on both crimes against persons with disabilities and on crimes that lead to disabilities (be they short- or long-term). Additionally, in their review of research regarding services provided by victim service agencies, under 8% had provided services to someone with a cognitive or physical disability and only 1% provided services to victims who were blind, deaf, or hard-of-hearing. Only 9% of agencies who responded to a survey in 2003 about services for crime victims with disabilities stated that they included budget items that would assist in their ability to serve this group.

It is clear that services to victims with disabilities will require more than a basic understanding of the issue and that some great work has been done toward that end. Federal grant funding now includes as an eligibility factor, the necessity that the victim service agency (public or private) be compliant with Americans with Disabilities Act (ADA) requirements. Most of the research on victims with disabilities has been done in the last decade, so there is a long way to go, but some great efforts have been made to better serve this diverse group of victims and a path has been laid to guide us in the right direction for continued improvement.

Rural Victims

Rural crime victimization carries with it a number of challenges that do not exist in the urban setting, specifically geographical dispersion, isolation, mistrust of authority (particularly government), informal social control and subcultural norms to work problems out on one's own, lack of knowledge about programs, and inability to access programs that do exist because of their urban setting or fear of stigma if spotted. According to Johnson, McGrath, and Miller (2014), rural areas are often more geographically dispersed and the residents are more likely to be isolated, homogeneous, and mistrustful of others, including government. They may have fewer neighbors, but they are more knowledgeable about who is in their community and the friendships they develop are deep. Johnson et al. (2014) also suggest that rural victims may feel more strongly about dealing with problems on their own and not reporting crime to police because they may believe that crime is a private matter. Yun, Swindell, and Kercher (2009) concur and suggest that lower rates of crime in rural community may simply be an artifact of lower reporting rates than urban communities. This may pose significant challenges to both criminal justice personnel and victim advocates as the people who need help may be reluctant to seek it out and/or accept it when offered.

Geographical Dispersion and Isolation

Yun et al. (2009) purport that for victim service providers there may be challenges in reaching rural victims because the area is spread so far apart. Fewer resources are available for other health and public health-related issues (medical, substance abuse, mental health) so the organizations that do provide them may have larger caseloads spread across a wide area, so direct service could be more time-consuming and clients may end up on waiting lists for longer periods of time than their urban counterparts. Additionally, victim service agencies might have to cover several counties, covering a large geographical space, so services that are offered may not be as available as they are in the urban setting.

For victims, whereas in urban communities neighbors may stop to provide assistance or call for help when they hear something troubling occurring, in rural areas neighbors may not hear anything ... ever ... because of the distance between houses; thus a victim does not have that potential safety net of the concerned neighbor (Walsh & Muscat, 2013). It's a bit troubling to note that Websdale and Johnson (1998) reported that rural intimate partner violence victims were more likely to report torture by the hands of their batterers and being "shot at" by their batterers because of the geographical isolation in which they lived.

Informal Social Control Networks, Mistrust of Authority, and Stigma

Law enforcement and victim advocacy personnel who also reside in the rural area may be familiar with, indeed neighbors, friends, or family of, the victim or offender, which means interactions could be uncomfortable for both the victim and the advocate, so rural victim service providers will need to be especially cognizant of confidentiality issues. Littel (2009) suggests that there may be a small number of officers on the road at any given time who are required to cover a large expanse. Because there may be relatively few officers on duty at any one time, it may be highly likely that a victim will know who is on duty and may be reluctant to call because of the fear of being disbelieved because of relationship between law enforcement and the batterer. Johnson et al. (2014) report that there is a general mistrust of government in rural areas as a bit of a cultural norm, so reliance upon a government official may be looked down upon by the community as a whole. Perhaps this is why Grossman, Hinkley, Kawalski, and Margrave (2005) found that rural victims in their study appeared to call law enforcement for assistance less than urban victims. They proposed it could be because of fear of the police or the general lack of resources rural law enforcement might have. Alternatively, Walsh and Muscat (2013) report that many rural households have police scanners, which means if a victim calls for assistance her neighbors and/or friends of the batterer may hear about it, and respond, before law enforcement can come to her aid. Because rural communities are smaller and everyone seems to know each other, it can be extremely difficult to find the courage to walk into a center to receive assistance for a victimization because of the lack of anonymity and relative confidentiality that exists in the community (Walsh & Muscat, 2013). This could be particularly detrimental, for instance, to a battered woman who is looking for information but may not be ready to leave. If it is reported to her batterer that she was seen entering a women's center, victim advocacy agency, or even a law enforcement office, she may be in grave danger when she returns home.

Lack of Knowledge About or Access to Programs That Do Exist

Walsh and Muscat (2013) report that victims in rural communities are often unaware of resources in their community or surrounding communities that could assist them, particularly as it relates to intimate partner violence. Indeed Grossman, Hinkley, Kawalski, and Margrave (2005) noted that a victim advocate may be the first social service person the victim has encountered. A needs assessment of the victim may highlight additional social services needs for survival so a rural victim advocate may also need to have a strong core of knowledge about all other public health and social service programs that could assist a rural victim. Additionally, Yun et al. (2009) note that there is a lack of public transportation available in rural areas, so it may be very costly for a victim to call for a taxi (if they could find one that serves their area) to be driven to a criminal justice facility, court proceeding, or victim service agency, rural or urban. Finally, rural victims are purported to have fewer economic resources, thus they may need to rely on a victim service agency (e.g., shelter) for a longer period of time, which could lengthen waiting times for other rural victims.

Funding and Client Base

According to the American Prosecutors Research Institute (APRI) (2006), in one state 26 urban counties received $7.3 million in VOCA funding whereas 76 rural counties had to split a pool of $1 million total and were recipients of only 10% of VAWA funding available. This may make intuitive sense as the urban counties may be serving more clients overall, but advocacy agencies in rural areas oftentimes have equally arduous tasks of providing services to a more geographically diverse pool of clients, so their service areas are significantly larger, and more costly, than their urban counterparts'. For example, Yun et al. (2009) report that directors of rural victim advocacy agencies in Texas reported that they may have fewer numbers of clients, but they might be serving multiple counties in the region. For that reason, they are unlikely to look "impressive" to grant-funding agencies because they can't compete with the numbers of clients that the larger urban counties have. It was noted that in Texas, seven urban counties make up over 50% of the state's population—but there are 254 counties in Texas, which means the overwhelming majority will be serving rural clientele. Additionally, respondents in their study reported that because they didn't provide service in the more populated urban counties they didn't have access to funding from the large corporations that chose to fund local programs only. Losing positions, therefore, in rural victim advocacy agencies may severely limit the ability of those agencies to serve all the rural victims that need their assistance and appears to have led to the loss of shelters and staff overall.

In rural prosecutors' offices, victim/witness advocates may be extraordinary overtaxed as they are more likely to have to carry larger caseloads of clients and shoulder additional duties in their job to assist in the prosecution of cases in their counties. For instance, the APRI study (2006) found that while 89% of an urban victim/witness advocate's time is spent directly dealing with victims, a rural victim/witness advocate can only spend 69% of his or her time working with victims, as the rest of their time must be devoted to other duties within the office, that are not case related (law enforcement coordination, clerical duties, community outreach etc.).

Human Trafficking

As you read about in Chapter 2, human trafficking has garnered more attention in recent decades and data reveals it to be a significant global problem. According to the 2013 Department of State Trafficking in Persons Report, an estimated 27 million people are in a trafficking situation at any given time. Also called modern-day slavery, human trafficking doesn't look the same today as it did in the past. When many American's visualize slavery, they see the chains that characterized the nation's history in the South. Today, however, chains are not always necessary. People are trafficked into sexual slavery, labor such as farming or fishing, as well as involuntary domestic servitude. Even in the United States, victims of trafficking may walk around apparently freely, all the while being forced to work in people's homes.

The State Department's 2013 report identifies and defines several categories of human trafficking such as sex trafficking, child sex trafficking, forced labor, bonded labor or debt bondage, involuntary domestic servitude, and forced child labor including the unlawful recruitment and use of child solders. The UNODC 2012 Global Report on Trafficking in Persons identifies several other forms of exploitation which fall under their definition of human trafficking, including begging (1.5% globally), removal of organs (0.2% in 2010), and illegal adoption. According to the UNODC 2012 Global Report on Trafficking in Persons, about half of all victims of human trafficking are trafficked from and exploited in the same region. Roughly 27% of trafficked victims were trafficked domestically, meaning they remained in the country of origin. For victims who were trafficked across national borders, 45% of victims were trafficked with in the same region of the world and 24% were trafficked transnationally.

Human trafficking has been identified as a three-step process involving the recruitment, transportation, and then exploitation of victims (Dammer & Albanese, 2014). The recruitment may take the form of the promise of work or a better life in a new place or country. Traffickers specifically target vulnerable populations, particularly children, women, and the poor. Children may even be sent into trafficking situations by parents who are misled into believing they are providing a better life for their children. The victims may agree to go willingly for the promise of work; they may enter an agreement to pay for the opportunity or to work off the cost of the move, a situation called debt bondage. Transportation may involve the victims crossing international boarders, but transportation is not necessary for a victim to be trafficked. The exploitation of the victims may take many forms. The US State Department's *2012 Trafficking in Persons Report* identified several common methods for controlling trafficking victims. They include restriction of movement, harmful living conditions, and harmful working conditions. Restrictions of movement may include removal of all personal identification including passports and visas so the victim can't be identified or are misidentified as illegal immigrants. Traffickers also may accompany victims at all times, including speaking for them and interpreting all conversations for them. This may also include telling lies to the victims, such as local police will not believe them or even harm them if they speak out. Often traffickers will intentionally take victims to a country whose language they are not familiar with just to maintain control by restricting language. Other strategies include isolation of the victims, forcing them to live and work in a small area, which limits their contact with outsiders who may identify them as victims of human trafficking. According to the State Department's 2012 report, harmful living conditions may include lack of access to food or clothing, forbidding healthcare access, and not providing time off or enough time to sleep. Harmful working conditions may include a fee to work which is unreasonable for the victim to pay off, requiring excessively long hours without breaks or days off, and providing very little, irregular pay.

At the international level, the United Nations has a Plan of Action to Combat Trafficking in Persons to serve as guidance to address human trafficking. The plan covers four areas: prevention of trafficking in persons, protection of and assistance to victims of trafficking, prosecution of crimes of trafficking, and strengthening of partnerships against trafficking. Prevention involves tackling the many factors which create vulnerable populations in society, such as poverty, inequality, and discrimination, as well as education about trafficking for potential victims, as well as addressing economic and labor issues which can create demand. Protection and assistance for victims includes areas such as protecting victims' rights; identifying, educating, and training those who may encounter victims to properly identify them as such; and providing a variety of recovery and long-term support services for physical, emotional, and economic harm caused by victimization. According to the UNODC 2012 Global Report on Trafficking in Persons, prosecution of human traffickers is incredibly low compared to other crimes and one reason for this is lack of strong and clear domestic laws to prosecute these individuals; therefore, creation of laws and strengthening prosecution is a necessary step for many countries. In addition, the plan recommends the ability of laws to target organized crime groups, their finances, and their trafficking routes. Finally, international cooperation is incredibly important to combating human trafficking, so strengthening the relationships and partnerships, not just among nations, but across a variety of societal institutions to work together towards prevention, protection of, and assistance to victims of trafficking, prosecution of crimes of trafficking, and strengthening of partnerships against trafficking is absolutely necessary to combat this global problem.

In the United States, there are several challenges to responding to human trafficking, especially as the response pertains to the victims. One of the priorities identified in the State Department's 2013 report is the importance of accurate identification of victims of trafficking. The report discusses some of the major downfalls of poor identification, such as misclassifying victims of trafficking as illegal immigrants or criminals, which re-victimizes them and doesn't provide them with services to recover from their victimization, or deportation, which may put them back into the same situation where they were trafficked from. In particular, the report discusses how male victims, who often are forced into labor, can often be misidentified by immigration officers or labor officials and treated as illegal immigrants, even though they can provide detailed accounts of the trafficking experience. Another example provided is that of law enforcement officials assuming a person participating in sex work is a criminal or perhaps a blameworthy victim, but failing to recognize the reach of human trafficking into what has traditionally been perceived as prostitution. Due to the recent identification of the variety of contexts where human trafficking can occur, the State Department recommends training on the identification of victims of trafficking in a large number of areas, including: government officials responsible for a variety of inspections, private sector employees who may encounter victims in a variety of service-related industries, and all law enforcement officials, including immigration and border patrol agents. In addition, individuals involved in healthcare, transportation, and education all have the potential to encounter victims of human trafficking and should be provided training on proper identification of trafficking and appropriate reporting avenues.

Immigrant Victims

In addition to being victims of human trafficking, immigrants to the United States, both documented and undocumented, can also be victims of more traditional crimes. Data on these victims is scarce due to several factors, including language barriers, fear of the police, or fear that they or family members might be deported.

Immigrants to the US experience a variety of forms of victimization. According to a study on immigrants in Houston, Texas, 59.3% of the individuals responding were a victim of crime in the past three years and 48% had been victimized multiple times (Kercher & Kuo, 2008). For those who had experienced victimization, 57% reported to the police. The study found that immigrants who lived in the US for 10

"In the News" Box 12.1

On May 19, 2014, Human Rights Watch reporter, Amy Braunschweiger, published an article entitled "Nashville Immigrants Too Scared to Call the Police." The article discusses the fear that illegal immigrants have in calling the police when a crime has occurred. The article highlights the case of a woman named Elena, whose daughter was assaulted in their apartment complex hallway. This is not the first crime to have occurred to Elena's family. Four days after returning from the hospital with her newborn son, a woman knocked on Elena's door presenting herself as an immigration official who was there to deport Elena and her family. The woman took Elena's newborn and other children and fled the house—thereby kidnapping Elena's kids through false representation of who she was. It took weeks for Elena to get regain custody of her children as the kidnapper alleged that she had sold her children to her. After much prodding by neighbors, Elena consented to letting a neighbor call law enforcement to report the crime so that the perpetrator wouldn't be able to hurt anyone else. The article notes that in Nashville, police have collaborated with Immigration and Customs agents to crack down on illegal immigrants, which has created a culture of fear among immigrants who happen to be crime victims. The programs instituted by the police and ICE have resulted in thousands of deportations and have veered from their focus on violent offenders to any offender, including minor traffic offenders. For some immigrants, the fear of potential harm (and death) in the country they fled from is too great to risk losing their livelihood in the United States, so they flee. In Elena's case, the perpetrator went to court and Elena and her daughter initially cooperated. She and her daughter were told about U visas that they might be eligible for due to the crime victim status. During the investigation, however, police raided Elena's apartment complex and she fled to avoid deportation.

To read the full article, visit: http://newamericamedia.org/2014/05/nashville-immigrants-too-scared-to-call-the-police.php.

years or longer reported to the police more often (62.5%), and those living in the US under 10 years were less likely to report (47.9%). The two most frequent crimes reported to the researchers were robbery and larceny; however, interviews with police officers revealed that domestic violence may have been underreported by the respondents (Kercher & Kuo, 2008). This is consistent with a National Institute of Justice report, which found domestic violence to be the largest reported category reported to researchers by recent immigrants (US Department of Justice, 1998).

All victims of domestic violence face a variety of challenges to reporting or leaving abusive situations, but female immigrants face a variety of additional hurdles. Women are more likely than men to come into the US on a spousal or dependent visa, which can have several consequences (Sreeharsha, 2010). First, their spouse may be in the country on a work visa, which can make the victim economically dependent on that individual and can be used as a mechanism to keep the victim in the relationship (Sreeharsha, 2010). Second, the victims' status may be dependent on the abuser, so threats of deportation by the abuser can be another strategy to keep the victim quiet about the abuse (Sreeharsha, 2010). Finally, language and cultural barriers can be obstacles to reporting or leaving abusive relationships for immigrants. The spouse who is on a work visa may have more education and better language skills than a victim, thus providing another mechanism to instill fear and intimidation in the victim to prevent them from reporting (Sreeharsha, 2010). Given the experiences victims may have in their home countries, such as governments treating abuse as a private matter or corruption and violence in police departments, abusers may use the language barriers combined with these types of past experiences to prevent victims from reporting abuse (Sreeharsha, 2010).

In 2000, Congress enacted the Victims of Trafficking and Violence Protection Act, which can provide a U visa or T visa for immigrants, both documented and undocumented, who are victims of crime (Pollock & Hollier, 2010). Both visas are intended to encourage victims of crime to report their victimization without fear of deportation. Furthermore, it enables ongoing cooperation with law enforcement to prosecute crimes and assist victims with accessing services they otherwise would be ineligible for by providing them with legal status (Ivie & Nanasi, 2009). The U visa and T visa can provide temporary legal status for individuals for a period of four years, during which they may also apply for permanent legal status (NY Anti-Trafficking Network, 2010). While it may appear from the title of the act that the visas are only intended for victims of human trafficking, it actually applies to victims of a variety of crime types, including many forms of sexual violence (rape, sexual assault, trafficking, sexual exploitation), domestic violence, being held hostage, and involuntary servitude (NY Anti-Trafficking Network, 2010).

Cultural Competency

A number of issues were addressed in the sections on victims of human trafficking and victims who are illegal or undocumented immigrants that can help us to better understand the role of cultural competency in best practices for victim service providers. The National Victim Assistance Academy addresses the topic of cultural competency in its training materials for victim service providers. They suggest that there are three main areas to be aware of when considering cultural competency in victim services: (1) communication, (2) appropriate relationship building, and (3) self-awareness. Umbreit and Coates (2000) also highlight these issues as important to providing strong multicultural services to crime victims.

Probably the most obvious issue surrounding communication (and potential barriers) is the necessity to have victim services providers (public and private) able to converse in the languages of the people in need of services. For law enforcement, courts, corrections, and juvenile justice this means having people within agencies who are bilingual or multilingual. This does not mean all criminal justice practitioners need to be able to speak languages other than English, but if the population that is being served has subsets that are not familiar with English or have a primary language other than English, there should be enough public servants available to be able to communicate with these populations with little delay in service. For the most part, criminal justice agencies have much larger staffs than community victim service agencies, but because crime victims may not want to utilize criminal justice services it is equally important for community victim service agencies to either have bilingual or multilingual staff and/or have the ability to bring in someone who is bilingual or multilingual and can assist with interpretation for the client and advocate. In some cases this may simply mean that victim advocacy agencies must form partnerships with community cultural organizations so they can share information and provide services to a wider variety of clients overall. Umbreit and Coates (2000) suggest that within our understanding of communication in situations where an advocate/ practitioner and a victim or a victim and offender may be from different cultures, it is important to understand each culture's particular communication styles so that differences will not be misinterpreted in any interactions that take place. Specifically, Umbreit and Coates (2000) remark that we must pay attention to proximity, body movements, paralanguage, and density of language. Many cultures have different preferences for the distance they prefer between people engaged in an interaction. For instance, they suggest that in general (though it is important not to overgeneralize and assume that everyone fits these general patterns) "Latin Americans, Africans, Black Americans, Indonesians, Arabs, South Americans and the French are more comfortable speaking with less distance between them than White Americans" (p. 7). Thus, it might be seen that a White American is backing away from an interaction, or backing up during an interaction and that may be interpreted as rude or aloof, rather than a general cultural difference.

Umbreit and Coates (2000) purport that body language or movements are often very telling in interpersonal interactions. For instance, we often assess one's engagement, interest, truthfulness, or comfort levels by the person's posture, eye contact, facial expressions, gestures, and other body movements. The authors suggest that White Americans have a tendency towards using a great deal of facial expressions to express themselves, whereas those from Asian cultures may have been taught to control their feelings, and their expression of them, more tightly. This could have significant implications for law enforcement interviews of victims as well. If a victim has been brought up to contain his or her emotions and thus does not express strong emotions after being victimized, some may find this lack of emotions puzzling and perhaps suspicious. In another example, Umbreit and Coats (2000) suggest that in some traditional American-Indian cultures looking one's elder directly in the eye is a sign of disrespect, so a victim within that culture may choose to avoid eye contact with law enforcement or even victim advocates if they are perceived to be authority figures in that context. Another interesting pattern reported by Umbreit and Coates is that Black Americans tend to make more frequent eye contact when speaking and less when listening, while conversely White Americans tend to make more eye contact when listening than when speaking. Unfamiliarity with these general patterns could result in miscommunication, offense, or even shut down by the parties involved and may hamper the recovery of crime victims.

Paralanguage includes tone of voice, pace, dialects, inflections, silences, and hesitations in speaking. Some cultures prefer faster paced dialogues whereas others rely on hesitations and silences to impart important points. It is important to understand these nuances among different cultures (including regional differences) so that when working with practitioners, the victim feels comfortable to present and receive information pertinent to his or her situation. Density of language refers to the overall volume of words used in a dialogue. Umbreit and Coates (2000) suggest that Black and White Americans are much more comfortable using fewer words to express themselves and may rely heavily on shared codes within their cultures to communicate large thoughts in a small amount of words. In one of the author's home states (Wisconsin) the colloquialism "oh sure" is often used to connote "yes, I understand, that makes sense," but outside of that general region some may mistake that phrase for sarcasm, as in "yeah right, you're pulling my leg." Additionally, there may not be a shared definition of "justice" between people of different cultural backgrounds, so when providing service to crime victims it is important to find out how the crime has affected them and their community, if applicable, and assess how they see "justice" being achieved.

Umbreit and Coates (2000) purport that while it is important to recognize, value, and accommodate multiple cultures when responding to crime victims, it is also important to not overgeneralize and start to expect specific communication styles when dealing with people from specific cultural backgrounds. The authors report that there are both differences among cultures and within cultures. They state that within the United States, the dominant White culture may value "individualism, competition, taking action, [and] rational linear thinking," (p. 9) but that doesn't mean that all White Americans share those same values or that those values are shared by all US citizens. Furthermore, persons within the same cultural group, but raised in different regions of the country or geographical spaces (urban, suburban, rural, small town) may share some characteristics and communication styles with others within their cultural group, but they may also have stark differences in communication as well. Finally, to be effective at working with crime victims, Umbreit and Coates (2000) remark that it is also important for each person to recognize his or her own cultural biases, prejudices, and assumptions about "other" cultures. The NVAA (2000) concurs and suggests that working with a victim, getting to know them, building rapport and trust, and paying attention to their cultural predilections will help to form a positive experience for the crime victim. Failing to assess what one could be bringing into an interaction or allowing for prejudices to creep into a relationship could lead to miscommunications and revictimization of crime victims and hamper their recovery overall.

New Developments in Victim Services

There have been a number of new developments in victimology and victim services that have resulted from an understanding of best practices in working with victims of crime. As was discussed in Chapter 11, "traditional" tools of victim advocacy agencies (crisis hotlines, individual and group counseling, support groups, shelters, accompaniment and companionship, direct advocacy, etc.) appear to be effective at assisting victims on their paths to recovering from the criminal incident, and there has also been a growth in understanding that alternative justice responses and recovery tools may also provide avenues of support. Collaborations among criminal justice practitioners and victim advocates have resulted in less revictimization of crime victims as the service workers both learn more about what the other does in response to the needs of crime victims and also there is a reduction in the redundancy of requests from crime victims that typically required them to revisit or relive the victimization in order to get the service provider to understand what happened to them. Presenting a united front, or collaboration between criminal justice and victim advocacy agencies, can also help the crime victim feel less anxious about the process and more empowered if he or she chooses to report the crime. To that end, this next section will focus on some new developments in victim services that have been shown to be effective at increasing victim satisfaction with the criminal justice process, have aided in the recovery of victims, and have acknowledged the need to provide comprehensive and convenient service to crime victims who may feel lost in the confusing world of crime victim services and criminal justice case processing.

Restorative Justice Initiatives

For a long time, victims have reported feeling that they have been excluded from traditional criminal justice processes and they haven't experienced the reconciliation or restoration that they have sought because they have been limited in their ability to control their own recovery process (Meyer, 2003). States presenting cases wherein the state is the victim, the traditional criminal justice system frowning upon interaction between a victim and offender, and prosecutors symbolically "hearing" a victim but not incorporating his or her preferences into the case processing have left victims feeling unfulfilled and ill at ease. Meyer (2003) notes that in the 1990s the justice principle of restoration was recognized. Meyer (2003) suggests that restoration was not a new concept, in fact there are elements of **restorative justice** philosophies in early justice codes wherein an interaction took place between a victim and offender in which recompense was required to occur to assist in restoring the victim to his or her state prior to the crime occurring. Additionally, ancient justice codes also allowed for victims to "pardon" offenders after discussing the victimization and coming to an agreed upon arrangement between the victim and offender that would both restore the victim to the pre-crime state and reintegrate the offender into the community. Umbreit and Coates (2000) suggest that there are six main principles to restorative justice programs: "the nature of the crime, the goal of justice, the role of victims, the role of offenders, the role of the local community, and the role of the formal criminal/juvenile justice system" (p. 3). The nature of crime reflects the stance that crime is a violation of both personal and social relationships that exist in our "social contract" and that it harms the social/community fabric overall. The goal of restorative justice is not punishment, like traditional justice practices, but instead is geared toward repairing the harm done and restoring relationships to pre-crime states. The victim must be a willing participant in the process, as forced participation will not lead to restoration overall. The involvement of the victim can be minimal, with little to no contact with the offender, or there can be a facilitated interaction; the choice is typically the victim's to make. The offender who chooses to participate in restorative justice practices is giving up some of his or her due process rights because they must accept responsibility for the harm that was perpetrated, but the returns may be great. The offender will engage in an interaction with the victim that he or she is comfortable with, and will be an integral part of the process by which reparation to the victim is determined and resolution between the victim and offender may occur. The community can be involved through the restoration process between the victim and offender and if its resources are used in the resolution that is determined between the victim and offender. Finally, the criminal or juvenile justice system is involved to the extent that it provides the opportunity for alternative justice paradigms and will monitor any agreed upon resolution to ensure it is carried out.

Some commonly used restorative justice programs include **victim-offender mediation** (probably the most commonly used), **family group conferences, community reparation boards,** and **circle sentencing.** Umbreit and Coates (2000) describe community reparation boards as community boards that monitor that restitution that has been agreed upon by the victim and offender, or determined by the board or a judicial agency, is carried out. The victim and offender may or may not have a great deal of interaction, but the focus of restoring the victim through restitution is a primary goal of these programs. Family group conferences focus on shaming and reintegrating the offender back into the community with an emphasis on re-educating the offender to live a law-abiding life, so as not to bring harm to the victim, or any new victims, anymore. Circle sentencing, alternatively, focuses exclusively on the needs of the victim, wherein the victim, community, and offender meet together to come to a consensus about a repair plan that will assist both the victim and offender in meeting their needs. Finally, victim-offender mediation is a process by which victims and offenders meet to discuss a plan that will repair the harm perpetrated against the victim. The mediator is a facilitator between the victim and offender and works with the two parties without imposing a resolution on them. Curtis-Fawley and Daly (2005) found that victim advocates felt that victim-offender mediation allowed victims to have a voice in the process and it allowed offenders to accept responsibility for their actions without fear of extreme reprisal by the system. They further suggested that it provided victims an opportunity to regain control over the situation as they were key parties to the decision-making process surrounding reparation to and restoration of them by the offender. Advocates in their study also had concerns

"In the News" Box 12.2

Psychology Class Hopes to Implement Restorative Justice

By Julia Chacko
Staff Writer, *Sonoma State Star*

A psychology course is spawning a wave of support for the implementation of Restorative Justice at Sonoma State University.

Partnering with Restorative Resources of Santa Rosa, two students from psychology professor Maria Hess's Intro to Community Mental Health class, Lauren Dillier and Cody Hoffman-Brown, presented their research concerning the topic at an open-forum presentation on Wednesday, April 23. At the forum presentation, held in the Bennett Valley room of the Student Center, Dillier and Hoffman-Brown voiced their hope for its application throughout the Sonoma State community in the future.

Restorative Justice can be defined as a community-based approach on how to deal with crime, the effects of crime and the prevention of crime. The approach is something that functions on the belief that the path to justice relies on problem solving and healing rather than punishment and isolation.

"[Hess] was looking for a way to engage her students with community organizations, and we [Restorative Resources] agreed to do an introductory training with her class and take on five students for a semester-long service learning project," said Jessica Hankins, volunteer coordinator and adult program coordinator for Restorative Resources.

"There, the idea was born that we could explore bringing Restorative Justice to Sonoma State, and Maria approved this [task] for [Dillier and Hoffman-Brown]. From there, the three of us met several times throughout the semester, identifying stakeholders on campus, generating interest on the subject and planning our presentation."

"I will admit that, at first, I was a little skeptical about seeing how [Restorative Justice] would all work," said Dillier, psychology major and Community Services Advisor. "But in our first meeting with Restorative Resources, we did a role-play activity where one [person] played a victim, another played an offender and a third was the mediator. Through this simulated process, I could see the healing that happened with both the victim and the offender."

Instead of simply punishing a perpetrator for a crime, the restorative justice model strives to bring reparation and resolution to all, in the form of a facilitated circle wherein the victim, offender and others affected are all brought together to discuss the circumstances and motivations behind the crime as well as a fitting way for the offender to make amends.

"Victims are given the opportunity to be heard and share what they need to move on. Offenders are given the chance to hear how their actions have affected others, and because of this, are less likely to repeat their offense in the future," said Hankins. "Restorative Justice is also a good idea because it teaches everyone involved how to communicate better and strengthens community by involving everybody at an equal level. Instead of pushing people out when they have made a mistake, it brings them back in and reminds them that they have a place in their community, just like everyone else."

If Sonoma State were to take on these practices, the university would be following in the footsteps of several other colleges and universities across the nation, including University of Colorado, Boulder (the first to do so), Skidmore College, University of Michigan and University of San Diego. One of the members of the group that implemented Restorative Justice process at the University of Colorado, Boulder was Matthew Lopez-Phillips, vice president for student affairs and chief student affairs officer at Sonoma State.

"We had amazing results with the program, and the community enjoyed being a part of the process as well," said Lopez-Phillips. "SSU could benefit from such a program as it brings the larger community together to address issues of harm. Repairing that harm is the cornerstone of Restorative Justice circles. It would be great to see a RJ program on campus."

The event, which Dillier, Hoffman-Brown and Hankins said is the first of many, drew a crowd of about 20 people, ranging from a few students, to faculty, to Sonoma State Chief of Police Nathan Johnson, all of whom voiced their support for a Restorative Justice program at Sonoma State University.

"Exactly where it would be situated, what kinds of issues would be brought to it, who would actually do it, etc., is unclear at this point," said Pat Jackson, professor of criminology and criminal justice studies. "My sense of our purpose now is to involve key persons and groups at SSU and the surrounding community to consider the idea and how it might work."

Some program requirements/necessities discussed at the event were the implementation of an on-site paid coordinator, and a designated space for Restorative Justice conferences (circles) and volunteers. So far, ideas of how to fund the program have spanned from the offender paying a fee, to the student body paying a small fee ($5 or less) as part of tuition, or the use of grants and off-campus funding.

"We're working on scheduling some time to sit down with Matthew Lopez-Phillips as well as the chiefs' of police for our campus, Rohnert Park and Cotati to discuss how we can advance or outline a restorative program for both the campus and local community," said Hoffman-Brown.

"We are also looking to talk to Associated Students and the school of education," said Dillier. "We do plan to try and continue these types of conversations over summer and see where things can go."

For more information on Restorative Justice, visit the Restorative Resources website, and for news on the latest in the push to implement Restorative Justice at Sonoma State, contact Dillier or Hoffman-Brown.

Link to the article: http://www.sonomastatestar.com/news/psychology-class-hopes-to-implement-restorative-justice-1.3165529?pagereq=2#.U3t-p3ahEo.

Reprint permission granted.

about restorative justice practices, however. The advocates noted concerns that the offender might be able to revictimized the victim through the mediation process and that they might be getting off easy (Curtis-Fawley & Daly, 2005). Smith (2003) gives another name to these types of programs and instead calls them victim-offender reconciliation programs. Smith (2003) notes that victim-offender reconciliation programs help to bring closure to the crime victims and can address conflict resolution between the two parties. Smith (2003) notes that research examining victim-offender reconciliation programs suggest that victims report very high levels of satisfaction with the programs in both the ways that the cases were handled and in the outcomes that resulted from the mediation sessions, and in the overall feeling of fairness they reported by the mediators themselves. In all cases, the satisfaction levels were higher than individuals who had been given the opportunity to participate in victim-offender reconciliation programs but chose not to and those who were only presented the option of the traditional court process.

Restorative justice can sort of be seen as the merging of two justice paradigms with members both within and outside of the criminal and juvenile justice systems. Typically, cases from the criminal court system are referred to outside nongovernmental organizations (NGOs) who conduct the restorative justice practice. The NGO then reports the outcome to the criminal or juvenile justice system representative and cases are either referred back or more often monitored by the traditional justice system. It is stated that this can "sort of be seen as the merging" of justice paradigms because the practices, particularly of victim-offender mediation (or victim-offender reconciliation programs) are cooperative efforts between governmental and nongovernmental personnel.

If there is one word to describe some of the most cutting-edge programs with best practices in serving crime victims, that word is collaboration. The twenty-first century is seeing some tremendous effects from collaborative efforts between criminal justice and victim advocacy agencies. **Sexual Assault Response Teams (SARTs)** and **Family Justice Centers (FJC)** are two of the most prominent examples of diverse multi-agency collaborations wherein various agencies that provide services to crime victims come together with the purpose of limiting the potential revictimization of crime victims and surrounding the victim with a supportive environment that can truly address the many needs she or he may have in a more comprehensive fashion.

Sexual Assault Response Teams (SART)

According to Campbell, Greeson, Bybee, and Neal (2013), the response to sexual assault victims by legal, medical, and mental health personnel were uncoordinated and oftentimes harmful to the victim. **Sexual Assault Response Teams (SARTs)** were created in an attempt to remedy the treatment of sexual assault victims and to both reduce the trauma of the assault overall and increase successful apprehensions and subsequent convictions of perpetrators of rape and sexual assault. SARTs are collaborations between law enforcement, medical (specifically SANE and/or emergency

Professional Profile 12.2

Duane Ruth Heffelbower

Fresno Pacific University

Q: How did you get involved with working with crime victims? Do you currently work with victims? Have you participated in a joint research/practice project? Please describe.

A: My first career was the general practice of law in a small town beginning in 1975. I handled criminal cases and also got involved with people who had been victimized in various ways. This ranged from fraud victims to those injured in automobile crashes with impaired drivers. My family law work often involved spousal abuse issues. I became involved with the first victim offender program in the West in 1982 and, as the name implies, worked with offenders and their victims while helping to get an organization going. It is still in operation as part of the university center I direct, and has handled well over 10,000 cases. Around the same time refugees from Laos began arriving in my city and I wound up helping them in various ways. I left the practice of law to enter seminary, after which my wife and I co-pastored a new church. This work brought us into direct contact with victims of various types of abuse, as well as victims of economic systems and public policies. In 1995, I accepted an assignment helping develop resources for a new unexploded ordnance disposal program in Laos, traveling there to meet with victims and to learn how to do the demining work. In 1996, I moved full-time to Fresno Pacific University's Center for Peacemaking and Conflict Studies, almost immediately landing a three-year grant from the federal Office of Refugee Resettlement to work with conflict among refugees, resettlement workers, and local residents at 12 sites around the US. The refugees came from the worst places on earth and had heartbreaking stories. The cross-cultural conflict issues they ran into in US cities left them feeling re-victimized. We were able to develop methods for working with these conflicts, and published a book describing our process. At the end of the research project I took a leave of absence to allow my wife and I to accept an assignment with a relief and development agency in Indonesia, living there 2 1/2 years, working all over that country with victims of inter-religious and inter-tribal violence, and helping to develop conflict resolution methods suitable for that context. Upon my return our center increased its efforts working with schools and court-connected cases, using restorative justice and other mediation principles to assist people with their broken relationships. Often both sides thought they were the victims. I continue with this type of work while directing our center and its graduate program in peacemaking and conflict studies.

Q: What advice do you have for students interested in working with victims?

A: Many students don't realize the breadth of the field. A recently reformed cannibal on a tropical island whose ancestral lands are being taken by the government to give to loggers or miners is a victim, and has much in common with a North American victim of domestic violence. Members of my Indonesian team have since worked at trauma healing after tsunamis, earthquakes, and volcanic eruptions. A refugee in Atlanta whose furnace isn't working because a slumlord won't fix it is a victim. A teenager whose drug addict parents push her into the sex trade is a victim. If you want to work with victims think beyond the usual crime victim focus to the world of people in need of healing after trauma.

Q: What are some challenges for working with victims, especially in the field of criminal justice?

A: Crime rates have been steadily dropping for over 20 years, even as corrections expenditures have risen. The age of mass incarceration in the US has peaked and is headed down. In its wake is uncounted human wreckage from broken families, abandoned children, and unemployable former prisoners. There are almost no resources devoted to this group of millions of people. If they are not properly served it will be difficult to sustain the falling crime rate. So far there has been no political advantage in trying to address this need. That must change, and recent economic difficulties have encouraged lawmakers to look for new ideas. That is the new cutting edge in victim services, and an excellent place to work if your desire is that there are no more victims.

Q: What obstacles have you encountered while striving to assist victims? Have things changed?

A: From a political point of view there are good and bad victims. Bad victims are those who in some way placed themselves in a position to become victims. People who hang out in sketchy places or with sketchy people become bad victims. People who engage in any kind of risky behavior are bad victims. People who live in bad neighborhoods become bad victims. There are very few completely innocent victims when viewed in this way. The problem becomes getting resources to spend on bad victims, since almost everyone falls into that category. Advocacy has to first move a group into the good victim category before it can even begin to marshal resources.

Q: What do you feel is the mark you will have left on the field of victim services? What do you consider as your "legacy" in the field of victimology/ victim services?

A: Much of my work falls under the heading of restorative justice. Seeing offenses as violations of people and relationships rather than as violations of law is my starting point. I hope to have left a mark on the field in that way. My biggest contribution has been in training and encouraging others, creating structures that allow them to work. The role I played in starting the demining program in Laos has resulted in 1,000 people doing demining work for the last 20 years, saving a life every time a bomb comes out of the ground. The Victim Offender Reconciliation Program has spread into more areas and continues bringing victims and offenders together to make things right. I have had the opportunity to see my efforts bear fruit, and am not too concerned about who gets the credit.

Q: What are some issues that you see in the fields of victimology/victim services?

A: Getting away from dividing victims into good and bad, or innocent versus involved in their own injury is one of the biggest issues we face. People who have suffered harm need assistance whether an onlooker thinks they are deserving or not. I have put a lot of energy into advocating for people who don't look like real victims to the powers that be. Another major issue is recognizing the injuries suffered by victims of crimes that don't leave visible marks. Thanks to budget cuts it is common for victim advocates to only serve those with bloody injuries. A physically uninjured victim of a carjacking may have greater needs than the victim with physical injuries. We have not yet begun to recognize the prevalence of PTSD among a broad range of victims.

Q: Are there groups of victims you think need to be served but are not? Why or why not?

A: Families of incarcerated offenders have needs that are often ignored. There are groups that work with these people, but not as victim advocates. Victims of oppression are rarely helped, partly because they are the victims of powerful people who affect budgets. Refugee service providers tend to focus on the physical needs and not on the PTSD. The same is true for victims of natural disasters. As I write this my area is experiencing a drought which will take thousands of agriculture jobs. That type of tsunami doesn't attract victim advocates. When advocates are strapped for resources they have to narrowly focus their efforts. The need is to advocate for a broadening the classes of persons who are being helped.

room representatives), and mental health professionals along with rape crisis victim advocates and other entities more specific to different communities. For instance, the Cumberland County, North Carolina, SART includes representatives from the local child advocacy center and Ft. Bragg SHARP program as child sexual abuse and military sexual assault are addressed in this collective supportive manner as well. In their provision of services to rape and sexual assault victims, SARTs work collaboratively to reduce the number of interviews a rape/sexual assault victim must undergo so as to reduce the trauma of telling and re-telling the story multiple times. SARTs are familiar with the different services available for victims and can provide victims with that information to aid in the recovery from the rape/sexual assault. SARTs also meet regularly to review cases, to discuss responses to rape/sexual assault victims, and to identify patterns or problems related to rape and sexual assault in their communities.

Effectiveness of SARTs can be measured using a number of different indicators. Most often SARTs are evaluated on how many cases are successfully prosecuted and how many perpetrators of sex crimes are convicted. Research is inconclusive on this point, as some research suggests that SART cases are more successfully prosecuted while other research suggests that there is no different between SART cases and non-SART cases (Campbell et al., 2013). Another indicator that is valuable, especially as it relates to best practices for working with crime victims, is the assessment of the program by victims themselves. One of the goals of SARTs is to reduce the trauma associated with the crime and to decrease the amount of revictimization that is experienced by the victim from criminal justice, medical, mental health, and victim advocacy personnel (Greeson & Campbell, 2013). It is thought that collaborations may enhance the sensitivity and understanding with which a SART team member might approach, treat, and ultimately assist a rape/sexual assault victim. Greeson and Campbell (2013) found that SARTs are typically effective at assisting rape victims with their needs, but that there is wide variation in the organization and structure of SARTs, which may contribute to some SART programs being more effective than others.

Family Justice Centers ("One-Stop Shops")

A relatively recent collaborative effort that shows great promise for assisting victims of interpersonal violence, sexual assault, stalking, and child and elder abuse is the **Family Justice Center** effort that has really begun to take off in communities. In October 2003, President George W. Bush created the President's Family Justice Center Initiative, modeled after the San Diego Family Justice Center. Twenty million dollars was devoted to the creation of "one-stop shops" that serve victims of family violence in multi-agency co-located domains. What this essentially means is that victims of interpersonal violence could go to one location and meet with a law enforcement officer and/or court representative (typically a victim/witness liaison), a domestic violence or sexual assault victim advocate from a victim service agency, an individual who would be able to assess the victims medical needs as they related to the victimization, a person who could assist the victim in filling out paperwork for victim compensation, a magistrate or paralegal who could assist the victim with filing a protective or restraining order, and a child advocate who could work with the children who have been exposed to violence and/or conduct supervised visitations with the offending parent. One challenge victims of interpersonal violence or sexual assault often faced was having to travel to many different offices to receive services and it was easy for victims to fall through the cracks and not receive the assistance they needed to recover. The Family Justice Center concept seeks to reduce that and to make it easier for victims to start and continue their recovery journeys without all the previous obstacles of figuring out who to see and how to get there. According to the National Family Justice Center Alliance (Strack & Gwinn, 2013), Family Justice Centers typically have the goals of reducing IPV homicides, increasing safety while reducing anxiety and fear of victims, empowering victims into becoming autonomous and self-sufficient people, and increasing both successful case processing within the criminal justice system and community support for victims and their families (see also: Office on Violence Against Women, 2007). The National Family Justice Center Alliance is an organization that has been designated by the US government to provide training and technical assistance to Family Justice Centers across the United States. In 2011, the CEO, Gael Strack, was recognized by US Attorney General Eric Holder with the Innovation in Victim Services Award for her devotion to the Family Justice Movement. Across the United States, Family Justice Centers may serve additional types of victims including rape/sexual assault victims, victims of child or elder abuse, and stalking victims in addition to victims of interpersonal violence.

Since 2002, a number of Family Justice Centers have grown across the United States and early results indicate that victims are very satisfied with the services and the format in which the services are offered. The San Diego Family Justice Center saw a 95% decrease in interpersonal violence-related homicides over a 15-year period, a staggering statistic to consider (Office on Violence Against Women, 2007). The Alameda, California, Family Justice Center saw 20% more interpersonal violence cases accepted by prosecutors from police over a two-year period and a 10% increase in felony domestic violence cases (where there was a history of charging more often at the misdemeanor level) (Alameda Family Justice Center report June 18, 2008, visited June 22, 2017). In their assessment of the Nampa Family Justice Center, Giacomazzi, Hannah, and Bostaph (2008) found that the agencies participating in the Family Justice Center felt that they were a true collaboration working together to assist victims of interpersonal violence and their families and victims' reports were very positive about the services they received from the center. Chaiken et al. (2001) found that prosecutors' offices involved in family justice center-type relationships with victim advocacy and other agencies benefitted from more cooperation from clients and greater numbers of successful prosecutions. Additionally, victims who experienced the work of the collaborative teams experienced less trauma associated with the processing of the cases and a decreased amount of re-victimization by all parties overall.

The National Center for Victims of Crime sponsored a similar type of initiative called the "Parallel Justice" project, in which three sites were given seed money to re-structure their approaches to justice to a more victim-centered approach. The parallel justice approach resulted in immense efforts to incorporate victim input and feedback into restructuring justice system responses to victims and truly put victim needs at the forefront of their missions (National Center for Victims of Crime, n.d.).

SARTs, Family Justice Centers, and Parallel Justice projects illustrate that when the needs of victims are put first there can be greater accomplishments by the criminal justice system, increased satisfaction in the role of victim service providers across agencies, greater satisfaction by clients and a reduction in stress, trauma, and revictimization experienced by victims overall.

Hot Topics

Crime Victims in Disasters

Experiencing a disaster of any kind can be an incredibly traumatic experience by itself, but becoming a victim of crime during any phase of a disaster can take that trauma to a whole other level. Frailing and Harper (2012) co-edited a book titled *Crime and Criminal Justice in Disaster* that highlights some of the main types of victimization that occur before, during, and immediately following disasters. The book focuses on three of the most prominent types of victimization that occur: looting (business and residential), rape, and fraud. Additionally, sometimes the disaster itself is considered the crime and the victims are typically large in scope and include humans, animals, and the environment.

Thornton and Voight (2012) report that rape happens in all phases of a disaster, the warning phase (prior to the disaster hitting, but during the time in which people are preparing for the disaster), the impact phase (during the disaster), the emergency phase (immediately following the impact and the initial stages of recovery), and response (the longer recovery period). During Hurricane Katrina, 47 rapes were reported to the National Sexual Violence Resource Center while at the same time only 4 rapes were reported officially by the New Orleans Police Department. Thornton and Voight (2012) remarked that women are especially vulnerable to rape in both natural and man-made disasters. In their own research study, they examined reports of rape from multiple sources, including law enforcement, newspapers, victim advocates, and victims themselves, and discovered that women were raped in every stage of the disaster. Women were victims of rape as they sought to evacuate from the city. Women were victims of rape during the disaster as they were vulnerable due to the lack of guardians and the chaos of the situation. One of their study participants reported that as the hurricane was underway, she walked to a convenience store to get food, water, and medicine for her children and elderly mother. She was attacked by men in the store who were attempting to break into an ATM machine and she was kicked and insulted after the rape. She did not report the offense to police. Immediately after the hurricane, rapes occurred as people evaluated the state of their homes, tried to find their loved ones, and sought shelter, food, and water. One report of a rape victim indicated that a man came into the house she and a number of other people had found shelter in and she was raped in a stairwell. The woman poured bleach over herself to try to ward off any infections or disease the perpetrator might have had. Finally, in the recovery and restoration phases, many women reported that they were attacked in the FEMA trailer parks, by people they thought were volunteers to assist with the clean-up (in one case a volunteer was raped), in the large capacity shelters, and by their partners. Thornton and Voight (2012) remark that disaster rape is not uncommon and is global in scope. Women who have sought refuge in camps following terrorist attacks have been raped at alarming rates.

Businesses and individuals have been victims of looting in disasters (Frailing & Harper, 2012). Frailing and Harper (2012) suggest that there is "bad" looting and "less bad" looting. "Bad" looting includes the stealing of property that is not pertinent to survival after a hurricane, such as entertainment devices, jewelry, etc. Both businesses and individuals were victims of "bad" looting as motivated offenders took advantage of the lack of law enforcement, shop owners, and residents to guard their belongings. "Less bad" looters are those that take items only necessary for survival, including food, water, clothing, medicines, etc. Frailing and Harper (2012) reported that the burglary (looting) rate for New Orleans the month following Hurricane Katrina was over 400% higher than the previous month's burglary rate!

Frailing (2012) reports that there are a number of different types of fraud that occur in the wake of disasters, including false claims by individuals who state they were disaster victims, price gouging, and contractor fraud. False claims are acts perpetrated against an agency and price gouging affected all citizens overall. However, contractor fraud was a specific deceitful act toward victims of the disaster wherein people contracted with an individual to fix their property, paid the contractor money, and the contractor either did no work or did shoddy work. Frailing (2012) reports that in some cases, contractors were also charging individuals up to 1,700 times the amount that it cost to actually execute the job.

It is clear that crime does not stop when disasters happen and that new patterns may emerge as people assess the overall situation and act out in antisocial ways. Frailing and Harper (2012) purport that it is time that we take a hard look at crime that occurs within the context of disasters. Crime victim service providers must be included in community disaster preparedness plans, and law enforcement and other criminal justice and government officials need to help citizens be aware of the different victimization risks that exist within the disaster context.

Using Social Media to Assist Crime Victims

Social media can be both a boon and scourge to crime victims. Who hasn't heard of someone "playfully stalking" someone on Facebook? Whether it's that new person that a friend is interested in or a colleague from school or work who has been saying nasty things about you—many people will check out each other's Facebook pages to see who people are, at least on social media, and what they're up to. Unfortunately, this makes it easier for not so funny stalking situations to actually occur and for

Figure 12.1: Pleasant Prairie, WI, Facebook Notice

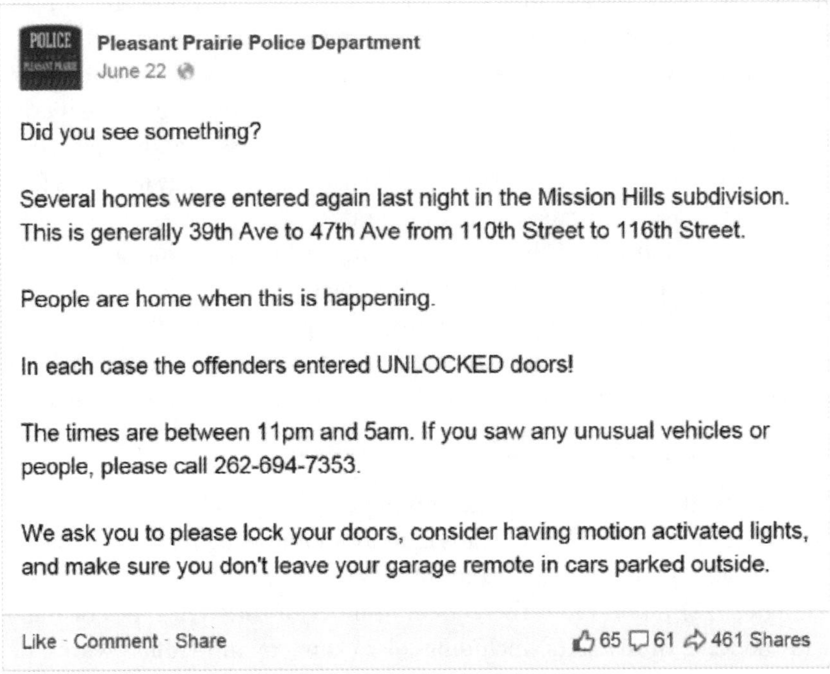

Pleasant Prairie Police Department
June 22

Did you see something?

Several homes were entered again last night in the Mission Hills subdivision. This is generally 39th Ave to 47th Ave from 110th Street to 116th Street.

People are home when this is happening.

In each case the offenders entered UNLOCKED doors!

The times are between 11pm and 5am. If you saw any unusual vehicles or people, please call 262-694-7353.

We ask you to please lock your doors, consider having motion activated lights, and make sure you don't leave your garage remote in cars parked outside.

Like · Comment · Share   65   61   461 Shares

abusive partners to be able to track down their victims, even if a victim has "unfriended" the perpetrator. Aurelia Sands Belle, executive director for the Durham Crisis Response Center in North Carolina, suggests that while social media can be great, it is a double-edged sword when abusers use it to further harm their victims (Sexual Assault Report, 2014).

Conversely, in the last few years, more and more police departments around the country have created Facebook pages and Twitter accounts by which they can inform citizens of police-community events, seek assistance in identifying wanted criminals, and alert people to crimes happening in their communities (Stuart, 2013; Wagley, 2014). For instance, on 6/22/2014, the Pleasant Prairie, Wisconsin, police department posted a crime alert/crime prevention tip on its Facebook page after a flurry of burglaries in one of its neighborhoods (see Figure 12.1).

Stuart (2013) reports that the Kentucky State Police posted pictures of jewelry, a tattoo, and a facial composite of a deceased person who had not been identified since being found 10 years previous. The pictures led to new leads, which led to the discovery of the identity of the person. This suggests that if used ethically (so as not to cause great distress to potential survivors on Facebook) social media could be a great tool for cold cases, particularly if a decedent cannot be identified. This could bring a sense relief to the family and friends of a loved one who has been reported missing and where foul play is suspected. While learning that a person may have passed away, naturally, accidentally, or from a homicide, will be traumatic, the ability to achieve closure could help the survivors of that person to recovery from the death and relieve the worry and anxiety of wondering what has happened to the individual. The crime prevention tips can truly help individuals prevent victimizations from happening to them and if a victim sees that the police are soliciting information on their cases this could make them feel more confident in the police and more validated, as they see that the police have taken their case seriously.

In the National Crime Victims' Rights Week materials for 2014, the Office for Victims of Crime included a "media tips" sheet which focused, in part, on how victim service providers (public or private) could use social media to advertise programs they were putting on to celebrate NCVRW and/or their services overall. The Vision 21 report by OVC also discussed the headway agencies can start to make as social media evolves (OVC, 2013). As discussed, funding is a big problem for victim advocacy agencies, but social media is one way to get the word out about services they offer and is free of charge.

Victims in Mass Casualties

In the last decade, the news media has reported extensively on a number of mass casualty crime incidents, including school shootings (discussed previously), the Aurora, Colorado, theater shooting, shootings against military personnel on military posts, the San Bernadino mass shooting, and the Orlando Pulse Nightclub shooting. As this text was being reviewed by the authors for final edits, a tragic mass casualty shooting occured in Las Vegas. At least 59 people were killed and no motive was yet known (Wagner, Rocha, & Willis, 2017). Not only is the community dealing with assault and murder—but assault and murder on a significantly large scale. In some instances the attacks are motivated by terrorist ideology (or suspected to be motivated by that), in others the mental health of the suspect(s) has been brought into question. No matter the motivator, the impact on individuals involved who may have been injured, but survived, survivors of homicide victims, and general public as a whole requires an immense effort to help victims recover from these events (OVC, 2005). Those called on to provide these services include, to name a few, representatives from the criminal justice community, medical community, victim and social service representatives, mental health professionals, and faith-based personnel. On a regular day, these organizations may be taxed dealing with traditional clientele, including singular crime victims. When incidents with mass casualties occur the impact often requires a response akin to a disaster or other emergency management-type response effort. The Office for Victims of Crime, in conjunction with the American Red Cross, created a guide for professionals on how best to respond to victims of both terrorism and mass violence. The effects of mass violence include severe, longer lasting psychological/emotional aftereffects. Mass violence, like disasters and terrorist attacks, can cause higher rates of PTSD, depression, anxiety, and a shift in the "just world philosophy" of survivors (OVC, 2005). Just as with singular acts of crime, physical, psychological, and financial consequences may occur. Social consequences may be even more extreme as a larger segment of the community is affected by the event, thereby taxing the services that are available and perhaps requiring assistance from neighboring communities. With the advent of social media (as discussed previously in this chapter) there have been sites created that allow for survivors to post safety messages to calm the fears of family and friends. In addition to state-administered crime victim compensation programs, the Office for Victims of Crime has additional funding available to victims of mass violence, including crisis response grants, consequence management grants, and criminal justice support grants. Additionally, the National Center for Victims of Crime created the National Compassion Fund, where 100% of donations go directly to victims of a mass violence event. The effort is a co-ordinated effort between victims of the incident and NCVC and was created, in part, to eliminate scams perpetrated by ne'er-do-wells intent on scamming those with charitable intentions (NCVC, visited March 4, 2017).

Future Considerations

Remaining Gaps in Service to Victims

Moriarty and Roberts (2008) indicate that all current victims' services and funding opportunities are greatly needed, but unfortunately they are only available to specific types of victims. For instance, Moriarty and Roberts (2008) state "(w)ith the exception of family members of homicide victims and sexual assault victims, the acute crisis episodes and trauma experienced by human trafficking, robbery, attempted murder, home invasion, carjacking, mugging, hazing and burglary victims have never been understood" (p. 127). There are a number of areas within victimology and victim services that need further investigation from researchers and practitioners and greater attention by legislative bodies and assistance organizations at the local and state levels. One such area is assistance for victims of property crime. Many of the victim advocacy agencies that exist focus on personal crime victims and state victim compensation programs only provide assistance to personal crime victims, but property crime victims suffer great financial losses too (as demonstrated in Chapter 3) and they have very few resources to assist them in getting back on their feet. A more concerted effort has to be made to assist these victims with being restored, especially since property crime victims account for the vast majority of crime victims overall.

Additionally, as you learned, males are the predominant category of victims for almost all crimes (excluding sexual assault and domestic violence), however, very few services exist to assist male crime victims and those that do exist are typically offshoots of female crime victim services, so they may not provide the gender-specific services that male victims need to assist in their recovery. If we truly want to make a dent in the harm produced by criminal victimizations, there must be greater attention paid to male crime victims to better understand what needs they have and what services can address those needs, be they similar to or different from those that currently exist for female victims.

Professional Profile 12.3

Human Right Awareness

Dr. Laura Moriarty
Monmouth University

Q: What got you into the field of victimology and/or working with crime victims?

A: While in the doctoral program at Sam Houston State University (SHSU), I took a "victims of crime" class with Dr. Teske and it had a very lasting impact on me. I wanted to learn more about victims and their rights and how I could help assist them. I also participated in an Academy of Criminal Justice Sciences (ACJS) victimology workshop with Bill Doerner and that really solidified my interest and research agenda.

Q: What advice do you have for students interested in working with victims and/or becoming victimologists?

A: While it is very rewarding to work with victims, especially when you see how they can overcome such adversity; you can easily get burned out, frustrated, overwhelmed. It is a good idea to find a balance in your approach to helping victims and perhaps find other outlets that are not so emotional. It's hard ... but very rewarding work.

Q: What are some challenges to studying crime victims that you have encountered or seen?

A: The system still is not as responsive to crime victims as you would expect in 2014. Thus, trying to study victim's services from a system-wide approach remains difficult. We have made progress but there is still a great deal yet to be analyzed.

Q: What obstacles have you encountered while striving to study crime victims?

A: Some of the obstacles are inherent in where the victim's services are located. When part of a court system, there is more of a specialty bent to victim services. Obviously, all victims need services, but sometimes those services are limited, especially when victims are reluctant to go through the CJS.

Q: What do you feel is the mark you will have left on the field of victimology? What do you want people to see as your mark? At the end of the day, what do you want your "legacy" to be in the field of victimology/victim services?

A: The *Controversies in Victimology* book—an edited volume—with some really good contributions from excellent scholars/researchers looking at controversial issues facing victims and/or the study of victimology is my legacy if

I have one. I am very proud of that book and hope it stimulates dialogue that results in moving forward with services for victims.

Q: What are some burgeoning issues that you see in the field of victimology?

A: Victimization over the Internet or online or in cyberspace has gained momentum as a research topic. However, it is relatively new in terms of our understanding of the medium and thus we don't really know what types and kinds of victimization are yet to surface. I think we have only scratched the surface here.

Q: What areas within victimology do you think are neglected?

A: Neglected is too strong of a word … but I do think we need to focus more on human rights victimization expanding the definition of victims of crime. Human rights victimization should be conceptualized as crime victims. I think we are moving in that direction but it seems to be more of a topic in political science, which is fine, we just need to get the dialogue going in criminal justice.

Similarly, you've learned that repeat victims experience a large proportion of all crime, yet there are really no services that exist that focus on this group of individuals and businesses. "Crime" would receive a strong "punch in the face" if we could stop continued repeat victimization from happening.

For practitioners, grant-funding has become more reliant on evidence-based practices; thus agency personnel, directors in particular, are going to have to spend more time on program evaluations and outcome analysis to justify continued funding from government agencies from year to year. Indeed, Campbell et al. (2013) noted that SART teams that were the most effective were the ones who engaged in program evaluation and thus continuous improvement, thus not only is evaluation necessary for funding, but to inform programs of what works and what doesn't so they can retain effective programs and eliminate those that are not. Partnerships with outside evaluators, particularly universities, will be necessary (and perhaps welcome) elements to their strategic plans and an understanding of statistics and reporting may be skills that the twenty-first century manager of a victim service agency will need to gain.

There need to be continued efforts to identify new and unique groups of victims so as to highlight the issues that may be specific to them and require creative approaches and solutions on a more global scale. For instance, victimologists should focus more attention on global human rights violations, specifically as they relate to homicide, assault, and rape as forms of human rights violations by governments and peace-keeping organizations. Additionally, it is important to make more of an effort to bring diverse groups of victims under the "victim" umbrella. For instance, victims of state and corporate crime, including environmental crime victims, are often dealt with outside of the traditional criminal justice system, thereby invalidating their claims of being actual *crime* victims, mainly because their perpetrators have typically escaped the focus of criminal justice and government authorities. In a similar vein, individuals who become victims of crime either by the hands of or while under supervision by criminal justice authorities are oftentimes ignored unless an outside organization such as a prisoners' rights group or the media become involved in the case. Victims of interpersonal violence who are married to police officers, prisoners who are raped by other inmates or correctional staff, and alleged suspects and/or offenders who are brutalized at the hands of criminal justice personnel may continue to be invisible as the various subcultures within criminal justice preserve the "code of silence" in the blue or grey "brotherhood."

Movement in the Field

Victimology is a fast growing area in both academia and the "real world." Over 300 institutions of higher education have at least one faculty member with a specialization in victimology, but only 11% of 679 schools require coursework in a victim-focused course (Bostaph et al., 2011). So, while the first part is encouraging, it seems we still have a little way to go to fully integrate the curriculum with victim-focused coursework. Perhaps we're already starting to see some real growth however, because more universities are starting to offer bachelor's and master's degrees in victimology, victims studies, and victim services management. For instance, Fresno State University has offered students the ability to concentrate in victimology within their criminology curriculum since 1992 (American Society of Victimology), Sam Houston State University offers both a bachelor's degree in victim studies and an online master's in victim services management, which started in the fall of 2013 (Sam Houston State University, visited June 22, 2017) and Boise State University provided students the opportunity to earn a victim services certificate at the graduate level starting in the fall of 2014 (Boise State, visited June 22, 2017). The University of New Haven offers a bachelor's in criminal justice with the possibility to complete a concentration in victim services administration (University of New Haven, visited June 22, 2017). The field is expanding and is becoming professionalized, just as its predecessors in the criminal justice field did.

Not only do we see this growth in academia, but we see continued and even more specialized growth in our national victim assistance organizations. For instance, the National Center for Victims of Crime recently began two large new initiatives, one focused on stalking (Stalking Resource Center) and another focused on the importance of DNA collection, especially as it relates to the backlog of rape kits for sexual assault victims (DNA Resource Center) (NCVC). These two centers highlight burgeoning issues in the field and as grants and legislation continue to highlight these issues we will need the vast repository of current information that NCVC will provide. While the momentum is strong, it is important to catch hold of the victimology wave and make some real strides in the field while we can.

Perhaps because of the grassroots nature of the growth of victimology and the prominent focus of developing an understanding of what works best for victims, there have been some significant efforts towards collaboration between researchers and practitioners. For instance, Dr. Christine Murray at the University of North Carolina-Greensboro, in concert with the North Carolina Coalition Against Sexual Assault and North Carolina Coalition Against Domestic Violence, worked to bring together researchers and practitioners across the state in February 2013 at the first annual Innovations in Domestic and Sexual Violence Conference. At this first conference, which one of the authors of this text attended, there was a great deal of discussion on how to cultivate researcher-practitioner relationships so that research that is being conducted is directly beneficial to those in the field and so that those in the field have influence on what is being researched. The second annual conference took place in March 2014 and the future is bright for this form of networking. In the Vision 21 report, it was noted that there is a lot of great information available, but there is no clear way to get that information straight to victim advocacy agencies, policymakers, and other stakeholders in the victim services and criminal justice fields. Therefore, another challenge we will need to face is how to both disseminate information to a larger variety of people and how to ensure that the research that is done illustrates the policy or program implications of the research—so as to truly inform the readers on best (and worst) practices in the field (OVC, 2013).

Summary and Conclusions

The research used in this textbook is a combination of researcher-based, practitioner-based, and researcher/practitioner collaborations, so you have been informed by the field as a whole. We still have work to do, but it seems fair to say that victimologists, victim service practitioners, and individuals working for large victim assistance organizations all have a passion to see fewer victimizations, a reduction in harm, and a better future for victims of crime.

Along the same lines, it is promising to see so many collaborations between criminal justice practitioners and victim advocates, but there is still a need to inculcate criminal justice practitioners into using research conducted by both academics and victim advocates to truly inform their treatment of victims that they respond to on a daily basis. Cutting edge research, like the neurobiology of sexual assault information, should be mandatory reading for law enforcement officers but it is unclear how well this information is trickling down to the street-level officer. Conversely, it is incumbent upon researchers to ensure that their work is distributed in works that may be more commonly read by criminal justice practitioners, such as trade journals or more agency-specific publications. Though progress is being made, there needs to be continued efforts to invite criminal justice practitioners to utilize the information available to ensure the best treatment possible for crime victims.

There are some incredible glimmers of progress in the field, such as T and U visas for trafficking victims; "Link" teams addressing violence recognition and coordinated response to animal cruelty, child abuse, and domestic violence; the growth of Family Justice Centers and other "one-stop" shops to provide comprehensive and convenient services to victims; SART programs across the country; and victim activism to both support victims and advance their rights. Victimology is young, but with youth comes passion, and passion is unbounded. Just think where we will be in another 50 years.

Key Terms

Restorative justice   Circle sentencing
Victim-offender mediation   Sexual Assault Response Teams (SARTs)
Family group conferences   Family Justice Centers
Community reparation boards

Discussion Questions

1. Where do you see the fields of victimology and victim services going in the next 20 years?
2. How do you think we could "bridge the gap" so that researchers can assist victim service practitioners with real-world research needs and practitioners can utilize the information produced by researchers?
3. What other types of collaborations between criminal justice, victim advocacy, academic, and other personnel do you think victims need right now?

Websites for Further Information

Family Justice Center Initiative: http://www.familyjusticecenter.org/.

National Center for Victims of Crime: http://www.ncvc.org/ Click on Our Programs to view more about the Stalking Resource Center and the DNA Resource Center.

References

American Prosecutors' Research Institute. (2006). Rural victim assistance: A victim/ witness guide for rural prosecutors. Washington, DC: US Department of Justice, Office of Justice Programs, Office for Victims of Crime. NCJ 211106.

Boise State University, Unique Online Victim Services Grad Certificate Approved, (https://news.boisestate.edu/update/2014/04/17/bosie-state-offer-unique-online-grad-certificate-victim-services, visited June 22, 2017.

Bostaph, L., Giacomazzi, A., Brady, P., & Beattie, C. (2011, October) Crime victims in criminal justice curriculum: Are we there yet? Conference of the Western Association of Criminal Justice, Reno, NV. Retrieved from http://works.bepress.com/lisa_bostaph/16. As cited on http://sspa.boisestate.edu/criminaljustice/victim-services/overview/.

Campbell, R., Greeson, M., Bybee, D., & Neal, J. W. (2013). *Sexual assault response team (SART) implementation and collaborative process: What works best for the criminal justice system? Final report.* Washington, DC: US Department of Justice.

Chaiken, M. R., Boland, B., Maltz, M. D., Martin, S., & Targonski, J. (2001). *State and local change and the Violence Against Women Act, Executive summary, Final report.* Washington, DC: US Department of Justice.

Curtis-Fawley, S., & Daly, K. (2005). Gendered violence and restorative justice: The views of victim advocates. *Violence Against Women, 11*(5), 603–638.

Dammer, H., & Albanese, J. (2014) *Comparative criminal justice systems* (5th ed.). Belmont, CA: Wadsworth Cengage Learning.

Davis, R., & Erez, E. (1998). Immigrant populations as victims: Toward a multicultural criminal justice system. US Department of Justice, National Institute of Justice Research Brief.

Frailing, K. (2012). Fraud in the wake of disasters. In D. W. Harper & K. Frailing (Eds.), *Crime and criminal justice in disasters* (2nd ed.), (pp. 157–176). Durham, NC: Carolina Academic Press.

Frailing, K., & Harper, D. W. (2012). Fear, prosocial behavior and looting: The Katrina experience. In D. W. Harper & K. Frailing (Eds.), *Crime and criminal justice in disasters* (2nd ed.), (pp. 101–121). Durham, NC: Carolina Academic Press.

Giacomazzi, A., Hannah, E., & Bostaph, L. (2008). Nampa Family Justice Center process and outcome evaluation. Retrieved from http://www.familyjusticecenter.org/index.php/jdownloads/finish/41-evaluation-a-outcomes/261-evaluation-a-outcome-s-nampa-fjc-process-and-outcome-evaluation-giacomazzi-et-al-05-08.html.

Greeson, M. R., & Campbell, R. (2013). Sexual assault response teams (SARTs): An empirical review of their effectiveness and challenges to successful implementation. *Trauma, Violence, and Abuse, 14*(2), 83–95.

Grossman, S. F., Hinkley, S., Kawalski, A., & Margrave, C. (2005). Rural versus urban victims of violence: The interplay of race and religion. *Journal of Family Violence, 20*(2), 71–81.

Harrell, E. (2014). *Crime against persons with disabilities, 2009–2012 — Statistical Tables.* Washington, DC: US Department of Justice, Office of Justice Programs, Bureau of Justice Statistics. NCJ 244525.

Ivie, S., & Nanasi, N. (2009) The U visa: An effective resource for law enforcement. *FBI Law Enforcement Bulletin.*

Johnson, M., McGrath, S. A., & Miller, M. H. (2014). Effective advocacy in rural domains: Applying an ecological model to understanding advocates' relationships. *Journal of Interpersonal Violence, 29*(12), 2192–2217.

Kercher, G., & Kuo, C. (2008). *Victimization of immigrants.* Crime Victims' Institute. Criminal Justice Center. Sam Houston State University.

Littel, K. (2009). Victim services in rural law enforcement. National Sheriffs' Association. NCJ 232746.

Meyer, J. (2003). Restoration and the criminal justice system. In L. J. Moriarty, *Controversies in victimology* (pp. 81–90). Cincinnati, OH: Anderson Publishing Co.

Moriarty, L. J., & Roberts, A. R. (2008). Introduction: Controversial and critical issues with crime victims: Current research begins to reconcile the debates. *Victims and Offenders, 3,* 127–130.

National Center for Victims of Crime (NCVC). (2014). *Stalking fact sheet.* Washington, DC: US Department of Justice, Office of Justice Programs, Stalking Resource Center.

National Center for Victims of Crime (NCVC). (n.d.). *Parallel justice: A new vision of justice for crime victims.* Overview of Pilot Site Activity. Washington, DC: US Department of Justice, Office of Justice Programs.

National Center for Victims of Crime (NCVC). (n.d.). *VOCA funding: Victim advocates speak out.* Washington, DC: US Department of Justice, Office of Justice Programs.

New York Anti-Trafficking Network. (2010). Immigration relief for crime victims: The U visa manual.

Office for Victims of Crime. (2005). *Responding to victims of terrorism and mass violence crimes: Coordination and collaboration between American Red Cross workers and crime victim service providers.* Washington, DC: US Department of Justice, Office of Justice Programs. NCJ 209681.

Office for Victims of Crime. (2008). *Crime and disability.* Promising practices in serving crime victims with disabilities. Retrieved from http://www.ovc.gov/publications/infores/ServingVictimsWithDisabilities_bulletin/crime.html.

Office for Victims of Crime. (2013). *Vision 21, transforming victim services, Final report—Executive summary & recommendations.* Washington, DC: US Department of Justice, Office of Justice Programs. NCJ 239957.

Office for Victims of Crime. (2014). Section 4: Communicating your message: Media tips & tools. In Office for Victims of Crime, 2014 NCVRW Resource Guide, *30 years: Restoring the balance.* Washington, DC: US Department of Justice, Office of Justice Programs, Office for Victims of Crime. Retrieved from http://ovc.ncjrs.gov/ncvrw2014/.

Office on Violence Against Women. (2007). *The president's Family Justice Center Initiative best practices.* Washington, DC: US Department of Justice. Retrieved from www.ovw.usdoj.gov.

Sam Houston State University, Master of Science in Victim Services Management, http://www.shsu.edu/programs/master-of-science-in-victim-services-management, visited June 22, 2017.

Sexual Assault Report. (2014, March/April). A view from the field: A conversation with Aurelia Sands Belle, *Sexual Assault Report,* p. 59.

Smith, M. R. (2003). Victim-offender reconciliation programs. In L. J. Moriarty, *Controversies in victimology* (pp. 103–116). Cincinnati, OH: Anderson Publishing Co.

Sreeharsha, K. (2010). *Reforming America's immigration laws: A woman's struggle.* Immigration Policy Center.

Strack, G., & Gwinn, C. (2013). *Final evaluation results: Phase II California Family Justice Initiative statewide evaluation, Executive summary.* San Diego, CA: Family Justice Center Alliance. Retrieved from http://www.familyjusticecenter.org/index.php/jdownloads/finish/41-evaluation-a-outcomes/751-evaluation-a-outcomes-executive-summary-of-california-family-justice-initiative-statewide-evaluation-july-2013.html.

Stuart, R. D. (2013, February). Social media: Establishing criteria for law enforcement use. *FBI Law Enforcement Bulletin.* Retrieved from http://www.fbi.gov/stats-services/publications/law-enforcement-bulletin/2013/february/social-media-establishing-criteria-for-law-enforcement-use.

Thornton, W. E., & Voight, L. (2012). Disaster rape: Vulnerability of women to sexual assaults during Hurricane Katrina. In D. W. Harper & K. Frailing (Eds.), *Crime and criminal justice in disasters* (2nd ed.), (pp. 123–156). Durham, NC: Carolina Academic Press.

Tyiska, C. G. (1998). Working with victims of crime with disabilities, *OVC Bulletin.* Washington, DC: US Department of Justice, Office of Justice Programs, Office for Victims of Crime, NCJ 172838.

Umbreit, M. S., & Coates, R. (2000). *Multicultural implications for restorative justice: Potential pitfalls and dangers.* Washington, DC: US Department of Justice, Office of Justice Programs, Office for Victims of Crime, NCJ 176348.

United Nations Office on Drugs and Crime. (2012). *Global report on trafficking in persons.*

University of New Haven, Criminal Justice, M.S., Victimology Concentration, http://catalog.newhaven.edu/preview_program.php?catoid=3&poid=344, visited October 27, 2017.

US Department of State. (2012). Trafficking in persons report.

US Department of State. (2013). Trafficking in persons report.

Wagley, J. (2014). Police embrace social media. *Security Management*. Retrieved from http://www.securitymanagement.com/print/9175.

Wagner, M., Rocha, V., & Willis, A. (October 3, 2017). Las Vegas shooting: Live updates. cnn.com, 4:18pm EDT.

Walsh, J. A., & Muscat, B. T. (2013). Reaching underserved victim populations: Special challenges relating to homeless victims, rural populations, ethnic/racial/ sexual minorities, and victims with disabilities. In R. C. Davis, A. J. Lurigio, & S. Herman (Eds.), *Victims of crime* (4th ed.), (pp. 293–324). Thousand Oaks, CA: Sage Publications, Inc.

Websdale, N., & Johnson, B. (1998). An ethnostatistical comparison of the forms and levels of woman battering in urban and rural areas of Kentucky. *Criminal Justice Review, 23*, 161–196.

Yun, I., Swindel, S., & Kercher, G. (2009). Victim services delivery: A comparison of rural and urban communities. *Southwest Journal of Criminal Justice, 6*(2), 145– 162.

Appendix

James Comey's Speech on Police Shootings[*]

James B. Comey
Director
Federal Bureau of Investigation
Georgetown University
Washington, DC
February 12, 2015

Hard Truths: Law Enforcement and Race

Remarks as delivered.

Thank you, President DeGioia. And good morning, ladies and gentlemen. Thank you for inviting me to Georgetown University. I am honored to be here. I wanted to meet with you today, as President DeGioia said, to share my thoughts on the relationship between law enforcement and the diverse communities we serve and protect. Like a lot of things in life, that relationship is complicated. Relationships often are.

Beautiful Healy Hall—part of, and all around where we sit now—was named after this great university's 29th President, Patrick Francis Healy. Healy was born into slavery, in Georgia, in 1834. His father was an Irish immigrant plantation owner and his mother, a slave. Under the laws of that time, Healy and his siblings were considered to be slaves. Healy is believed to be the first African-American to earn a PhD, the first to enter the Jesuit order, and the first to be president of Georgetown University or any predominantly white university.

Given Georgetown's remarkable history, and that of President Healy, this struck me as an appropriate place to talk about the difficult relationship between law enforcement and the communities we are sworn to serve and protect.

---

[*] Source: https://www.fbi.gov/news/speeches/hard-truths-law-enforcement-and-race, visited 3/17/2017.

With the death of Michael Brown in Ferguson, the death of Eric Garner in Staten Island, the ongoing protests throughout the country, and the assassinations of NYPD Officers Wenjian Liu and Rafael Ramos, we are at a crossroads. As a society, we can choose to live our everyday lives, raising our families and going to work, hoping that someone, somewhere, will do something to ease the tension—to smooth over the conflict. We can roll up our car windows, turn up the radio and drive around these problems, or we can choose to have an open and honest discussion about what our relationship is today—what it should be, what it could be, and what it needs to be— if we took more time to better understand one another.

Current Issues Facing Law Enforcement

Unfortunately, in places like Ferguson and New York City, and in some communities across this nation, there is a disconnect between police agencies and many citizens— predominantly in communities of color.

Serious debates are taking place about how law enforcement personnel relate to the communities they serve, about the appropriate use of force, and about real and perceived biases, both within and outside of law enforcement. These are important debates. Every American should feel free to express an informed opinion—to protest peacefully, to convey frustration and even anger in a constructive way. That's what makes our democracy great. Those conversations—as bumpy and uncomfortable as they can be—help us understand different perspectives, and better serve our communities. Of course, these are only conversations in the true sense of that word if we are willing not only to talk, but to listen, too.

I worry that this incredibly important and incredibly difficult conversation about race and policing has become focused entirely on the nature and character of law enforcement officers, when it should also be about something much harder to discuss. Debating the nature of policing is very important, but I worry that it has become an excuse, at times, to avoid doing something harder.

The Hard Truths

Let me start by sharing some of my own hard truths:

First, all of us in law enforcement must be honest enough to acknowledge that much of our history is not pretty. At many points in American history, law enforcement enforced the status quo, a status quo that was often brutally unfair to disfavored groups. It was unfair to the Healy siblings and to countless others like them. It was unfair to too many people.

I am descended from Irish immigrants. A century ago, the Irish knew well how American society—and law enforcement—viewed them: as drunks, ruffians, and criminals. Law enforcement's biased view of the Irish lives on in the nickname we still use for the vehicles we use to transport groups of prisoners. It is, after all, the "paddy wagon."

The Irish had tough times, but little compares to the experience on our soil of black Americans. That experience should be part of every American's consciousness, and law enforcement's role in that experience—including in recent times—must be remembered. It is our cultural inheritance.

There is a reason that I require all new agents and analysts to study the FBI's interaction with Dr. Martin Luther King, Jr., and to visit his memorial in Washington as part of their training. And there is a reason I keep on my desk a copy of Attorney General Robert Kennedy's approval of J. Edgar Hoover's request to wiretap Dr. King. It is a single page. The entire application is five sentences long, it is without fact or substance, and is predicated on the naked assertion that there is "communist influence in the racial situation." The reason I do those things is to ensure that we remember our mistakes and that we learn from them.

One reason we cannot forget our law enforcement legacy is that the people we serve and protect cannot forget it, either. So we must talk about our history. It is a hard truth that lives on.

A second hard truth: Much research points to the widespread existence of unconscious bias. Many people in our white-majority culture have unconscious racial biases and react differently to a white face than a black face. In fact, we all, white and black, carry various biases around with us. I am reminded of the song from the Broadway hit, Avenue Q: "Everyone's a Little Bit Racist." Part of it goes like this:

> Look around and you will find
> No one's really color blind.
> Maybe it's a fact
> We all should face
> Everyone makes judgments
> Based on race.

You should be grateful I did not try to sing that.

But if we can't help our latent biases, we can help our behavior in response to those instinctive reactions, which is why we work to design systems and processes that overcome that very human part of us all. Although the research may be unsettling, it is what we do next that matters most.

But racial bias isn't epidemic in law enforcement any more than it is epidemic in academia or the arts. In fact, I believe law enforcement overwhelmingly attracts people who want to do good for a living—people who risk their lives because they want to help other people. They don't sign up to be cops in New York or Chicago or L.A. to help white people or black people or Hispanic people or Asian people. They sign up because they want to help all people. And they do some of the hardest, most dangerous policing to protect people of color.

But that leads me to my third hard truth: something happens to people in law enforcement. Many of us develop different flavors of cynicism that we work hard to resist because they can be lazy mental shortcuts. For example, criminal suspects routinely lie about their guilt, and nearly everybody we charge is guilty. That makes it easy for some folks in law enforcement to assume that everybody is lying and that no suspect, regardless of their race, could be innocent. Easy, but wrong.

Likewise, police officers on patrol in our nation's cities often work in environments where a hugely disproportionate percentage of street crime is committed by young men of color. Something happens to people of good will working in that environment. After years of police work, officers often can't help but be influenced by the cynicism they feel.

A mental shortcut becomes almost irresistible and maybe even rational by some lights. The two young black men on one side of the street look like so many others the officer has locked up. Two white men on the other side of the street—even in the same clothes—do not. The officer does not make the same association about the two white guys, whether that officer is white or black. And that drives different behavior. The officer turns toward one side of the street and not the other. We need to come to grips with the fact that this behavior complicates the relationship between police and the communities they serve.

So why has that officer—like his colleagues—locked up so many young men of color? Why does he have that life-shaping experience? Is it because he is a racist? Why are so many black men in jail? Is it because cops, prosecutors, judges, and juries are racist? Because they are turning a blind eye to white robbers and drug dealers?

The answer is a fourth hard truth: I don't think so. If it were so, that would be easier to address. We would just need to change the way we hire, train, and measure law enforcement and that would substantially fix it. We would then go get those white criminals we have been ignoring. But the truth is significantly harder than that.

The truth is that what really needs fixing is something only a few, like President Obama, are willing to speak about, perhaps because it is so daunting a task. Through the "My Brother's Keeper" initiative, the president is addressing the disproportionate challenges faced by young men of color. For instance, data shows that the percentage of young men not working or not enrolled in school is nearly twice as high for blacks as it is for whites. This initiative, and others like it, is about doing the hard work to grow drug-resistant and violence-resistant kids, especially in communities of color, so they never become part of that officer's life experience.

So many young men of color become part of that officer's life experience because so many minority families and communities are struggling, so many boys and young men grow up in environments lacking role models, adequate education, and decent employment—they lack all sorts of opportunities that most of us take for granted. A tragedy of American life—one that most citizens are able to drive around because it doesn't touch them—is that young people in "those neighborhoods" too often inherit a legacy of crime and prison. And with that inheritance, they become part of a police officer's life, and shape the way that officer—whether white or black—sees the world. Changing that legacy is a challenge so enormous and so complicated that it is, unfortunately, easier to talk only about the cops. And that's not fair.

Let me be transparent about my affection for cops. When you dial 911, whether you are white or black, the cops come, and they come quickly, and they come quickly whether they are white or black. That's what cops do, in addition to all of the other hard and difficult and dangerous and frightening things that they do. They respond to homes in the middle of the night where a drunken father, wielding a gun, is threatening his wife and children. They pound up the back stairs of an apartment building, not knowing whether the guys behind the door they are about to enter are armed, or high, or both.

I come from a law enforcement family. My grandfather, William J. Comey, was a police officer. Pop Comey is one of my heroes. I have a picture of him on my wall in my office at the FBI, reminding me of the legacy I've inherited and that I must honor.

He was the child of immigrants. When he was in the sixth grade, his father was killed in an industrial accident in New York. Because he was the oldest, he had to drop out of school so that he could go to work to support his mom and younger siblings. He could never afford to return to school, but when he was old enough, he joined the Yonkers, New York, Police Department.

Over the next 40 years, he rose to lead that department. Pop was the tall, strong, silent type, quiet and dignified, and passionate about the rule of law. Back during Prohibition, he heard that bootleggers were running beer through fire hoses between Yonkers and the Bronx.

Now, Pop enjoyed a good beer every now and again, but he ordered his men to cut those hoses with fire axes. Pop had to have a protective detail, because certain people were angry and shocked that someone in law enforcement would do that. But that's what we want as citizens—that's what we expect. And so I keep that picture of Pop on my office wall to remind me of his integrity, and his pride in the integrity of his work.

Law enforcement ranks are filled with people like my grandfather. But, to be clear, although I am from a law enforcement family, and have spent much of my career in law enforcement, I'm not looking to let law enforcement off the hook. Those of us in law enforcement must redouble our efforts to resist bias and prejudice. We must better understand the people we serve and protect—by trying to know, deep in our gut, what it feels like to be a law-abiding young black man walking on the street and encountering law enforcement. We must understand how that young man may see us. We must resist the lazy shortcuts of cynicism and approach him with respect and decency.

We must work—in the words of New York City Police Commissioner Bill Bratton—to really see each other. Perhaps the reason we struggle as a nation is because we've come to see only what we represent, at face value, instead of who we are. We simply must see the people we serve.

But the "seeing" needs to flow in both directions. Citizens also need to really see the men and women of law enforcement. They need to see what police see through the windshields of their squad cars, or as they walk down the street. They need to see the risks and dangers law enforcement officers encounter on a typical late-night shift. They need to understand the difficult and frightening work they do to keep us safe. They need to give them the space and respect to do their work, well and properly.

If they take the time to do that, what they will see are officers who are human, who are overwhelmingly doing the right thing for the right reasons, and who are too often operating in communities—and facing challenges—most of us choose to drive around.

One of the hardest things I do as FBI Director is call the chiefs and sheriffs in departments around the nation when officers have been killed in the line of duty. I call to express my sorrow and offer the FBI's help. Officers like Wenjian Liu and Rafael Ramos, two of NYPD's finest who were gunned down by a madman who thought his ambush would avenge the deaths of Michael Brown and Eric Garner. I make far too many calls. And, there are far too many names of fallen officers on the National Law Enforcement Officers Memorial and far too many names etched there each year.

Officers Liu and Ramos swore the same oath all in law enforcement do, and they answered the call to serve the people, all people. Like all good police officers, they moved toward danger, without regard for the politics or passions or race of those who needed their help — knowing the risks inherent in their work. They were minority police officers, killed while standing watch in a minority neighborhood — Bedford-Stuyvesant — one they and their fellow officers had rescued from the grip of violent crime.

Twenty years ago, Bed-Stuy was shorthand for a kind of chaos and disorder in which good people had no freedom to walk, shop, play, or just sit on the front steps and talk. It was too dangerous. But today, no more, thanks to the work of those who chose lives of service and danger to help others.

But despite this selfless service — of these two officers and countless others like them across the country — in some American communities, people view the police not as allies, but as antagonists, and think of them not with respect or gratitude, but with suspicion and distrust.

We simply must find ways to see each other more clearly. And part of that has to involve collecting and sharing better information about encounters between police and citizens, especially violent encounters.

Not long after riots broke out in Ferguson late last summer, I asked my staff to tell me how many people shot by police were African-American in this country. I wanted to see trends. I wanted to see information. They couldn't give it to me, and it wasn't their fault. Demographic data regarding officer-involved shootings is not consistently reported to us through our Uniform Crime Reporting Program. Because reporting is voluntary, our data is incomplete and therefore, in the aggregate, unreliable.

I recently listened to a thoughtful big city police chief express his frustration with that lack of reliable data. He said he didn't know whether the Ferguson police shot one person a week, one a year, or one a century, and that in the absence of good data, "all we get are ideological thunderbolts, when what we need are ideological agnostics who use information to try to solve problems." He's right.

The first step to understanding what is really going on in our communities and in our country is to gather more and better data related to those we arrest, those we confront for breaking the law and jeopardizing public safety, and those who confront us. "Data" seems a dry and boring word but, without it, we cannot understand our world and make it better.

How can we address concerns about "use of force," how can we address concerns about officer-involved shootings if we do not have a reliable grasp on the demographics and circumstances of those incidents? We simply must improve the way we collect and analyze data to see the true nature of what's happening in all of our communities.

The FBI tracks and publishes the number of "justifiable homicides" reported by police departments. But, again, reporting by police departments is voluntary and not all departments participate. That means we cannot fully track the number of incidents in which force is used by police, or against police, including non-fatal encounters, which are not reported at all.

Without complete and accurate data, we are left with "ideological thunderbolts." And that helps spark unrest and distrust and does not help us get better. Because we must get better, I intend for the FBI to be a leader in urging departments around this country to give us the facts we need for an informed discussion, the facts all of us need, to help us make sound policy and sound decisions with that information.

* * *

America isn't easy. America takes work. Today, February 12, is Abraham Lincoln's birthday. He spoke at Gettysburg about a "new birth of freedom" because we spent the first four score and seven years of our history with fellow Americans held as slaves—President Healy, his siblings, and his mother among them. We have spent the 150 years since Lincoln spoke making great progress, but along the way treating a whole lot of people of color poorly. And law enforcement was often part of that poor treatment. That's our inheritance as law enforcement and it is not all in the distant past.

We must account for that inheritance. And we—especially those of us who enjoy the privilege that comes with being the majority—must confront the biases that are inescapable parts of the human condition. We must speak the truth about our shortcomings as law enforcement, and fight to be better. But as a country, we must also speak the truth to ourselves. Law enforcement is not the root cause of problems in our hardest hit neighborhoods. Police officers—people of enormous courage and integrity, in the main—are in those neighborhoods, risking their lives, to protect folks from offenders who are the product of problems that will not be solved by body cameras.

We simply must speak to each other honestly about all these hard truths.

In the words of Dr. King, "We must learn to live together as brothers or we will all perish together as fools."

We all have work to do—hard work, challenging work—and it will take time. We all need to talk and we all need to listen, not just about easy things, but about hard things, too. Relationships are hard. Relationships require work. So let's begin that work. It is time to start seeing one another for who and what we really are. Peace, security, and understanding are worth the effort. Thank you for listening to me today.

Index